D1373269

THE ULTIMATE HOUSE-HOLDER'S BOOK

OVER 4,000 INVALUABLE TIPS TO SAVE YOU TIME & MONEY

By the Editors of Consumer Guide

THE ULTIMATE HOUSE- HOLDER'S BOOK

A&W Publishers
New York

Copyright © 1982 by Publications International, Ltd.

All rights reserved. No part of this work may be repro-
duced or transmitted in any form or by any means,
electronic or mechanical, including photocopying, recording, or any information storage and retrieval system, without permission in writing from the publisher.
Permission is never granted for commercial purposes.

Published by
A&W Publishers, Inc.
95 Madison Avenue
New York, NY 10016

Manufactured in the United States of America

Art by Jeff Mangiat

Designed by Denise C.Schiff

1 2 3 4 5 6 7 8 9 10

Library of Congress Cataloging in Publication Data

Main entry under title:

The Ultimate householder's book.
2. Home economics.
    Includes index.
    1. Consumer education. I. Consumer guide.
TX335.U44   640   82-6754
ISBN 0-89479-113-3   AACR2

17.95
10/11/82

TABLE OF CONTENTS

INTRODUCTION

We humans are creatures of habit, yet each one of us is also blessed with imagination—that marvelous capacity to see the new in the old, to adapt, to invent a better way, to make the most and the best of what's at hand. Most of us have had the experience of discovering a new and easier way of doing things, another way to save the day. "Now why didn't I think of that?" we say. And we, in turn, enjoy passing on those little tricks for making life easier that are part of our store of knowledge.

These hints can make the difference between success and disaster. So when it's time to cope with the myriad emergencies and dilemmas that come up around the house, don't throw up your hands in despair: If your own heritage of hints doesn't save the day, you're bound to find the answer in this book. With *The Ultimate Householder's Book,* you can cope with most of life's minor catastrophes—you can make do, improvise, salvage, and discover how much fun it is to operate on the "hint" principle.

HINTS FOR THE WHOLE FAMILY

None of us knows all the possibilities, but it's probably true that each of us could write our own compendium of helpful hints. We know only that little bit that's been passed down through our own families, or that we've chanced to discover along the way. That's why your way of cleaning, or your neighbor's way of cooking, still holds so many surprises for the rest of us. And that's what *The Ultimate Householder's Book* is all about—collecting all those individual hints into one complete survival handbook.

The Ultimate Householder's Book gives you access to over *4,000* time-tested hints, for everyone in the family and every aspect of daily life. While most hint collections focus almost exclusively on kitchen and cleaning hints, we've gathered tips on every facet of your life—not just cooking and cleaning, but also carpentry and home repair, painting, decorating, and gardening; first aid, health and diet; your grooming and wardrobe; kids, pets, sewing; your family car.

But don't be fooled by these categories—the world of hints is too big to stay within those limits, and it can inspire you to further refinements and improvisations. For example, you can tack a shoebag to the table where you do baby's diapering, and keep it stocked with pins, ointment, talc, and cloth. When an older child goes off to summer camp, let him take a similar bag to hang alongside his bunk for storing comb and brush, toothpaste and books. If you slip rubber bands over the ends of hangers so your clothes won't fall off, why not also put rubber bands around cups and glasses that can so easily slip from a child's grasp? *The Ultimate Householder's Book* is more than a handbook; it's a starting point to a whole new way of life.

KEEPING HOUSE WITH HINTS—THE EASY WAY

Start your hint parade with "Hints for the Whole House" and dozens of hints that will follow you upstairs, downstairs, to the basement and the attic, out to the garage, and even up on the roof. Here are hundreds of ideas for home planning and organization; cleaning and problem solving; laundry; lighting, plumbing, and shop projects; painting and decorating; indoor and outdoor repairs. You'll learn how to get more mileage out of the storage space you already have, and how to find more space in unsuspected nooks and crannies. You'll learn all the sneaky things that people have discovered over the years—that nylon fishing line makes an invisible picture hanger, that you should paint alternate steps of a stairway so you'll have a way out, and more.

When you need to silence a leaky faucet or unclog drains and toilets, this is where to find help, and whether your windows stick or it's the time of year to wash them, there are always easier and better ways. There are hints too for cleaning and painting walls, hanging wallpaper, and organizing a move from one home to another. Spots and stains—ring around the collar, ring around the bathtub, and rings left on furniture by glasses—also get the full treatment. With hints like these, how can you go wrong?

The tips on outside repairs alone would make *The Ultimate Householder's Book* a valuable reference. When the roof leaks, shingles come loose, gutters need cleaning, or the house needs painting, you'll find answers to your questions here. This is the place to look for tips on the tricky art of painting downspouts, or what to do about house paint that blisters, peels, wrinkles, or "alligators."

And once the outside is in shape, you can make your home energy efficient with a little help from Part II, "Energy Savers." This section will give you the knack of saving, of conserving, of maximizing the overall energy efficiency of your home. You'll find hints for specific ways you can save on heating, cooling, electricity, and your water system—practical tips and a lot of common sense. For example, a large group of people generates heat, so turn down the thermostat next time you have a party. You'll get more sunlight and use less heat by keeping your windows sparkling clean in winter—and you'll lower your electric bills in summer by placing your air conditioner in the shade. In fact, you'll find that you can save energy all over the house, as simply as lowering the water heater's setting or wrapping hot-water pipes with insulation.

CASH ON THE LINE—MONEY HINTS THAT WORK

A hint is something that tells you a better way—and when the subject is money, most of us can use all the help we can get. *The Ultimate Householder's Book* can help you win in today's economy—with a whole section of hints on money management from family budgeting to tax and investment advice.

Almost everyone has met someone with the Midas touch, turning everything into gold. Now, with these special, savvy tips, you can polish up your own touch as you get into more hintwise money management. Your pocketbook will show the results—and so will your bank account—as you pick up these tips on general money-saving, housing and real estate, investing, borrowing, insurance, taxes, and retirement planning. The idea of money hints may be a funny one, but you'll laugh all the way to the bank.

BLUE PLATE SPECIAL: TIPS FOR THE KITCHEN

In a special section on kitchen hints, *The Ultimate Householder's Book* presents some of the best tips yet for coping with the perils and pleasures of your kitchen. Here are hints that make food preparation easier and meals taste better; they show you how to salvage kitchen calamities, how to save money, how to handle the cleanup, and what to do with leftovers. From soup to nuts, here is a wealth of proven kitchen helpers.

If you already know how to keep the lumps out of gravy and the tears out of slicing onions, you'll still want to check out our hints for keeping fruits, vegetables, meats, and other foods fresh for as long as possible, and for tips on what foods you can substitute when you suddenly discover you're out of an ingredient in a favorite recipe. You'll learn how to firm up soft potatoes, how to freeze bananas, stretch butter, and keep cottage cheese fresh twice as long. For the cook who takes special pride in the advanced aspects of cooking, there are over 100 gourmet hints to instill confidence and inspire culinary creativity. And for every unfinished meal, you'll find a great way to serve it on another day— from simple leftovers to melted ice cream served over cereal. Here's the place to look for the best hints on kitchen cleanup, too. Stop drudging at stubborn jobs like cleaning the oven or the blender; there's an easier way to do the job—and it's here.

SPECIAL TOUCHES, FESTIVE WAYS—FOR PARTIES, HOME, AND YOU

Hints are great for practical information, but there's a lot more to the hint principle than this. A special section on entertaining and parties gives you a wealth of ideas for decorating and serving, during the holidays and all year-round. Whatever the occasion, you'll find just the right touch with our festive gift-giving, planning, and preparation hints.

Special touches mean a lot for everyday, too. Even if you're short on time and money, *The Ultimate Householder's Book* will show you how to decorate your home to get the look you've always wanted. It tells how *you* can be your home's best designer—how to make a room look bigger, how to give a room a quick facelift, how to make your own good-looking and inexpensive decorations. And once you've finished sprucing up your home, move on to a complete section of health and diet tips. We've found tips on losing weight that don't require counting a single calorie, tips on first aid and time-tested home remedies for some of the most common ailments. There are ideas on grooming and personal care to keep you looking your best. Skin, hair, and total body care are thoroughly covered; a special section on the art of makeup application will clue you in on the secrets of professional models.

Our practical suggestions on dressing and wardrobe will help you maintain your considerable clothing investment. Planning a wardrobe, keeping the whole family's clothing neat and clean, and improvising clothes from unlikely sources are just some of the valuable topics covered. You'll also learn the secrets of preventing runs in nylon stockings, keeping angora from shedding, making buttons stay on longer, and more. And whether sewing is a budgetary necessity or an enjoyable hobby for you, our sewing and needlework hints will help you sew with professional expertise, eliminating many of the tedious aspects without sacrificing the quality or the excitement of creating your own designs.

KEEPING KIDS AND PETS HEALTHY AND HAPPY

You've covered a lot of ground so far, and found a huge array of practical and fun hints. But there's still a lot more to *The Ultimate Householder's Book,* starting with a section on kids. There's a whole treasury of hints especially for babies, toddlers, and older children, from feeding time to playtime—mealtime with a picky toddler will never be a problem again when you serve lunch in a muffin tin; you can speed up a reluctant sled by spraying the bottom of its runners with vegetable oil; and much more. Everybody's good ideas are here, collected into one indispensable volume of hints.

There's still another very special section—a collection of hints about pets, who bring us so much friendship, affection, and sometimes, protection. These practical and authoritative hints will help with the everyday grooming, feeding, health, and safety needs of your pet, and make it easier to deal with discipline and other problems. Cat owners will want to try out tips for the perennial problems of keeping cats from digging into houseplants or jumping up on the furniture; dog owners will welcome our sure-fire ways to make Fido swallow a pill without a struggle; people with other kinds of pets will find great tips on caring for them. Love a cat; love a dog; give your kid a hug today—you'll enjoy all these clever hints.

AND A MYRIAD MORE . . .

Finally, besides all these home-, family-, people-, and pet-related hints, *The Ultimate Householder's Book* takes you back out into the world again, with the most complete coverage of other areas around. Spending time out in the yard? You'll find a complete section on yard, garden, and patio tips—from easier ways to clean the grill to quick, natural weed killers. Indoors, keep your window on the world healthy—pamper your plants with our many hints for potting, feeding, and tending.

And when you're ready to take to the road, we're right with you with sections on your car: Here are all the tricks for increasing your car's gas mileage, tips for buying a new or used car, advice on body and engine work to keep your car younger, longer.

THE HINT CONNECTION: ENJOY IT NOW!

You can see that hints are much more than just random bits of information—they're part of a store of knowledge that's grown through generations of trial and error, generations of people experimenting and failing and sometimes finding a better way. To the modern mind, hints sometimes seem funny—yet they work. What's more, the rising cost of energy has brought home the fact that we must again learn to value and protect resources, extend the life of goods and possessions, and brush up on skills that used to be part of everyday survival not so long ago. The old Yankee ethic—use it up, wear it out, make it do, or do without—is back again, and we need all the help we can get. *The Ultimate Householder's Book* provides that help—all along the line.

Necessity is the mother of invention; this book proves it again. Some of these hints are traditional; some were invented in our own time; but every one of them is up-to-date, and will help you cope creatively and pleasurably with the problems of your day-to-day life. Whatever your situation, whatever your own personal challenge is, *The Ultimate Householder's Book* is a great way to brighten up your day, a great introduction to the art of making—and taking—life easy.

Part I

HINTS FOR THE WHOLE HOUSE

For most of us, our home is probably the one possession that will bring us the greatest joy over the years. But home repair problems and organizational hassles can quickly turn the joy into a cry of "How do I cope?" One very smart way to keep the pleasure and eliminate the problems is to keep *The Ultimate Householder's Book* nearby and consult it often.

"Hints for the Whole House" begins with a host of ideas for efficient organization and smooth daily living for your whole family. An organized home is a harmonious one, and you can adapt some of the clever ideas business people use to keep your home running smoothly.

It's a law of nature that there's never enough space—and making space in today's often cramped living quarters is always a problem. We have hints for miraculously turning wasted space into valuable storage areas, for making the most of even a tiny storage potential. And even if you think you're getting the most from your closet space, you'll be pleasantly surprised to read the hints for increasing storage efficiency.

When you move, the section on "Planning a Move" will be especially worthwhile. Everything is covered—from smart packing suggestions to organizing a moving sale *before* you go to get rid of unwanted items that would cost money to move. And once you're in that new home, you can turn it into a showplace with our imaginative tips on painting and decorating.

Hints on laundry and cleaning show you how to breeze through routine maintenance, and how to meet special challenges like removing difficult stains from clothes or smoke stains from a fireplace wall. And a chapter on cleaning and problem solving gives you dozens of worthwhile tips on cleaning, repairing, and maintaining the many valuable parts of your home—a real money saver.

You can learn how to make the work areas of your home *really* work for you with helpful suggestions for organizing safe, efficient basements, shops, and garages. With tools and work areas well managed, money-saving home repairs become easier than ever. Our hints on electrical, plumbing, and exterior home repairs will save you plenty in service bills.

The final chapter in this part, "Pest Control," will help you cope with all kinds of unwanted guests—a life-saver when you need a quick answer. When it comes right down to it, your home is probably your biggest investment. Take care of it right—and easily—with these handy pointers.

Chapter 1

GENERAL HOUSEHOLD HINTS

UPSTAIRS AND DOWN, MAKE EVERY PART OF YOUR HOME MORE COMFORTABLE, EFFICIENT, AND SAFE WITH THESE TIME-TESTED HINTS.

Home Planning

If you have trouble getting started in the morning, get organized the night before. Lay out your clothes, measure the coffee, and set the breakfast table before you go to bed.

Kids can help you get the day going by making their own lunches. While you get breakfast, the kids can create sandwiches with lunch meats and spreads left out on a tray.

Discover the time of day when your energy level is highest and do your least favorite chore then. You'll find you can get through much easier. Wind down the day with one of your favorite things, no matter how simple.

When lining garbage cans with plastic trash bags, nest several bags into a can at the same time. Then remove the bags, one by one, as they fill.

Walk around the house with a candle on a cold windy day to see where cold may be entering doors and windows.

Pin the menus for the week on a bulletin board—with the recipe titles and cookbook page references—for everyone in the family to see. The first one home can start the meal.

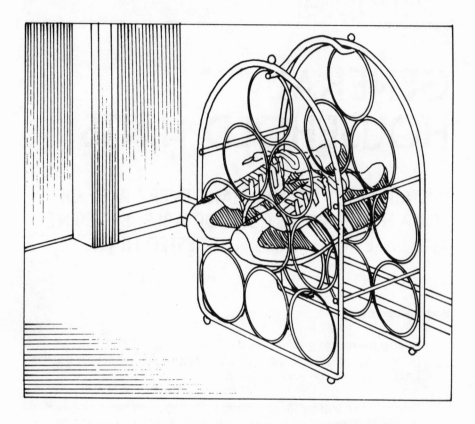

Put a wine rack next to the door and use it to store your sandy beach shoes and muddy running or gardening shoes.

Take a check from your checkbook and put it in your wallet, and you'll always have an extra when you find yourself down to your last check—or if you've forgotten your checkbook. Be sure to record the amount of this check in your checkbook when you use it.

Make out your shopping list in the same order as the food is stocked in the store aisles, and you'll save time and energy at the grocery store.

Keep a large empty drawer, storage box, or laundry basket handy for instant cleanup when an unexpected guest is on the way.

Put extra pieces of carpeting to use by cutting out square coasters. The foam will absorb the moisture.

Organization

Assign a color to each family member and color code items throughout the house. Schoolbags, umbrellas, ponchos, coat hooks, storage boxes, and lunchboxes can all be color coded this way.

Add shelves above your washer and dryer and put colored plastic baskets—one color for each family member—on them. When you take clean clothes out of the dryer, sort each person's clothes into the appropriate basket. Family members can then pick up their baskets and fold and put away their own clothes.

Instead of using an address book, keep a record of names and addresses on index cards stored in a file box. If someone moves, just substitute a new card with the current information. This method also gives you more room to keep records of birthdays, anniversaries, and clothing sizes.

So that slide and photo showings are more enjoyable, label the film as soon as it's developed, with place, date, and any other information needed for identification.

Designate one area of your home for filing business bills, letters, and clippings, even if it's only one drawer somewhere.

Use the back of junk mail letters and envelopes for shopping lists or telephone messages.

Organize your records by category with the help of stick-on colored dots. All your classical records can be coded with one color, rock music with another, musicals with another, and so on.

There are many uses for little printed address labels: Use them to fill in your name on coupons; label items that you've lent; label your bowl or casserole brought to a pot luck or dinner; identify an item left for repair.

If you gather your appliance warranties, manuals, and receipts all in one folder, you'll have everything at your fingertips when you need the information.

As you pack things in boxes for storage, list where and what you're storing in a record book. That way you can find it again in a jiffy.

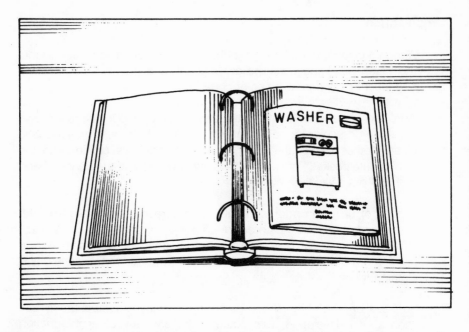

The instruction booklets that come with appliances won't be so easily misplaced if you keep them handy in a notebook. Paste the back cover of each booklet against one of the notebook's three-hole-punched sheets, and you'll have the information handy when you need it.

Large detergent boxes cut on the diagonal are perfect for filing special issues of magazines you want to save.

Easy Carrying

An empty soft drink carton is a good carryall for cleaning compounds as you work from room to room. Then take the whole kit and put it away neatly below the sink.

Canvas feedbags available from riding stores make good shopping carryalls.

Making Space

If your home is built with studs and drywall, you can add cabinets between the studs, anywhere you need them—they won't take up any space at all. For example, put a liquor cabinet over your bar, or fashion a canned-goods pantry in your kitchen.

Pegboard is most often used on walls, but it can be used as a room divider, or even to make the inside of a closet or cabinet door more functional. When installing it, remember to provide space behind the panels for the hooks.

If you're short on wall space for books, you can pull a sofa away from a wall and surround it with arm-height bookcases.

To increase the capacity and efficiency of a drawer, outfit it with a lift-out tray. Fill the tray with items you frequently use—then fill the space beneath the tray with articles you seldom need.

Nail coffee cans to the wall to make bins for clips, pins, or any small items.

Glass baby food jars are ideal for storing nails and screws. Better yet, nail the caps to a wood base or wall plaque, and just screw the jars into place.

Lining Shelves

If you have troubles with bubbles and creases when applying adhesive-backed paper to shelves or drawers, try smoothing the paper with a blackboard eraser.

To make self-adhesive paper fit exactly in drawers and on shelves, first make patterns with sheets of newspaper.

An iron is a useful tool when removing adhesive-backed paper. Place a towel over the paper and iron it. The warmth will loosen the adhesive's grip, and you'll be able to pull up the paper easily.

Doubling Up

Sometimes hallways can double as storage areas. If they're wide enough, line them with shelves or shallow cabinets.

The area in front of a never-used window or door can be used to store small items. Block off the back of the opening, and line the cavity with shelves.

Put the space under a stairway to work as a storage area. Construct a wheeled, wedge-shaped container that fits into the farthest area beneath the steps.

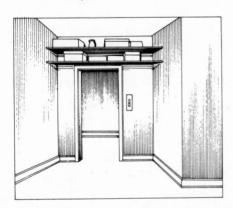 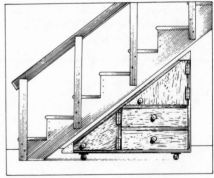

Another way to use a stairway as a storage area is to replace ordinary nailed-in-place steps with hinged steps. Use the space under the hinged steps to hold boots or sports equipment neatly.

If you're in need of an extra closet for storing items like golf clubs, skis, and camping equipment, angle a decorative folding screen in an extra corner of the house.

For a double-duty ottoman, build a plywood box with a hinged cover.

Paint the outside or cover it with fabric, and then cover the top with scrap carpeting. Add a cushion for comfortable sitting, and store your magazines in style.

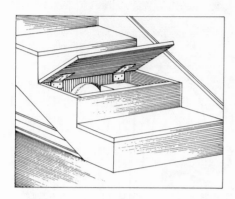 

Closets

For extra closet storage, see if your closets can accommodate a second shelf above the existing one. And, if you install the main clothes-hanging rod high enough, you may be able to install another rod beneath it on which to hang shorter items such as slacks and shirts.

Hooks, shelves, or hanging bins can transform the inside surfaces of closet doors into useful storage areas.

Install two rows of clothing and coat hooks on your closet doors—one down low for a child to use, another higher up for you to use. (See illustration on p. 10)

Convert an ordinary closet or chest into a cedar closet or chest by installing thin cedar slats over inside surfaces. Then weatherstrip to contain the scent.

If your cedar chest or closet no longer smells like one, lightly sand its surfaces. Sanding opens the wood's pores and releases a fresh cedar scent. Remember that the scent doesn't kill moths; it merely repels them. So, it's best to clean all clothes before storing to remove any moth eggs.

Keep a stool and a hooked pole handy for use in a tall closet.

Bathroom

Make your bathroom work for all family members. For the little child in the house, store a stool under the sink vanity.

Hang a wicker backpack on the bathroom wall for storing towels, tissues, soap, and bath toys.

Bedroom

Add more storage space in your bedroom by building a headboard storage unit. You can place books, lamps, or a radio on the lid of the unit and inside you can store extra linens and blankets.

Use flat, roll-out bins for under-the-bed storage. They can hold bed linens, sewing supplies, and other infrequently used items.

Clothing

A good place to store small clothing items is in large, metal potato-chip cans—after the cans are washed.

When storing heirloom linens or baby clothing, preserve them in "mint" condition by washing and rinsing them, then rinsing again in a vinegar and water solution. Avoid starching and ironing and, if possible, dry them in the sun. Finally, wrap each item separately in tissue paper, placing extra paper between folds.

Film and Negatives

You'll always know where your photo negatives are if you store them behind corresponding prints in your photo album.

Photographic film will stay fresh longer if stored in your refrigerator.

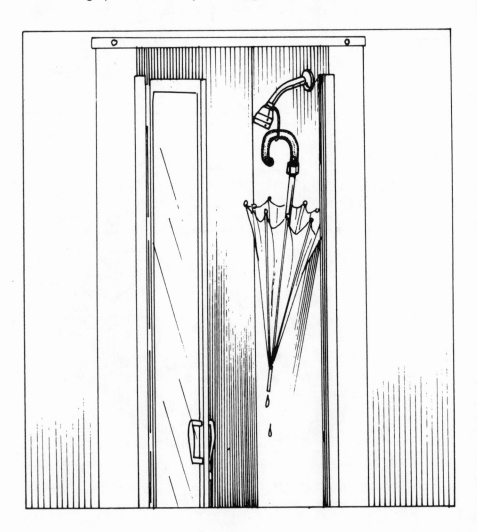

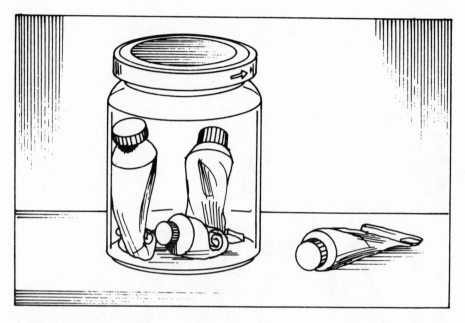

A Place for Everything

Hang a basket near the front door and keep your keys in it, so you'll always know where they are. This is also a good place for bills and letters that need to be mailed. When you grab your keys, you won't forget to take the mail.

Keep flashlight batteries fresh by storing them in a sealed plastic bag in the refrigerator.

To keep a broom from resting on its bristles and thus becoming lopsided, drill a hole in the broom's handle and hang the broom on the wall.

Extension cords won't get tangled when stored in a drawer if you wind them and secure them with rubber bands—or slip them into a toilet-paper or paper-towel tube.

Keep your wet umbrella in the shower where it can drip away without making a mess. This is especially handy when you have company on a rainy day, and everyone has an umbrella.

Partially used tubes of glue won't dry up before you're ready to use them again if you keep the tubes in tightly closed glass jars.

Keep place mats flat and out of the way by hanging them on a clipboard hung from a hook inside a cabinet or pantry door.

When storing suitcases, put a cake of unwrapped soap inside each one to keep musty odors from developing.

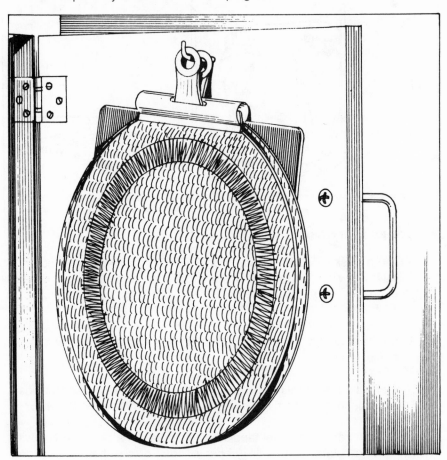

Planning Your Move Ahead of Time

Moving will go more smoothly if you make a master checklist of everything that must be done in connection with the move. So that you don't fall behind, schedule a deadline for each task.

When notifying people about your move, be sure to include utilities, post office, social security, publications to which you subscribe, doctors, insurance companies, and the phone company. If you also go through your address book, you'll be less likely to overlook someone who'll want or need to know you're moving.

Take a survival package along with the family so you can camp in your new home till the moving van arrives. Include instant coffee, cups, spoons, soap and towels, a can-and-bottle opener, some light bulbs, a flashlight, toilet paper, cleansing powder, and a first aid kit. Also be sure that daily medications travel with you, not the movers.

Packing Up

Save space by not packing the unbreakable content of tightly loaded drawers. Simply tape the drawers in place with strips of wide masking tape. To minimize tape marks, remove the tape as soon as the furniture arrives at your new home.

Get carpets and slipcovers cleaned before you move. They'll come back wrapped and ready to go.

Small linens such as towels, washcloths, and pillowcases also can serve as packing material for dishes and glassware—and they don't waste space.

If you pack books so their spines are alternated, they will take up less space. (It may be cheaper to ship books via the United States mail, since the Post Office offers an inexpensive, fourth-class book rate.)

Plates are less likely to break if they are stood on edge when packed. To minimize breakage of glass items, place the heavier ones on the bottom and the more delicate ones on top. Excelsior or pieces of crumpled newspaper make good packing material. If you have several days to pack before moving, dampen the excelsior so it will shape itself to the china and glassware.

To prevent odors from developing in the refrigerator or freezer during the move, put several charcoal briquettes inside the unit to absorb them. Or fill the refrigerator or freezer with wadded-up newspapers. The paper will absorb any moisture and help prevent odors.

As you tape up each packed box, place a piece of kite string underneath the tape, leaving about an inch sticking out. When it's time to unpack, just pull on the string, which will slit right through the tape.

Because furniture casters sometimes fall out when a piece is lifted, remove them ahead of time. Keep them together with heavy twine, and tag them so you know which piece they fit.

Involving the Kids

If you're going to move a considerable distance, get your youngsters "into the act." Encourage them to look up facts on your new location at the library, and let them help you plot the most convenient route on a map. If you're simply moving a short distance, let them examine the new house and neighborhood before the move.

When leaving your previous home, empty the children's rooms last, and restructure their rooms first when you've arrived at your new home. This helps them adjust psychologically.

Moving In

If you have access to the new home a day or so before the van arrives, you could set off a bug bomb or spray. (Even if you don't see bugs, there probably are some.) This way, you won't worry about the family, your pets, foods, or furnishings during the spraying.

If you're going to arrive before the movers, consider bringing a book, radio, or portable television with you.

To save time and eliminate confusion when the movers arrive, draw a floor plan of your new home ahead of time. Sketch in and number your furnishings the way you want them arranged. Tag furniture pieces to correspond to the floor plan so the movers know where to put each piece.

If you drive to your new location and arrive late, spend the first night at a motel rather than trying to "settle in" when everyone's tired. Everything will be much more fun in the morning.

A Moving Sale

If you hold a house or garage sale to dipose of unwanted items before moving, you'll not only make money, you'll save money by not having to pay for transporting those possessions.

To get the most money for your castoffs at your moving sale, clean and shine the objects you're selling—and display them creatively.

Your sale will be more organized if you categorize odds and ends in bins. For example, have one bin for kitchen gadgets, another for books, and another for records.

To display the clothes you're selling, rig up a clothesline. You can also throw an old sheet over part of the clothesline for a makeshift dressing room.

To keep pairs of shoes together, tie them with yarn or string.

Make sure you have plenty of newspapers, old boxes, and grocery bags for packing up the items purchased.

A Safe and Skidfree House

To avoid accidents, wipe up spilled water, grease, and other liquids from your kitchen, bathroom, and garage floors as soon as possible.

Anchor rolled up sections of carpet firmly to prevent someone from tripping.

Secure throw rugs with nonskid pads and keep them away from the tops and bottoms of stairs.

If your basement stairs are to be painted, add a little sand to the paint for a better grip. Or install rubber or abrasive treads.

If you staple burlap to the bottom step of a ladder, you'll have a scraper for your shoes. This way you won't have any slippery substances left on your shoes.

To keep someone from running into the edge of a bedroom door in the middle of the night, paint the door edge with luminous paint.

Kitchen Safety

Keep the handles of pots and frying pans turned inward on the kitchen range. A child could easily tip one over by accident.

To prevent grease fires, keep the stove clear of pot holders, paper napkins, and towels when frying food.

Don't put hot tea, coffee, or other hot liquids on a table cloth that hangs way over the side of the table. Someone could trip on the cloth and spill the scalding liquid.

When handing a knife to someone else, always hold the point turned away from him or her.

Keep the gas cooktop away from open windows where curtains can blow into the flames or where wind could extinguish the cooking flames.

Keep baking powder on hand for extinguishing emergency kitchen fires.

Safety for Children

Check all your child's toys to be sure any eyes, noses, knobs, or other parts will not come off when pulled or chewed.

Never leave a small child alone in the bathtub. Face your child toward the hot water faucet so he won't accidentally bump into the hot metal.

Don't hold a child on your lap while you drink or pass a hot beverage, or while you smoke.

Keep home workshop tools disconnected and lock switches and power supplies so a child can't turn them on.

Store all your poisonous materials on high shelves, out of the reach of children. And remember to label the containers.

Tie a bell around all bottles and containers that hold poisonous materials in the house to alert you if your child has gotten into something dangerous.

It's best never to place pillows in an infant's crib and to keep the crib completely away from the cord of a Venetian blind.

Never place a plastic bag or thin plastic covering near the bed of an infant or small child.

Remove the plastic spray nozzle from old aerosol cans when you discard them. You lesson the risk of children finding the cans and spraying chemicals into their own or their playmates' eyes.

Fire Rules to Remember

Never spend more than 30 seconds fighting a fire. If the fire can't be extinguished, warn others and get out of the house.

Walk your family through a fire drill so everyone knows what to do and where to go in case of fire.

Every room in the house should have at least two escape exits.

Never reenter a burning house for any reason.

Fire Prevention

Replace frayed electrical cords before they burn or cause a fire.

Don't overload circuits with appliances.

Don't run extension cords under the rugs. The cords wear easily and may short out, causing a fire.

Create a special closet for combustible materials and dangerous tools you don't want your children to play with. Put a good lock on the door and a heat detector inside to alert you of any fire danger.

Keep combustibles away from the furnace, which can give off flames or sparks at times.

Forewarned Is Forearmed

If you make your living or have your residence in a high-rise building, locate the fire exits on your floor. If an alarm sounds, remember that you should always use the fire stairs, not the elevator.

Learn to distinguish the sound of a fire alarm in your building from the sound of an elevator alarm bell. If you think someone's trapped in the elevator when, in actuality, the building is starting to go up in flames, you could be in serious trouble.

Never enter a public place, including a restaurant, without noting where all exits are. If they're chained, barred, or locked, complain to the management. If you get the cold shoulder, turn on your heels and leave. Management will soon get the message.

Smoke Detection

For basic protection at minimum expense, locate one smoke detector in the hallway near each separate sleeping area. (More complete protection calls for a detector on every level of a home.)

Don't mount a smoke detector in areas where the alarm can be triggered inappropriately such as by smoke from cooking, steam from the shower, or in the garage where combustion products from the car's engine can set it off.

Smoke detectors are unreliable below 40° F.

Fire Fighting

Never use water on electric, oil, or grease fires. Water will only spatter the flames.

If you can't shut off the gas before fighting a gas fire, get out immediately.

If you can't remove the fuel from a wood, paper, or fabric fire, cut off its air by smothering the fire with a coat, or heavy woolen blanket. You might also cool the fire with water, a fire extinguisher, sand, or earth.

Distribute fire extinguishers in key areas such as the kitchen, bedrooms, workshop, and garage.

Even if a fire is confined to a frying pan or wastebasket, never spend more than 30 seconds fighting the fire. Small fires can grow with frightening speed.

Electrical Safety

Never place an electric appliance where it can fall in water.

Never touch an electric appliance while standing in water.

Don't place electric heaters near combustibles.

As a safety precaution before leaving the house on vacation, unplug all electrical appliances except for those lights connected to automatic timers.

Safety from the Storm

Alert your local police department if you discover downed power lines. Set up barricades to keep others away from the area until help arrives.

A lightning protection system should offer an easy, direct path for the bolt to follow into the ground and thus prevent injury or damage while the bolt is traveling that path.

Grounding rods (at least two for a small house) should be placed at opposite corners of the house.

Keep an eye on large trees—even healthy ones—that could damage your house if felled in a storm. Cut them back if necessary.

When a major storm is imminent, close shutters, board windows, or tape the inside of larger panes with an "X" along the full length of their diagonals. Even a light material like masking tape may give the glass the extra margin of strength it needs to resist cracking. Exception: When a tornado threatens, leave windows slightly ajar.

If you live in a storm-prone area, nail down roof shingles or use adequate adhesive to keep them from blowing off in a violent wind. For roofs with shingles that are not the seal-down type, apply a little dab of roofing cement under each tab.

In your storm shelter, store a lantern, pick, shovel, crowbar, hammer, screwdriver, and pliers. If the exit became blocked, you might have to dig your way out. Store canned food and bottled water too.

The basement is not a good shelter during a tornado because it's too close to gas pipes, sewer pipes, drains, and cesspool. A better shelter would be underground, far from the house (in case the roof falls) and away from the gas and sewer system.

In a hurricane, don't go out unless you have to. However, if flooding threatens, seek high ground and follow the instructions of civil defense personnel.

Water Safety

A spare tire in the trunk of your car can be used as a life preserver in an emergency. Just make sure the tire is in good shape.

Handling Insecticides

Never spray insecticide near a flame, furnace, lighted stove, or pilot light.

Keep insecticide spray away from food, pets, dishes, cooking utensils, and children.

Avoid contact with the pesticide and don't inhale its fumes.

Don't go overboard when fumigating. Use only the amount of pesticide required for the job.

Never smoke while using pesticide and wash your hands before handling a cigarette afterwards.

Change clothes after doing the spraying and store insecticides in a safe place.

Never flush insecticides down the toilet, sewer, or drains.

Do not reuse insecticide containers. Rinse and dispose of them.

Never hang a chemically treated pet strip in a room where people will be present for any length of time, especially sick or old people or children.

As soon as you have used a space spray (bomb), leave the room. Close it up tightly for at least half an hour, then ventilate.

General Security Measures

Plan to burgle yourself. In this game, you'll discover any weaknesses in your home protection system that may have previously escaped your notice.

Before turning your house key over to a professional housecleaner for several hours, make sure the person is honest and reputable, as well as hard-working. Check all references thoroughly by calling them. If the housecleaner is from a firm, call your local Better Business Bureau to check on their reputation. Make sure the firm insures its employees against accidents and theft.

Ask for credentials from any salesman who wants entry to your home—even security system salesmen. Many professional burglars use this cover to check out homes. If you want to buy an electronic alarm system, make your own contacts with reputable firms.

Instead of keeping a spare key in a mailbox, under the door mat, or on a nail behind the garage, wrap the key in foil—or put it in a 35mm film can or a pipe tobacco can—and bury it where you can easily find it if you need it.

Lock up your home, even if you go out only for a short time. Many burglars just walk in through an unlocked door or window.

If your plans to be away from home have been publicized through a funeral, wedding, or similar newspaper notice, hire a housesitter. Burglars often read the newspapers to see who's planning to be away from home all day or for several days.

If a check or money is being sent to you, try to have a family member at home when the mail arrives.

Your house should appear occupied at all times. Use timers to switch lights and radios off and on when you're not at home.

Try to vary your daily schedule of departures and arrivals, etc. so that it isn't easily predictable.

Safeguard your home by not leaving notes for workmen or family members on the door.

If you're going to be away from home for several days—or even for just one day—adjust your telephone ring to its lowest volume. To a prowler, an unanswered phone is a quick tip that your home is empty.

Ask your neighbors to use your garbage cans when you're on vacation, so your absence won't be so evident.

Have a neighbor pick up your mail and arrange to have newspaper delivery stopped when away.

Let neighbors know of any suspicious-looking person or strange cars you notice lurking about.

Keep your curtains drawn or remove valuables to rooms where they can't be seen from outside.

To prevent burglars from stealing ladders stored outdoors, padlock them to something unmovable.

To keep your tools from being stolen, paint the handles. Thieves overlook items that are easy to identify.

Trees located near windows or shrubbery that might shield a burglar from view can be major flaws in your home protection plan.

Burglar Alarms and Watchdogs

For the most effective alarm system, conceal all wiring. A burglar looks for places where he can disconnect the security system.

Dogs are among the best deterrents to burglars; even a small dog can be effective.

Secure Your Doors

To help burglar-proof your home, install 1-inch throw deadbolt locks on all exterior doors.

A door with too much space between the door and the frame is an invitation for the burglar to use a jimmy. Reinforce such a door by attaching a panel of three-quarter-inch plywood or a piece of sheet metal to it.

If there are door hinges on the outside of your house, take down the door and reset the hinges inside. Otherwise all a thief has to do is knock out the hinge pin.

You can burglar-proof your glass patio doors by setting a pipe or metal bar in the inside bottom track of the door slide. The pipe should be the same length as the track.

It's easy for a burglar to pry his way through rot, so replace rotted door frames with new, solid wood.

It's simple for a thief to break glass panels and then reach in and open a door knob from the inside. Fortify such a door in another way or get a new door.

Attach your telephone number instead of your address to your key ring. If they're lost, a thief won't be able to find your house to use the keys.

Window Security

Protect your windows with one or more good locks, an iron grill or gate, an alarm system, burglar-resistant glass, or many small panes instead of one large area of glass.

When putting window locks on, have all the locks keyed alike and give each family member a key. Keep a key near the window where children can get it (but a burglar can't reach it) in case of fire.

After installing a window lock, drip some solder onto the screw heads. That will stop a burglar from unscrewing the lock after he cuts a small hole in the window pane.

It can be a problem to lock an aluminum sliding window in a ventilating position. A locking sliding window bolt allows high security as it fails entry even if the glass is broken.

Protect your basement windows by putting up grills, or even nailing them shut.

When you move into a new house, it's a good idea to change all the locks and tumblers.

Change your lock cylinders from time to time, just in case someone has gotten hold of a set of your keys. If you lose your keys, change the cylinder immediately.

A spring-latch lock is good for burglars who are "loiding" experts. Loiding is the method of slipping a plastic credit card against the latch tongue to depress it and unlock the door. A deadbolt defies any such attack. It is only vulnerable when there is enough space between the door and its frame so that an intruder might bring power tools or a hacksaw to bear. But that takes time—to the burglar's disadvantage.

In a rented house, install a double cylinder lock that requires a key to open from the inside as well as the outside. If a thief breaks through the panel and reaches in, he still has the lock to deal with instead of just a knob.

Stashing Your Valuables

You can keep your jewelry safe by installing a wall-outlet safe. When the safe is closed, if looks just like an electrical outlet. When buying a wall safe, be sure it's fireproof as well as burglar-proof.

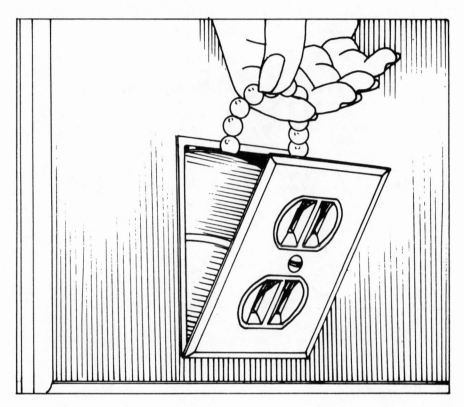

If you don't need a safe, find good hiding places in your home for your valuables. An acoustical tile ceiling offers good hiding possibilities. Remove a tile and restore it afterwards with magnetic fastener or a similar device. However, be careful not to leave finger marks. (See illustration on p. 28)

A chiseled-out space in the top of a door makes a great "safe" for small valuables. Or you might devise a false closet ceiling.

Fireplace logs can be hollowed out to make hiding places, too. Other ideas include the underside of desktops, linings of drapes, underneath insulation in the attic, inside a lamp. Avoid the obvious places such as mattresses, drawers, inside figurines, behind pictures, and under carpets.

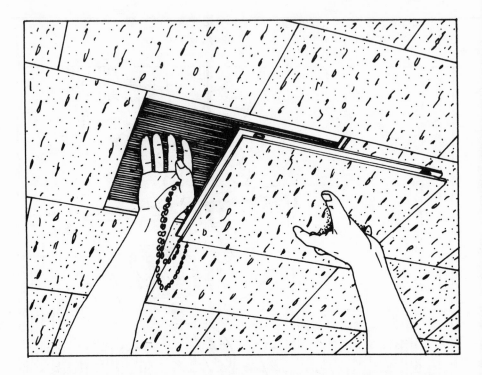

Hollow out the leg on a table or chair for hiding small objects. Drill from the bottom, then cap all the legs with rubber tips.

Garage Security

If you frost or cover your garage windows, burglars won't be able to tell if your car is gone.

Keep your garage door closed and locked even when your car is not there.

Are you worried about someone entering your house through your attached garage? A C-clamp can provide extra security if the garage door lifts on a track since the door cannot be opened if you tighten the C-clamp on the track next to the roller.

Another way to increase garage security is to install a peep hole in the door separating the house from the garage. If you hear suspicious sounds, you can check without opening the door.

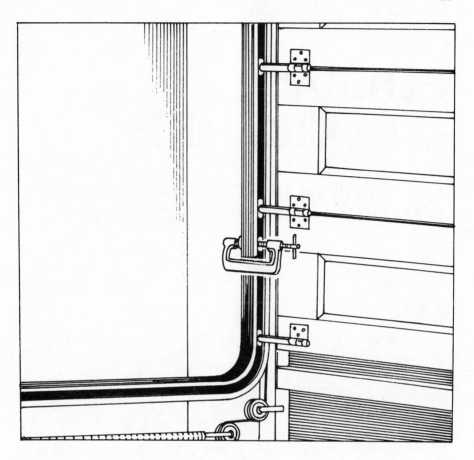

Shopping Security

When shopping, watch for pickpockets in places like the checkout counter where you normally plunk down your purse or parcel. Also be alert at store entrances, on escalators and in elevators, in bargain areas or demonstration areas.

When shopping, it's best to carry a zippered shoulder bag, with any outside pockets facing toward you. Divide your cash among the purse, your eyeglass case, and inner clothes pockets.

Chapter **2**

GENERAL CLEANING HINTS

A BUCKETFUL OF HINTS TO HELP YOU BREEZE THROUGH ALL YOUR EVERYDAY CLEANUPS

Dusting

Worn-out cotton sweat socks—particularly those with terry-lined feet—make excellent dusting mitts.

Instead of buying dust cloths chemically treated to "attract" dust, make your own from cheesecloth. Dip the cloth in a solution of two cups of water and one-quarter cup of lemon oil and allow it to dry before using.

Paint brushes make excellent dusters for small or hard-to-reach areas. Flick them along door jambs, around windows, and into corners where dust cloths won't fit.

So you won't snag or harm delicate fabric when dusting ruffled or pleated lamp shades, use an old shaving brush or a baby's hair brush. The bristles are soft and effective.

Want to dust furniture quick as a flash? Dampen two old cotton gloves or socks with furniture polish, slip them over your fingers, and then dust with both hands.

Vacuuming

It's annoying, when vacuuming from room to hallway to room, to discover that the cord often doesn't extend as far as you want it to. Rather than have to look for other wall sockets (usually located behind furniture), just add an extension to your cleaner's present cord.

You can use a straightened wire hanger to unclog a jammed vacuum cleaner hose. Leave a small hook at the end of the hanger and maneuver it back and forth; then, see if the hose is free of debris by dropping a coin through it. If the coin rolls out the other end, you're ready to vacuum again. If it doesn't, you'll have to maneuver the hanger some more. Another way to unclog a vacuum cleaner hose is to push an ordinary garden hose through it.

To prevent a dust cloud from forming, empty a vacuum cleaner bag into a large plastic garbage bag; hold the mouth of the bag shut as you dump the dust inside it.

It's best to empty vacuum cleaner bags when they're about two-thirds full; a full bag reduces suction power.

Mend a torn reusable vacuum cleaner bag by pressing iron-on patches over holes.

You can vacuum dust and lint from mops and brooms by holding them under the hose attachment.

Pictures

When cleaning picture glass, carefully dust the glass, and then polish it with tissues designed to clean eyeglasses. Avoid liquid cleaners because they could seep under the edge of the glass and spoil the photo or artwork. If you do use liquid cleaners, apply them to a cloth, *never* directly to the glass.

To clean deeply carved picture frames, use a clean, dry, plastic squeeze bottle, pumping the bottle like a small bellows to blow dust from tiny crevices.

To make a tarnished gilt frame gleam again, wipe it with a turpentine-dampened rag.

To avoid damaging a picture or painting when polishing its wooden picture frame, spray the polish on a cloth, not the frame, and then carefully apply to the frame.

Lampshades

Lampshades affixed to their frames with glue should be dry cleaned.

When lampshades aren't glued to their frames, wash them in the bathtub with warm water and a spray hose. Dry them quickly after washing so the frames won't rust. An electric fan or hair dryer can speed the process.

Telephone

To keep a phone clean and germfree, rub it with an alcohol-soaked paper towel.

Knickknacks

To wash fragile objects without breaking them, put them on a tray in the sink and spray them first with window cleaner or foam bathroom cleaner, and then with water. Let them air dry on a towel.

You can wash knickknacks more quickly than you could dust them. Swish them in water containing a touch of liquid detergent, rinse and drain on a towel. If you want to make sure every crevice is dry, use a handheld hair dryer.

Ivory

Always keep ivory objects where light can reach them, because steady darkness causes ivory to yellow.

To clean a yellowing ivory object, cut a lemon in half, dip it in salt, and rub it over the ivory surface. When the surface is dry, wipe it with a damp cloth, then buff dry for bright finish.

You can remove stubborn stains from ivory or plastic piano keys with a damp cloth dipped in baking soda, being careful not to let the soda fall between the keys. Wipe the keys off with another cloth, and buff them dry.

Luggage

Do you have black scuff marks on your luggage? They'll rub off with lemon extract.

Clean colored-leather luggage with mild soapsuds and a damp sponge or soft-nap cloth.

The best way to clean regular leather luggage is to use a soft, clean rag to rub in a few drops of baby shampoo, a small area at a time. Repeat until all surfaces are covered. Use the same cloth to buff the luggage to a natural sheen.

Tobacco Stains and Odors

Clean and sweeten ashtrays by washing them in baking soda and water, mixed one tablespoon to the quart.

To get rid of stale cigarette or cigar smoke, leave a dish of vinegar or ammonia in the room overnight. It also helps to dampen a towel with diluted vinegar and wave it through the room.

Cleaning and Protecting Books and Records

To keep vinyl and imitation leather-covered books looking good as new, wash them periodically with a mild detergent and then treat with a light coat of petroleum jelly or a vinyl dressing.

It is easy to clean lightly soiled records on the turntable. Gently hold a clean dust cloth on a record and allow the disc to turn at least three revolutions under the cloth. You'll be cleaning with the grooves, not across them, and so won't damage the record.

Periodically treat leather bound books with a light oil so the leather won't dry out and crack.

If you arrange books at the front of shelves, air will be able to circulate and prevent mustiness.

Protect books from direct sunlight, because it can fade and deteriorate the bindings.

In order to remove grease stains from books, rub the affected areas with soft, white breadcrumbs.

Sprinkle damp book pages with talcum powder or cornstarch until the moisture is absorbed, then shake or brush the powder away.

Precious Metals

To restore luster to a dried-out emerald or jade, dip a toothpick in olive oil and gently rub it over the stone's surface. (Use this method only if the piece won't be resold, since the stone may darken.)

An inexpensive way to clean gold is to mix one teaspoon of cigarette ashes with enough water to form a paste. Rub the paste onto the gold's surface with a soft cloth, rinse, and buff dry with a chamois. If there's no smoker in the house, use baking soda instead of cigarette ashes.

An easy way to clean silver is with ordinary baking soda. Make a paste from three parts soda to one part water. Using a soft cloth, rub the paste gently on the silver surface. Tarnish will disappear rapidly. After rinsing, buff the silver with a soft cloth to bring up the shine.

To clean tarnished silver, place the items in a glass dish, add a piece of aluminum foil, and cover with a quart of hot water mixed with one tablespoon of baking soda. A reaction between the foil and the silver will remove any tarnish. Don't use this process on raised designs, however. You'll lose the dark accents of the sculpture.

Tips to Remember

The acid in vinegar makes it a good preventive wash for areas where mildew might form.

To remove the discoloration of a yellowed bathtub, rub the tub with a solution of salt and turpentine.

So you don't have to guess when trying to mix correct solutions of cleaning compounds, plainly mark pint, quart, and gallon levels inside a bucket with red fingernail polish.

You can eliminate tiny scratches on glass by polishing the affected areas with toothpaste.

When a spray bottle's suction tube doesn't reach the liquid because most of the liquid has been used up, drop marbles or pebbles into the bottle till the level of the liquid rises enough to cover the tube end.

An automobile snow brush is perfect for cleaning under a refrigerator.

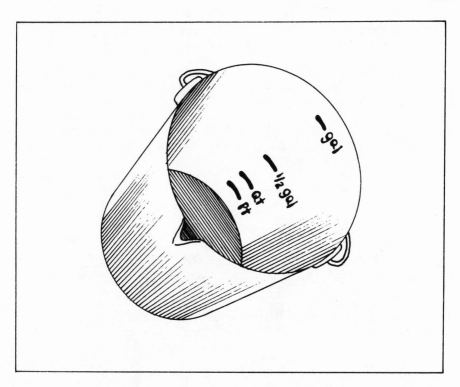

Old toothbrushes can be put to good use as hair dye applicators, or as cleaning brushes for silverware, combs, and typewriter keys.

You can get stale odors out of sponges by washing them in the dishwasher, or by immersing them overnight in a bowl of bleach. (Rinse them well the next morning.)

Make an efficient cleaning apron from a compartmented shoe bag by attaching strings and filling the pockets with rags, polishes, brushes, and other lightweight supplies.

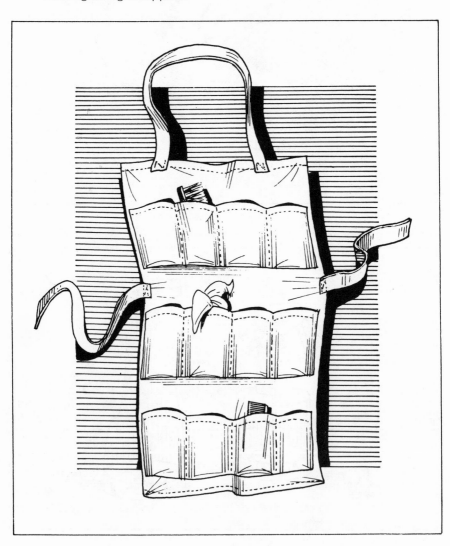

Special Challenges

It is possible to clean a chandelier without taking it down—here's how. In a glass, mix a solution that's one part denatured alcohol and three parts water. Cover the floor or table under the chandelier with newspaper or plastic and set up a ladder so you can reach the fixture's pendants. Individually submerge the crystals in the glass for a few moments, swishing them back and forth a little, and then simply let them air dry.

If candle wax has dripped on a table or cloth, hold an ice cube against the wax until it's brittle, and then pry it off with a knife or your fingernail.

If silver candlesticks accumulate wax drippings, place them in the freezer; when the wax freezes, you'll be able to peel it off.

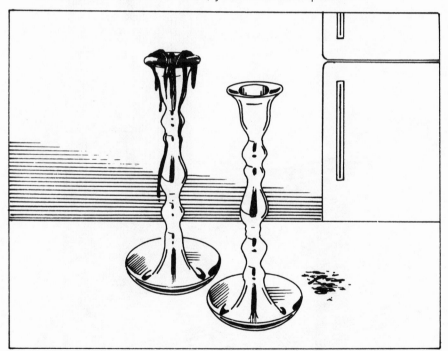

To make a copper/brass/bronze cleaner, stir together 1 tablespoon of table salt and 1 tablespoon of flour. Continuing to stir, add 1 tablespoon of white vinegar. Apply the resulting paste with a damp cloth or sponge, rub gently, then rinse and wipe dry.

Sometimes a slightly tarnished aluminum surface can be cleaned by rubbing it with crumpled aluminum foil.

Remove traces of rust on iron by rubbing with an emery cloth, or with steel wool moistened with a few drops of turpentine or kerosene.

Fireplace smoke stains can be removed by washing them with one-half cup of trisodium phosphate (TSP) mixed in 1 gallon of water. (Wear gloves to protect your hands.) You also can remove fireplace smoke

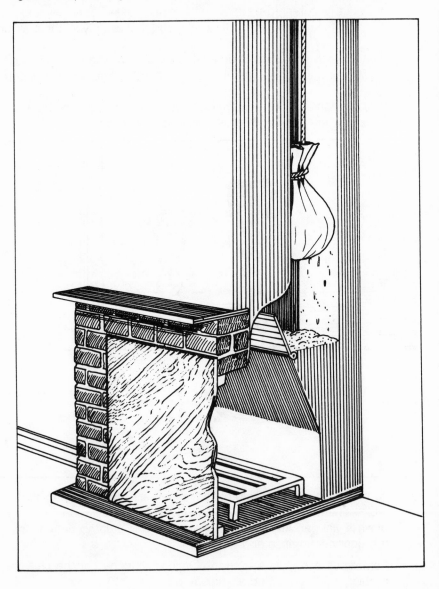

stains by rubbing them with an art gum eraser, or by applying a paste of cream of tartar and water. When the paste dries, brush if off, along with the stains.

Why pay a chimney sweep to clean your chimney? Do it yourself this way: Open the damper. Seal the hearth from the room with scrap lumber or a drop cloth secured with masking tape. If the flue is straight, fill a burlap bag with wadded paper and two bricks and fasten it to a long rope. Go up to the roof and slide the bag up and down the chimney's interior five or six times to remove all soot. If the flue is curved, use two feet of tire chain or other heavy chain at the end of the rope, rather than a burlap bag. Slap the chain against the flue's sides as you raise and lower the rope five or six times. For the most efficient use of your fireplace, do this once a year.

To see if your chimney is sootfree after you've cleaned it, wait an hour or so for the dust to settle and then examine the flue using a large hand mirror and a flashlight.

Chapter 3

CLEANING AND PROBLEM SOLVING

FEEL LIKE CLIMBING THE WALLS WHEN IT'S TIME TO WASH THEM? HERE'S HOW TO TACKLE ALL THOSE BIG CLEANING JOBS WITH CONFIDENCE.

WALLS AND CEILINGS

Cleaning Walls

There's no need to purchase expensive wall cleaner. Make your own by mixing one-fourth cup of washing soda, one-quarter cup of white vinegar, and one-half cup of ammonia in a gallon of warm water.

It's best to wash walls from the bottom up; otherwise, water trickling over the dry, unwashed areas creates hard-to-remove streaks.

You can make washing walls less of a wet, messy task by decreasing the amount of water and using thick suds created with an egg beater.

To prevent water from running down your arm when washing walls, fashion a bracelet from a sponge or washcloth held in place with a thick rubber band.

For cleaning rough-textured walls, old nylon stockings or socks are better than sponges or cloths because they won't tear and leave behind difficult-to-remove bits and pieces.

Lift crayon marks off a painted wall by gingerly rubbing them with a cloth or sponge dampened with mineral spirits or lighter fluid. Remove any shine left on flat paint by sponging lightly with hot water.

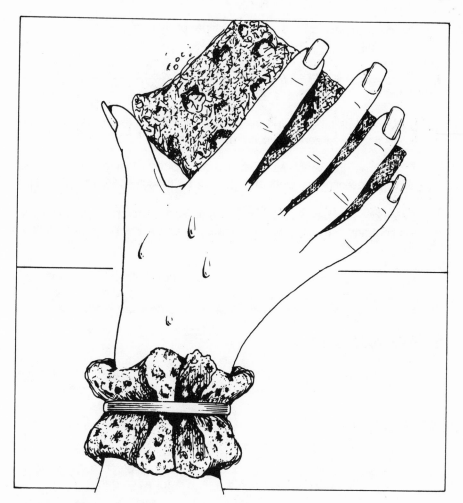

Cleaning Wall Coverings

You can sponge washable wall coverings with a mild detergent, and even scrub some vinyls. To find out how much elbow grease your paper can take, first work on a scrap.

To remove crayon marks on wallpaper, rub gingerly with a dry soap-filled, fine grade steel-wool pad. Or, use a wad of white paper toweling moistened with dry-cleaning solvent, and delicately sponge the surface. Carefully blot and lift in small areas to prevent the solvent from spreading and discoloring the paper.

Remove ordinary soil marks from wallpaper by gently rubbing them with an art gum eraser.

Lift grease stains from washable wallpaper with a paste made of cornstarch and water. Or, rub dry borax over stains.

Clean nonwashable wallpaper with rye bread. Make a fist-sized wad of bread and rub it across discolorations and dirt.

To remove grease stains from a grass-cloth wall or ceiling covering, apply an aerosol dry cleaner, following instructions carefully.

To remove a grease spot on nonwashable wallpaper, place a blotter over the spot and press it with a moderately hot iron. The blotter will soak up the grease. Repeat as required.

You can also eradicate a grease spot on nonwashable wallpaper with talcum powder. Use a powder puff to dust the spot with talc, leave it for an hour, and then brush it off. Repeat the procedure if necessary.

Cleaning Wood Paneling

To remove white water marks from wood paneling, rub mayonnaise into them. Wipe it off 12 hours later—the marks will have vanished.

Removing Tape

It's easy to remove transparent tape from a wall without marring the paint or wallpaper if you press the tape—through a protective cloth—with a warm iron to soften and loosen the tape's adhesive backing.

Hanging Wallpaper

If you're planning to paper all walls in a room, choose the least conspicuous area as your starting–finishing point. It's almost inevitable that the pattern won't match perfectly as you return to the start.

If there are stubborn grease spots on walls you're going to paper, seal them with clear nail polish or shellac so the grease won't soak through the new wallpaper.

To make wallpaper hanging easier, a right-handed person should work from left to right. If you're left-handed, work from right to left.

So you can see precisely where you've applied the wallpaper paste, tint it slightly with food coloring.

Save time when applying wallpaper paste by using a short-napped paint roller.

Save time when hanging the wallpaper itself by smoothing it with a clean, dry paint roller. If you attach the roller to a long handle, you can reach the ceiling or the tops of walls without climbing a ladder.

Eliminate bubbles and wrinkles in vinyl wall coverings with a squeegee.

To eliminate a bubble in freshly hung wallpaper—while the paste is still wet—puncture the blister with a sharp needle or pin. Press the blister inward from its edges toward the puncture, squeezing out excess paste. Wipe this excess off with a damp sponge, and then press the area flat with a seam roller or the back of a spoon.

To eliminate a bubble in wallpaper after the paste has dried, take a razor blade and slit the blister twice across its center, forming an "X." Peel back the slit's four tips, dab paste under them, press down, and smooth with a seam roller or the back of a spoon.

Take the headaches out of wallpapering a ceiling—hang the paper crosswise since strips are shorter in that direction. Accordian-fold each strip, paste against paste, then unfold as you go along, supporting with one hand and smoothing with the other.

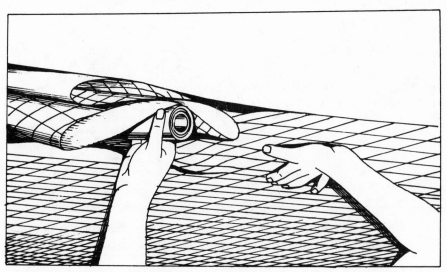

When papering over wall anchors, or places where you plan to reposition shelves or pictures, insert toothpicks in holes left by screws or picture hooks. As you cover these sections, force the toothpick points through the paper to mark reinstallation places for screws or hooks.

After wallpapering a room where there'll be a lot of moisture—such as kitchen or bathroom—it helps to cover all seams with clear varnish to guard against peeling.

Repairing Wallpaper

It's a good idea to save leftover wallpaper for patching. Let it "weather" and fade at the same rate as the paper on the wall by taping a piece or two on a closet wall. If you do this, it will correspond—in color density as well as pattern—to the paper on the wall that later might need patching.

To repair a damaged wallpaper section, *tear*—don't cut—a patch from a piece that's been "weathered." Because less-defined torn edges blend imperceptibly with paper already on the wall, the patch will be virtually invisible. Note: Don't remove damaged wallpaper before placing a patch on it. Paste the patch directly over the damaged surface.

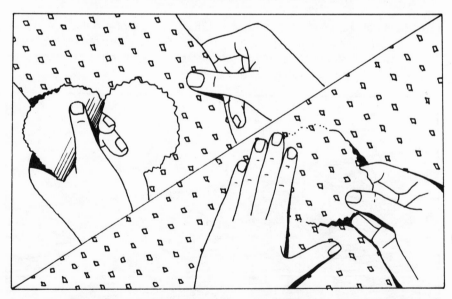

If you lack wallpaper scraps for patching, try touching up the design in worn areas. Carefully use felt-tip pens to restore rubbed or faded colors.

If you don't have a seam roller to use to tame a loose wallpaper seam, rub it with the back of a spoon. White glue can substitute for wallpaper paste.

Removing Wallpaper

When preparing to remove old wallpaper, soak it first with very hot water applied with a paint roller; add a touch of detergent to the water to hasten the process. If the paper is foil, or vinyl-coated, score its surface so water can penetrate to the backing.

When removing old wallpaper with a steamer, save the ceiling for last. As you work on the walls, steam rising from the applicator will loosen the ceiling paper. Much of it will start sagging from its own weight, and peeling it off will be easy.

Fabric Wall Coverings

If you're stapling fabric to a wall and you want to mask the staples at the top and bottom, glue a band of fabric—or even a wide, contrasting ribbon—over these seams. You also can cover the staples with molding strips.

Putting Up Paneling

When paneling a room, let the panels acclimate to the room's humidity for 48 hours before positioning them. This helps prevent them from being installed too tightly or loosely.

When applying wood paneling to a wall, you can attach panels directly to the studs. However, panels attached this way tend to give a little and are not as soundproof as those installed over either a plywood or a gypsum board backing.

When you're installing wood panels, first lean them against the wall as you think they should be placed. This gives you a chance to arrange the wood graining in the manner that pleases you most. When they're positioned the way you want them, number the panels for reference and proceed with the project.

When using a hand saw or a table saw to cut a wood panel, cut the panel with the face up. When using a hand power-saw, cut the panel with the face down.

Installing Wallboard

Do you want to discourage nails from "popping" out of wallboard? Drive them in in pairs, spaced 2 inches apart. Each strengthens the holding power of the other. If you're driving nails into a stud where 2 wallboard edges butt up against each other, stagger the double nailing on each side of the interface.

Instead of carrying large wallboard sheets into the house and possibly damaging them when navigating awkward corners, measure and cut them to fit before bringing them inside.

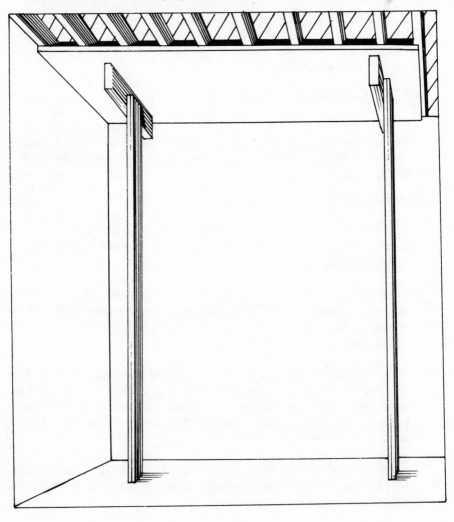

To save your arm muscles when installing ceiling wallboard, construct two "deadman" supports. These consist of 2 × 4's of the proper floor-to-ceiling length, including T-bars at their tops. The deadmen effortlessly support the panels while you do the final positioning and securing.

Acoustical Tiles

To help absorb noise, install acoustical tiles on doors to playrooms. You could also reduce noise in your home by using such tile to line the rooms or closets that house central heating and air conditioning units.

Wall Repairs

A saucepan lid—turned upside down—makes a good container for joint compound, since the lid's knob lets you hold the "bowl" easily during application. (When you've finished, make sure you rinse out the lid before any residue hardens.) Other easy-to-hold containers are a bathroom plunger or half a hollow rubber ball.

To patch a small hole in drywall, you can use a tin can lid covered by a plaster patch. Thread a wire in and back out through two holes in the can lid, and then slide the lid behind the wall through horizontal slits cut out

from each side of the hole. Pull the lid flat on the inside, and hold it in place while you apply plaster.

It will be easier to fill a large hole in the wall if you first jam a piece of wallboard into the hole, and then mar the wallboard's surface so it's rough. The spackle will adhere tightly to the wallboard piece and won't sink in and require further applications.

A beer can opener makes a good tool for cutting loose plaster out of a wall before patching a large crack. Use the pointed end of the opener to undercut and widen the opening.

It's best to fill wide cracks in plaster from the inside out, pressing fresh plaster in with a putty knife or a trowel.

Adding a tablespoon of white vinegar to the water when mixing patching plaster will keep the compound from drying too quickly, allowing you more time to work.

If a screw hole in the wall has worn-down grooves, stuff the hole with a cotton ball soaked in white glue, and let it dry for 24 hours. You'll then be able to insert a screw securely using a screwdriver.

Ceramic Tile

To fit a ceramic tile around the stem of a shower pipe, cut the tile in half and then cut semicircles out of each half with tile nippers.

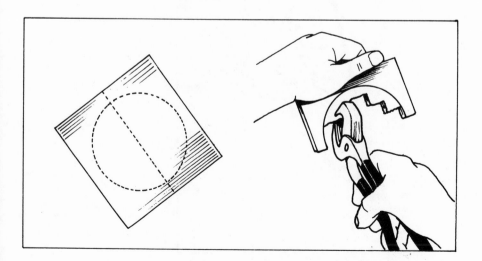

You'll be able to remove a damaged ceramic tile easily if you first drill a hole through its center and score an "X" across it with a glass cutter. Then chisel out the pieces.

When replacing an individual ceramic wall tile, it helps to tape it securely to surrounding tiles until its mastic dries.

Hanging Heavy Objects

Hang heavy objects without special anchors by driving nails directly into the wooden studs behind walls. There are several ways to locate studs. You can tap a wall gently with your knuckles or a hammer. A wall sounds hollow between studs; solid on top of them. Or, move an electric razor (turned on) along a wall; a razor registers a different tone over studs. If

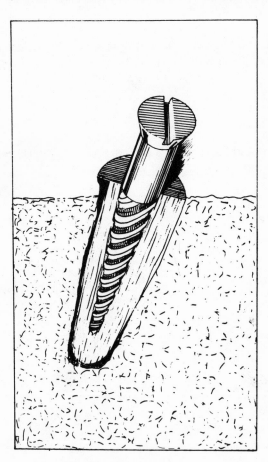

nails were used to attach drywall to studs, a magnet will indicate the location of the nails, and, therefore, the studs.

To prevent a toggle bolt from slipping into a wall cavity before a hang-up is in place, insert a washer under the bolt's head. (The hole needed for the bolt is normally larger than the bolt's head.)

To hold a heavy bolt in a masonry wall, taper a dowel and drive it into a small hole. Then drive the bolt into the dowel.

WINDOWS AND DOORS

Cleaning Windows

A liquid cleaner for glass can be made by mixing 2 cups of water and 2 tablespoons of liquid dishwashing detergent with 2 cups of isopropyl rubbing alcohol (70 percent). Stir until thoroughly mixed and then pour into a clean, pump-spray bottle. The alcohol keeps the cleaner from freezing on the panes in winter.

To make an ammonia-based glass cleaner, mix two cups of water, one cup of isopropyl rubbing alcohol (70 percent), and 1 tablespoon of household ammonia. Pour into a clean, pump-spray bottle.

To remove built-up cooking grease or soot from window glass, use a solution of two cups of kerosene and one gallon of warm water. Rub it on with a soft rag, and wipe the panes dry with a clean towel. Caution: Kerosene is flammable; don't pour it or use it near an open flame. The same cleaning solution (2 cups of kerosene to 1 gallon of warm water) also protects window exteriors. Water drops will bead just as they do on a highly waxed car.

Pure vinegar will remove stubborn hard-water sprinkler spots and streaks from a window.

Cloudy days are preferable to sunny days for window washing because direct sunlight dries cleaning solutions before you can polish the glass properly.

If you can wash one side of a window with horizontal strokes and the other side with vertical strokes, you'll be able to tell which side a streak is on.

An old auto wiper blade makes a good squeegee for washing windows.

When washing windows, a soft toothbrush or a cotton swab is a useful tool for cleaning corners.

It is possible to clean upstairs window exteriors without using a ladder. Use a garden hose spray bottle attachment containing automatic dishwasher detergent; the spray leaves only a few spots.

To give an extra shine to window glass, polish it with well-washed cotton T-shirts or old diapers.

Polish windows to a sparkling shine with crumpled-up newspaper. The paper also leaves a film that's resistant to dirt.

Rubbing a clean blackboard eraser over a freshly washed (and dried) window gives it a diamond-bright shine.

Hints to Remember

Spattered rain and dirt will easily wipe off window sills that have a protective coat of wax.

Applying a reflective vinyl coating on the inside of your windows will both protect your furniture upholstery or drapery fabric from the fading effects of strong sunlight and help keep your home cooler in the summertime.

To free a window that's been painted shut, use a scraper, knife, or spatula to cut the paint seal between the sash and the window frame. Then, working from the outside, insert the blade of a pry bar under the sash and pry gently from the corners in. Lever the bar over a block of scrap wood.

If you try to open a window and it refuses to budge, tap a hammer on a block of wood at various places on the sash. (Don't hit the sash directly with the hammer, or you'll leave dents.) The tapping may jar the sash loose.

Window Repairs

When replacing a broken sash cord, consider using a sash chain, which has a much longer life.

Soften old putty for easy removal by heating it with a soldering iron, propane torch, or handheld hair dryer. Or, if you prefer, soften it with linseed oil, and then scrape it away.

To make dried-out putty workable again, sprinkle it with a few drops of raw linseed oil, and knead it till it's soft and pliable.

Before attempting to chisel dried and hardened putty from a wooden window frame, brush raw linseed oil over the putty's surface. Let it soak in and soften it.

To prevent a window pane crack from spreading, score a small arced line with a glass cutter just beyond the crack, curving around it. Usually the crack will travel only as far as the arc.

To remove cracked glass from a window without excess splintering, crisscross the pane on both sides with several strips of masking tape before rapping it with a hammer. Most of the pane will be held together.

You can fill a pellet gun hole in a window pane with clear nail polish or shellac. Dab at the hole; when the application dries, dab again—and reapply till the hole is filled. The pane will appear clear. A pellet-gun hole in stained glass can be filled the same way.

When installing a new window pane, speed up the process by rolling the glazing compound between the palms of your hands to form a long string the diameter of a pencil. Lay the "string" along the frame, over the glass, and smooth it in place with a putty knife.

When glazing windows, prevent the wood from drinking the putty's oils. First brush the frames where the putty will lie with boiled linseed oil.

If, when glazing a window, the putty knife sticks or pulls at the glazing compound, you can "grease" the knife by dipping the blade into linseed oil. (Wipe off the excess.)

When painting glazing compound, lap the paint slightly over the edge of the compound and onto the glass to completely seal the compound to the pane.

Screens

To keep aluminum screens from pitting, clean them outdoors (never indoors) with kerosene. Dip a rag in the kerosene, and rub both sides of the mesh and the frames, then wipe off the excess. This is a particularly

good rust-inhibitor for older screens. (Since kerosene is highly flammable, it should always be stored in a cool place and never in large
amounts.)

To repair a small tear in a wire window screen, push the wire strands
back into place with an ice pick. If the hole doesn't close completely,
sparingly brush clear nail polish or shellac across the remaining opening.
Let the sealer dry, and reapply till the pinhole is transparently sealed. (Be
careful not to let any sealer run down the screen. Immediately blot any
excess.)

If there's a clean cut or tear in a window screen, you can stitch it together.
Use a long needle and a strong nylon thread or a fine wire. Zigzag stitch
across the cut, being careful not to pull the thread or wire so tight that the
patch puckers. After stretching, apply clear nail polish to keep the thread
or wire from pulling loose.

To close a large hole in a window screen, cut a patch from a scrap piece
of screening of the same type as the damaged screen. Zigzag stitch the
patch into place, and then apply clear nail polish to the stitching.

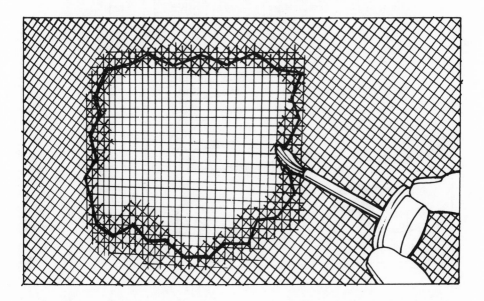

Repair fiberglass screening by laying a fiberglass patch over the hole or
tear and running a hot iron around its edges; the heat fuses the patch to

the screen. Put a scrap of foil over the screen itself to prevent the iron from touching it.

Clean awnings in the direction of the seam, not against it. (As fabric awnings age, their seams weaken.)

Lower rolled-up awnings after a storm to allow them to dry.

You can rejuvenate faded canvas awnings with a special paint available from awning dealers or a paint store.

Door Repairs

If a door's hinge screws are loose because the screw holes have become enlarged, fill the holes with pieces of wood toothpicks dipped in glue. When the glue dries, reinsert the screws. Or, wrap hinge screws with steel wool and reinsert.

If you're trying to remove a door's hinge pin and the pin won't budge, press a nail against the hinge bottom and tap upward against the nail with a hammer.

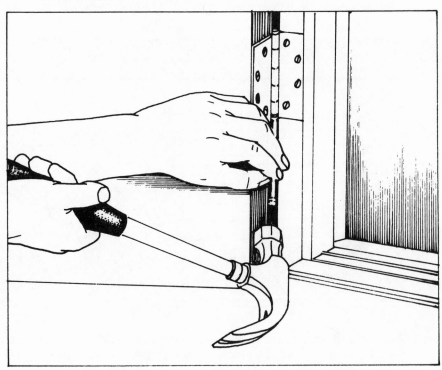

For better control when lifting a door off its hinges, remove the bottom pin first. When replacing a door on its hinges, insert the top pin first.

You needn't remove a door to plane its bottom if it scrapes the threshold or the floor. Place sandpaper on the threshold or floor; then move the door back and forth over the abrasive. Slide a newspaper or magazine under the sandpaper if it needs to be raised to make contact.

If a door binds on the knob side when the door is closed, its hinges may be misaligned. If the top of the knob side binds, try putting a cardboard shim behind the bottom hinge. Should the bottom corner bind, slip a cardboard shim behind the top hinge. To shim a door hinge, loosen the screws on the door frame side. Cut a shim from thin cardboard with slots to fit around the screws, slide it behind the hinge, and tighten the screws.

When you've fashioned a door to the exact size for hanging, bevel the latch edge backward just a bit to let it clear the jamb as it swings open and shut.

If you have to remove some wood at a door's binding points, use a block plane on the top or bottom of the door and a jack plane to work on the side. Work from the ends to the center on the top or bottom edge, from the center out on the sides.

If a door sticks at the sides, try to plane only on the hinge side. The latch side is beveled slightly and planing could damage the bevel. Plane from the center toward the ends.

Before you replace a door you've planed, seal the planed edges. If you don't, the raw wood will absorb moisture and the door will swell and stick again.

General Door Hints

Cardboard shields will protect a door's finish when you clean and polish door hardware. Fit the shields around the pertinent metal parts, holding them in place with masking tape.

To prevent people from mistaking a closed sliding glass door for an open one, apply an eye-level decal—at both adult and child levels—to alert people before they walk into the pane and possibly injure themselves. You can use the same trick to mark lightweight screens.

Children old enough to answer the door should be able to see who's there, just as you do. Install a second peep hole low enough for youngsters to use.

If a doorknob bangs against a wall, protect the wall by covering the knob with a slit-open powder puff.

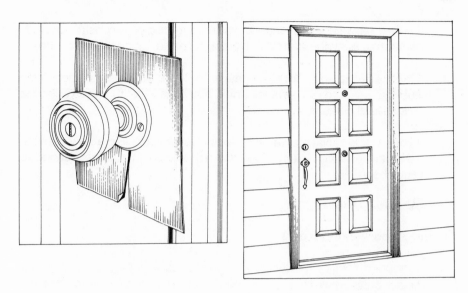

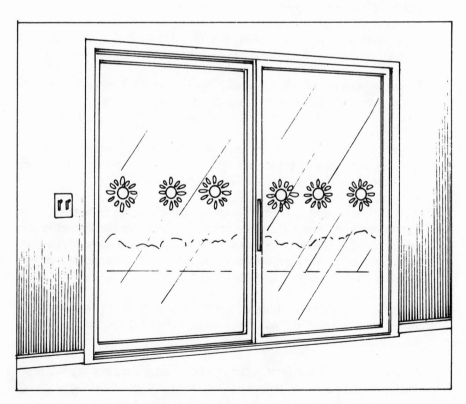

If you quiet a squeaky hinge by lubricating its pin with petroleum jelly rather than oil, you needn't worry about floor drippings.

Graphite from a soft pencil can be used to lubricate a resistant door lock. Rub the key across the pencil point, and then slide it in and out of the lock several times.

If you want to replace an existing lock but you can't find a new one that will fit the existing holes, cover the old holes with a large decorative escutcheon plate.

FLOORS AND STAIRS

Cleaning and Waxing Floors

A mopped floor occasionally dries with a luster-dulling film, but if you mop it again—this time using water containing a cup or so of white vinegar—the floor will glisten.

A few drops of vinegar in the water you're using to clean the kitchen floor will help remove cooking-grease particles that have settled from the air.

A pencil eraser or fine, dry steel wool often are effective in removing scuff marks left by shoe heels on resilient flooring. Lift crayon marks by rubbing with a damp rag containing toothpaste or silver polish.

A portable blow dryer can soften wax that has dripped onto wooden surfaces. Wipe away the wax with a paper towel, then rinse the area with a mixture of vinegar and water. Dry thoroughly.

Dust and other debris often collect in hard-to-reach corners, such as behind large appliances, but you can reach into these corners with ease with a yardstick. Make a yardstick "duster" by covering the end with a sock, secured with rubber bands, or by fastening a small sponge to the end of a yardstick with staples or rubber bands.

To clean your radiators, hang a damp cloth behind the radiator, then blow on the radiator with your hair dryer to force hidden dirt and dust onto the damp cloth.

If you're tired of buying new dust mops because the old ones get dirty so quickly, cover your mop with an old nylon stocking. When the stocking gets soiled, simply discard it and replace it with another.

To clean up raw egg dropped on a floor, sprinkle it with salt, let it sit for 15 to 20 minutes, and then sweep it with a broom.

When cleaning an asphalt tile floor with water, use a well-wrung cloth or sponge, since excess water can seep into the seams and loosen the adhesives that hold the flooring.

To prevent dulling the shine of highly waxed floors when washing them between waxings, use a solution of one cup of fabric softener in one-half pail of water.

When it's time for a new coat of wax on a linoleum or tile floor, remove the old wax by mopping with a solution of three parts of water to one part of rubbing alcohol. The floor will be clean and ready for a new waxing.

Instead of using commercial preparations, you can "wax" a floor by adding 2 tablespoons of furniture polish and one-half cup of vinegar to a bucket of warm water.

For a fast shine between floor waxings, put a piece of waxed paper under your mop and slide it around your floor.

After you've waxed a floor, you can wrap a bath towel around each foot and shuffle around the room to polish the floor in a flash.

Instead of using a rag to apply paste wax to floors, slip a glove-type potholder or workmen's glove over your hand for a better grip and to protect your skin. Such gloves have the added benefits of being sturdy and easy to clean.

Rather than wax floors on your hands and knees, stand and use a long-handled paint roller. A roller not only speeds up the waxing process, it makes it easy to reach under a radiator or built-in furniture.

Floor Repairs

If you have a squeaky wood floor under tile or carpet, you might be able to eliminate the squeak without removing the floor covering. Try to reset loose boards by pounding a hammer on a block of scrap wood in the area over the squeaky boards. The pressure may force loose nails back into place.

You might be able to silence squeaky hardwood floors by using talcum powder as a dry lubricant. Sprinkle powder over the offending areas, and sweep it back and forth till it filters down between the cracks.

Try filling dents in a hardwood floor with clear nail polish or shellac. Because the floor's color will show through, the dents will not be apparent.

Sometimes you can flatten bulges or curled seams in a linoleum floor by placing aluminum foil over them and "ironing" them with your steam iron. (The heat will soften and reactivate the adhesive.) Position weights, such as stacks of books, over treated areas to keep them flat until the adhesive cools and hardens.

To patch a gouge (not a dent) in a resilient floor, take a scrap of the flooring and grate it with a food grater. Mix the resulting dust with clear nail polish and plug the hole.

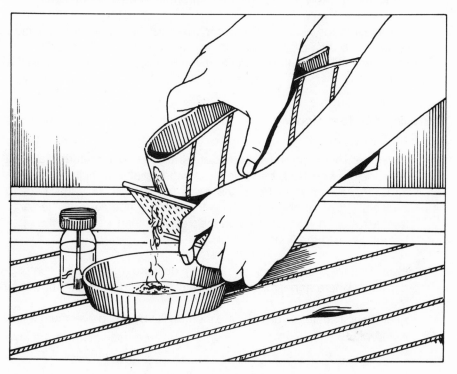

Another way to camouflage a gouge or hole in a resilient floor is with crayon wax. Choose a crayon that matches the floor color, melt it, fill the gouge or hole, and then wax the floor.

If you want to replace a damaged area of resilient flooring, make a perfect patch from scrap flooring with this method: Place the scrap piece over the damaged area, so that it overlaps sufficiently, and tape it to hold it. Then, cut through both layers at the same time to make a patch that is an exact duplicate. Replace the damaged area with the tightly fitting patch.

To remove a damaged resilient tile, soften it with a propane torch fitted with a flame-spreader nozzle. (Be careful not to damage surrounding tiles.) When the tile is soft, pry it up with a paint scraper or putty knife and scrape the adhesive off the floor so the new tile bonds cleanly.

You also can remove a resilient tile by covering it with dry ice, wearing work gloves to protect your hands. Let the dry ice stand for 10 minutes and then remove any remaining ice. The cold will make the tile brittle, so it will shatter easily. Chisel out the tile from the edges to the center.

To remove a resilient floor tile for replacement, lay a piece of aluminum foil on it and then press down with an ordinary iron set at medium. The iron's heat will soften the mastic, and you can easily pry up the tile with a putty knife.

Installing Resilient Flooring

Laying resilient floor tile will be easier if the room temperature is at least 70°F before you start, because tile is more pliable at higher temperatures. Put all boxes of tile in the room for at least 24 hours prior to positioning tiles on the floor. Keep the room temperature at the same level for about a week after laying the tiles, and then wait at least a week before washing the floor.

Install floor tiles from the center of a room outward, because the center of a room is where appearance and perfect matching are most important.

After laying floor tiles, you can help them lie flat by going over them with a rolling pin.

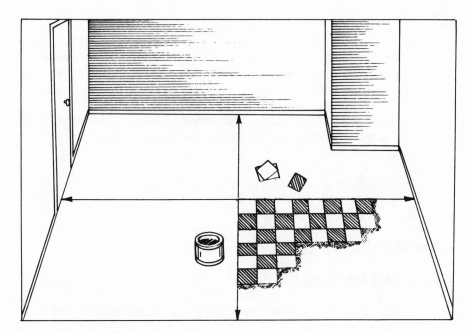

Protecting Your Floor

To prevent scratching the floor when moving heavy furniture across uncarpeted areas, slip scraps of old carpeting, face down, under all furniture legs.

So chairs won't scratch a hardwood floor, glue bunion pads to the bottoms of the chair legs.

Thumbtacks pressed into the bottom ends of wooden chair legs will also allow them to slide more easily across a wood or tile floor.

If you're going to use flagstone or slate as indoor flooring, these porous materials should be sealed to keep them looking their best.

Brick flooring can also be sealed and waxed to protect its porous surface from staining. It is especially helpful to treat brick this way if it is used for flooring in a kitchen.

Solvent-based cleaners and polishes preserve cork tile floors and should be used instead of water or water-based products.

Stairs

Try eliminating squeaks in stairs by using packaged graphite powder or talcum powder in a squeeze bottle, applying the lubricant along the joints in the problem area.

To stop squeaks at the front of a stair tread, drive pairs of spiral flooring nails, each pair angled in a "V," across the tread and into the top of the riser below it.

If an application of graphite powder or talcum powder fails to eliminate a stair squeak, go under the stairs and drive wedges into the gaps between the moving components.

FURNITURE

Cleaning and Protecting

Leftover tea makes a good cleaning agent for varnished furniture.

While waxing furniture, also wax the insides of ash trays. This makes them easier to clean.

To avoid leaving fingerprints while polishing furniture, wear cotton gloves.

After polishing furniture, sprinkle on a little cornstarch and rub to a high gloss. Cornstarch absorbs oil and leaves a glistening, fingerprint-free surface.

Paste furniture wax or oil furniture polish will camouflage tiny furniture scratches.

To treat scratches on natural wood or antique finishes, polish with a mixture of equal amounts of turpentine and boiled linseed oil. Apply with a clean, soft, damp cloth.

Rub walnut or pecan meat over scratches in finished wood; the oil often hides them. Liquid shoe polish often covers scratches, too.

Any scratch made by a match can be removed by rubbing it with a lemon wedge.

There are several ways to remove white spots, such as those left by wet drinking glasses. You can rub them with toothpaste on a damp cloth. Try this on other surface stains, too. Or rub them with paste furniture polish or any mild abrasive or oil. Appropriate abrasives are ashes, salt, soda, or pumice; suitable oils are olive oil, petroleum jelly, cooking oil, or lemon-oil furniture polish.

Prevent rusting on chrome kitchen chairs with a coat of wax.

Paper stuck to a polished table can be lifted after saturating the paper with cooking oil.

Decals will easily lift off painted furniture if you sponge them with vinegar.

It's best to position a piano where the sun won't shine on it and where it's least likely to be exposed to changes in temperature or humidity.

An old piano bench with a few inches sawed off its legs makes a "conversation piece" coffee table.

Repairing Furniture

You can unstick wooden drawers by rubbing contact surfaces with a bar of soap or a candle.

Tighten a cabinet or dresser knob by dipping its screw or screws in fingernail polish or shellac and reinserting the knob. When the polish or shellac hardens, the screws will be set and the knobs will be tight.

You can tighten a loose furniture leg caster by wrapping a rubber band around its stem and reinserting it.

When wood fibers in a piece of furniture are merely bent, but not cut, straighten out any dents with an electric iron and a damp cloth. Place the damp cloth on a dent, hold the iron on it till the cloth begins to dry, redampen the cloth, and repeat the process as needed. Make sure the iron is at a medium setting.

If a chair wobbles because one leg is shorter than the others, steady the chair by forming an appropriately shaped piece of wood putty to "extend" the short leg. When the putty dries, sand and stain it to match the leg and glue it in place.

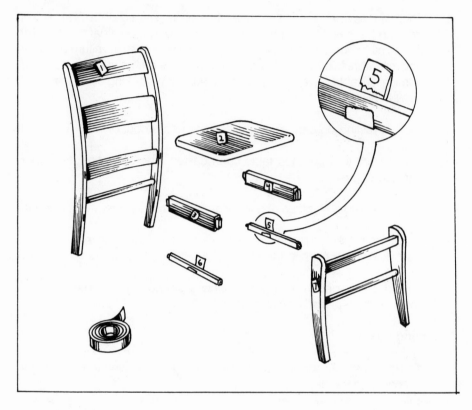

When disassembling a piece of furniture for repair, label or number the parts with bits of masking tape so you'll know how to put them together again.

If you need to pound apart sections of a chair that needs regluing, a soft mallet will be much kinder to the wood than a hammer, while providing enough power to do the job.

Thread can serve as packing around a chair rung before regluing it.

To tighten wobbly wicker furniture, wash it outdoors with hot soapy water, rinse with a hose, and let it air dry. The wood and cane will shrink and tighten.

To hold a freshly glued chair rung firmly in place, form a tourniquet. Clamp the glued rung with a heavy cord wrapped around the pertinent

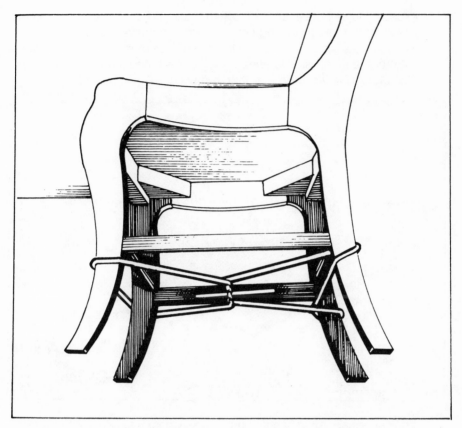

chair legs. Use a dowel to twist the cord till the proper tension is reached, then prop the dowel to maintain pressure.

Saggy wicker or cane seats can be similarly treated by sponging on hot water.

If a loose cane on a rattan chair is snagging your clothing or stockings, tame it with clear transparent tape, or blunt it by dabbing on clear nail polish.

When gluing dowels, a dowel that's exactly the size of the hole it fits into can push much of the glue to the bottom of the hole and therefore not hold as well as it should. To avoid this, cut a few grooves in the dowel so the glue distributes along its surface for a more secure bond.

Sometimes a warped table leaf or other board can be straightened by exposure to wet grass and hot summer sun. For this treatment, water a grassy area thoroughly and set the board, concave side down, on the wet grass. As the dry side of the board absorbs moisture from the grass, the moist (convex) side is dried out by the sun and the board unwarps. This process takes no longer than a day.

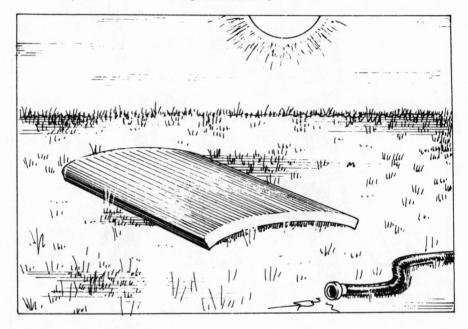

You can usually rub cigarette burns out of wooden furniture with very fine sandpaper or steel wool. Then color the area, if necessary, with shoe polish to match the rest of the surface.

Refinishing Furniture

Before varnishing furniture in a house with central heating, switch off the system so dust circulation is kept to a minimum. However, your work space should be ventilated and have a constant temperature over 70°F; finishes and glues don't work properly in a cooler environment.

When using paint stripper on furniture with legs, place a tin can under each leg to catch the stripper as it drips. This protects the floor and collects the excess for reuse.

If you use newspaper to protect your floor or workbench when refinishing a piece of furniture, drive nails partially into its leg bottoms. Otherwise the paper may adhere to the legs when the finish dries.

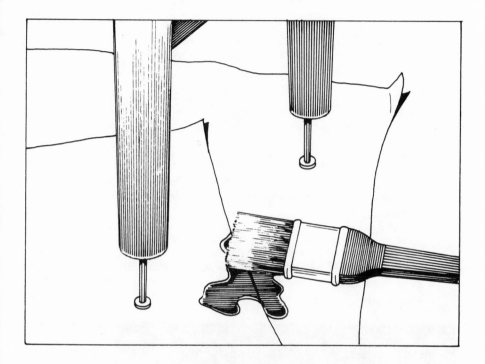

When working with varnish, hold the container as still as possible so you won't create bubbles that will spoil the finish's appearance.

If you'd like to know how your unfinished furniture would look if stained, try the "wet test." Dampen a cloth with turpentine and wipe it over the surface; the moisture will bring out the grain, showing any contrasts and giving the wood the appearance it would have if stained.

Many small items are useful for cleaning furniture crevices and cracks when you're refinishing. Enlist the aid of a nut pick, a plastic playing card, a plastic credit card, the broken end of an ice-cream stick, the tine of an old fork, an orange stick, wood toothpicks, or an old spoon.

If you need an unusually shaped smoothing tool for use on wet spackling compound and other wood fillers, try whittling an ice-cream stick to the required contour.

A heavy string is useful when stripping the narrow turnings of a furniture leg's spindle. Gently "saw" the string back and forth to remove the finish.

To avoid gouging wood when using a putty knife to strip furniture, round the putty knife's sharp corners with a fine-toothed file. If you're working on large flat surfaces, dull a paint scraper the same way.

For scraping small areas when refinishing, consider using such unconventional tools as a coin, bottle cap, golf tee, screwdriver, or your thumbnail. Even a car windshield scraper can be pressed into service.

When refinishing, a flat rubber kitchen spatula can be a useful scraper for removing paint from curved or rounded surfaces, especially since it can be used even on delicate carvings. For greater versatility, buy both wide and narrow sizes.

Sanding concave curves will be easier if you hold the sandpaper around a piece of dowel the same diameter as the curve or smaller. Or, slit a length of rubber garden hose and wrap the paper around it, with the ends held in the slit.

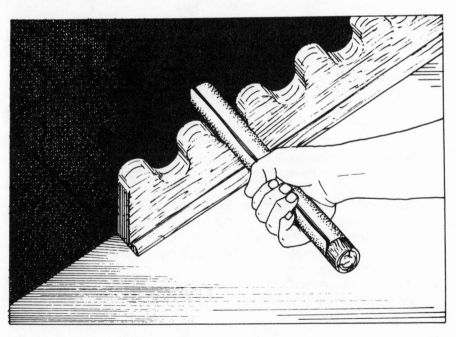

To smooth wood evenly and thoroughly in the refinishing process, work with successively finer sandpaper grades. Between sandings, brush off or vacuum the sanding debris; then wipe the wood clean with a tack cloth.

To sand a furniture spindle or rung without flattening it, hold a sandpaper strip behind the part, one end in each hand, and saw the ends back and forth to buff–sand the wood.

If wood still shows ink stains, white water marks, splotches, or traces of any previous stain or filler after stripping, try wiping them away with liquid laundry bleach. To remove black water marks or to lighten chemically darkened wood, use oxalic acid (available in paint stores and drugstores).

Remember that treatment with any bleach raises the wood grain, even when the furniture piece already has been thoroughly sanded. To prevent the raised grain from affecting the finish, resand to the level of the wood surface after the wood dries.

To obtain a smooth, evenly finished surface on open-grained woods, treat them with a filler after staining. First apply filler in the direction of the grain; then work across the grain to fill all pores completely.

If large knots in unfinished furniture are loose, remove them, apply carpenters' glue around their edges, and replace them flush with the surface. If small knots (pin knots) are loose, remove and discard them and plug the resulting holes with plastic wood or water putty.

For the most professional patching job, use shellac sticks to fill cracks and gouges since they leave the least conspicuous patch.

Small blisters on a veneered surface sometimes can be flattened with heat. Here's how: Lay a sheet of smooth cardboard over the blistered area and press firmly with a medium-hot iron, moving the iron slowly and evenly till the blisters soften and flatten. Leave the cardboard in place and weight the smoothed-out area for 24 hours.

It will be easier to apply paint or varnish remover to a piece of furniture if all hardware has been removed. If you label the hardware along with a sketch of the furniture, it also will be easier to reassemble it correctly.

If hardware is spotted with paint or finish, drop it into a pan filled with paint remover. Let it soak while you work on the wood, then wipe it clean.

To help slow evaporation after applying a coat of paint remover—and give it more time to work—cover the surface with aluminum foil. Keep in mind, though, that paint remover stops working in any case after about 40 minutes.

You can make a template for a patch for damaged veneer this way: Lay a sheet of bond paper over the damaged area and rub a soft lead pencil gently over the paper. The edges of the damaged area will be precisely indicated on the paper and you can cut a pattern from this.

For more durability, top an antiqued finish with a coat of semigloss or high-gloss varnish.

If you apply a protective shellac coating to cane chair seats, they'll last longer and be easier to clean.

Upholstering

When you reupholster furniture, put fabric scraps in an envelope and staple the envelope to the underside of the newly covered piece. That way you'll have the scraps you may later need for patching.

For speed and convenience, you can cut foam rubber upholstery padding with an electric carving knife.

To hammer decorative furniture tacks without damaging their heads, place a wooden spool over each tack and pound on the spool.

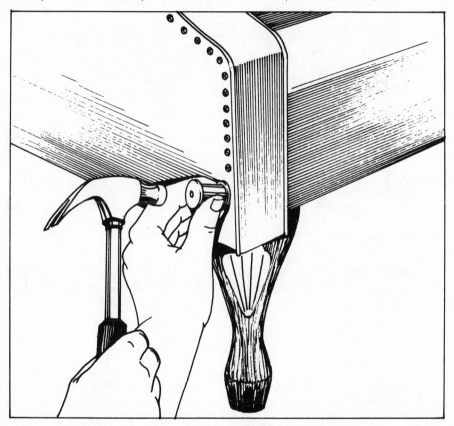

When using ornamental tacks for upholstery, push extras into the frame in an inconspicuous spot so you have replacements if needed.

Before covering kitchen chair seats with plastic, warm the plastic with a heating pad so it will be more pliable and easier to handle.

Moving Furniture

Instead of straining your back when rearranging a heavy piece of furniture, simply position a child's roller skate or skateboard under each end, and then wheel it effortlessly.

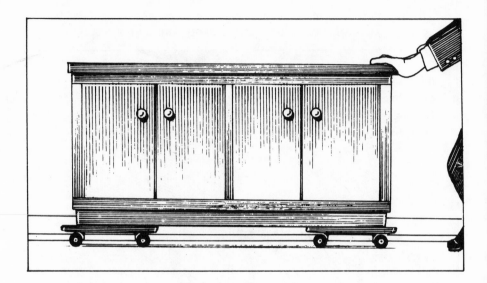

Always remember to tape the drawers shut before moving a piece of furniture—and remember to remove the tape quickly, too, or it will leave marks.

For Peace and Quiet

Heavy, lined curtains will absorb the excess noise in a room. Placing heavy furniture against the wall facing noisy neighbors will also help cut down on sounds.

Cover hardwood floors with area rugs to cut down on noise in your home. Upholstered furniture also absorbs noise, while glass, chrome, and wood reflect noise.

To insulate your home from street noise, double glaze the windows, insulate the walls and ceilings, and install wall-to-wall carpeting.

To reduce noise in your home and also cut energy costs, weatherstrip all doors and windows.

CARPETING AND UPHOLSTERY

Cleaning Spots and Stains

Acid stains on a carpet or upholstery should be immediately diluted and neutralized with baking soda and water, or with club soda. The same solutions work to keep vomit stains from setting.

If someone spills an alcoholic drink on carpet or upholstery, instantly dilute the spot with cold water so the alcohol hasn't time to attack dyes. If red wine is the culprit, dilute it with white wine, then clean the spot with cold water and cover it with table salt. Wait ten minutes, then vacuum up the salt.

Dampen blood stains on carpet or upholstery with cold water. (Hot water *sets* the stains.) Then apply carpet or upholstery shampoo and follow this treatment by applying dry-cleaner fluid.

Some homemakers use a paste of laundry starch and cold water to lift blood stains from carpet or upholstery. They allow the paste to dry and brush it away.

You'll be able to absorb butter stains—and other greasy household stains on a carpet or upholstery—with cornmeal, dried and ground corn cobs, or dry-cleaning fluid.

Chewing gum that is stuck on the carpet can be removed by pressing an ice cube against the gum. The gum will harden and can then be pulled off. Treat any past traces of gum with a spot remover.

Blot coffee stains quickly and dilute with plain water.

Use dry-cleaning fluid on tar spots, but apply it sparingly and blot regularly.

If there's candle wax on carpet or upholstery, put an ice cube in a plastic bag and hold it against the wax. When the wax becomes brittle, chip it away with a dull knife.

Here's another way to remove candle wax from carpet or upholstery: Place a blotter over the wax spot and press with a warm iron until the blotter absorbs the melted wax. Move the blotter frequently so it doesn't oversaturate.

You can occasionally remove crayon marks on carpet or upholstery by using the iron-and-blotter treatment that's effective with candle wax, but you also could try dabbing at them with a cloth moistened with dry-cleaning fluid.

To remove nonbutter-type grease stains on carpet or upholstery, scrape up as much spilled grease as possible and apply dry-cleaning fluid with a cloth. Or, rub with paint thinner, cover with salt, and vacuum. Another alternative: Sprinkle with cornmeal, leave overnight, and vacuum.

Use hair spray to lift ballpoint ink stains from carpet or upholstery. Use dry-cleaning fluid, applied with a cloth, on other ink stains. Here's another way to cope with ink stains: Sprinkle them with salt. As soon as some ink is absorbed, brush the salt away and sprinkle again. Repeat as necessary.

Try to remove mildew from carpet or upholstery with white vinegar. If spots remain, rub with dry-cleaning fluid. Note: Eliminate moist conditions or the mildew will return.

Allow mud spots to dry before softly brushing to loosen the dirt before vacuuming.

Lift nail polish with prepared polish removers or acetone, but apply these gingerly because they can damage the carpet or upholstery.

To remove wet latex paint spots on carpet or upholstery, dab with water. To remove wet oil-base paint spots, dab with turpentine, then absorb the turpentine with cornmeal. In either case, follow with an application of dry-cleaner or shampoo.

If your pets have accidents on carpet or upholstery, blot the stains with water, then clean with club soda. A mix of equal parts of white vinegar and water is just as effective.

You can remove soot stains by sprinkling generously with salt, allowing the salt to settle for several minutes, and vacuuming both salt and soot.

You'll be able to remove animal hair from furniture by wiping with a damp sponge. Dabbing with pieces of Scotch tape also works well.

The best way to clean vinyl upholstery is with baking soda on a damp cloth, followed by a light washing with a dishwashing soap. Never use oil; it will only harden the upholstery.

If your carpet sweeper misses bits of lint, string, and other small debris, just dampen the brushes.

Carpet odors can be eliminated by sprinkling baking soda on the carpet before vacuuming, or by doing the same thing with one cup of borax mixed with two cups of cornmeal. (Let the latter mixture stand for an hour before vacuuming.)

Repairing Carpets and Rugs

When a carpet thread is loose, snip it level with the pile. If you try to pull out the thread, you'll risk unraveling part of the carpet.

To repair a large burned area in a carpet, cut out the damaged area and substitute a patch of identical size and shape. Secure the new piece with double-faced carpet tape and latex adhesive.

You needn't hide a carpet burn with furniture. If the burn isn't down to the backing, just snip off the charred part with fingernail scissors. However, if a carpet burn does extend to the backing, snip off the charred fibers and put white glue in the opening. Then, snip fibers from a scrap or an inconspicuous part of the carpet (perhaps in a closet). When the glue gets tacky, poke the fibers into place.

Should your spot-removal efforts alter the color of carpet or upholstery, try touching up small places with artists' acrylic paint. If that doesn't work, try a felt marker, or a permanent ink marker of the appropriate color—and go slowly.

Installing Carpets and Rugs

For a perfect bathroom carpet fit, make a precise pattern with paper. Lay overlapped sheets on the bathroom floor, tightly butted up against corners, walls, and obstacles. Tape the sheets together and cut. Turn the pattern over, face down, on the back of the carpet, trace with a pencil, and then cut.

Caring for Your Carpets and Rugs

Has the pile on your shag rug flattened? You can raise it with a lightweight bamboo yard rake.

Just as fabric softener takes static cling out of your laundry, it can remove the static "shock" from your carpet. If you spray your carpet lightly with a mix of five parts water to one part liquid softener, you won't have to worry about shocks when you touch metallic objects.

To raise depressions left in carpets by heavy furniture, try steaming them. Hold an iron close enough for steam to reach the carpet, but don't let the iron touch the fibers, especially if they're synthetic, since they could melt. Lift the fibers by scraping them with the edge of a coin.

Rugs will last longer if you occasionally rotate them to change areas of wear or rearrange furniture to alter traffic patterns.

To prevent small area rugs from slipping out from under you, hold them in place with strips of double-faced carpet tape under their corners.

DRAPES, BLINDS, AND SHADES

Draperies and Curtains

To prevent a curtain rod from snagging when sliding it through a curtain, slip a piece of aluminum foil or a thimble over its tip.

To keep draper hem folds in position, insert wire solder or plastic-covered wire. Bend the wire into desired shapes after hanging the draperies.

Do your draperies gap in the middle when you close them? They won't if you sew a small magnet into both center seams at the same height from the floor.

Old keys can make good drapery weights.

To make sure that curtain tie-backs are exactly opposite each other when installing them, use the bottom edge of the window shade as your guide.

Before washing a curtain, it's a good idea to shake it outdoors to remove accumulated dust.

Venetian Blinds

If you wear cotton gloves when washing Venetian blinds with mild soap and water, you can use your fingers to rub the slats—better than any brush. Another way to wash Venetian blinds is to hang them from a clothesline and turn a hose on them. Or, wash them under the shower.

If you're interrupted while cleaning Venetian blinds, clasp a clothespin to the last slat you cleaned so you'll know where you left off.

To prevent Venetian blind tapes from shrinking when cleaned, rehang the blinds before the tapes dry.

Make yellowed Venetian blind tapes white again by applying white, liquid shoe polish.

To install a new Venetian blind cord, tape or sew the end of the new one to the old one. Slowly pull out the cord and you'll pull the new one into place.

To keep Venetian blind pulleys working smoothly, spray them with a silicone lubricant.

Window Shades

To lift spots from window shades, use wallpaper cleaner or an art gum eraser.

If an unwashable window shade needs cleaning, rub it with a rough flannel cloth dipped in cornmeal or flour.

A window shade that has too much tension can be removed from its bracket and unrolled by hand two or three revolutions to make it less tense after it is replaced.

A shade that won't lift properly needs more tension. Remove it, roll it up two or three revolutions, and reinstall it.

Use a silicone spray instead of oil on a window-shade mechanism. (Oil will soak through the wood roller and ruin your shade.)

You can sometimes repair small window shade tears with clear nail polish.

BED AND BATH

Beds and Bedding

Sometimes you can silence squeaky bed springs with a coat of spray wax. If bed squeaks are caused by springs touching the frame, pad the frame with pieces of sponge.

If bed slats sometimes slide out of place on the frame, keep them from moving so easily by slipping wide rubber bands over the slat ends.

If your innerspring mattress is showing uneven wear, turn it over and around, end to end, once a month.

Hand wash quilts filled with cotton batting, because machine washing is too harsh and will cause the batting to bunch.

Launder a patchwork quilt using the method recommended for the most delicate fabric in the quilt.

When storing linens, it's best to roll them around cardboard tubes rather than fold them.

When you purchase a new bedspread, you could buy a larger size than you need and then cut the excess to make a matching headboard.

Place an unwrapped bar of soap in a drawer or linen closet to give lingerie and linens a pleasant scent.

To give a guest room a clean and inviting scent, place an unwrapped bar of sweet-smelling soap under each bed pillow.

To enjoy maximum heat from an electric blanket, cover it with a thin sheet.

An adjustable ironing board placed beside a bed makes a perfect bed table for someone who's ill.

Buying a Mattress

When buying an innerspring mattress, make sure it has thick, strong wire along its borders, and a machine-stitched tape covering its outside edges.

Before purchasing a mattress when you're married, lie down on it with your spouse to be sure it gives both of you the desired support side-by-side, at your heads, shoulders, and hips. If one person rolls over, the mattress definitely shouldn't sway. If it does, try another mattress.

Because handles are seldom included on mattresses today, when you turn one from head to toe or from side to side, keep it as rigid as possible.

Make sure any mattress you buy is warranted against defects in workmanship and details for 10 to 15 years. Some guarantees aren't valid if the mattress isn't positioned on a frame that meets with manufacturer's specifications.

When outfitting a guest room that's used infrequently, economize by choosing a cheaper mattress. It won't have to withstand daily use.

When shopping for a mattress, be sure that the clerk offering you advice is employed by the store and not by any particular bed manufacturer. A manufacturer's representative will have a vested interest in selling you his brand, which might not be right for your needs.

Bed manufacturers don't share a common system for rating mattress firmness. You'll have to judge each mattress by testing it, not by relying on a "soft," "medium," or "firm" tag.

Cleaning Bathroom Tiles

To make your own ceramic tile cleaner, put one-quarter cup of baking soda, one-half cup of white vinegar, and 1 cup of household ammonia in a bucket. Add 1 gallon of warm water, stirring till the baking soda dissolves. Wear rubber gloves, and apply with a scrub brush or sponge, rinsing afterwards. Mix a fresh batch for each cleaning.

To make your own heavy-duty grout cleaner, put 3 cups of baking soda in a medium-size bowl and add 1 cup of warm water. Mix the contents to a smooth paste and scrub into grout with a damp sponge or toothbrush, rinsing thoroughly afterwards. Mix a fresh batch for each cleaning.

A typewriter eraser from the stationery store is an excellent way to clean the grout between bathroom tiles.

To make your bathroom walls sparkle, rub ceramic tile with car wax, and buff after 10 minutes.

You can remove most mildew from the grout between tiles by rubbing it with a toothbrush or nailbrush dipped in laundry bleach. (Don't use abrasive powders or steel-wool pads or you'll scratch the tile.) Rinse with clear water after cleaning. If spots remain, you could camouflage stained grout with a white fingernail pencil or white liquid shoe polish. (If you get polish on the tiles, let it dry and then wipe it off with a rag.)

Cleaning the Toilet Bowl

One-quarter cup of sodium bisulfate (sodium acid sulfate) can be sprinkled into a wet toilet bowl for a single scrubbing and flushing. (Wear rubber gloves.) Let it stand for 15 minutes, and then scrub and flush as usual. (Don't use with chlorine bleach because the resulting fumes would be toxic.)

Rust stains under a toilet bowl rim sometimes yield to laundry bleach—but be sure to protect your hands with plastic or rubber gloves. (Note: Never combine bleach with toilet-bowl cleaners; the mix can release toxic gases.) Rub off truly stubborn stains with extra-fine steel wool, or with wet–dry sandpaper (available at hardware stores).

Cola that has gone flat can be spilled into the toilet bowl. Left to soak for an hour, the soft drink will clean the bowl.

Chemical toilet bowl cleaners should never be used to clean the bathtub and sink as the chemical will ruin their finish.

Cleaning the Bathtub

A ring-around-the-tub can be rubbed away without cleaners with a nylon-net ball or pad. Cover a stubborn ring with a paste of cream of tartar and hydrogen peroxide. When the paste dries, wipe it off—along with the ring. To enjoy your bath without worrying about leaving a tub ring, add a capful of mild liquid dishwashing detergent to the bath water.

To get rid of a bathtub's rust stains, try rubbing them with a paste of borax powder and lemon juice. If the stain persists, use a dry-cleaning solution.

An old nylon stocking rolled with a ball becomes a nonscratch scrub pad for cleaning sink and tub.

Clean a rubber or vinyl bathtub mat by tossing it into the washer with bath towels. The terry cloth scrubs the mat, and all come out clean.

Shower enclosures are a chore to keep clean—but they can be less so if you follow these suggestions. Keep mildew from taking hold by wiping shower walls with a towel after each shower, while you're still in the tub. When the walls need a thorough cleaning, run the shower water at its hottest temperature so the steam will loosen the dirt. Then, using a sponge mop, clean in a jiffy with a mixture of one-half cup vinegar, 1 cup clear ammonia, and one-quarter cup baking soda in 1 gallon of warm water. After cleaning, rinse with clear water. Note: Never use harsh abrasive powders or steel-wool pads because they'll scratch tile or fiberglass.

Having trouble getting mineral deposits off a shower head? Remove the head, take it apart, and soak it in vinegar. Then brush deposits loose with an old toothbrush. Clean the holes by poking them with a wire, pin, toothpick, or ice pick.

Lemon oil will remove water spots on metal frames around shower doors and enclosures.

Glass shower doors will sparkle again if you clean them once a week with a sponge dipped in white vinegar.

To prevent shower curtains from wrinkling after washing, put them in the washing machine with one-half cup of detergent and one-half cup of baking soda, along with two large bath towels. Add a cup of vinegar to the rinse cycle, then hang the curtains up immediately after washing, and let them air dry.

Keep a new shower curtain fresh-looking by using the old shower curtain as a liner. Hang the new curtain on the same hooks, but in front of the old curtain. The old curtain will take the beating from water and soap scum while the new one stays squeaky clean.

When you clean a plastic shower curtain, keep it soft and flexible by adding a few drops of mineral oil to the rinse water. Maintain the curtain's softness by wiping it occasionally with a solution of warm water and mineral oil.

Mirrors

To make your bathroom mirror sparkle, polish it with a cloth dipped in a borax-and-water solution or in denatured alcohol. Or, polish with dry facial tissue, a lintfree cloth, paper toweling, or old nylon stockings.

Rubbing alcohol will wipe away hair-spray haze on a mirror.

You can defog a bathroom mirror in a jiffy by "spraying" it with hot air from a handheld dryer.

Mirrors in your bathroom won't steam up if you run an inch of cold water in the bathtub before adding hot water.

Soap Savers

Even when soap bars wear down, they're still useful. Slit a sponge to make a pocket to hold the slivers, wet and squeeze the sponge for foamy suds. Or, fill a sock with soap slivers and use it the same way.

A bar of soap will stay high and dry in a soap dish if it rests on a small sponge.

To remold leftover soap slivers into bars of soap, place them in a small saucepan, cover them with water, and heat the water to the boiling point. Lower the heat to simmer, and stir the mixture to melt the soap pieces. When the mixture has the consistency of thick, smooth syrup, remove the pan from the heat. Pour its contents into lightly oiled, small containers, such as jar caps or plastic soap dishes. Let the mixture stand for at least 3 days till hard before tapping the mixture out of the molds.

Thin, leftover soap bars can be tossed into a blender with water and transformed into creamy, liquid soap. Pour this substance into empty squeeze bottles, and keep one at each sink.

Organizing and Storage Tips

To give yourself more storage space in a small bathroom, erect shelves in the "dead" wall space beside the vanity, over the toilet, or behind the

door. Such shelves offer convenient storage without intruding on floor space.

Make your shower curtain rod do double duty—attach extra curtain hooks to hold a back brush, a net bag for bath toys, each family member's wash cloth, or a shower cap.

Your medicine cabinet will stay neat and clean with "shelf paper" made of blotters that can absorb medicine or cosmetic spills. And, so you won't misplace frequently used items, glue small magnets on the medicine cabinet's walls to hold nail files, cuticle scissors, clippers, and other small metal objects.

Keep toothbrushes handy but neatly out of the way on cup hooks attached to a wall or under a cabinet.

If you color code cups and toothbrushes in the bathroom—with each

family member choosing a different color—there'll be no confusion over what belongs to each person.

To keep a spoon handy for taking medicine, use an extra slot in the toothbrush holder.

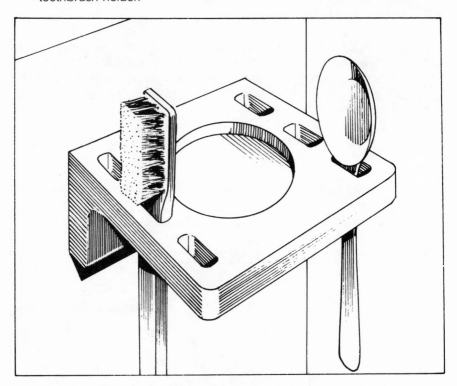

When toothbrush-holder slots become clogged with toothpaste or toothpowder residue, clean them with cotton swabs dipped in vinegar.

If you save the tops to shampoo bottles and toothpaste tubes, you'll have a handy replacement should a top from a new container get lost.

Window Cover-Ups

If you want to cover your clear bathroom window without putting up curtains, render the glass opaque by brushing on a mixture of 4 tablespoons of epsom salts and a half pint of stale beer. Alternatives: Glue on stained-glass pieces, silver Mylar, or wax paper. Double-duty alternative: Cover the panes with mirrored squares, which, as a side benefit, will make the bathroom seem larger.

Chapter **4**

LAUNDRY

GOT THE WASH-DAY BLUES? TOSS THEM INTO THE SUDS ALONG WITH THESE WINNING WAYS WITH LAUNDRY.

REGULAR LAUNDRY

Sorting and Separating

Always sort your laundry by color. Put all white or predominantly white articles in one pile, light colors and pastels in another pile, and bright and dark-colored items in a third pile. Separate the bright and dark piles into two piles; one for colorfast items and one for noncolorfast items. Finally, separate each pile into three smaller piles: lightly soiled, moderately soiled, and heavily soiled. You should also separate white synthetic articles and wash them only with other white fabrics. Separate synthetics, blends, and permanent-press fabrics from natural-fiber fabrics without special finishes.

When preparing the wash, turn all pockets inside out to get rid of debris; turn down cuffs at the bottom of sleeves and pants, and brush away the loose soil; and tie and buckle all sashes and belts to prevent tangling. Finally, mend seams, tears, holes, or loose items to prevent further damage during the wash cycle.

Automatic Washer Hints

Load an automatic washer to capacity, if possible, to save time and energy. However, to keep wrinkling to a minimum, don't wash large loads of permanent-press or synthetic-fiber knits.

For the best circulation when using an automatic washer, mix small and large items in each load.

Before washing a garment, check the label to see if the item has been pretreated for shrinkage. "Sanforized" clothing shrinks less than 2 percent after washing, but a preshrunk item may shrink as much as 5 percent. That much shrinkage can really affect the look and fit of a garment, so you'll want to adjust washing and drying temperatures accordingly.

To make an overabundance of soap suds in your washer disappear, sprinkle table salt into the water.

To prevent buildup of fabric softener, use it only every third time you wash towels, diapers, or other fabrics you wish to remain absorbent.

Give your washing machine a periodic cleaning to get rid of accumulated soap scum and hard-water minerals. Run the machine through a warm water cycle to which you've added a gallon of distilled vinegar.

Bleaching

Laundry bleach should be poured into the wash water or otherwise diluted when used—never poured directly onto fabrics.

When bleaching, always bleach the whole item, not just a single stain.

Use the hottest water possible when using a bleach, as this improves its performance.

To bleach delicate fabrics safely such as silk, use one part 3 percent hydrogen peroxide mixed in eight parts of water.

Tough Jobs

You can prevent fabrics from bleeding by adding 2 or 3 teaspoons of salt to the wash and rinse cycles.

To remove dirty rings from shirt collars, scrub the area with an old toothbrush and a bit of shampoo before laundering.

When laundering greasy work clothes, add a cup of kerosene to the soapy water for a cleaner wash. Or pour a bottle of cola into the wash water. Cola loosens grease stains.

You can treat grease and grime on shirt collars and cuffs by rubbing in a thick coating of chalk; allow this to sit overnight and launder as usual.

To boost detergent effectiveness for heavily soiled or greasy wash loads, add 1 cup of ammonia to the wash water.

To help prevent face and hair creams and oils from staining pillow cases, lightly starch the cases.

A White Wash

To make soiled white socks snow white again, boil them in water containing a lemon slice.

White socks will come cleaner if soaked in baking soda and water to help loosen dirt before washing.

Enjoy truly white handerchiefs again. Add a touch of cream of tartar to the wash water.

Never launder white nylon with colored fabrics, because a color transference may take place.

Dark Clothes

If you wash dark clothes separately, you won't have light-colored lint to cope with.

Dark clothes and corduroy won't show lint after washing if you turn these garments inside out before washing.

Black lingerie and other black clothing tends to look brownish after several washings. To restore the pure black color, add bluing, coffee, or strong tea to the rinse water.

If you want jeans to retain their color instead of looking faded, wash, dry, and iron them inside out.

Fabric Finesse

To prevent nylon from yellowing, presoak in a baking powder and water solution.

A general rule to follow in cleaning synthetic fabrics: Wash the clothes in warm water, rinse in cold water, and tumble dry at low temperatures.

Silk can be hand washed in cool water with a mild soap. Air dry the fabric away from direct heat or sunlight.

Wash and dry cottons in hot temperatures, but be sure the garments are completely dry before storing. Otherwise, you could be inviting mildew damage.

When washing linen, use hot water for white and pastel colors, and warm or cool water for dark colors. Iron linen garments while they're still damp.

Woolen and Knits

Woolen garments should be washed in lukewarm water to prevent shrinking. Lay them flat to dry so they won't lose their shape.

To prevent stretching, knit garments should be washed by hand and laid flat to dry. Place the wet garments on heavy towels, and replace the towels twice a day until the clothing is dry. Never put knit garments in direct sunlight, as it will fade them.

Adding fabric softener in the final rinse water will reduce clinging when you wear your knit garments.

Turning sweaters inside out when machine washing helps prevent fuzz balls from forming.

Hand Washables

If you trace around a wool sweater on a large piece of paper before hand washing, you'll have a pattern to use when reshaping the sweater for drying. Cut out and discard the paper "sweater" and use the outside frame as your guide.

When hand washing a sweater, it's best to reach under it to lift it; if you pull it out of the water, it might stretch.

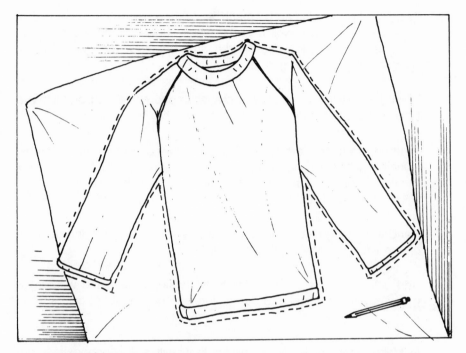

For extra softness when hand washing sweaters, put a capful of cream hair rinse in the rinse water.

Machine Washing Fragile Items

To machine wash fragile garments, put them in a pillowcase and close it with a plastic-bag tie. Wash the bundle on a gentle cycle.

If you place fabric belts and other small items in a mesh bag before washing in a machine, they will be less likely to get tangled or damaged.

To prevent fraying, wash a foam rubber pillow in its case. Then air dry the pillow. Do *not* use a dryer.

Glycerin will keep plastic items such as shower curtains and baby pants soft and pliable if several ounces are added to the rinse water when washing these items.

Plastic or rubber rainwear should be air dried, not put in a clothes dryer.

Nylon fabrics can be machine washed and dried at low temperatures. Add a fabric softener to the final rinse water to reduce static cling.

Down-filled garments can be machine washed using cold water and a mild detergent. Rinse well until the water shows no more suds, then machine dry at very low heat. Add a large bath towel or sneaker to the dryer to help rotate the garment.

When hand washing silk, use a hair shampoo containing protein. The protein in the shampoo feeds the protein in the silk.

When doing hand washing, use towels to blot off excess moisture from sweaters, stockings, panties, and bras. Hang to dry only if the weight of the water won't stretch these items out of shape. Otherwise dry them on a towel-covered flat surface.

Hand wash rayon fabrics in warm water and drip dry. Iron the garment on the wrong side while it's still damp.

Add a few pinches of table salt to the water when hand washing a garment with both light and dark colors so that the darker colors won't run.

Felt fabrics can be cleaned by wiping them with a dry sponge. If a more thorough treatment is necessary, hold the material over a teakettle's steam and then brush lightly with a dry sponge or lintfree cloth to smooth the surface.

Rinsing

If you want to eliminate suds from a sink so you can rinse, simply sprinkle salt on the suds.

There will be no soap residue on clothing if you add a cup of white vinegar to the washer's final rinse water. For hand washing, add a proportionately smaller amount of vinegar to the rinse.

A few drops of vinegar added to the rinse water will reduce static electricity in synthetic fabrics or curtains.

Bath salts added to the final rinse water will give your underwear a nice fresh fragrance.

Leather Gloves

Hand wash leather gloves in saddle soap while wearing them, but without rubbing them. Rinse them well and remove them. If they're hard to remove after washing, run a stream of water into them.

Before drying leather gloves you've just hand washed, blow into them to help reshape the fingers. When the gloves are almost dry, put them on once more, flexing the fingers so they won't be stiff. Then take them off again, and dry them flat.

Tennis Shoes

If you spray new tennis shoes with starch before wearing them, dirt can't become embedded in the canvas and the shoes will always be easy to clean.

When washing white tennis shoes, bleach them ultra-white by adding lemon juice to the final rinse.

Tennis shoes can be cleaned in the washing machine, or by hand with a soap-filled plastic scouring pad.

You won't lose shoelaces in the wash if you string them through the buttonholes in a shirt and tie the ends together.

Line Drying

Line dry white and light-colored items in the sun to bleach them snowy white. Line dry bright-colored items in the shade.

Instead of running your clothes dryer in winter, hang your laundry in the basement to humidify the house and cut your energy costs.

Always wipe a clothesline with a damp cloth before using it.

Attach items to a clothesline by their sturdiest edges.

Smooth clothes as you hang them on a clothesline, running your fingers down seams and along collar fronts and cuff edges. This eliminates a lot of ironing later.

Wash plastic clothespins in mild soap and warm water in the sink, or in the automatic clothes washer, using a mesh bag. Wash wooden clothespins in hot water and dishwashing detergent.

A permanently pleated skirt will keep its freshly pressed look after washing if you gather the pleats together tightly and carefully slip a nylon stocking down over the skirt before hanging it up to dry.

When using a wire coat hanger to drip dry clothes, cover the hanger with a towel or aluminum foil so the clothes don't get rust spotted.

Special Drying Tips

When machine drying, shake out each article before placing it in the dryer to speed up drying time and reduce wrinkling.

Polyester knits should be removed promptly from the clothes dryer to prevent wrinkling and shrinking.

Machine washable slipcovers will fit smoothly after laundering if they're put back on the furniture while still slightly damp. As they dry completely, they'll shrink into place.

TREATING SPOTS AND STAINS

Work Fast

Treat stains right away. The longer a stain sets, the more likely it is to become permanent.

Remove as much of a stain-producing agent as possible before treating it with a stain-removal product. That way, you'll avoid the possibility of enlarging the stain.

Handle stained items gently. Rubbing, folding, wringing, or squeezing can cause the stain to penetrate more deeply and may damage delicate fibers.

Keep a cool approach to stain removal since heat can set a stain. Keep stained fabrics away from hot water, a dryer, or an iron.

After washing a garment, be sure all stains are completely removed before ironing. Heat-set stains are often impossible to remove.

Steps to Success

Pretest any stain-removing agent in an inconspicuous spot, such as the seam allowance or hem of a garment, the part of a rug that's hidden under a table or chair, or upholstery under a seat cushion. Always run a sample test, since even water may damage some surfaces.

When you flush a stain—particularly on a nonwashable fabric—carefully control the flow of flushing liquid with an adjustable plastic-trigger spray bottle, a plant mister, or an ordinary eyedropper.

When stain removal instructions call for sponging, place the fabric stained side down on an absorbent pad. Then dampen another pad with water or a stain remover and blot lightly from the center of the stain outward to the edge to minimize the formation of rings. Sponge in an irregular pattern around the outside of the stain. Change the absorbent or sponging pads when there's any sign of the stain transferring to them, so the stain won't be redeposited on the fabric. For ring-prone fabrics, barely touch the stain with the sponging pad, so the stain absorbs the cleaner slowly. When the spot has been lifted, use a dry pad on either side to blot up as much excess moisture as possible.

Tamping is a good way to remove stains if the fabric is sturdy enough. The best tamping instrument is a small, dry brush with a handle, such as an old toothbrush. Place the stain on the work surface without a pad underneath, raise the brush about 3 inches, and bring it down squarely on the fabric, much like using a small hammer. The action should be light—never, enough to bend the bristles. Use only the amount of tamping needed to remove the stain.

An effective way to loosen many stains is by scraping with a teaspoon. Place the stain directly on the work surface, and grasp the spoon by the side of the bowl. After adding the stain remover to the stain, move the edge of the spoon's bowl back and forth, in short strokes, without pressing hard on the spoon. This procedure shouldn't be used on delicate fabrics.

You'll get the best results if you work from the center of a stain outward. Moving outward helps avoid leaving a ring around the cleaned area.

To avoid spreading very small stains, use a medicine dropper or a glass rod to apply cleaner preparations.

If, in the cleaning process, you have to use more than one stain-removal agent, thoroughly rinse each one away before applying the next.

Safety First

Never transfer a stain-removal product to a new container. Keep it in the original container, which is correctly labeled and features full instructions regarding the product's use.

When using stain-removal products, be sure they're kept well out of your child's reach.

Unbeatable Techniques

Flushing releases the staining substance and removes the chemicals used to treat the stain so they don't damage the fabric later. To flush, place a clean pad under the stain, and drop small amounts of the cleaning agent on the stain with a medicine dropper or with a container that allows very slow pouring. Don't add the stain remover faster than the pad underneath can absorb it, and change the pad several times while flushing. As soon as the stain disappears, use dry pads to remove any excess moisture. If water is used for flushing on a washable article, dip the stained area up and down in a bowl of warm water. Change the water at least twice during the process.

Homemade Spot Cleaners

A soapless spot cleaner can be created by mixing 2 cups of isopropyl rubbing alcohol (70 percent) and three-quarters of a cup of white vinegar. Pour the mixture into a clean bottle and cover it tightly. To use, blot the soiled area until it's dry, apply the cleaner with a cloth or sponge, let it stand for several minutes, then blot the area dry again. Repeat if necessary. Blot with water after using.

To make a wet spotter for nongreasy stains, combine 1 cup of water, 2 tablespoons of glycerin, and 2 tablespoons of liquid dishwashing detergent in a small bowl, stirring until the mixture is thoroughly blended. Pour the mixture into an ordinary clean bottle, or a squeeze bottle, and cover the container tightly. When using, blot the soiled area dry, apply the spotter, let the spotter stand for several minutes, and them blot the soiled area dry again. Repeat if necessary.

Grease

To remove grease spots on cotton garments, try using salad oil. Rub the oil into the grease; then wash in hot, sudsy water.

Remove grease from fabrics by applying cornstarch or by dampening them with salt dissolved in ammonia.

Perspiration

Perspiration stains will come out of clothing if it is first soaked in salt water and then washed. Another way to remove perspiration stains is to apply a baking-soda paste and let it sit for a while before laundering.

To remove deodorant stains from fabrics, apply rubbing alcohol to the affected areas. Test for colorfastness before doing so.

Blood

There are several ways to remove blood stains from fabrics. One way is to wash immediately with cold water. (Hot water sets the stains.) A second way is to cover still-wet spots with a coating of dry starch. When the fabric dries, brush away the starch—and the spots. A third method is to apply a paste of meat tenderizer and cold water, which will lift the stains. A fourth way—if ammonia won't harm the fabric—is to soak blood stains in a solution of 1 tablespoon of ammonia per pint of cold water.

Cosmetics

Here are three ways to remove a lipstick smear from a fabric. The first is to rub it with a slice of white bread. A second is to dab the smear with petroleum jelly, then apply a dry-cleaning solution. A third way is to pat salad oil on the smear, and launder the fabric after 5 minutes.

Makeup marks disappear from dark clothing if rubbed with bread.

Nail polish spots on a fabric? Lift them by applying polish remover to the fabric's underside. (First check an inconspicuous place to make sure you won't damage the fabric.)

Mildew

If you have badly mildewed clothing, soak it in buttermilk overnight, then launder. Should there be no buttermilk available, dry clean the clothing. Applying vinegar and exposing clothing to sunshine also helps.

Mildew spots disappear from white fabrics if rubbed with a mixture of lemon juice and salt. Place the fabric in the sun to dry before washing.

Food

There are several ways to remove chocolate or cocoa stains from fabrics. You could soak the stains thoroughly with club soda before washing, or rub talcum powder into the stains to absorb them. Or, apply milk to the stains, since milk keeps them from setting. A fourth way is to rub shortening into them, then launder.

Remove fruit stains by pouring a mixture of detergent and boiling water through the fabric. Or sponge the affected area with lemon juice. You can also rub the cut sides of a lemon slice over the stain.

To remove egg stains from a fabric, soak the fabric for an hour in cold water before laundering.

Grass

To remove grass stains from fabrics, rub lard into them. if you don't have lard handy, you can rub them with denatured alcohol or a diluted solution of ammonia before laundering.

For removing grass stains, combine one-half cup of isopropyl rubbing alcohol (70 percent) and one-half cup of water with 1 teaspoon of household ammonia and stir. To use, saturate the stained fabric with this mixture, let it stand for several minutes, rub to remove the stain, and launder as usual. (Use only on washable fabrics, and test fabrics for colorfastness before applying.)

Scorch Marks

A scorch stain on linen can sometimes be removed by rubbing it with the cut side of an onion. Afterward, soak the linen in cold water before laundering.

Put scorched cotton in cold water immediately and let it soak for 24 hours. Often the scorched area will vanish without further treatment.

Treat scorch marks by rubbing them with an onion slice, soaking them in cold water, and laundering. Another way to treat fabric scorch marks is to dab them with an ammonia-dampened cloth, soak them in cold water, and launder. Or, try removing scorch marks by kneading them with a slice of dampened, stale white bread.

Pen and Pencil

Treat an ink-stained fabric by soaking it overnight in sour milk or buttermilk. Speed the milk's action by first rubbing salt into the stains. Ink spots also respond to applications of lemon juice, hair spray, or denatured alcohol.

Remove ballpoint pen stains by sponging them with milk.

Another way to remove ballpoint pen stains or stamp pad stains (except red) is to sponge the affected area with water, or dampen them with a light mist of hair spray. Then apply a few drops of white vinegar, blotting every 5 minutes with a clean absorbent pad.

Erase pencil marks around shirt pockets before washing because they're more difficult to remove once wet.

Removing Super Stains

Hardened stains sometimes can be loosened up by placing a pad dampened with stain remover on top of the stain and allowing it to penetrate for an hour or more. Also place a pad under the stain, and keep the top pad damp by adding more stain remover as needed.

You can remove shoe polish from clothing by applying rubbing alcohol. If traces of polish remain, add a tablespoon of borax powder to the water when laundering.

Try to rub soot from clothing with an art gum eraser. You also can sprinkle salt on a soot spot, let it settle, and then brush away both salt and soot with a stiff brush.

To eliminate a tar spot on fabric, apply shortening, let the tar soften for 10 minutes, scrape it away, and launder.

Rub out mud spots in fabrics with a slice of raw potato.

Water marks on clothing? Rub them with the rounded back of a silver spoon.

Nonoily spots on leather can be removed by buffing with an art gum eraser. Sponge with damp cheesecloth and saddle soap to remove surface dirt.

IRONING

Setting the Stage

If you do your ironing in the bedroom, you'll be able to use the bed to sort things out and have hangers close at hand in the closet.

When ironing, keep thread, needle, and extra buttons handy for making necessary repairs before an item is pressed and stored in the closet.

Always arrange your ironing paraphernalia according to whether you're right or left-handed. If you're right handed, pile up the clothes to be ironed on your left, and position the clothes rack to your right. If you're left handed, reverse these directions.

When ironing, progress from articles or garments needing the lowest temperature to those requiring the highest temperatures. And start with small areas, such as cuffs, before progressing to larger areas.

A Good Fit

To make your ironing board cover fit perfectly, place it on the board while it's still damp from the washer, and it'll dry in place.

A piece of lightweight muslin or batiste makes a perfect, inexpensive pressing cloth.

Cooling Off a Scorcher

To avoid scorching the fabric you're ironing, put it between two sheets of aluminum foil. The iron will glide smoothly over the foil and its heat won't scorch the fabric.

If you've scorched white fabric with an iron, sponge the stain gently with a cotton pad soaked in peroxide.

Time-Tested Methods

To prevent wrinkles, keep moving freshly ironed surfaces away from you.

To prevent collars, cuffs, and hems from puckering, iron them on the wrong side first.

Iron collars and cuffs from the ends toward the center for the best results.

Iron double-thickness fabric on the inside first, then on the outside.

So that shirtsleeves or tablecloths won't drag on the floor while you're ironing, slide a card table under the narrow end of your ironing board.

If you don't have a sleeve board, insert a rolled-up towel in sleeves so they can be pressed without leaving creases. Or make your own sleeve board from a heavy cardboard tube covered with a soft fabric.

A thick magazine wrapped in heavy-duty aluminum foil makes an ideal iron rest.

Down-Home Spray Starch

Quick spray can be made at home by slowly adding one-half teaspoon of cornstarch and 1 1/2 teaspoons of wheat starch to 1 cup of cold water. Stir until the starch is dissolved and pour the blend into a clean, pump-spray bottle. You can use it to spray fabrics lightly when ironing.

Tricky Ironing Jobs

Unwanted creases in a permanent-press fabric can sometimes be banished by pressing with a cloth moistened with a solution of two parts water and one part white vinegar.

Because acrylic knits stretch out of shape if moved when wet and warm, press each section dry and let it cool completely before moving it on the ironing board.

Hold pleats in place with paper clips when ironing.

You can refresh velvet by moving the fabric's back side over an iron's heated surface; you can revive the nap of velvet or corduroy by pressing it face down on a piece of the same fabric.

When pressing badly wrinkled corduroy, hold the iron just above the garment and steam the fabric thoroughly. Then, while the corduroy is still damp and hot, quickly smooth it along the ribs with your palm. This technique will eliminate even bad creases.

To keep from giving your wash-and-wear garments a sheen when you do touch-up ironing, turn the clothing inside out and iron the wrong side.

You can restore a shiny look to chintz by ironing the fabric right-side-down on wax paper. This also adds body to the fabric.

So that you won't flatten embroidery or eyelets when ironing, iron them face down on a thick towel. A towel is a good cushion for napped fabrics, too.

To remove wrinkles from a tie, insert a piece of cardboard cut to fit the tie's insides. Cover the tie with cheesecloth, and press lightly with a steam iron.

In Good Working Order

To avoid clogging the insides of a steam iron with mineral deposits from tap water, use distilled water. Better yet, use water collected from defrosting the freezer or from the air conditioner condenser—it works just as well.

If your iron is sticky from pressing starched clothes, clean it by running it across a piece of aluminum foil, fine sandpaper, or paper sprinkled with salt. If your iron is plastic coated, though, avoid salt or other abrasives.

Remove cleaning-product residues from the soleplate vent areas of an electric iron with a cotton swab or a pipe cleaner.

Chapter **5**

LIGHTING AND ELECTRICITY

TO BE SAFE AND SURE ABOUT HOME LIGHTING NEEDS, LET THESE HANDY HINTS LIGHT THE WAY.

Safety First

To make sure that no one accidently flips the circuit breaker back on while you're making electrical repairs, put a piece of tape—and a sign to let people know what you're doing—over the circuit breaker's handle. The same precaution applies to a fuse box.

Wait to tinker with a switched outlet or lighting fixture—even though you've flicked off the switch—until you also have deactivated the circuit. In many switching systems, parts of the circuit are still energized when the switch is off.

When working with electricity, insulate your pliers by slipping a length of small-diameter rubber hose on each handle. Wrap other metal parts with electricians' tape. Insulate a screwdriver's shank by slipping a section of rubber or plastic tubing over it. Be sure to cut the tubing so it extends from the handle down to the blade.

Replace a fuse with one of the same amperage as the one you took out. If you use one rated to carry more amps or if you try to bypass the fuse in any way, you are risking causing an electrical fire.

For safety's sake, stand on a dry board when working with a fuse box or a circuit-breaker box. Also avoid getting shocked when working with electrical wiring by using a wooden, rather than aluminum, stepladder.

It's a good idea for everyone in the family to know how to throw the master switch that cuts off all electrical current. Any time there's a chance of water–electricity contact, avoid wading in water until the master switch has been shut off.

When maneuvering a section of electrical cable through a wall, play it safe and use roughly 20 percent more than a straightline measurement indicates you need. Often there are unexpected obstructions and the cable must be fished around. You can always cut off any extra cable.

Troubleshooting

Save time *ahead* of time. Determine which circuits activate which outlets in your home; then diagram or print the information on a card attached to

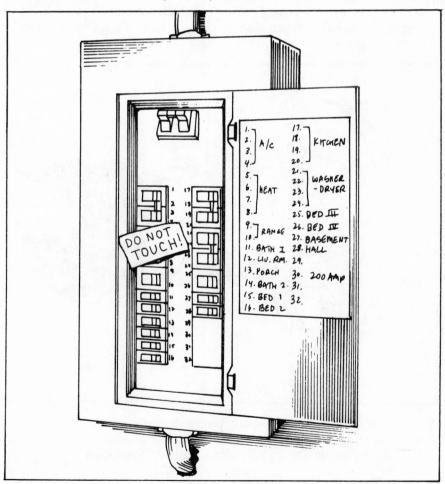

your circuit-breaker or fuse box. When your electricity falters, you'll be able to solve the problem quickly.

A blown fuse or a tripped circuit breaker is a signal to look for trouble. Locate and eliminate the problem before you replace a blown fuse or reset a tripped circuit breaker. Otherwise, the problem will only recur.

Changing Light Bulbs

So you won't be left in the dark if a bulb burns out in the basement, light the area with a two-socket fixture. If one bulb burns out, the other still will enable you to see.

Finding it hard to remove a broken light bulb because there's little left to grasp? Turn off the switch. Jam a sponge-rubber ball against the jagged glass and twist.

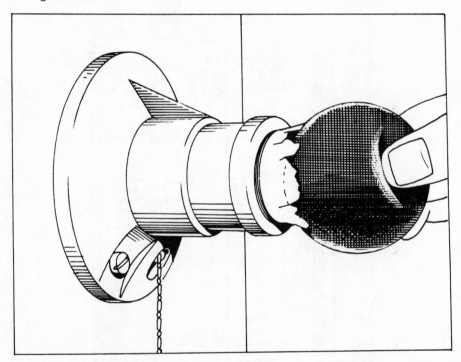

Any change in a fluorescent lamp's normal performance—such as flickering or growing noticeably dimmer—is a warning to replace the bulb. Failure to do so can strain parts of the fixture; for example, repeated flashing wears out the starter and deteriorates the starter's insulation.

Improved Lighting

If you're distracted by shadows that reduce visibility in your kitchen or home workshop, replace incandescent fixtures with fluorescent lamps, which provide even, shadow-free illumination.

If you're planning to replace a lamp socket, consider installing a three-way socket for greater lighting versatility. Wiring a three-way socket is as simple as wiring a standard on/off version.

Chapter 6

PLUMBING

NOT EVEN CLOGGED DRAINS, LEAKY FAUCETS, OR SLUGGISH TANKS ARE A MATCH FOR THE FOREARMED HOME PLUMBER.

Clogfree Drains

You can keep drains clogfree and odorless by once-a-week pouring 3 tablespoons of washing soda (sal soda) into them and then slowly running very hot water to dissolve any build-ups.

For better suction when plunging a clogged drain, cover the plunger's rubber cap with water and plug the fixture's vent opening with wet rags.

If a plunger doesn't work when you try to unclog a drain, try using a straightened wire coat hanger, bent at one end to form a small hook. Using the hook, try to loosen or remove the problem-causing debris.

A garden hose can sometimes be effective in unclogging floor drains, such as those in basements and showers, especially if the debris isn't close to the opening. Attach the hose to a faucet, feed the hose into the drain as far as it will go, and jam rags around the hose at the opening. Then turn on the water full force for a few moments to blast the debris away.

For a homemade, noncorrosive drain cleaner, mix 1 cup of baking soda, 1 cup of table salt, and one-quarter cup of cream of tartar in a small bowl. Stir thoroughly, and pour into a clean, covered jar. When using the mixture, pour one-quarter cup of it into a drain, immediately adding one

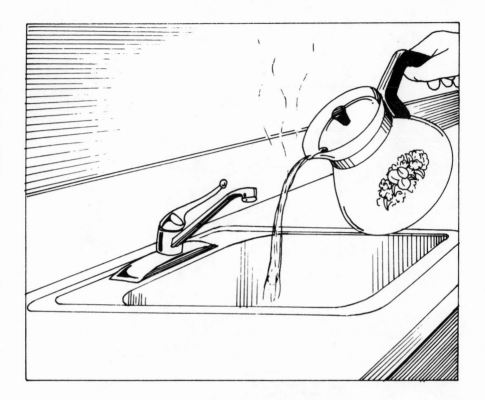

cup of boiling water. After waiting 10 seconds, flush with cold water. Do this weekly to keep drains clogfree and odorless. (One blending of this mixture equals 2¼ cups of cleaner.)

Faucets

If you hear a squealing noise when you turn a faucet handle, the metal threads of the stem are binding against the faucet's threads. To fix this, remove the handle and stem and coat both sets of threads with petroleum jelly. The lubrication should stop the noise and make the handle easier to turn.

Should a dripping faucet get on your nerves before the plumber arrives or before you have time to fix it yourself, tie a 2-foot-long string around the nozzle, and drop the string's end into the drain. As the faucet drips, the drops will silently run down the string and away.

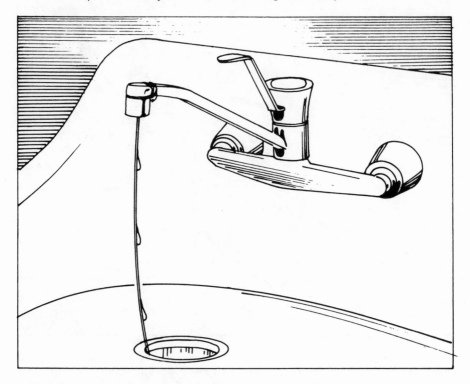

Toilet Bowl and Tank

What can you do if too little water comes from the tank to flush the toilet bowl clean? Check the water level in the tank to see if it's too low. If the water level doesn't come to within 1½ inches of the top of the overflow tube, bend the float arm up slightly to allow more water to enter the tank.

If there's very little water in a clogged toilet bowl, flushing will only cause the bowl to overflow. Instead, use a plunger to unclog the toilet—and bring water from another source to cover the plunger cup for better suction.

To make a septic tank activator, combine 2 envelopes of active dry yeast with 1 pound of brown sugar in a large bowl. Add 4 cups of warm water, stirring till the mixture completely blends. Set the mixture in a warm place for 10 to 20 minutes till it's foamy and its volume increases. Then, flush it down the toilet.

Noisy Pipes

If your water pipes bang and faucets leak, the water pressure in your home might be reaching or exceeding 70 to 80 pounds per square inch, and you might need to install a pressure-reducing valve. You can measure the average water pressure in your house by attaching a pressure gauge to a cold-water faucet nearest the main shutoff valve.

You can silence a noisy water pipe (if the noise is caused by the pipe banging against a wall) by wedging the pipe off the wall with a wood block and clamping the pipe to the wedge with a pipe strap.

Frozen Pipes

If you have a stretch of water pipe that often freezes, consider investing in heat tape (sometimes called heat cable). You can buy the tape, which is wrapped around the pipe, with an automatic thermostat to start the heat when the temperature outside drops to about 35°F.

When thawing a frozen pipe, start at the tap end and open the tap so that melting ice and steam can run off or dissipate harmlessly. If you start at the middle of a pipe, steam from melting ice may burst the pipe.

Sweat Soldering

Good sweat solderers gain their expertise through practice. It might be a good idea to buy a few short lengths of copper pipe and some fittings and try your hand before you tackle the real project.

To clean copper pipe before sweat soldering, wrap an emery cloth strip around the end of the pipe and move it back and forth as if you were buffing a shoe.

Most amateur plumbers are so proud of their first sweat-soldered joints that they immediately turn on the water—a big mistake. Allow the joint to cool naturally because the sudden cooling effect of rushing water can weaken the joint and cause it to crack.

Preventive Plumbing

If a pipe springs a leak, consider replacing an entire section rather than patching just the leak. A pipe that is corroded enough to leak in one location often starts leaking in other places as well.

Whenever you secure a pipe, be careful to anchor it so it still can expand and contract with temperature changes. If you place a bracket on a pipe, include a rubber buffer fashioned from garden hose, radiator hose, foam rubber, rubber cut from old inner tubes, or kitchen sponges.

To avoid scarring a chrome-plated plumbing fixture with wrench teeth when installing it, first wrap the fixture with a double coating of plastic electrical tape.

It's a good idea to turn the water shutoff valve off and then on again once every 6 months to keep it in working order.

Make sure everyone in the family knows where the main shutoff valve is in your home—and make sure everyone knows how to use it. This could prevent flooding in an emergency.

When you're using hot-water faucets regularly, there's no danger of hydrogen gas building up in your hot-water heater. But if you've been away for an extended period, there *is.* If you've been away for awhile, open all hot water taps for a few minutes after reentering your house to prevent the danger of a possible explosion.

Chapter 7

BASEMENT, SHOP, GARAGE

NO MATTER WHERE YOU'VE PUT YOUR WORKSHOP, HERE'S A NUTS-AND-BOLTS GUIDE TO MAKING EVERYTHING HANDIER.

GENERAL SHOP

Trade Secrets

Loosen a stubborn screw, bolt, or nut with a shot of penetrating oil. If you don't have oil, use hydrogen peroxide, white vinegar, kerosene, or household ammonia. Should these prove ineffective, heat the metal with an iron, rap it sharply with a hammer while it's still hot, and again try to loosen it.

You can work most rusted bolts loose by pouring a carbonated beverage on them.

If a bolt repeatedly loosens due to vibrations, coat its threads with fingernail polish and reinsert it. It won't loosen again. Should you have to remove it, you can break the seal with a little effort.

You can prevent a knot in nylon rope from working loose by holding it briefly over a small flame. The heat will melt and bond the fibers.

Dipping the ends of a rope in shellac will keep them from unraveling.

To hide a screw head, drill a counterbored hole, seat the screw, glue a piece of doweling into the counterbore, and sand it flush.

Avoid burning your fingers when lighting a pilot light with a short match. Simply clamp a match in an alligator clip at the end of a straightened coat hanger.

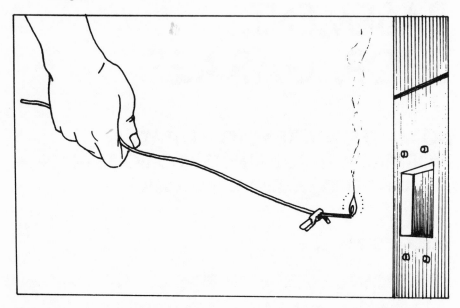

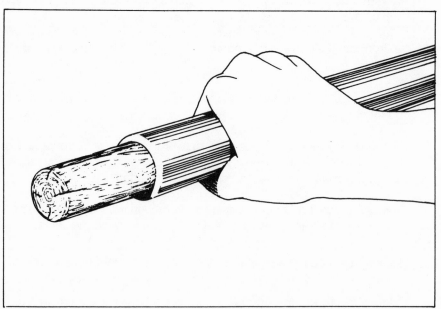

To prevent metal tubing from denting when sawing it, insert a round dowel that tightly fits the tube's interior.

Easy Measuring

If you know the exact width of your hand with thumb and fingers spread, you'll be able to make rough measurements, if necessary, without using a ruler or tape measure.

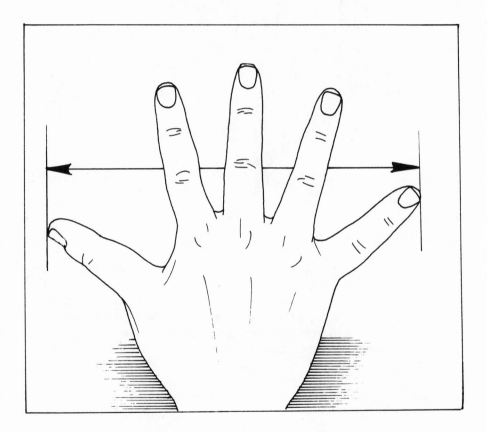

As an aid in measuring lumber or pipe, paint lines a foot apart on a concrete floor.

For easy workshop measuring, fasten a yardstick to the edge of your workbench so you can just hold items against it. Cut keyhole slots in the yardstick so you can remove it when you need it elsewhere.

Handy Substitutions

If you're out of penetrating oil, you can substitute hydrogen peroxide, lemon juice, or kerosene.

You can use a coping saw blade to remove a broken-off key from a lock. Slide the blade in beside the key, turn it toward the key so its teeth sink into the key's soft brass, and then pull the blade out along with the key fragment.

An old nylon stocking makes an effective strainer if you're out of cheesecloth.

Space Savers

In your workshop, use a pocketed shoebag for such items as cans. The bag holds more in less space than does a shelf.

An empty soft-drink carton makes a convenient "tote" kit for holding and carrying lubricants.

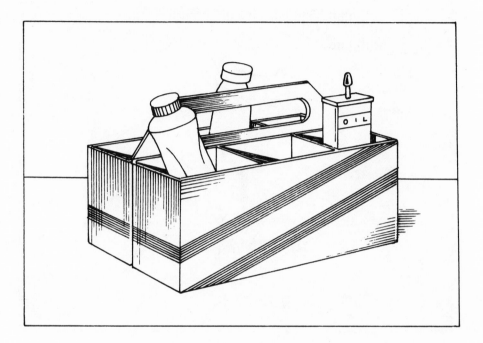

Empty hand-cream jars are great storage containers for nails. The greasy film left on the sides of the jar will prevent the nails from rusting.

If you need more workbench storage space, slide an old dresser under the bench and keep items in its drawers.

Time Savers

To keep the pores of your hands dirt- or grease-free, wipe on a thin coat of shaving cream before starting a messy task.

You won't waste time when picking up spilled nails, screws, or tacks if you collect them with a magnet covered with a paper towel. When the spilled items snap toward the magnet because of its "pull," gather the towel corners over the pieces to collect them. Then pull the towel "bag" away from the magnet.

Using Tools

Don't take a chance on hitting a thumb or finger when hammering a small brad, tack, or nail. If you slip the fastener between the teeth of a pocket comb, the comb holds the nail while you painlessly hold the comb. You also can use a bobby pin or a paper clip.

To transform a hammer into a soft-headed mallet, cover the head with a rubber tip from a crutch, or a chrome-plated furniture leg.

To prevent a screwdriver from slipping, rub chalk on its blade.

If you don't have a carpenter's level, you can substitute a tall, straight-sided jar with a lid. Fill the jar three-quarters full with water. Lay it on its side on the surface you're testing and when the water is level, the surface is, too.

If you want to remind yourself to unplug an electric drill when changing its accessories, fasten the chuck key near the plug end of the cord.

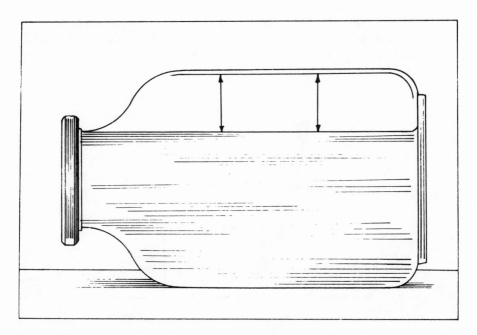

Tool Care and Storage

To retard moisture and rust, keep mothballs with your tools. If rust spots appear, rub them away with a typewriter eraser.

To protect tools, it's best to store them so they aren't subjected to moisture. Keep a thin coating of oil on metal parts, wrap them in plastic wrap, or keep carpenter's chalk in the tool box. (Carpenter's chalk absorbs dampness.)

To sharpen a pair of scissors, use it to slice up several pieces of sandpaper.

A piece of slit garden hose is a handy protective cover for the teeth of a hand saw between projects.

Snow won't stick to your snow shovel if you give the shovel a coat of floor wax.

To make a rust-preventive coating for tools, combine one-quarter cup of lanolin and 1 cup of petroleum jelly in a double boiler over low heat. Stir till the mixture melts and completely blends, and then remove from heat and pour into a clean jar, letting it cool partially. Use the mixture while it's still warm, applying it to tools, outdoor furniture, and other metal objects. Don't wipe it off, just let it dry. If there's any extra, cover it tightly, rewarming it when you use it again.

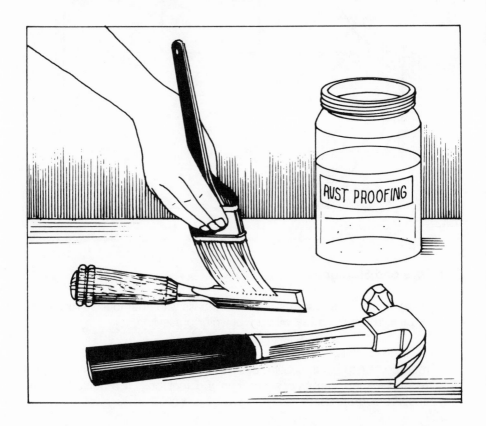

If you paint all tool handles with an unusual, bright color, or wrap reflective tape around them, they'll be easy to identify if borrowed or left in the wrong place.

If you don't have a tool box, carry tools in a large plastic bucket.

To guard the teeth of circular saw blades when not in use, store the blades in record album covers. You could even store them in an ordinary record rack in your shop.

If you hang tools on pegboard walls, outline each tool with an artist's brush so you'll know at a glance where each tool goes. You'll also know when a tool hasn't been replaced.

Keep screwdrivers handy. Slide the blades through the mesh in plastic berry baskets nailed to the shop wall.

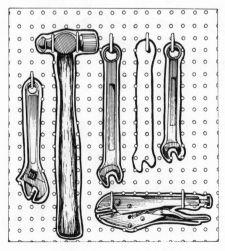
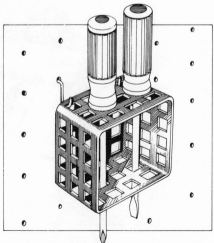

WOODWORKING

Plywood

Plywood frequently splits when you begin sawing it. You can prevent this by applying a strip of masking tape at the point where you plan to start.

To prevent splintering or splitting when sawing, you can also prescore the top layer on both sides, at the cutoff point, with a sharp chisel or pocket knife.

If you're buying plywood to use where only one side will be visible, you can save money if you ask for a piece that's less expensive because it's perfect on only one side.

Use expensive waterproof bond plywood only for outside use; less expensive water-resistant bond plywood when panels will be exposed to weather infrequently; and relatively inexpensive drybond plywood when panels will be used indoors.

Sawing

You can saw a board into almost perfectly equal lengths without measuring it. Simply balance it on a single sawhorse. Saw at the point where it stops teetering.

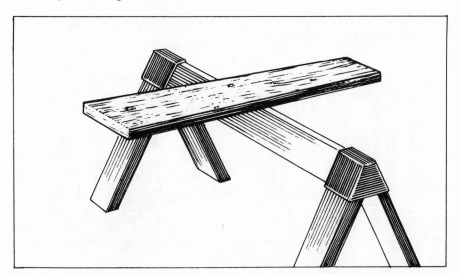

To render any sawing task smoother and easier, frequently lubricate a saw's blade by running a bar of soap or a candle stub over its sides.

To prevent a saw from binding when ripping a long board, hold the initial cut open with a nail or wedge. Move the nail or wedge down the cut as you continue to saw.

Saws cut easier *across* the grain than with it. In ripping cuts, there's a tendency for the blade to follow the grain, rather than a marked or scribed line, so watch carefully when making rip cuts or the cut might turn out wavy.

Removing Nails

To prevent dimpling a wood surface when removing a nail with a hammer, protect the surface with a small block of wood or a shim, which, incidentally, will increase your leverage.

To extract a nail without widening its hole or denting surrounding stock, use long-nose pliers and roll the pliers in your hand.

Drilling

When you drill through any kind of wood, a certain amount of wood splintering will occur at the breakout point. (This is true regardless of the type of bit used, since wood has a composition that causes it to fracture rather than break.) You can prevent this breakout splintering by backing the stock with a piece of scrap.

Sanding

You can check that wood is perfectly smooth after you sand it by covering your hand with a nylon stocking and rubbing it over the surface. You'll be able to detect any remaining rough spots.

Sandpaper clogs fast, and usually before it's worn out. You can clean clogged sandpaper and give it new life by vacuuming it or rubbing a fine-bristled brush back and forth across its grit.

Gluing

When gluing two pieces of wood together, position the grain in the same direction. If the pieces are cross grained and later swell due to moisture absorption, the joint will pull apart.

Screws and Bolts

Whenever there's danger of splitting a narrow section of wood with a screw, predrill a hole. Then the wood won't crack when you insert the screw.

Tips to Remember

Though a hacksaw is designed to cut metal, the thin blade is well suited for accurately cutting small pieces of wood.

A plastic playing card or credit card can serve as a scraper for removing excess wood filler from a surface undergoing repairs.

A salt shaker makes a good applicator for distributing pumice evenly on a wood surface.

Tack rags will last longer if they're stored in an airtight container since they won't dry out. Airtight storage also prevents spontaneous combustion. (This safety tip applies equally well to other rags, coveralls, work gloves, and any other clothes that might absorb flammable oils and solvents as you work on various home repair projects.)

BASEMENT

Special Tips

You will have better daytime visibility in the basement if you paint window wells, basement walls, and basement ceilings white to reflect more outside light.

To guard against tracking dust or sawdust upstairs, carpet the basement steps. The carpet nap will brush dust or sawdust off the soles of your shoes.

Basement Moisture

If you have a moisture problem in your basement, you need to know whether the cause is seepage or condensation. To determine which one you have, tape a hand mirror against a wall in the middle of a damp spot. Leave it overnight. If the mirror is fogged the next morning, condensation is the culprit.

To get rid of condensation, either air the basement frequently or use the opposite approach: Keep its doors closed and install basement storm windows to keep moisture out.

If your problem turns out to be seepage, you'll probably need professional help, but in either case, wrap exposed cold-water pipes with nonsweat insulation and install a dehumidifier.

GARAGE

Easier Parking

Luminous stripes painted on the rear garage wall can help you center your car when parking.

If you never are quite sure when to stop when you pull into your garage, a ball suspended on a string from the garage ceiling can act as a parking guide. Hang the ball so it almost touches the windshield at eye level when you are seated at the steering wheel. Then when you drive in, stop just before the windshield touches the ball.

A "padded" garage can help you avoid scratching your car when pulling in and out. Attach sections of inner tube to both sides of the entranceway if that is your problem area.

To avoid damaging your car doors after you've driven into the garage, staple inner-tube sections, foam rubber, carpet scraps, or rubber mats to the garage walls where doors might hit when opened.

To soften the blow in case you accidentally collide with the garage's rear wall when parking, cushion the wall with an old tire hung at bumper height.

Cleanups

To keep the garage floor free of grease and oil spots, place a drip pan under the car. Make your own from a cookie sheet filled with cat litter, which will need to be replaced when it's saturated. Or, cut a piece of corrugated cardboard to fit the cookie sheet and change it as necessary. If you need a drip pan larger than a cookie sheet, fashion one from aluminum foil stapled to a piece of corrugated cardboard.

Garage floor oil and grease spots can be cleaned with paint thinner. Apply thinner and cover overnight with cat litter, dry Portland cement, or sand; sweep; repeat if necessary.

Some automotive oil spots can be lifted with baking soda or cornmeal. Sprinkle on and sweep off; repeat as necessary.

As a last resort, try removing a garage floor stain with full-strength laundry bleach.

If all else fails, you can camouflage garage floor drippings with paint. Apply a black stripe the width of the space between the car's tires. The stripe doubles as a parking guide.

Garage Doors

If your wooden garage door is hard to open, it could be because it is not completely painted or sealed and so has swollen. (An unpainted door can bind at the edges and seem heavy.) To remedy this, let the door dry out thoroughly over several dry days, and then seal it by painting all surfaces, including edges.

More Storage Space

If you need to maximize garage floor space, try hanging items such as rakes and shovels on the walls. Gain more room by filling the top half of the garage's rear wall with shelves or cabinets in which to stash small tools, automotive supplies, and garden accessories. (Your car's hood can be tucked under these cabinets.) Overhead, lay a platform across the garage's ceiling joists so you can put the space between the ceiling and roof to work for storage, too.

Save space on your garage floor by stashing storm sash or screens overhead in a simple storage rack constructed to attach to existing ceiling joists.

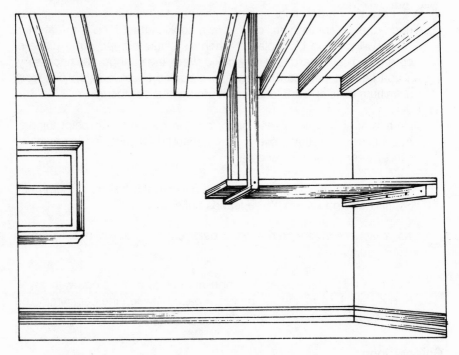

Maximize garage floor space by painting white lines on the floor to outline parking areas for bicycles, the lawn mower, and other large objects. They'll never be in the car's way.

Chapter **8**

PAINTING AND DECORATING

INDOORS OR OUT—THESE ARE SURE-FIRE WAYS TO MAKE ALL YOUR DECORATING SIMPLE AS WELL AS SPIFFY.

Indoor Painting Tips for No Drips

Prevent drips when painting a drawer front by removing the drawer and painting it when it's face up.

Keep paint off window panes when painting by masking pane edges with tape. If you have no tape, do the same thing with strips of newspaper dampened so they will stick to the glass. Peel off the paper as you finish each frame.

To avoid smearing when painting cabinets, paint the insides of the cabinets first. Then paint the tops, bottoms, and sides of doors before painting the door fronts. If you proceed in this sequence, you won't have to reach over already painted areas.

If you don't want to—or can't—remove hardware when painting adjacent areas, coat the hardware with petroleum jelly before painting. Should you accidently get paint on the metal, you'll be able to wipe it off.

Protect door knobs when painting by wrapping them with aluminum foil or by slipping plastic sandwich bags over them.

If your wall-switch cover plate was painted over along with the wall and you now need to remove it, avoid flaking or chipping any paint by cutting carefully around the plate's edge with a single-edge razor blade. Remove the screws and lift off the plate.

Glue paper plates to paint-can bottoms to serve as drip catchers. The plates move along with the cans and are more convenient than newspapers.

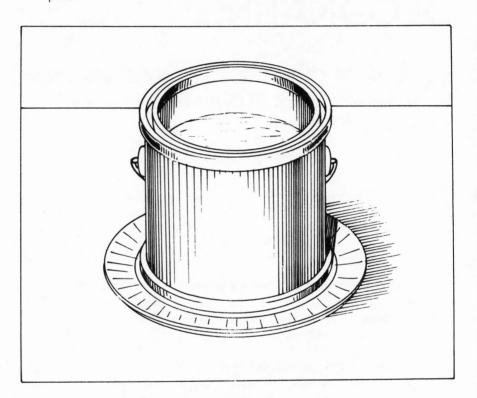

Stairs

When painting stairs, paint alternate steps so you'll have a way out. When those dry, paint the others. Or, paint one side of each step at a time. Use the other side for foot traffic till the painted side dries, then reverse the process.

Where appearance isn't important, steps will be safer, if you mix in a little sand when painting them (so they'll be less slippery) and edge them with luminous paint (so they'll be more visible).

Ceilings

You'll be able to reach the ceiling when painting if you stand on a handy scaffold made by laying a wide plank across two sturdy chairs.

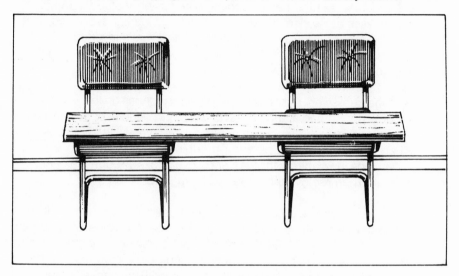

Before painting a ceiling, turn off the light fixture, and loosen it, and let it hang down. Then wrap it in a plastic bag for protection against paint splatters.

Paint Odors

If the odor of a freshly painted room bothers you, you can eliminate it in one day by leaving in the room either a dish of ammonia or vinegar, or onion slices in a bowl of water.

To cut the smell when you're decorating with oil-based paint, stir a spoonful of vanilla extract into each can of paint.

Hanging Pictures

Picture hanging can be frustrating if you simply try to "eyeball" the right spot to put the hook. Instead, place a picture exactly where you want it the first time with the following method. Cut a sheet of paper to the exact size of the frame. Position the pattern on the picture's back side, pull up taut the wire the picture will hang from, and mark the inverted "V" point on the pattern. Adjust the pattern on the wall, and then poke through it to mark the "V" point on the wall. If you nail the hook there, the picture will hang precisely where you wanted it.

If the picture isn't too heavy, another time-saving method is to hold the picture itself by its wire and decide where you want it positioned. Wet a fingertip and press it on the wall to mark the wire's inverted "V" point. The fingerprint mark will stay wet long enough for you to drive a nail and hook on target.

Take the guesswork out of arranging several pictures on the wall, the way the pros do. Spread a large sheet of wrapping paper—or several taped-together newspapers—on the floor and experiment with frame positions. When you decide on a pleasing grouping, outline the frames on the paper, tape the paper to the wall, and drive hooks through the paper into the wall. Then remove the paper and hang the pictures.

Sometimes a picture that was positioned correctly has a mind of its own and won't hang straight. Give it some gentle guidance by wrapping masking tape around the wire on both sides of the hook so the wire can't slip. Or, install parallel nails-and-hooks a short distance apart; two hooks are better than one for keeping pictures in their places. Squares of double-faced tape affixed to the frame's two lower back corners also will keep pictures from roving. (If you don't have double-faced tape, make two loops with masking tape, sticky side out. Apply to each of the lower back corners and press the picture against the wall.)

Don't lose a perfect picture grouping when you repaint a room—insert toothpicks in the hook holes and paint right over them; when the paint dries, remove the toothpicks and rehang your pictures.

To prevent a plaster wall from crumbling when driving a nail and hook into it, first form an "X" over the nail spot with two strips of masking tape or transparent tape.

Other Common Hang-Ups

If you're hanging a picture from a molding but don't like the looks of exposed picture wire, substitute nylon fishing line. The transparent nylon does a disappearing act that allows your picture to star on its own.

Sometimes a picture that has been hanging for more than a year will leave darkish outlines on the wall when removed because dust and dirt have collected against the frame. To prevent such build-up, allow better air circulation by holding pictures slightly away from the wall with thumb tacks pressed partially into the backs of their frames. Or, attain the same result by affixing small tabs of self-sticking foam weatherstripping to the picture backing.

If a wooden picture frame becomes loose, it doesn't necessarily need to be reglued. Save yourself time and trouble by stapling it instead. Turn the frame face down on something that has a 90-degree angle, such as a magazine or sheet of paper. Align each corner on the paper guide and staple, making sure the staples span the joints.

Hanging Mirrors

Hang mirrors to reflect *you* but not the sun, because some mirror backings are adversely affected by direct sunlight.

When hanging a mirror with screws that go through mounting holes in the glass, don't tighten the screws all the way. Leave enough play so the mirror won't crack if the wall shifts.

House Painting

Spring is the ideal time to paint a house's exterior. Do it as soon as the weather turns warm enough, but before the temperature gets too hot. When the heat is blistering, paint dries too quickly and leaves marks where strokes were overlapped.

When painting the outside of your house, fold newspapers over the tops of doors and then close them. You won't paint the doors shut.

Wrinkling occurs when too much paint is applied or when the paint is too thick. You can correct wrinkling easily by sanding the surface and brushing on paint of a lighter consistency.

Don't try using a flame to soften alligatored paint. The flame can shoot into a crack and ignite the sheathing.

Paint will not bind on a surface wet from morning dew or on a prime coat not thoroughly dry. And without proper bonding, paint will peel. Be sure to wait for dew to dry before painting.

If using an oil-based paint, add a mildew inhibitor to it when painting an area that has suffered mildew. (This isn't necessary with water-based paints, which don't have the oil that fungus feeds on.)

Don't wipe your paintbrush against the lip of the paint can. The lip will soon fill up with paint, which will run down the side and drip off. Use a coffee can to hold the paint instead.

Painting gutters is easy, but downspouts can be tricky. To protect the downspout's interior against rust, drop a string with a weight on it down through the spout, and tie a sponge to the string's bottom end. Use a sponge that must be compressed to fit inside the spout. Using plenty of paint, soak the sponge, and then pull on the string to squeeze the sponge up through the spout. The paint will spread evenly from bottom to top as the sponge goes up.

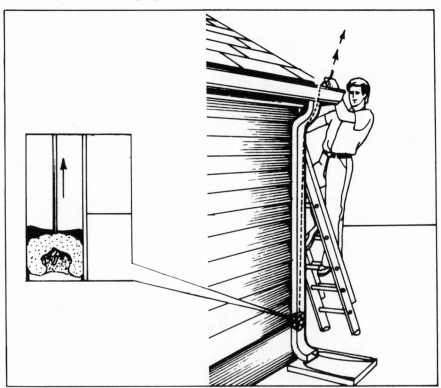

To keep your hands free when painting, you can make a paint holder from a coat hanger. Open the hanger and bend it in half; then bend it into an "S" to hook over the ladder and hold your paint can.

To avoid marring a paint job when leaning a ladder against clapboard siding, cover the top ends of the ladder with heavy woolen socks. The paint will remain unblemished.

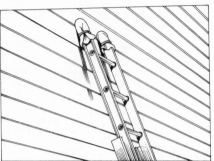

If you have hollow porch posts or columns, and their paint is blistering, trapped moisture could be the problem. Cure it by boring small ventilating holes at the top and bottom of each post or column.

Surface Problems

When sanding to remove paint from wood siding, don't use a sander with a revolving disc. It will gouge the surface.

To prepare old wood for paint, it's not necessary to remove the old paint. Simply seal all knots with thinned shellac and sand when dry. If the knot is loose, tighten it with wood caulking. After the caulking has dried, coat the spot with shellac and then sand.

To remove loose and peeling paint from curved metal surfaces, use a wire brush. A scraper or putty knife will take such paint off flat surfaces. Use steel wool on rust spots, and a mirror to inspect the undersurfaces not visible from without.

Protecting Trees and Shrubs

Plant or prune shrubbery or trees so branches don't touch paint exterior surfaces. The undersides of leaves hold moisture long after a rain, and prolonged moisture causes paint to blister and peel.

To protect nearby shrubs from paint splatters when painting the exterior of your house, cover them with suit bags from the cleaners.

Good Timing

It's best to paint galvanized metal after it weathers at least 6 months because raw metal is coated with a protective, oily film that will keep paint from adhering properly. If you prefer not to wait for the metal to weather, strip the film by washing the metal with pure white vinegar. Rinse the metal with water and allow to dry before painting.

If you want to be able to use a previous coat of exterior paint as a base for a new coat, the old paint should be no more than 5 years old. If you wait longer than that, you'll have a major job of scraping, sanding, and spackling.

Getting the Right Color

Artificial light darkens color, so your paint will look lighter in the daylight. If in doubt when at the paint store, take the container outside to examine the color.

Color can saturate your eyes. When mixing paint, look away from the mix at a white surface for several minutes to allow your eyes to adjust for accuracy.

All paint dries to a lighter shade than the one you see when it's first applied to the surface you're painting.

Ladder Safety

For safety's sake when positioning a ladder against a house or tree, it is best to place the base of the ladder so the distance from it to the object or structure is one-fourth the ladder's extended length. Otherwise the ladder may fall forward or tip backward.

If you are on a ladder working in front of a closed door, lock it so no one can inadvertently swing the door open and send you sprawling.

Cleaning Up

For easy cleanup of your paint tray, line the tray with a plastic bag before pouring in your paint. After the job's done, you can discard the bag without having to clean the roller tray.

To avoid having to clean a paint roller pan, press a sheet of aluminum foil into it before using. When you're finished, simply wrap up the foil and dispose of it.

Why buy new paint thinner when you can reuse the old? Here's how: Pour paint thinner into an empty coffee can. After you've cleaned your brushes, cover the can tightly and let it stand for several days. When paint from the brushes settles to the bottom as sediment, drain off the "clean" thinner into another can and store for reuse.

When you buy a new oil paint brush, soak it for a day in a can of linseed oil before using it. The brush will last longer and be easier to clean.

To clean a paintbrush without making a mess of your hands, pour solvent into a strong, clear plastic bag, and insert the brush. Your hands will stay clean as you work the solvent into the bristles through the plastic.

To keep a brush as soft as new, after cleaning it, dip it in a final rinse containing fabric softener.

An empty coffee can with a plastic lid makes a perfect container for soaking brushes, since the brush can be suspended without the bristles resting on the bottom. Just make two slits in the center of the plastic lid to form an "X," push the brush handle up through the "X," and replace the lid. The lid seals the can so the solvent can't evaporate.

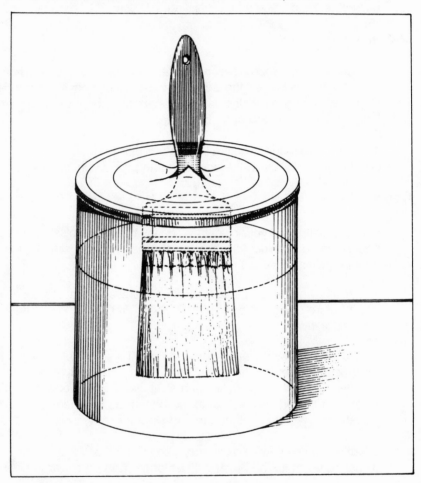

If you must leave a paint brush for a short time and don't want to clean it, wrap it in foil or a plastic bag to keep it soft and pliable. Put it in the freezer to save it for a longer time.

To clean a paint roller after use, roll it as dry as possible, first on the newly painted surface and then on several sheets of newspaper. Then slide the roller from its support and clean it with water or a solvent, depending on the type of paint used.

Storing Paint

Before capping leftover paint for storage, mark the label at the level of the remaining paint so you'll know at a glance—without opening the can—how much is left inside. Label the cans by rooms so there's no question which paint to reorder or use for touchups.

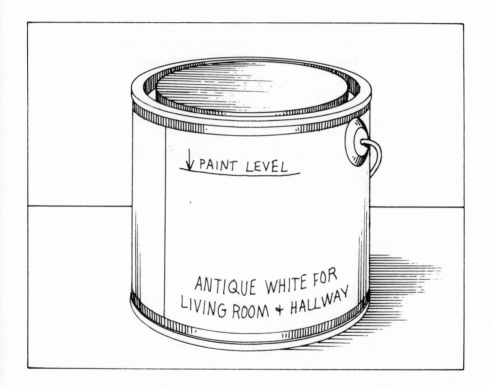

↓ PAINT LEVEL

ANTIQUE WHITE FOR LIVING ROOM + HALLWAY

If you store a partially used can of paint upside down, "skin" won't form on the paint's surface. (Be sure the lid is tight!)

Leftover paint that is lumpy or contains shreds of paint "skin" can be strained through window screening to remove such impurities.

Professional Secrets

To get the correct "feel" for spray painting and to determine the correct spray distance from the object to be painted, first experiment with a sheet of cardboard as the target area.

To avoid painting a window shut, gently slide the sash up and down as the paint hardens but before it forms a seal.

Do tiny spots need a paint touch-up? If you use Q-tips instead of a brush, you won't waste paint and you won't have to clean a brush.

Record how much paint is required to cover each room by writing the amount on the back of a light-switch plate. When you remove the switch plate before repainting, you'll have your handy guide.

White paint won't yellow if you stir a drop of black paint into it.

A paste-type paint remover will remove paint spots from brick.

You can remove paint splatters from your hair by rubbing the spots with baby oil.

Chapter 9

OUTSIDE REPAIRS

LEAKING ROOF? LOOSE SHINGLES? PEELING PAINT? SOLVE THESE AND ALL YOUR OTHER OUTDOOR HOME REPAIR DILEMMAS.

Leaky Roof

If there's an unfinished attic or crawl space below a leaky roof, finding the leak shouldn't be too hard. Climb into this space and look around with a flashlight—don't turn on a fixture or trouble light; it's easier to see a leak in the semidark. When you find the leak, outline the wet area with chalk. If possible, push a piece of wire up through the bad spot, so it protrudes out the roof. This makes it easier to find the bad spot when you're working outside.

Repairing Shingles

When repairing shingles, wait for a sunny day, if possible. A wet roof is dangerously slippery.

You can temporarily repair split shingles even if you don't have any flashing. Put a piece of cardboard in a plastic bag and then slide the bag under the shingles.

You don't have to replace a cracked asbestos shingle if all the pieces are still in place. After pulling out the obstructing nails, slide a piece of roofing felt or roll roofing under the shingle until it is behind the cracks. Drill holes for the new nails needed, then drive in the nails gently. Cover the nail heads with roof cement.

For emergency repair of a shingle, cut a patch to fit from a piece of sheet metal and slip it well under the shingle above the one you're repairing. Apply a coat of roof cement to the bottom of the patch, and tack in place. Cover the tackheads with cement. When you come back to do more permanent repair later, pry up the patch.

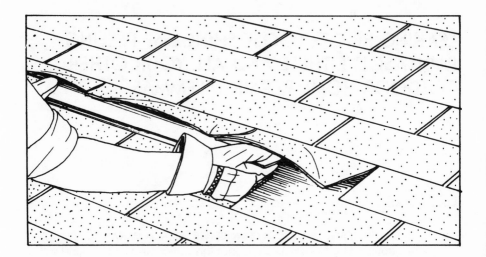

If black roofing drips tar down on shingles when you're patching, soak a rough rag or brush in kerosene and scrub the stains off right away.

To make it easier to slide a new shingle up into place, round its back corners slightly with a sharp utility knife. Then lift the corners of the overlapping shingles and drive in a roofing nail at each corner.

New asphalt shingles can be put down over old asphalt, wood, and roll roofing if it's only one or two layers. If it's in three layers, the old roofing must be stripped off. Cedar shakes, however, must be taken off, as must slate shingles or tiles.

To eliminate a new-looking, unweathered patch in repaired shingles or shakes, take replacements from an inconspicuous area of the house and use new shingles or shakes on that spot.

If you want to replace a damaged shake and it doesn't come out easily, split it into several pieces with a hammer and chisel. Remove the pieces and extract the nails.

If the deck under old shingles is spaced sheathing, begin at the ridge so that debris does not fall through the spaces into the house.

Do not store asphalt shingles directly on the ground or on the roof overnight. Stack on pieces of 2 × 4. When storing shingles, cover them with tarp rather than plastic, as moisture can condense under plastic. Stack shingles no higher than 4 feet.

Protecting Gutters

For best wear and protection, paint the outsides of gutters with oil-based exterior house paint, and coat the insides with asphalt roofing paint, which will render them rust resistant.

Never rest a ladder on a gutter. It will bend the gutter out of shape, causing low spots where pools of water will collect when it rains.

Cleaning Gutters

When cleaning gutters, inspect each hanger for bent straps and popped nails, as you work your way along the gutter. If the house has a fascia or board trim, check the gutter's alignment with it. The gutter should rest firmly against the fascia for maximum support.

Clean gutters by hand, then hose them down after you've removed the debris. This flushes out the remnants and gives you an opportunity to observe the flow of water and see low spots or improper pitch.

Clearing Downspouts

To keep downspouts clear, flush them frequently with a garden hose. If necessary, remove stubborn clogs with a plumber's snake.

Check the nails or screws in the straps holding the downspout to your house. These can work themselves loose when a downspout has been used as a ladder support, or as a result of use or age.

Using a spray-on auto undercoating is a quick and easy way to repair your rain gutters. If you notice any gaps in the gutter, simply spray. If you have to patch a small hole, put a piece of screen wire over the hole and then spray the undercoating.

If you are replacing only a section or two of gutter, take a cross-sectional piece with you when buying a new one. You'll need an exact match of shape and metal.

When installing a new gutter, get help for lifting the gutter sections. Positioning long sections into place cannot be done by one person.

Siding Repairs

Cracked, warped, or loose siding should be repaired as soon as you notice it. Water works its way through such defects into the interior wall where rotting can take place undetected. If you don't have time for a thorough repair, seal splits with oil-based caulking compound and clamp them together by driving nails and clinching them over the boards. This is an effective expedient but temporary only.

Caulking

Never caulk when the temperature falls below 50°F. For an emergency job in cold weather, use polybutane cord.

The best time to caulk is when painting the house. Apply primer to the seams first, then caulk. Primer helps the caulking stick. Allow the caulking to cure for a couple of days, then apply a finish coat. Be sure to use a compound that will take paint.

If you caulk in very hot weather and the caulking gets runny, place it in the refrigerator for an hour or two. Change to a fresh tube every time you go in for a beer.

Removing Mildew

To remove mildew from house siding, scrub the surface with a bleach and water solution (1 cup of bleach to a gallon of warm water). Flush the area with clear water and allow it to dry thoroughly before painting.

To remove white powdery surfaces on brick or concrete surfaces, go over them with a stiff brush. Wet the surface with a weak 5 percent solution of muriatic acid and water. After the solution has been on for 5 minutes, brush the wall and immediately rinse with clear water. Work a 4-foot-square section at a time.

When mixing acid and water, always add acid to water and *never* vice versa. Wear goggles, gloves, and an apron before mixing, and leave them on till after you rinse off.

Water Seepage

To keep water from collecting where a paved area meets your home's foundation, undercut the joint, fill it with mortar, and then shape the mortar into a smooth curve with the back of a spoon.

If water is seeping into your basement, inspect to see if water collects on the ground adjacent to your home's foundation. Soil should slope away from a house, so if the ground is level, or slopes in toward the foundation, you may be able to solve your seepage problem by regrading the soil so it slopes properly.

Concrete Work

When you're pouring concrete steps, be sure to use solid objects as fillers; hollow objects buried in concrete, such as pieces of pipe, have a tendency to float to the surface.

A smooth concrete surface is a hazard on outdoor steps. After the concrete has settled, but is still workable, run a stiff broom across the steps to create some roughness.

If you put sand on top of asphalt sealer, it will prevent the sealer from sticking to your shoes.

You can prevent wooden forms from sticking to concrete by painting with oil the parts that will be in contact with the cement.

An old metal Venetian blind slat can be used as a finishing trowel on small concrete jobs.

If a hollow glass block in your garage wall breaks, clean the opening and soak some pieces of brick. Put the pieces into the opening and pack the hole solidly with concrete mix. You must use brick or the mix will fall out.

Make drilling in masonry easier by making a pilot hole with a masonry nail at the exact spot you want to drill.

Water System

If you're shutting down your house for the winter, turn off the house water supply at the underground street valve. Be sure you're through using the water before doing so, however.

Here's a fast way to clean the house water pipes of water when shutting down a house. After the water heater has been drained and everything else is empty, there may be water left in low spots in the horizontal mains. Just stick the end of a running air compressor hose into an opened outdoor hose faucet. The air pressure will shoot the water out wherever there is an opening. When only air comes out, you're done. This beats crawling under the house to drain the pipes.

When shutting down your water system, open all the faucets and outdoor hose spigots to drain. Flush the toilet and sponge out remaining water from tank. Drain or blow water out of fixture traps, including the toilet. After removing all the tap water from the sink and lavatory traps, fill the traps with a mixture of a little kerosene and a lot of denatured alcohol. Kerosene will keep the alcohol from evaporating.

Other Outdoor Projects

If putting in a skylight, plan it for the northern or eastern slope of your roof. Make sure the attic is well ventilated because a skylight can really heat up a room on a sunny day.

If you camouflage telephone poles or clothes lines with black paint, they seem to disappear.

When installing an antenna, situate it in a place where it won't fall across a power line.

When you can't find repair information in how-to manuals, check with the appropriate U.S. government department for information. Call the local citizen service office.

Tools at Hand

Need a place to hold your hammer when you're on the roof? Attach a shower curtain ring to your belt and slip the hammer through it.

To keep your hands free while you're outside making repairs, make a holster for the nails and screws you'll need. Take a paper cup and make two vertical slits in the cup—about an inch apart—starting under the rim down to the width of the belt. Slip your belt through the slits and you're set.

Keep your tools on a sheet of plastic foam when working on a steeply sloped roof. They won't slide off.

Up the Ladder

If you're planning to work on a ladder extended to its full height, gain stability by lashing the bottom rung to two stakes driven into the ground under the ladder, at its sides.

When working on a ladder, before climbing up, test its bottom rung to make sure it is solidly footed.

The best way for a lone worker to raise a ladder is to pin its feet against the base of the house and push the ladder up from the other end, hand over hand, until it's upright.

Before extending or lowering ladder height, get it into position. It's dangerous to yourself and others to try to maneuver any extended ladder.

Make sure your ladder has firm support at the top. Placing it against a window sash or close to an edge means a slight shift could send you sailing.

Keep your hips within the ladder's rails. Extend the top two rungs higher than the place where you're working. The ladder should always extend up above the roof.

When using an aluminum ladder, watch out for power lines: aluminum *conducts* electricity.

Chimney Repair

Your home's chimney should be inspected each year just before the cold season to reduce the chances of fire and increase chimney efficiency.

Inspect the chimney from the top to see more. On a bright day, reflect sunlight down into it with a mirror. If you can't look down a chimney, inspect it with a strong flashlight and mirror from a fireplace or flue opening for a stove pipe.

If the chimney has crumbling mortar, go easy as you chip away cracked, loose mortar in preparation for tuckpointing or remortaring. A chimney in bad shape could topple at any time.

Preventing Ice Dams

Help prevent ice dams by installing insulation between the rafters in your attic. Use insulation with a vapor barrier and leave air space between the vapor barrier and roof boards under an underhang. The insulation should be 6 inches deep.

You can also prevent ice dams by providing ventilation for the attic through the soffit vent between lookout beams, which can be located by nail heads in the soffit.

Chapter **10**

PEST CONTROL

WHEN BUGS OR OTHER PESTS TAKE UP THE SIEGE, THESE NO-NONSENSE TIPS WILL COME TO THE RESCUE.

Ants

You can keep ants away from your home with a concoction of borax and flour. Mix 1 cup of flour and 2 cups of borax in a quart jar. Punch holes in the jar's lid and sprinkle its contents outdoors around your home's foundation.

Bothered by ants and other tiny insects in your cupboards? Scrub the cupboards and then leave several bay leaves in each to discourage return visits.

Bats

Bat-proofing your property is a good idea if you've been infested once and want to eliminate future colonies. The strong odor a colony leaves behind attracts other bats even after the first group has been evicted.

If you see a bat in your house, try to knock it to the floor with a tennis racquet or broom. Once it's stunned, pick it up wearing gloves, or scoop it up with a piece of paper, and deposit it in the trash. Never handle a bat with your bare hands because of the risk of rabies.

Bees, Hornets, Wasps

If bees are nesting in a wall, and you want to find out where, tap the wall at night and decide where the buzzing is loudest. Since the nest interior is usually about 95°F, you may also be able to feel its heat through the wall. Double-check by drilling a small hole in the suspect area. If the drill bit comes out with honey or paraffin on it, you've found the nest.

If there are wasps around your house and one stings you, have someone else exterminate the nest. You may develop a dangerous hypersensitivity after one sting and shouldn't risk another.

If there's a hornet, wasp, bee, or other flying insect in your house and you have no insect spray, kill it with hair spray.

Fleas

If, thanks to your pets, your home becomes infested with fleas, vacuum rugs thoroughly before spraying and throw out the dust bag at once.

Mealworms

Mealworms, which are attracted to open packages of spaghetti, noodles, or macaroni, are repelled by spearmint chewing gum. You won't be bothered by the pests if you place a few sticks of wrapped gum in, or adjacent to, the packages. (Note: The gum must be wrapped so it won't dry out and lose its scent.)

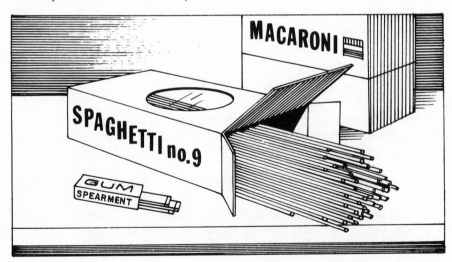

Mice and Rats

The scent of peppermint repels mice. If you place sprigs where the rodents are likely to enter the house, you won't see them again. (You can achieve the same effect by soaking pieces of cardboard in oil of peppermint and leaving them in appropriate places.)

Raw bacon or peanut butter makes good bait for a mousetrap; so does a cotton ball saturated with bacon grease. So a mouse can't get the bait without springing the trap, make sure he will have to tug to remove it. If you're using peanut butter, dab some on the triggering device and let it harden before setting the trap. If bacon is your bait, tie it around the triggering device.

To keep rodents out of your house, seal every opening they could squeeze through. Some need less than a one-quarter inch space. Put poison in deep cracks or holes, and stuff these with steel wool or scouring pads pushed in with a screwdriver. Close the spaces with spackling compound mixed with steel wool fragments.

Mosquitos

Since mosquito larvae thrive in water, changing birdbath water every 3 days will help cut down the population.

Raccoons

Because raccoons are walking fleabags, take immediate action if one sets up housekeeping in your attic or chimney. Chemical repellents such as oil of mustard are temporarily effective, but the obnoxious smell may bother you as much as it does the raccoon. Your best bet is to let the animal leave, and then cover its entrance hole with wire mesh.

Roaches

You can also control roaches with a mixture of one-half cup of borax and one-quarter cup of flour. Sprinkle this powder along baseboards and doorsills, or spoon it into clear jar caps positioned under sinks or under cabinets.

A Word to the Wise

Remember that supermarkets and grocery stores almost always have roaches, so check bags and boxes when unpacking food at home.

If you live in a multiunit building, any pest control measures you take individually ultimately will be ineffective, since insects can travel from one apartment to another. The entire building should be treated at one time to eliminate bugs completely.

In spring, moving leftover firewood away from the house will help keep possible insect infestations at a distance.

The presence of centipedes in your house may indicate there are other insects as well, because centipedes prey on other bugs.

The presence of carpenter ants indicates another problem. Because they're fond of damp wood, you should check for water leaks, inspecting your pipes, roof, and window sills.

You can distinguish termite damage from other insect damage by examining any holes you find in wood. Termites eat only the soft part of wood, leaving the annual rings intact.

Part II

ENERGY SAVERS

"Rising energy costs"—we hear and read this phrase all too often these days. No longer can any of us afford to be energy wasters, for the expense is just too great for all of us. Part II tells you what you can do right *now* to decrease the bite energy costs take from your earnings, and to conserve as much energy as you can. Many of these tips involve no extra expense; all it takes is a little extra energy consciousness.

In Chapter 1, "General Energy Efficiency," you'll learn how to maintain your heating system for maximum efficiency. Knowing where to locate and when and how to use major appliances effectively can mean real savings when you use your refrigerator, washer, dryer, and other mechanical servants. The major energy expense in cold winter climates is home heating, and Chapter 2 gives you some chill-chasing ideas for lowering your thermostat painlessly. You'll also learn how to dress for warmth, how to insulate your home, and how to capitalize on sun and oven warmth.

There are more illuminating ideas in Chapter 3, "Electricity,"—great hints on cutting your electric bills, from basic suggestions on selecting the right light bulb to tips for monitoring lights in remote parts of your home. "Cooling," Chapter 4, deals with an energy use that's potentially as expensive as heating, and tells you how to get the most from your air-conditioning system, without paying high cooling bills.

The last chapter in this section talks about a daily necessity all year round—hot water. You'll learn that insulating your water heater and pipes can considerably lower your water heating bills. And, besides clever ways of using water wisely, you'll also find out how an off-peak meter can save you money by turning your water heater on at times when the power company has power to spare. You *do* have the power to save money—and here's how to do it.

Chapter 1

GENERAL ENERGY EFFICIENCY

WHERE CONSERVATION IS CONCERNED, YOU DON'T HAVE TO BE AN EINSTEIN TO MAKE THESE ENERGY FORMULAS WORK FOR YOU.

Home Heating Efficiency

To check the efficiency of the heating system of a home you're considering buying, change the thermostat setting—raise it if it's cold outside and lower it if it's warm—and then see how fast the room heats up or cools down. It should take no more than half an hour for the home to reach the desired temperature.

Periodically cleaning the squirrel-cage-type blower in a forced-air heating system will improve its efficiency and lower the system's operating cost. A vacuum cleaner hose attachment and a stiff brush are effective cleaning tools.

Your heating system will operate at peak efficiency only if it's clean, so save on fuel bills with regular maintenance.

Next time a banging radiator drives you crazy, make a quick check with a level. The radiator should slope down on one side, toward the pipes and the boiler. If it doesn't, you can stop the banging by propping up the outside legs.

A fireplace draws air from the house to keep the fire going, so if your furnace is operating and warming up the air while the fireplace is going, the net effect is that you're paying to heat air that is going right up the chimney. The best way to eliminate this problem is to install an outside air vent directly in front of the fireplace. The fireplace then will operate on outside air instead of on your heated air. It's also a good idea to close the doors to the room where the fireplace is being used to reduce the amount of heated air drawn from the rest of the house.

When you're not using the fireplace, be sure you're not losing your home's heated air through the chimney; remember to keep the damper in the fireplace closed except when you're enjoying a fire.

Wood Stoves

When installing a woodburning stove, select a brand made of steel or cast iron for safety. Be sure that the stove carries a label indicating that it's been tested for reliability.

When purchasing a used stove, carefully check the condition of the hinges, grates, draft louvers, and the sturdiness of the legs. Reject any stove with cracks.

A stove should be installed only over a fireproof material such as brick, stone, or an asbestos plate covered with metal, made especially for the purpose.

Position your stove a safe distance away from easily flammable materials, such as newspapers and magazines, wooden furniture, and firewood logs.

Before operating a newly installed stove, read the instruction manual for safety tips, or contact your local fire department for safety specifications on the stovepipe and flue.

Make it an annual habit to have the elbows, joints, flue, and chimney of a stove pipe thoroughly cleaned.

Never use lighter fluid or other flammable liquids to start a fire. Place kindling wood and crumpled pieces of newspaper under your logs to help fan the flames.

The only suitable material to burn in a wood stove is dry, seasoned firewood.

Before leaving the house, or going to bed at night, always extinguish the fire in a wood stove.

Lower Thermostat Settings

For each degree you set your thermostat above 70°F, you can expect a 3 percent rise in energy cost. For most families, a 65°F daytime setting and a 55°F nighttime setting will be acceptable—and these offer considerable savings.

It helps to reduce the thermostat setting before retiring at night; cutting back for several hours will measurably decrease fuel consumption.

It takes less energy to run a thermostatically controlled electric blanket than it does to maintain daytime thermostat settings throughout the sleeping hours.

To avoid having a thermostat turn the heat on or off when it shouldn't, make sure it doesn't misinterpret the true warmth of your home. It will if it's positioned in a drafty area, placed on a cold outside wall or near a fireplace, or installed too near a heat-producing appliance, such as a TV set or a lamp.

Take advantage of the fact that a large group of people generates heat— reduce the thermostat setting when you're entertaining a crowd.

An electronic clock thermostat that automatically conserves energy by turning up or down your heating and cooling system per your presetting, qualifies for an income tax credit as an energy saving device.

To conserve heat energy, turn the thermostat to its lowest setting if you won't be at home for a few days. If there's no danger of pipes (and plants) freezing during that interval, you can turn off the heating system completely.

Do exercise caution in setting indoor thermostat temperatures too low, however. Older people may require temperatures above 65°F to avoid hypothermia, a possibly fatal drop in body temperature. People with circulatory problems or those taking certain types of drugs may also be vulnerable. In such instances, ask your doctor about recommended winter and summer thermostat settings.

Weatherstripping

A portable hair dryer can be helpful in checking where doors or windows need additional weatherstripping. Move the air stream along the interface between a door and its frame or a sash and its frame. Have someone on the other side of the door or window follow the dryer's movements with his hands. Where he feels heat leaking through, you need a patch job.

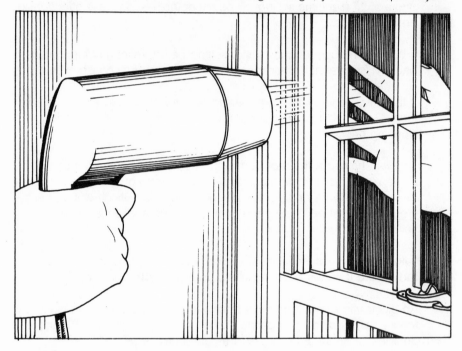

Many types of weatherstripping require nails for installation. You can use any type of hammer, but a magnetic tack hammer works best when driving small brads in cramped areas.

To speed the installation of weatherstripping, try stapling it instead of nailing.

Caulking

Keeping your home well caulked is one of the best ways to save energy. When you caulk, make sure joints are thoroughly dry—you can dry deep crevices with a cloth stretched over the blade of a putty knife, or with a blast of hot air from a hair dryer.

When caulking several joints, start with the smallest joint and recut the tube's nozzle as necessary for successively larger joints.

Washers and Dryers

About 95 percent of the energy used by a washing machine goes into heating the water. A machine with a cold rinse cycle will save some of that energy and cost you less to operate.

You'll use less electricity when running your washing machine if you select the shortest cycle appropriate for the type of fabric being washed and the coldest water setting that will do the job correctly. The amount of detergent you add is important, too, since oversudsing can overwork the machine.

Front-loading washing machines cost more to purchase than top-loading models, but they require less water to operate and save you money in the long run.

If you use a clothes dryer's fluff-air cycle whenever possible, you'll save because it doesn't require heated air.

If possible, run loads of similar fabrics in your clothes dryer, because some fabrics require less drying time than others.

Save energy by drying clothes in consecutive loads, because the dryer retains heat from one load to the next.

Refrigerators

To lengthen the life of your refrigerator and increase the unit's efficiency, periodically vacuum the dust that collects on the coils at the back of the refrigerator.

It's a good practice to position a refrigerator in a portion of the room where there's plenty of air circulation. A refrigerator uses more energy when located near a stove or a heating vent.

Television Sets

Color television sets use almost twice the amount of electricity that black and white sets do. If you have both, it will cost less to watch a black and white movie on a black and white set.

If you want a mini-TV that's truly portable, make sure it operates on both AC or DC current. However, if you don't plan to use it outdoors, consider getting a larger set, with a larger screen, that operates on household current only. Though still portable, it'll cost less than a true mini.

Before you buy any TV set, study the picture it produces under lighting conditions similar to those of the room in which you'll place the cabinet. If the picture isn't what you think it should be, examine another set. Never buy a pig in a poke.

Cable TV

Roughly 500 cable systems operate in the United States without a local franchising authority to govern them. So as not to be taken advantage of costwise and program-wise, check out your local cable system with the FCC. The franchisee should keep all of his preinstallation promises.

Chapter **2**

HEATING

ESCAPE THE COLD—AND THOSE BIG HEATING BILLS TOO—BY INSULATING EVERY NOOK AND CRANNY.

Heating the Home

You can save on heating costs by dressing to retain body heat. Wear lightweight basic garments, such as a shirt or blouse or short-sleeved sweater, covered by heavier garments, such as a sweater vest, and topped with a warm jacket or sweater jacket. Each item is removable if you become too warm—allowing you to adjust your own thermostat.

Loose-fitting windows can lose heat up to five times faster than windows that fit properly. To check a window for air leaks, feel around its edges for air movement on a windy day. Or, light a candle or match and move it around the edges; if the flame flickers, heat is being lost and weather-stripping is needed. Weatherstripping also is needed if ice or condensation builds up on a storm window since this is a clue that air is seeping around the interior window.

A room will stay warmer in cold weather if curtains fit tightly against the window's frame so warm room air doesn't move across the cold window surface. A fixed valance at the top and sides of the curtains will help, and so will weighting or fastening the curtains at the bottom.

A simple thing like keeping your windows sparkling clean in winter can help warm your home. Spotless window glass lets in more sunlight than grimy panes.

To maintain your home's temperature, latch the windows—instead of merely closing them—for a tighter seal.

It's best to remove window screens before winter arrives because fine-mesh screen can reduce the amount of warming sunlight entering your home by up to 20 percent.

Installing a window greenhouse for one or more of your house's south-facing windows is an unusual (but effective) way to gain extra heat for your home in winter, to reduce the loss of heat to the outdoors in the evening, and—not incidentally—to grow plants. Such greenhouses can fill even east or west windows if you install reflectors to catch more of the sun's rays.

If you plan to install new shades or mini-blinds to help keep your home warm, consider mounting them outside the frames. If they're installed inside window frames, air can "leak" along the edges, but outside mountings help reduce the flow of air against cold window glass.

Solar reflective films applied over your windows in warm-weather months will reduce the amount of light and, therefore, heat that enters your home.

During winter months, roasting foods slowly in the oven at low temperatures will not only save fuel and make the meat or fowl more nutritious, but as a bonus, the extra heat will help warm the house.

Hot bath water will help keep your bathroom warm in cold weather months if you allow it to cool before draining the tub. The water will add humidity that also will contribute to your home's comfort.

Aluminum foil placed behind a radiator helps to reflect heat into the room. Tape a piece of foil to the wall directly behind the radiator, shiny side out; use duct tape all around the edges.

Because a great deal of heat is conducted through large, overhead garage doors, a significant amount of heat can escape from a home that has an attached garage but no insulation between the house and the garage. An insulated and weatherstripped garage door, therefore, can save you money, even if the garage is unheated.

Chapter 3

ELECTRICITY

ADDING THESE BRIGHT IDEAS WILL HELP YOU SUBTRACT FROM YOUR ELECTRIC BILL.

Conserve Electricity

To save energy, convert incandescent fixtures to fluorescent wherever practical. Fluorescent tubes illuminate more efficiently than do incandescent bulbs. For example, a 40-watt fluorescent gives more light than a 100-watt incandescent while using less than half the current.

When possible, save electrical energy by using three-way bulbs, which, like dimmers, let you adjust lighting intensity to your needs. If a fixture won't take a three-way bulb, reduce the size (wattage) if you need the bulb only for general light.

If you install bright security lights, consider controlling them with a photoelectric cell or timer that turns the lights on at dusk and off at dawn so you can avoid burning the lights unnecessarily.

Make sure that bulbs in remote places (attic, basement, garage, or closets, for example) haven't been left burning by installing automatic switches that shut off lights in a room when the door is closed.

To monitor lights in remote areas of the house, another possibility is to install a switch with a red pilot indicator on it. When the red light glows, you'll know lights in the basement, garage, etc. have inadvertently been left on. These remote switches are available from hardware stores.

It is important that light fixtures be kept clean, because a dusty or dirty light fixture will absorb light, decreasing the amount of illumination reaching areas where it's needed. A dirty fixture may therefore cause family members to turn on additional lights that aren't necessary, wasting electricity and money.

The elimination of a decorative outdoor gas lamp can easily save you from $40–$50 a year in energy costs. However, if you actually require outdoor light, consider converting a gas lamp to electricity. This will reduce energy consumption considerably, especially if it's turned on only when necessary.

To save energy, it's better to use one large bulb rather than several smaller ones. It requires six 25-watt bulbs to produce the light of a single 100-watt bulb.

If you turn a three-way bulb to the lowest level while watching television, you'll reduce glare in the room and use less energy, too.

White or light-colored lampshades capitalize on the light produced by lamp bulbs. With such shades, a lower-wattage bulb will produce the same amount of light as a higher-wattage bulb screened with a dark-colored shade.

The smallest diameter recommended for a lampshade is 16 inches. Anything smaller will waste electricity by not diffusing light enough to be functional.

For directional lamps, such as pole or spot lamps, 50-watt reflector floodlights are recommended. They require half the wattage of standard 100-watt bulbs, yet provide nearly the same amount of illumination.

In high-intensity portable lamps, you can substitute 25-watt reflector bulbs for the 40-watt normally used, and you'll get approximately the same illumination while consuming less energy.

Chapter **4**

COOLING

WHEN THE TEMPERTURE RISES, YOU CAN STILL PLAY IT COOL WITH THESE ENERGY SAVING TIPS.

Cooling Your Home

Since cold air falls, you'll get better air circulation from a room air conditioner if you aim its vents upward.

If you have a forced air heating system but use window air conditioning units, be sure to close the heating system vents so cold air doesn't escape through the ducts and fall to the basement.

To keep air conditioning to a minimum, be sure you're not needlessly overheating your home. Draw your draperies against direct sunlight, and switch off lighting fixtures when you're not in the room. Consider barbecuing so you can keep the kitchen cool.

If you install your air conditioner thermostat away from heat-producing appliances and direct sunlight, it won't "think" the room is warmer than it really is and work overtime. For that reason, place any outdoor portions of your unit or a central unit where they'll receive the least direct sunlight.

Keep furnishings away from air conditioning vents so cold air can circulate freely.

Odors emitted by a central air conditioner usually indicate condensate drain fungus. You can eliminate the smell by pouring laundry bleach into the condensate pan to kill the fungus.

You'll save on energy costs by turning off your air conditioning unit when you leave home. If you're gone every day, install a timer control to keep the unit off until shortly before you return in the evening. (You can manually override the timer on weekends or other days home.)

Using a patio cover will reduce the load your air conditioning unit bears in the summertime. The cover shields the concrete from sunlight that then reflects and radiates into your home. Conversely, removing the cover in winter months lets you take advantage of heat generated by reflected sunlight.

Awnings and canopies can keep your home cooler in the summertime.

Chapter 5

WATER SYSTEM

TURN EFFICIENCY ON AND TURN WASTE OFF WITH THESE SIMPLE STEPS TO THE BEST USE OF YOUR HOME'S WATER SYSTEM.

Water System Efficiency

Expand your water heater's efficiency by spreading the family's baths, dishwashing, and laundry throughout the day. Also consider showering rather than tub bathing because a short shower consumes 4 to 8 gallons of hot water, while a bath uses 20 gallons or more.

Another way to make your water heater still more efficient is to use cold, rather than hot, water for washing clothes. Many modern fabrics and soaps are actually designed for cold-water washing.

A moderate temperature setting further increases a water heater's efficiency, since the "normal" setting, usually about 140°F, supplies all the heat most families need.

If your water heater is warm to the touch, it is not well insulated and is wasting energy. To start saving energy dollars immediately, wrap insulation around the tank.

To prevent water from cooling as it travels to your plumbing fixtures, wrap hot water pipes with insulation.

You can further conserve energy by turning off your water heater if you plan to be away for a few days.

Sediment buildup can slow your water heater's recovery rate. If you notice a marked drop in recovery time, drain sediment from the tank.

To prevent sediment from building up in your water heater, drain it periodically. Perform this maintenance step early in the morning, before anyone has used hot water and disturbed the water in the tank.

Hot water cools very quickly as it makes the long trip from the basement to a second-floor bathroom. Consider locating a water heater centrally, even if it means building a small closet in the kitchen. It's also important to have the water heater in a place as warm as is practical. The warmer the environment, the less the water has to be heated.

Locating a dishwasher near your water heater is one way to reduce heat loss, since shorter water lines lose less heat than longer ones.

If you have an electric water heater, check with the power company about obtaining an off-peak meter. This means your heater will operate at times when the company has power to spare, and you may be able to buy electricity at a lower rate.

To economize on your water bills, fill your swimming pool with rain water. Attach an elbow connection to your house's gutter spout and run a pipe from the elbow connection to your pool.

Part III

MANAGING MONEY

In today's often confusing economic climate, it's not enough just to earn a good income to keep up with the cost of living—you've also got to know how to make your money work for you through smart investments for future security.

In Chapter 1, you'll find "General Money Hints" covering the gamut from basic budgeting, supermarket strategy, and savings and checking accounts, to credit ratings, economical travel ideas, and smart negotiating practices. With these super-saver ideas, you'll make every day a bargain day.

Since a house or condominium is probably going to be your biggest single investment, you'll want to bone up on the timely housing and real estate tips in Chapter 2. Here's where you'll learn how to get the best return on your investment, including hints on getting the best mortgage and the biggest tax breaks and tips for boosting the resale value of your home. And for those who've gone into real estate for its solid investment potential, you'll find a whole section devoted to this complex topic.

If you're more of a gambler, Chapter 3 with its wealth of general investment hints is for you. Starting with basics like intelligent risk-taking and how to rate a stockbroker, this chapter also fills you in on some of the finer points of investing money, too.

Next time you need to take out a loan, peruse the hints on "Borrowing Money" in Chapter 4. Here's collateral know-how, plus hints on how to avoid the pitfalls of paybacks before you borrow.

How much insurance is enough? It's better to be safe than sorry, but you don't want to overdo it either. Chapter 5, "Buying Insurance," gives you the know-how to get the right life, health, and auto insurance for your needs—without having to tie up more of your income than necessary.

Everyone needs to know how to pay less tax, and Chapter 6 will tell you. You'll want to learn how to get late-year deductions, how to be sure you haven't paid too much Social Security, and what kinds of investment tax shelters make the most dollars and sense.

There's no time like retirement time—especially if it's been well planned and provided for. No matter how near or how far you are from retirement, the hints in Chapter 7, "Retirement Planning," should be part of your financial strategy.

With the array of money hints in this section, you'll be able to manage your finances with the savvy of a pro.

Chapter **1**

GENERAL MONEY HINTS

HEAD OFF INFLATION WITH THESE SHARP STRATEGIES TO SAVE YOU MONEY.

Wise Budgeting

When you budget, be sure to set goals: both short- and long-range goals. Goals might include a new car next year, a university education for a child in 10 years, and retirement for yourself in 25 years. Having goals gives you the incentive to control your spending.

A simple way to budget if there's more than one worker in your household is to use one of your paychecks each month to meet a big expense, such as an installment payment or the rent, and to use all other paychecks to cover other monthly expenses.

When budgeting, you needn't trace every expenditure down to the last penny. This wastes too much time—and often causes family arguments. Instead, overlook the inevitable small items that you can't seem to track down. Most budgeters have a few dollars' worth of such unaccountable expenses every month. Attempting to pinpoint them entails useless bookkeeping.

Are you financially constricted because several large household payments fall due within a short time? Consider arranging a more convenient payment time for some of them. For example, if taxes *and* an insurance premium are due the same month, contact the insurance company to see about rescheduling your premium due date.

So that too many family expenditures don't occur simultaneously, stagger the medical and dental checkups of family members.

It may be cheaper to buy prestamped envelopes from the post office than to buy the stamps and envelopes separately—check the price of your envelopes. Use the prestamped ones for paying bills.

To sidestep added-on service charges, pay the bulk of a month's bills between the tenth and fifteenth day of the following month. If most of your credit card companies and department store accounts demand payment before then, establish a bill paying period earlier in the month. Paying your bills this way should take no more than 2 hours monthly.

Rule of thumb: The maximum amount of installment debt payable monthly should never exceed 25 percent of your monthly gross salary before deductions.

Supermarket Strategies

You'll get much more for your shopping dollar if you don't automatically associate brand names and high prices with high-quality merchandise. Some of the best bargains (still high quality) are lower priced and generic.

It pays to use "Cents Off" coupons when buying food. Bit by bit, the savings add up over a year's time. Look for such coupons in your daily newspaper as well as in shopper "throwaways."

Save on supermarket costs by preparing shopping lists for a full week of planned menus. Always plan menus so you can make good use of leftovers. Doing this will enable you to reduce food costs by 10 to 20 percent.

You'll come out ahead, budget-wise, if you avoid buying nonfood items offered for sale in supermarkets. Shop for such items in discount outlets that specialize in nonfood products—where you'll usually find these products priced lower.

Every Penny Counts

Trade your extra food discount coupons with neighbors and friends, or form a club in your neighborhood which meets once a month to exchange coupons.

Keep the labels, box tops, and "proofs of purchase" from all the groceries you buy. You may be able to cash them in to the manufacturer at a later date when a refund offer is made for using the product.

File your food coupons according to product category, and review them often to discard those with expired dates.

Bargain Time

Money-wise shoppers take advantage of storewide clearance sales after Christmas, Easter, and July 4th. You'll find bargains galore in linens, clothes, and scores of other items.

The optimum time to buy economical back-to-school clothing for young-sters is at the *end* of September.

November is a good time to buy men's and women's overcoats at reduced prices; that's when merchants offer bargains to hype pre-Christmas business. Mid to late January, after the Christmas rush, is also a good time for bargains.

Cut down on long-distance phone call expenditures by calling on weekends or rather late in the evening—*always* dialing direct. Doing this will deflate your costs to less than half of what you'd pay for the same calls on weekdays.

You can curtail hospital expenses if you avoid being admitted on a Friday. Friday admissions result in longer stays than admissions on any other day. For the shortest length of stay, have yourself (or any family member) admitted on a Tuesday.

When you purchase furniture, you save money by buying only the best quality. Cheap furniture doesn't last long, or goes out of style quickly—necessitating the purchase of more cheap furniture. Top-quality furniture remains in style and in good condition for many years. The best time to buy is in June.

Cut down on your magazine subscription bills by trading magazines with your neighbors and friends.

Shop like a Pro

To conserve money, pay cash for things you'll soon use up, such as food items and cleaning supplies. Use credit only for things you'll continue to use after you've finished paying for them, or for emergencies such as medical bills.

To avoid dissatisfaction, never purchase on credit any item that doesn't have a utility or value that will outlast the installment payments.

When shopping for durable items, save on gasoline and wear-and-tear on your car by using mail order catalogues. Another advantage of shopping by catalogue is that each item is described in elaborate detail. You can pick and choose at leisure the product whose features best suit your needs.

If you enter a discount store with a specific item in mind and on which you've already done some checking, confidentially ask a salesperson, "Tell me...what's your *lowest* price?". If it's 85 percent or less of the already discounted ticket price, buy the item at once. If it isn't, thank the salesperson and leave.

Avoid wasting money on a service contract when you buy an expensive appliance. The contract price will typically be low for the first year, since nothing in the appliance is likely to go wrong. However, for each succeeding year, when things probably will go wrong, the contract *will* cost you more than it's worth paying.

When a repair is estimated to cost more than 15 percent of an appliance's replacement cost, seriously consider buying a new appliance. You'll be money ahead in the long run.

Don't let yourself become financially strapped by letting a door-to-door salesman fast-talk you into signing a sales contract. If the item costs $25 or more, federal law lets you cancel the contract within 3 business days and receive a full refund within 10 days.

If you have children of high school age, and the universities in your own state don't appeal to you, you might consider sending them to live with relatives in another state in order to qualify, at a lower cost, for truly topnotch public universities in that state. Check the regulations at the school and in the state to make sure this is legal there.

Savings Accounts

Put your money in a bank where interest is compounded semi-annually or quarterly, rather than yearly. Your money will work much harder for you.

If possible, never withdraw funds from a savings account before the stated interest payment date. If you do withdraw prematurely, you'll lose all the interest due you for that particular interest period.

In case you're hit by unforeseen big expenses—such as unexpected home repairs or a sudden illness in your family—have an emergency fund in your savings account equal to at least 2 months' income.

Even after you've paid off a loan, continue paying out the same amount to your own savings account every month. You'll never miss it.

When you receive a check, don't temporarily place it in a drawer. Deposit it at once. Many banks won't honor checks that are 2 or 3 months old.

If it's burdensome for you to save money, force yourself to do so by purchasing United States savings bonds under a payroll savings plan where you're employed, or by means of a bond-a-month plan at your local bank. You can build sizable savings over the years by authorizing small, regular deductions from your paychecks. There may be shrewder ways to invest, but there are no better ways to save. When you've built up a nest egg, divide it among several sound investments.

A good way to save money is to put aside, at the end of each day, every bit of change you have in your pockets, or in your purse or wallet, including single dollar bills. Faithfully deposit this amount in a bank or a savings association once a week.

Checking Accounts

Because you always want your money to be working for you, never keep more than is necessary in a no-interest checking account. (Enough reserve to cover expenses for a month is sufficient.) See to it that "extra" money earns interest in a savings account or elsewhere.

To remain on good terms with your bank, remember that endorsing a check and depositing it doesn't mean you instantly have that cash to draw on. Before being credited to your account, the check is sent back to the bank that sponsors the account against which it was originally written. If that bank is at some distance, several days may pass before the money is actually placed in your account. Ask the teller, when making the deposit, how long the check will take to clear, so you'll know when you'll be able to write your own checks against it.

It doesn't pay to postdate a check, because a bank may refuse to accept such a check, or may hold it until its date is reached. The bank's caution is understandable: If the check is charged to your account before you expected it to be, it might cause other checks you've written to bounce.

If you're shopping with a friend who's left her checkbook at home, don't generously lend her one of your checks. No matter how meticulously you scratch out the original titles and numbers on your preprinted personal check, machines processing the account will invariably read the original printing and the money will be extracted from your account.

How's Your Credit Rating?

It's smart to obtain maximum lines of credit well in advance of need. If a credit card grantor opens your account with several hundred dollars' worth of credit, request an increase after 6 months, even though you may not actually need it. Continue to pump up your credit availability until you achieve the maximum line. That way, it's there when and if you need it.

Planning to move out of the area covered by your local credit bureau? You may have trouble reestablishing credit quickly. For fast action on new credit applications, have in your possession several copies of your credit file from the bureau covering your former geographical residence.

Maintain your credit standing if you're temporarily unable to make a payment on a debt. See your creditor and discuss rearranging the payment schedule with him. Most creditors are understanding about this. They're *not* understanding if you try to avoid them.

In order to avoid being irritated by a collection notice that you know is due to a creditor's error (a not uncommon occurrence), pay the item in question if it's less than $25. Immediately forward your statement, with a complete explanation of the error, to the creditor. Almost invariably, your account will reflect a correction within 30 days.

Buying on Credit

Don't shoulder legal liability for a significant amount of money for which you're not covered by specific life insurance. This includes oversize department store bills and extended time-purchase agreements.

A good way to keep out of credit binds is to completely pay off a series of payments before committing yourself to a new series of payments for something else.

It isn't wise to put down less than a one-third cash payment when purchasing a car, and it's still less wise to let the financing extend past 36 months. With less than one-third down, a car's depreciation is likely to reduce its market value faster than you can shrink the balance of the loan.

Puzzled as to where you stand with your credit accounts? You needn't be. Simply set aside a special place for storing all credit slips. Periodically review the slips to see how much you owe, and to determine whether or not you can afford to buy more on credit at that particular time.

Whatever you do, don't sign a credit contract that contains a "balloon" clause. A balloon clause stipulates a final payment that's much larger than any of the installments that preceded it. If you discover such a clause too late, you may lose property after having paid a hefty part of its price, or be forced to refinance at extremely disadvantageous terms.

Cutting Car Costs

If you really don't need a second car, make do with one car only, rearranging your schedules and appointments accordingly. You'll save a hefty sum of money each year.

Consider leasing a car rather than buying it. Not only will you tie up less capital, you won't be burdened by insurance and maintenance costs.

Travel for Less

Planning to take a package tour of several European countries? If you go in October, odds are you'll pay at least $100 less than you would in June, July, or August.

To save money on vacations, try home-swapping for a stated period of time. For example, if you live on the Canadian border and would like to spend a week or two in Tampa, Florida, try to locate someone in Tampa who would like to spend a week or two on the Canadian border. Thousands of people do this each year.

Because hotel rooms are overly expensive, don't be afraid to ask for a room by price when you make a reservation. Hotels generally have three room categories: economy, standard, and luxury. Settle for an economy room. Smart travelers do it all the time.

Let's Make a Deal

For the sake of bargaining psychology, take a pocket calculator with you when shopping for a big ticket item. Just ask to be permitted to "work out the numbers" in front of the salesperson who wants to serve you. Then frown thoughtfully while tapping the calculator's keys. This procedure is almost guaranteed to restore an atmosphere of reasonable give-and-take in a bargaining situation.

If you have something difficult to negotiate—a concrete item that can be stated numerically, such as price, interest rate, or salary—cope with it at the *end* of a negotiation. By this time, the other side has already made a hefty expenditure of energy and a substantial time investment.

Never enter a financial negotiation without options. Having options places you in a better bargaining position.

Whenever you create competition for something you possess, the item rises in value. Obviously, when buying a product or service, the more people who want your money, the further your money will go.

Chapter **2**

HOUSING AND REAL ESTATE

WHEN BUYING, SELLING, REVAMPING, OR REFINANCING YOUR HOME OR RENTAL PROPERTY, DO IT LIKE A FINANCIAL WIZARD.

OWNING YOUR HOME

Buying a Home

Your object in a home investment should be to accumulate wealth. When inflation gallops ahead and everything else costs more, your home investment will go up in value, because it can't be duplicated or replaced for less. In fact, many home investors acquire a substantial nest egg without any real knowledge of real estate.

Rule of thumb for determining whether or not you can afford to purchase a home: Your family's gross income should total at least five times the home's projected collective mortgage payments.

If you expect your income may fluctuate, be interrupted in any way, or possibly terminate, don't invest in a home.

Look Before You Leap

To gauge the going prices for houses in any given area, and to measure the price levels in one area against the price levels in another, study classified ads in newspapers. This enables you to narrow your choices among the sections of town you might be interested in. Should the advertised prices in a given section be consistently higher or lower than what you'd like to pay, rule out that particular area.

Before buying a home, determine what zoning regulations cover the site on which it stands. For example, if you plan to expand the house in the future, will you be able to do so? Sometimes a house in its present form uses up the maximum space allowed by the local zoning ordinance.

It really doesn't make sense to purchase an expensive house in a neighborhood that heavily features less expensive houses. If you want an expensive house, you'll get more for your money in a neighborhood where all houses are in the high-price range.

If you want to hire an architect but his job fee seems outlandish, try buying his advice on an hourly basis.

Be a Choosy Buyer

When examining homes, it's best not to take small children with you. They're too much of a distraction. What's more, the owners of the homes you inspect (as well as the realtor) can offer you a better look at the premises, and provide more helpful information, if children aren't underfoot.

Corner lots were once considered desirable, but they aren't today. In addition to having the equivalent of two front lawns to maintain, corner lots pose a safety hazard for small children because of the increased traffic at corners.

When examining houses, don't be overly smitten by cosmetic touches or window views. Above all, you should be looking for adequate separation between the house's living, sleeping, recreation, and service areas.

If you stubbornly hold out for a lower price when a house's asking price actually is reasonable, you may inadvertently deprive yourself of owning the house you want most.

Getting the Best Mortgage

It's almost always more advantageous for a home investor to seek the longest mortgage term available. A term of 30 years or more to repay is better than a term of 20 or 25 years.

Consider the possibility of assuming the mortgage held by a house's seller, if one is outstanding. An existing mortgage probably carries a lower interest rate than the general going rate. Remember, though, that you'll need the lender's consent before you can assume the seller's mortgage.

Would you like to begin home ownership with lower monthly payments than a conventional mortgage allows? Get a graduated payment mortgage (GPM) through an FHA-insured program or through a federally chartered savings and loan association. While the total cost of your graduated payment mortgage will be higher over the life of a 25- or 30-year mortgage, you'll be able to purchase a home sooner if your income is modest but rising.

If you can manage to pay relatively large monthly payments, the odds are that you'll be able to get a larger mortgage loan, pay it off faster, and pay reduced finance charges.

Creative Mortgaging

Good houses have been appreciating about 10 percent a year, so if you've lived in your house 10 or more years, it's probably doubled in price. You can get your hands on some of this inflated value by refinancing the mortgage.

Refinancing is an excellent way for a homeowner to realize a return on real estate without selling it. Some homeowners, especially those who live in areas where property values have steadily increased for many years, routinely refinance each time the equity in their homes rises sufficiently so that the ratio of the loan to the equity dips below 60 percent. They hike the loan back to 75 percent of the value of a new mortgage and use the money they derive from doing so for other financial ventures.

An open-end home mortgage enables you, the borrower—after paying off part of the loan—to reborrow up to the amount of your original mortgage. This is a financially sound way to pay for modernization, repairs, remodeling, or home expansion.

Insuring Your Home

The ideal insurance policy should protect the homeowner against all of the hazards itemized in the basic HO-1 (homeowner's) policy, plus $100,000 or more of personal liability, plus any perils that frequently occur in the area, such as snow damage or floods. The policy should provide living expenses in case the home is damaged by fire or other disaster, and it should cover the full replacement cost of personal property that might be stolen or damaged. It makes sense to interview three separate agents before deciding on a policy.

As the value of your home increases, make sure your insurance company provides an "inflation rider" in its policy. An inflation rider automatically increases coverage as the value of your home increases.

You should be prepared to prove any insurance claims. One of the best ways is to take some photos of the insured property—inexpensive photos of every wall in every room—and store them somewhere outside the home for safe keeping. If a claim has to be made someday, these pictures will show exactly what the property looked like before it was damaged.

Take a Tax Break

For depreciation purposes, the IRS assumes that most residential properties have a 40–45 year lifespan.

When you sell your house and reinvest the proceeds of the sale in the purchase of a new house, you can postpone the payment of income tax on the gain from the sale for an indefinite period.

When engaging in income tax computations after you've sold your house, deduct the expenses entailed in the selling efforts. These expenses include the lawyer's fee, the broker's commission, any appraisal charges you've paid, and any advertising costs shouldered by you.

Real Estate Taxes

Sometimes the simple act of protesting a real estate tax levy results in a reduction. It's been estimated that as many as 20 million property owners are overassessed.

Your home-ownership budgeting will be relatively painless if you include a monthly portion of annual fire insurance costs and annual real estate taxes in each mortgage payment.

Boosting Resale Value

When improving a home for resale, never make an improvement unless it will bring more on the sale price. As a rule of thumb, don't invest money in improvements unless you'll get back $2 for every $1 you've put in.

Owners who keep their property for less than 3 years after making an improvement seldom recover their entire remodeling costs, so plan well ahead when you consider major improvements.

As a general rule, a new or greatly modernized kitchen, an additional bathroom, a finished family room, or an extra bedroom will return only 50 to 75 percent of its cost if the home is sold within a year or two. The idea is to make improvements that—in addition to making the home a more pleasant place in which to live—will pay for themselves in the home's overall appreciation over several years.

Keep a schedule of repairs to your home that cost more than $100. You receive no tax benefit for these repairs, but if you sell your home, adding such major repairs to your cost increases your tax basis.

What options are open to the homeowner comtemplating an improve-ment but reluctant to pay the prevailing labor rate? Try talking to the maintenance engineer in a nearby apartment building. These people often have plumbing and carpentry skills, and are happy for part-time work. An advertisement in the classified section of the newspaper can also help you locate someone with good repair skills who won't charge the top union wage.

Selling Your Home

Unless you're an experienced, almost hardheaded businessman, it's best to use a broker when you sell your house—and this is required by law in many areas. There's an incredible maze of unexpected paperwork that accompanies the transaction. Only a realtor can expertly guide you through this labyrinth.

A realtor can cull out people who are just "window-shopping" for houses, and aren't really serious about buying. When you advertise a house yourself, you attract crowds of meddlesome lookers who waste vast amounts of your time.

Trying to appraise your own home objectively is almost an impossibility. You'll be subjective and off base in spite of yourself. For instance, portions of your home that you regard as distinct assets may be sneered at by buyers as distinct liabilities. Let your realtor guide you.

Remember that a realtor doesn't necessarily want the selling price of a home to be as high as possible. A broker's primary concern is to close the sale. This entails seeing to it that the buyer and the seller agree on a mutually acceptable figure. He makes no deal and earns no money unless he can mediate a compromise between the seller's asking price (normally too high) and the buyer's offering price (normally too low).

There's really no advantage in placing your house for sale through an open listing that entails using more than one broker. If you list your house with several realtors, each will be psychologically disinclined to mount a major selling effort for your particular property. An exclusive listing works best for both the seller and the realtor.

Nine times out of ten, selling a home is easier if you use a realtor. But you may be able to sell your home on your own without much effort during a strong sellers' market. If you're in a community that's had a limited amount of new construction but a large influx of population, you should be able to sell without too much difficulty.

Making the Sale

There's no better time to sell a home than in early spring, late summer, or early fall. The urge to buy and to move are the most intense in the spring.

However, the urges are almost as intense in late summer and early fall, because families want to get resettled in time for the new school year.

When having an open house to show your home to prospective buyers, be sure to clean the house from top to bottom. Trim your bushes and mow your lawn; flick on the air conditioner if it's a hot day; open all curtains and draperies; have plenty of cookies, tea, and coffee available; and—perhaps most important of all—put up cardboard signs that point up features of special interest in your house.

When you have prospects in to examine your house, try to keep the premises as quiet as possible. Switch off the TV set, put your pets in the backyard, and request that your children play quietly (if they're younger) or turn off the stereo (if they're older). This erases the possibility that distractions in your home will prevent visitors from forming a valid opinion of the structure itself.

Don't fall victim to the "one more fool" theory. This theory emphasizes that, regardless of the price, someone will come along who'll eventually pay even more than the present bidder. It isn't necessarily true.

Ten percent above market value is probably too high for an owner-sold home. Just slightly above market value is more realistic.

RENTING AN APARTMENT OR HOME

Before deciding to live in rented quarters, ask yourself the following: What happens if you're forced to leave before the lease expires? Are you allowed to sublet? Is there a subletting fee? Remember that, normally, you must carry out the terms of a lease if a replacement tenant fails to do so. (Unless the landlord offers a lease to the new tenant.) Is it possible to have a clause written into the lease which eliminates your responsibility if you're transferred before the lease expires?

When dealing with a landlord regarding renting, make sure that all agreements are written into the lease. Don't rely on anything verbal. If a landlord makes promises that aren't in the printed lease, insist that they be written and attached to the lease. This applies to such promises as responsibility for maintenance, decorating allowances, property repairs, and your right to sublet.

REAL ESTATE

The Investment Outlook

Good real estate has been appreciating 10 percent or more a year and is one of the best inflation hedges. You can make money in real estate in several ways: (1) buying improved property (land with buildings) that produces income or grows in value; (2) buying unimproved land that will increase in value; and (3) investing in mortgages.

The odds are heavy that the value of any land you buy will continue to outpace the rate of inflation by a more than respectable margin.

If you're a small investor, real estate—more than any other option open to you—lets you cash in on the concept of leverage. To put it simply: The more money you borrow to acquire a piece of property, and the less you put into the purchase from your own financial resources, the greater the return on the dollar you'll receive.

The chances of making money in land investment—if you try to do it strictly on your own—are approximately the same as in roulette. A more sensible approach is to invest, as a joint venture, with a small group of like-minded people. At least one group member should be an experienced real estate broker or land investor.

A Sizable Investment

Because real estate investments usually require more capital than other investments, you must have sufficient resources—before purchasing real estate—so an emergency won't force you to sell at a loss to the first buyer who shows up.

If you have a lot of money to invest, remember that most wealthy investors tend to shun savings accounts. They put their excess cash to work for them via real estate investments, plus investments in tangible and intangible property.

Investing in real estate requires that you commit a sizable sum of money (at least $10,000) if you want to realize a profit worth mentioning. If you've got less than $10,000 to invest, you can still get a reasonably good stake in securities instead.

The Question of Liquidity

A major problem with most real estate investments is lack of liquidity. If you need to sell in a hurry, you may have to sell at a loss, or wait several years. Because of this, you should look upon any real estate investment as a long-term holding.

Financial rewards regarding cash flow and future appreciation of property are sufficient to make up for any lack of liquidity in a long-term real estate investment.

Houses are more flexible and "liquid" than land, apartment buildings, or commercial property as an investment. If you need cash, and you own several houses but choose not to borrow against them, all you have to do is sell one. Your other properties will remain undisturbed and continue to work for you.

Shrewd Strategies

If you're an income-property investor who repeatedly applies the same investment formula without reexamining it in the light of changing economic circumstances, you may eventually find yourself in real trouble.

A powerful incentive for pyramiding income-property investments every few years—as opposed to holding several small properties for a lifetime—is that larger apartment or commercial complexes are more efficient to maintain and manage than scattered fragments of property that quickly exhaust their depreciation potential.

If you're curious about which neighborhoods are gaining in resale values at an accelerated rate compared to others, spend some time at your community's property tax assessment office. With a bit of simple computation, you can plot street or neighborhood price movements with great precision.

Consider the Possibilities

The safest way to invest in mortgages is by investing in government agencies such as the Federal National Mortgage Association ("Fannie Mae") or the Government National Mortgage Association ("Ginnie Mae").

The "right" motel in the "right" locale can be one of the most trustworthy of real estate investments in terms of income production.

Since condominiums are sometimes viewed as transitional homes, they're more vulnerable, in sales-value terms, to economy ups and downs than are conventional detached homes.

Making the Best Deal

When buying or selling real estate, don't make any concessions without getting equal—or larger—concessions from the other side.

When it comes time to negotiate any real estate transaction, don't parade your enthusiasm. Always act hesitant—even though you may be eager— and always behave as though you're under no pressure whatsoever and have all the time in the world.

Reluctance on the part of a property seller to complete a requested questionnaire within a reasonable time period is a strong indication that the property isn't all it's made out to be.

You can almost always negotiate interest rates downward in the final few minutes before signing an earnest money agreement. The reduction may amount to little more than a fraction of 1 percent, but it adds up over the years and is worth fighting for.

Real estate closings can be disasters unless you're appropriately pre- pared. Appropriate preparation means that all documents must be submitted to all involved parties in advance, so there's time to find errors, raise and resolve objections, and make corrections.

There's no such thing as a standard real estate contract. There are certain printed forms that sellers (such as subdividers) insist upon. Legally, however, contracting parties are free to phrase their agreements in any manner they please—as long as the agreements are valid in the eyes of the law.

When purchasing urban property, be sure to obtain title insurance. A title insurance policy doesn't insure against every conceivable loss that might occur, but it does insure against defects that might normally appear in the records.

Best Bets in Rental Property

A wondrous way to live rentfree and beat inflation in the process is to purchase a duplex, a triplex, or a quadruplex. Live in one of the units yourself and defray—or completely pay for—its cost by renting the other units.

Don't put your money into rental property if you can't cope calmly and rationally with frozen pipes, overflowing toilets, malfunctioning heating and cooling systems, and nonpaying or destructive tenants.

When searching for rental properties, avoid those that are overequipped (and therefore overpriced) for their adjacent areas. Rather, seek out houses with no more features, equipment, or amenities than your prospective renters want. Remember, it's easy to add amenities and raise rent, but it's hard to remove amenities and lower rent.

If you're looking for properties to rent, concentrate your efforts in the lower-to-middle range of the local price structure. Why? Because higher-cost single-unit houses frequently return less in rent—proportionate to the outlays they require—than do lower-priced houses.

Purchasing a house to rent to others can give you a substantial annual yield for each dollar you invest. The correct house, with the correct financing, can return 20 to 40 percent or more to you each year via tax shelter, rental income, and capital appreciation.

Don't expect the impossible. A rental property will rarely—if ever—be at its optimum level of general maintenance and repair at all times.

Maximizing Your Property Investment

Don't invest in an apartment building if its vacancy rate is 8 percent or higher.

If you're renting out a building, an effective way to depreciate it is to put the building itself on one depreciation schedule—let's say 25 years—but put its major components, such as central air conditioning—on shorter, more realistic schedules.

Many "pyramid" builders (those who use property to buy other property) don't hold on indefinitely to every property they acquire. Rather, they purchase speculative properties, rehabilitate them, push the rents upward, and sell them (roll them over) to other investors at a hefty profit.

If you're the owner of a rented home, the rental income you receive can offset the monthly mortgage payments. In fact, a home with an older mortgage at a low interest rate can often bring in rental income that's substantially more than the mortgage payments, thereby putting cash in the owner's pocket.

To maximize the rental potential of a second home (or "vacation" home), make sure it has four-season occupancy potential. If the structure will be snowbound two-thirds of the year, forget it.

Getting the Best Tenants

Insist that prospective tenants for rental property have gross monthly incomes of no less than three-and-a-half times the rent you're charging. If their monthly income is only three times the rent you're charging, regard that as a red light warning and immediately back off.

When renting property to others, painstakingly spell out all operating rules in your leases. These rules should include the maximum number of occupants allowed in a given unit. Nine people in a house intended for three can have deplorable effects on both the unit and your annual balance sheet.

Never offer to rent property without first obtaining a detailed written application. Otherwise, you may be making yourself vulnerable to a professional deadbeat who'll quickly move out without paying, or possibly be setting yourself up for a housing discrimination suit.

Rental tenants will stay with you longer and will take better care of your property—possibly even *improve* it—if they feel you're giving them a fair shake. However, as soon as they take the least advantage of you, immediately commence eviction proceedings.

Tax Advantages

What distinguishes income-producing properties from almost all other forms of investment is their capacity to create tax shelters. (Depreciation is another term for essentially the same thing.) Through depreciation, a loss on paper can be transformed into a gain in terms of real income.

The tax shelter you can create for an overpriced high-risk property usually won't compensate for the higher risk.

If you invest in real estate, you can deduct 100 percent of the expenses in the year they occur. However, you must depreciate capital improvements over their lifetime.

As far as your income tax is concerned, land isn't depreciable. Therefore, for extremely valuable land, such as a downtown parking lot in a large metropolitan area, it can be advantageous to lease the site, then deduct the rent for income tax purposes. If you purchased the land rather than leased it, you wouldn't be able to deduct the lease payments as an income tax expense.

Condominiums that are used for business purposes, such as residential units held for capital gain or income, qualify for the same favorable tax treatment as conventional rental homes.

The owner of a rented home doesn't give up any of the tax advantages of ownership. Interest on the mortgage and real estate continues to be deductible.

The tax advantages available through renting out a home are even greater than in regular ownership and occupancy; a home used as an investment is assumed by the government to depreciate as it gets older.

Investing in Land

Thinking about investing in land? Keep in mind that the bigger the land developer's promotion, the less of a bargain there is. Steer clear of undeveloped property smack in the middle of nowhere, especially when it's being touted via slick, high-pressure promotions.

Instead of buying a piece of land that's already been subdivided, why not purchase a tract and subdivide it yourself? Be smart. Take the best lot for yourself, then sell the remaining to people you'd like as neighbors.

Average farm land—not necessarily top crop-producing land—increases in market value at an annual rate of close to 20 percent every 10 years.

Because of the expectation of construction in the near future, loans for development lots are generally easier to obtain than loans for raw land or farm acreage.

Chapter **3**

INVESTING MONEY

LET THESE EXPERT INVESTMENT TIPS HELP YOU SPREAD THE RISK, DIVERSIFY, PYRAMID—AND THEN REINVEST YOUR PROFITS.

GENERAL INVESTMENT TIPS

Words to the Wise

To maintain a fingertip sensitivity to financial and tax matters, consult the *Wall Street Journal* daily. Always collect, and file for ready reference, the column, "Your Money Matters," that appears on the last page, generally on Mondays.

There is no one type of investment that's superior to all others. The "perfect" investments for you are those you specifically select in response to your individual combination of income, tax, liquidity, and risk considerations.

If you truly have no "feel" for managing investments by yourself, and can't make heads or tails of investment advice, you're better off keeping all your money in the bank, splitting it among the various types of savings accounts.

One approach to creating personal capital is to borrow money today for asset acquisition, repaying it later with cheaper money. Caution: For this formula to work, an asset's appreciation must exceed the interest cost of the money it took to purchase it.

Invest for safety first, then growth. As you increase your capital, move from money market funds to bonds or bond funds, and then to mutual funds. This progression stresses income first, then growth.

It's financially better in the long run to miss out on a sure money maker than it is to impetuously rush into a money loser.

How Much to Invest?

Investment funds should be the resources you have remaining after providing for life insurance, health insurance, and a cash reserve. A good guideline for an immediate cash reserve is 2 months' income.

Everyone needs three kinds of money—an emergency fund, a guaranteed income, and investment capital to offset the effects of inflation. You must plan your investment strategy to provide all three kinds of money, and to cover every aspect of your life.

It's a money management maxim to use current income sources to meet current requirements. Using working capital to cope with current requirements sidesteps any disruption of your longer-range investments as well as possible adverse tax consequences.

If you've had little or no investment background, wait until you've accumulated about $10,000 in excess savings before beginning an investment program.

Invest as much as you can, preferably at least 10 percent of your gross income each month.

Intelligent Risk-Taking

Don't ever put all your financial eggs in one basket. Invest in different types of securities and in different securities of any one type.

You needn't, and probably shouldn't, live in an ivory tower when building your estate. You can join a mutual funds organization or an investment club. This spreads your risk and puts you in touch with a broader range of shrewd investments than you probably could muster or master by yourself.

When much is at stake financially, always consider sharing or "syndicating" the risk involved. When you spread a risk so that it's on others' shoulders as well as your own, you defuse and diffuse that risk.

If you have a balanced stock portfolio, individual stock losses aren't particularly important. What *is* important is the overall performance of the portfolio as a whole.

Intelligent risk-taking involves a knowledge of the odds, plus a philosophical willingness to shrug your shoulders and absorb a manageable loss without complaint.

In an investment situation, your degree of risk should be proportional to what you already have in the way of assets.

THE STOCK MARKET

Watch Your Step

Buy stocks only when you have adequate life insurance and enough savings in cash, or the equivalent, to pull you through an unforeseen financial emergency. Without this extra disposable income, you can't afford to invest in stocks.

If you dislike buying individual securities, you should purchase a *portfolio:* many securities grouped under one management. You'll get income both in the form of dividends and of capital gains.

Keep in mind that most successful investors "cull" their stocks the way a cattle rancher culls a herd, selling off all nonproducers.

On the average, stock prices have failed to match the upswing in consumer prices. Because of this, an investment in common stocks can be a second-rate hedge against inflation.

If you have less than $10,000, many stock experts advise against buying more than two or three different stocks. However, if you have up to $100,000 at your disposal, the same experts advise you to purchase about six different stocks.

Bearish or Bullish?

A Wall Street aphorism is to be bullish when the outlook is bad and cautious when the outlook is good. For example, the future appeared dismal during the Depression, but it was the best conceivable time to buy stocks.

Invariably, each time there's a new stock market trend, some previously unknown investment counselor seeks the limelight by announcing a foolproof method of acquiring riches. Regard all such schemes with a jaundiced eye.

Generally speaking, don't change more than 15 percent of your holdings in a single year. Overtrading can—and usually does—lead to large losses.

Hang on to money market funds as long as they offer rates that surpass those of savings deposits. When interest rates begin to dip, bail out.

If you have sizable profits in a stock and the market becomes shaky, consider taking profits and investing them in high-grade corporate commercial paper or in U.S. Treasury bills.

When other people think a stock is going to advance, try to not trail along with the crowd, since overbuying has already raised the stock's price excessively. On the other hand, when everyone is discussing a company's troubles, check into the possibility of its stocks being a bargain.

One way to keep a finger on the market pulse is to keep an eye on corporate directors and officers. It's a good sign if they invest most of their personal fortunes in their own organization's stock. In doing so, they're usually striving to improve earnings per share to make their stock an attractive investment. Since such people tend to be money wise, regard their activities favorably and consider investing in the same stocks.

In a falling market, buy stocks on a Friday afternoon, because the market may have dipped to its low point, with investors dumping because of the prospect of a weekend with more adverse news. If a stock or fund is on the upswing and the weekend news has been bullish, sell on a Monday afternoon, because that's when enthusiasm will be highest.

Wondering how to reinvest your dividends? More than 500 companies offer dividend reinvestment plans. Usually operated by banks, the plans allow you to invest your dividends in additional shares for no, or a low, service charge.

Investment Strategies

Invest in short-term securities. Money market funds may well be your best bet. Long-term investments can cost you money as interest and inflation rates go up.

If you invest in longer-term securities, stagger the maturities. If you invest so that some of your securities mature every year, or every other year, you can adapt your investment to accommodate changes in the interest rate.

If you purchase stocks during a recession, focus on the stocks of companies that provide the necessities of life—goods and services that people need *whatever* the economic climate.

Preferred stocks don't provide the safety of bonds or the growth potential of common stocks, but some types of preferreds can work to your advantage. Sinking-fund preferreds give you good dividends. When you buy participating preferreds, you share—normally 50/50—with common stocks and profits above a specified figure.

Rating Your Stockbroker

How to measure your broker's true capability: If he receives his advice on what to do from others, rather than figuring it out for himself from available indicators, the odds are that his performance will only be about average. What you want is a broker who's *above* average in performance.

If you happen to meet the $100,000 minimum money standard for retaining an investment counsel, request that he present you, in writing, with representative portfolio records covering the past 5 years. These should have been assembled for persons with investment objectives similar to yours. If the investment counsel (sometimes called a portfolio manager) can't or won't comply, don't retain him.

Tax Tips

A great income tax advantage of owning stock is that, when it appreciates in value, you may select the year in which to pay the tax on the gain.

Because the maximum tax on a long-term capital gain is only 25 percent, it sometimes pays to hold a security longer than 6 months in order to cash in on the favorable tax treatment granted on long-term gains.

BONDS

Bonds should form the foundation of your guaranteed income program. They can substitute for savings accounts, especially when they're yielding 2 or 3 percentage points above savings.

To compute a bond's current return, divide the dollar amount of interest by the bond's price.

For a long period of time, the low interest return on "E" bonds made them an unpopular investment choice, to say the least. Today, however, because the maturity date has been telescoped, they're excellent savings vehicles for middle-income families.

Include municipal bonds in any investment plan. The interest on such bonds is exempt from the federal income tax, and often—if you're a resident of the issuing locality—from state and local taxes.

Municipal bonds offer a much lower yield than AAA-rated corporate bonds, but the tax advantage they offer often makes the effective yield on municipal bonds higher for individuals with higher-bracket incomes.

For short-term profits, purchase high-quality, long-term bonds at a discount. When the interest rates slide, prices will rise, allowing you to take capital gains at a later date. If you follow this strategy, you can gain 15 to 18 percent combined interest and capital gains.

In weak markets, concentrate on convertible bonds in utilities, food processors, dairy products, and finances. In strong markets, concentrate on convertible bonds in machinery, steel, aerospace, and construction.

Buying less than five to ten bonds might cost you a stiff commission rate that cuts into your yields. You might be better off buying bonds through closed or open-end funds in which you can buy a portfolio of them for as little as $1,000 initial investment.

U.S. TREASURY ISSUES

The safest investments around are U.S. Treasury issues: bills, notes and bonds. They are the safest because they're backed by the "full faith and credit" of the U.S. government.

U.S. Savings bonds are perfect for building nest eggs, but Federal Agency and U.S. Treasury issues offer safety, shorter maturities, and higher current income. It's hard to go wrong when you invest spare cash in 13-week Treasury bills. Should interest rates remain high, simply roll over the bills and enjoy continued high rates. Should interest rates drop, purchase higher-yielding long-term bonds and/or other fixed income securities.

COLLECTIONS AND COLLECTIBLES

You can make money buying and selling collectibles. For instance, antiques don't have to be confined to the rare and expensive—or even to objects that are over 100 years old. Investors today make money investing modest sums in weather vanes, "action" banks, glass of all kinds, wind-up Victrolas, Currier and Ives prints, violin bows, cameo brooches, barometers, globes, religious objects, clocks, and spoons.

Literary collectibles—books, atlases, letters, maps, autographs—have appreciated 10 to 50 percent annually over the past 5 years. You can generally buy these items for prices ranging from $10 to $100, making literary collectibles less expensive than art works or antiques. However, most dealers will give you only half the price they think *they'll* be able to get. You might get a better price by contacting an auction house.

By selling collectibles, you can convince the Internal Revenue Service that you're an investor rather than just a collector. As an investor, you can claim certain tax advantages, including travel and selling expenses. You also can write off expenses associated with holding the assets against other income you incur during the year.

The vast majority of "limited edition" collectibles, such as commemorative medallions, never increase in value. Even more demoralizing, when you attempt to resell them, 80 percent are worth less than on the day you purchased them. They're a poor investment to put it mildly.

Consider buying and selling coins instead of collectibles. Some coins are better than cash. Rare coins have appreciated over the last 10 years at an annual rate of 13 percent.

GOLD AND SILVER

In days of skyrocketing inflation, gold and silver investments can more than preserve your purchasing power. Precious metal prices zoom upward when paper money values take a nose dive. It pays to have at least 15 to 25 percent of your investments in gold and silver to protect yourself against losses in stocks and bonds, as well as losses in the dollar's purchasing power.

The best time to purchase gold is when it's at a low point of a cycle. On the average, gold prices are lowest during warm weather months, in the middle of the month, and on Mondays.

Buying silver as an investment? Consider its long-term potential, despite possible extreme swings in market value. (During a recession, industrial demand for silver drops, as does the price. You can buy more for less.)

ANNUITIES

Annuities have some tax advantages because taxes are deferred on interest built up until you actually get the increase in annuity payments. And the payout that represents return of capital is usually tax exempt.

OIL AND GAS

Despite alluring advertisements to the contrary, it's hard to profit from a typical oil and gas tax shelter. With rare exceptions, gas and oil shelters have failed for as long as 15 years to return a dollar for each dollar invested.

Chapter 4

BORROWING MONEY

IF YOU NEED TO BORROW, BE SURE TO PROTECT YOURSELF AND YOUR COLLATERAL.

Collateral Know-How

Thinking about taking out a second mortgage to finance a vacation, an automobile, or to consolidate bills? Although your home could be used as security for such a loan, it's probably best to take out a personal installment loan instead. Second mortgages have their place, but not for the more casual kind of expenditure.

Offer the best security you can when taking out a loan. When you secure a loan with top-notch collateral, you usually get it at a cheaper rate than on your signature only.

Always make sure that all collateralized loan balances are less than the collateral's value. For instance, auto loans that entail a lien on the car should be reduced more rapidly than the decline in the car's resale value.

It's foolhardy to use emergency funds as collateral for a loan. If you default in payment and the funds are seized, you'll have painted yourself into a corner should any catastrophe occur.

Keep away from any loan that permits repossession of the property purchased without providing cancellation of the full amount of the indebtedness at the time of repossession.

Paying Back a Loan

Having trouble making monthly loan repayments? Consider slicing the remaining payments in half by extending them over a longer time period.

To save on interest charges when borrowing money, make the largest down payment possible and repay the balance in the shortest time span feasible. (It's always expensive to make a small down payment and to extend the life of a loan excessively.)

Taking out a loan to finance a vacation? For the sake of personal psychology as well as your budget, make certain you can pay it up within one year. If you can't, you may grudgingly be paying off this year's vacation when next year's vacation time rolls around.

Let the Borrower Beware

It doesn't pay to borrow money from small loan companies, because their interest rates are two to three times higher than those of banks or established savings and loan associations.

Avoid commercial debt poolers. They'll charge you as much as 35 percent of your debts for lumping them together and collecting one regular periodic payment from you.

Chapter 5

BUYING INSURANCE

NEITHER TOO LITTLE NOR TOO MUCH IS YOUR BEST BET WHEN BUYING INSURANCE.

Life and Health Insurance

Rule of thumb for how much life insurance you need: the equivalent of 4 to 5 years' pay.

Avoid having too many different life insurance policies. Consolidate your program into a few policies rather than buying half a dozen different policies. Your premium will be considerably lower.

If you're carrying more whole life insurance than you need, you can switch to a universal life policy for a better return on your money.

Getting the Right Policy

Shop around when buying a health insurance policy. Compare the loss ratios of different companies. A loss ratio is the percentage of premiums that a company pays back to its policyholders in benefits. A high loss ratio means a good value for you. A company which returns 60 percent of its premiums to policyholders is a better value than one returning only 30 percent. The difference can mean several hundred dollars more in benefits for you.

Unless you're totally satisfied with the transaction, you're under absolutely no obligation to purchase an insurance policy. Keep in mind that the inflated price sometimes quoted by one insurer over another is purportedly due to so-called "service." Never accept this as a valid reason for an extreme cost difference between two policies that are otherwise roughly identical. Make certain the price you pay is truly competitive.

It's best to have an insurance agent who's roughly your own age. If his or her insurance needs are probably quite similar to your own, the agent can draw a fine bead on your requirements.

You may be able to save a noteworthy amount of money by paying insurance premiums annually, rather than quarterly or twice a year.

Auto Insurance

Maintain only the auto insurance coverage you need. Get rid of collision and comprehensive coverage on older cars if you can afford to pick up any possible losses yourself.

Buy substantial deductibles on auto insurance, if you want to save money on your comprehensive and collision coverage. Doing so enables you to reduce your premium anywhere from 45 to 56 percent.

Are you 65 years of age or older? Take advantage of the fact that in the majority of states auto insurance rates are substantially lower for people in this age bracket.

Chapter **6**

PAYING LESS TAX

BEFORE YOU PAY THE PIPER, FIND OUT HOW TAX BREAKS AND DEDUCTIONS CAN WORK FOR YOU.

Tax Shelters

Start an IRA (Individual Retirement Account) up to April 15, or, if you have self-employment earnings, start a Keogh retirement plan before December 31. You can make your actual income tax contribution to the plan as late as your income tax filing deadline and still take a deduction on form 1040 for the preceding 12 months.

Saving money to send a child to college? If so, then you can reduce your income tax liability by transferring stocks, bonds, or cash into a custodian account for the child. That way all the dividends and interest are part of the child's income, not yours. A child will owe no federal income tax unless the annual investment income exceeds $1,000 (or $1,200 when at least $200 is from dividends or interest, if the new exclusion for dividends and interest is claimed).

You can reduce your income tax by establishing a short-term trust for a beneficiary who is in a lower tax bracket. The procedure involves putting income-producing assets—stocks, bonds, real estate, or savings accounts—into a trust for 10 years and a day. When the trust ends, you regain your property. But during the life of the trust, any taxes on the income are the responsibility of the beneficiary, whose lower tax bracket makes the whole concept a tax-saving strategy.

Tax shelters usually postpone taxes, rather than escape them. This is a factor that should be weighed by a young investor whose tax bracket when the shelter starts generating income will likely be loftier than it was for the early years when the shelter produced losses. But that same shelter may be just the thing for an older investor who doesn't have to report the shelter income until after he retires (and is in a lower tax bracket).

Know Your Deductions

Pay the accumulated interest on outstanding life insurance loans by December 31 and take the income tax interest write-off for that year.

Buy a new car or some other big ticket item by December 31 and take that year's income tax deduction for the sales tax you pay.

Charge late year outlays for medical expenses, charitable donations, and other deductible items on your credit card and you're entitled to deduct those expenses on that year's income tax return. It's immaterial that you don't actually pay the bill for these expenses until the following year.

Install energy saving devices in your home before year end and you qualify for a credit that you can subtract directly from your tax bill.

For the sake of your income tax reporting, selectively choose any charity to which you donate used personal property. Most charities have varying degrees of tax knowledge about how to evaluate a gift. If you feel that a charity has undervalued yours, speak to the charity's appraiser and get everything straightened out.

Check Your Records

If you get a big tax refund from the government every year, it's probably wiser to claim a bigger personal exemption. This way the extra money can be working for you all year long.

Organize your receipts and cancelled checks for tax-deductible items by subject in labeled, legal-size envelopes.

If you switch jobs during the year, check to see if you paid too much Social Security tax. If so, claim a refund when you file your income tax return.

The IRS requires you to report the gross income credited from all savings accounts. Should you withdraw your savings prematurely and be required to forfeit some of the interest, you can deduct the penalty for early withdrawal when computing your adjusted gross income. Make sure your bank notifies you as to what these amounts are.

Chapter **7**

RETIREMENT PLANNING

YOU'LL ENJOY YOUR RETIREMENT MORE IF IT'S BEEN WELL PLANNED.

A Secure Retirement

Check your Social Security account every 2 years to make sure you're being credited for the proper amount of contributions. Contact the Social Security office nearest you to obtain a statement of your "account."

Plan to have other income besides Social Security after you retire. The higher your salary, the less of your earnings Social Security usually replaces—even less if you retire at 62, and less again if your spouse is younger.

Even if you plan to work past retirement age, apply for Social Security 3 months before the month in which you'll be 65. That way you should be admitted to Medicare Part A and Part B without losing any months of coverage.

If you take early retirement (before age 65), your Social Security benefits are fixed at a lower rate for the rest of your life, unless you stop collecting the early benefits. You'll get cost-of-living raises, but the raises will be calculated on a lower base. (If you stop collecting early benefits or return to work, you can start collecting against a higher rate when you're 65.)

If you work part time after retiring, you might want to limit your earnings so you can collect your full Social Security benefits. Contact your local

Social Security office to find out if you'd be better off earning less money.

Be wary of "work-at-home" schemes that focus on retired people as their market. Only a tiny fraction of the population has ever made money addressing envelopes at home, or selling "much needed items" to their neighbors. These schemes are basically scams.

Home Sweet Home

Generally, it pays to buy, rather than rent, a retirement home. Buying gives you equity and a significant tax advantage over renting.

If you're going to buy a retirement home, don't get a house that's too big for you. One-and-a-half baths and two bedrooms are usually more than adequate.

You can save a considerable amount of money—if you purchase new living quarters when you retire—by being close to public transportation. Doing so can eliminate automobile operating and insurance expenses.

Think twice before renting an apartment in which to retire. Because you don't own your apartment, you have few legal rights regarding your tenancy. You can lose your apartment or be priced out of it at the end of the lease, and possibly—if the building is sold—even before the lease expires.

Your Insurance Needs

Don't rely on Medicare to cover all your hospital costs. As comprehensive as it is, Medicare pays for only 40 percent of the average beneficiary's bills. It's up to you to plug the gaps with a supplemental health insurance policy.

Retired people who don't qualify for Medicare, or who can't afford to pay the Medicare gaps, generally can receive medical assistance through Medicaid. Medicaid is comprised of medical aid programs, financed jointly by federal and state governments.

Be gun-shy of mail order insurance companies that zero-in on retired people as their market. Retired persons are deluged with mail claiming that certain policies are being offered at reduced premiums with "no age limits" and "no medical examinations required." Drop all such mail in the nearest wastebasket. Most of these policies are effective only if you've been in the hospital for 60 to 100 days. Most people are not hospitalized that long.

Set the Record Straight

Consult with an attorney before you retire to see if there are any steps you should take to maximize your self-protection, both legally and financially. And don't stop there. Reconsult him periodically. If you should move to another state, look up another competent lawyer at once.

It's a "must" before you retire to put all your records in order. Be sure to know where your insurance policies, property and investment records, various bank accounts, birth and marriage certificates, and other important papers are. Make a copy of each and keep the copies in a convenient place in a three-ring binder. Keep the originals in a safe deposit box.

You should always draw up, or revise, a will when you retire—but have an attorney do it. Don't try to do anything like this on your own. Words and phrases composed by an amateur are subject to controversial misinterpretations and can result in costly litigation for those you're trying to protect.

Know Your Tax Rights

Many states and counties permit exemptions for older citizens. Since these vary from state to state, contact your local tax offices to determine what exemptions are available to you.

Part IV

KITCHEN HINTS

"Kitchen Hints" is one of the heftiest parts of this book—and with good reason. Since a well-run kitchen is the hub of home activity, you'll welcome the range and depth of hints included here. These are the kind of tips that make a modern household function at peak performance for the whole family. Whether you've got a question on space-saving, energy efficiency or gourmet cooking, you'll find the answer here.

With kitchen space in many apartments and homes becoming tighter and tighter, the planning and organization tips in Chapter 1 are especially handy. Even the most cramped kitchen can be streamlined for best use if you know how to deal creatively with the space you've got. Delve into the dozens of ideas for maximum efficiency of every square inch of the work and storage areas in your kitchen.

Chapter 2, "General Food Storage," takes you one step further. Knowing how to store the many kinds of food you use saves you money and time by virtually eliminating waste from your kitchen. More savings will be yours when you learn to make surprisingly simple adjustments on your stove, refrigerator, and freezer in order to trim your energy bills. Chapter 3 on energy efficiency will show you how.

The next chapters cover every imaginable aspect of cooking and kitchen work—all with the goal of making the kitchen a fun place to be. See Chapter 4, "General Kitchen Hints," for all the ways to smooth out the sticky, squeaky, inconvenient problems that are so common in the kitchen. Chapter 5, with its general cooking hints, brings you the latest word on making all your cooking jobs a little easier. Chapter 6, "Food Hints", is a compendium on purchasing, storing, and cooking every kind of food from soup to nuts. Chapter 7, "Gourmet Cooking," offers you a chance to put a new emphasis on cooking as a pleasurable art. The more than 100 hints included here make complicated kitchen artistry as simple as everyday cooking. Chapter 8 brings you wonderful, economical tips for home canning and preserving.

The last chapters in this section make short work of two of the thorniest kitchen problems. When you borrow some of the magical hints on what to do with leftovers from Chapter 9, your family will be calling for encores. And with the hints from Chapter 10, "Cleaning Up," you'll polish off the worst kitchen chores with ease.

With these hundreds of ingenious and helpful hints, you're equipped with a veritable survival course for the kitchen.

Chapter **1**

PLANNING AND ORGANIZATION

THE BUSIEST ROOM IN YOUR HOUSE CAN ALSO BE THE BEST-ORGANIZED WITH THESE SURE-FIRE HINTS.

Space Savers in the Kitchen

If your kitchen is too tiny to keep a table and chairs out in the open, install a pull-out extension table or workspace that slides back into a "drawer." Or, make a flip-up counter and eating area that folds back down when not in use.

If you don't have cabinet space for your pots and pans, put a small wooden ladder—painted to match your kitchen—in a corner, and place them on the steps.

If you keep your brooms, mops, and buckets hanging on hooks inside the broom closet, they won't fall every time you open the door.

To make the most of available space when storing tapered glassware, position every other glass upside down.

If your dishpan leaks, you needn't throw it away. Put it to work as an under-sink storage bin for waxes, brushes, and soaps. You can slide it in and out like a drawer.

To gain more elbow room in the kitchen, hang pots, pans, and other items from the ceiling. Use hooks meant to hang swag lamps and screw them directly into the joists.

Counter Cues

If you lack drawer space for kitchen linens and towels, just put them in pretty baskets on the counter.

To economize on drawer space, arrange wooden spoons and other utensils bouquet-style in a handsome pitcher, canister, or wooden bucket at your range or mixing center.

A wall-hung canvas "apron" can hold all sorts of kitchen gadgets and utensils, and it's decorative.

You can cut counter clutter with stackable plastic canisters or a four-in-one turntable canister.

Organize your kitchen so that the items you use every day are within easy reach.

Pots and Pans

If your kitchen and dining room area are combined and you dislike looking at the pots and pans while you eat, install a venetian blind from the ceiling to separate the two areas.

Since pots and pans and casseroles are heavy, store them at lower levels.

If you store cast iron pots and pans with their lids inverted or slightly ajar, there will be enough air circulation to discourage rust formation.

Dishes

If you store your dishes in open dish racks—instead of in cabinets— position the rack over the sink. That way you can wash the dishes, put them in place, and they'll drip dry into the sink.

Hanging mugs on cup hooks underneath your cabinets saves precious shelf space.

A napkin, paper towel, or cloth protector placed between pieces of fine china when stacking will help prevent scratching.

To prevent cracking, wait to stack dinnerware for storage until it's cool.

Mending Dishware

Milk can mend a crack in a china cup. Just immerse the cup in a pan of milk, simmer for three-quarters of an hour, and then wash and dry it. The protein in the milk is what works the miracle.

Modeling clay can be shaped to support pieces of broken cups, glasses, or other objects while they are being glued.

To mend a broken plate, fill a pan with sand. Embed the largest broken portion of the plate in the sand, with the broken edge straight up. The glued pieces will be held in place by gravity. If necessary, use clothes-pins to clamp the pieces together.

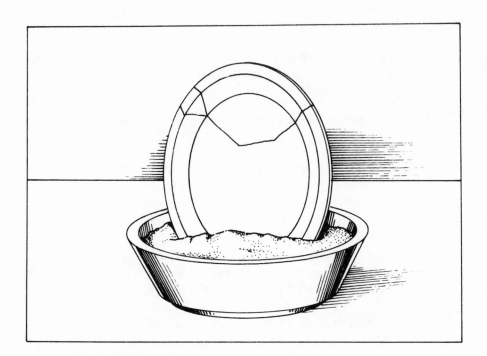

Freezer and Pantry

Most plastic food containers can be recycled for storing or freezing food.

Mesh bags, wire baskets, and even old nylon stockings make good storage containers for potatoes and onions because they allow the necessary air circulation.

When buying food storage containers, it's best to choose ones that do several jobs. Freezer-to-oven casserole dishes are more economical than freezer containers that store casseroles adequately but can't be used in the oven.

Toss a few extra plastic clothes pins into your kitchen drawer. Use them to seal packages of partially used foods such as pretzels, chips, noodles, rice.

Save screw-top glass containers from coffee and peanut butter for storing dry goods in the pantry.

Use the plastic lids that come with some tins as separators when you freeze hamburger patties.

Floor tiles make perfect linings for pantry shelves. They last longer than self-adhesive paper and are easier to fit in place.

Knives

If you hang your sharp knives inside or on the side of a cabinet, you'll save drawer space and they'll be out of the children's reach.

Make a knife holder out of your empty thread spools. Insert screws in the spool holes and attach them to a cabinet door. Place the spools in a row, one butted right next to the other. Gaps between the spools are for the knife blades while their handles rest on the spools.

If you store your sharp knives in drawers, they should be kept in a holder to prevent the blades from getting dull.

Notes and Messages

If you've nowhere to hang a memo board for your notes, paint part of your kitchen door with three coats of blackboard paint.

A phone center with a writing surface can be installed between two wall studs in your kitchen. Cut the wall between the two studs and build the center to fit the space.

Chef's Secrets

Keep an aloe growing in your kitchen. The gel squeezed from a leaf can soothe and heal burns, bites, prickly heat, or sunburn.

You don't need mixing bowls to mix foods. To save time and dish washing, pour all your ingredients into a sturdy plastic bag, close it, and shake to mix the food.

Washing your ice cube trays occasionally in hot soapy water will keep the cubes from sticking and they'll pop out that much easier.

Protect your wall behind your stove from grease splatters. Install a washable vinyl shade. Position it upside down so the roller is hidden by the stove. When cooking, pull the shade up and fasten it to a hook several feet above the stove. When finished, roll the shade down out of sight.

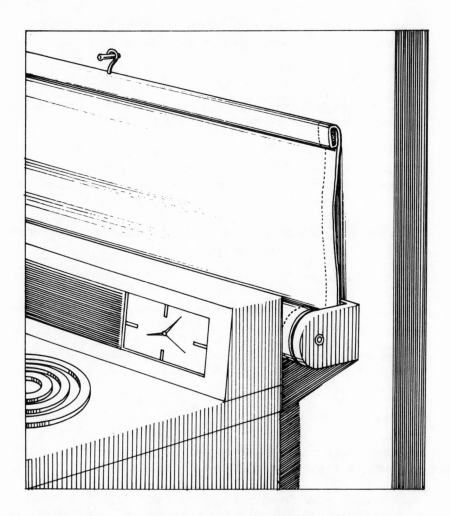

A rubber-coated plate rack makes a great cookbook holder.

Create your own kitchen sink splashback by cutting a piece of clear plexiglass to size. Drill two small holes in it and nail up on wall.

Alphabetize your spice rack so you'll never be at wit's end trying to find just the right one.

Kitchen Cabinet Storage

If you want to cover open shelves without going through the expense of installing cabinets, use colorful shades that pull up and down.

Reorganize cabinets located over the wall oven or refrigerator for storage of bulky items not in everyday use, such as platters, deep bowls, and baskets.

Lazy Susans make it easier to reach items in corner cabinets. In wall cabinets, they make spices and condiments easier to find; in base cabinets, they make quick work of retrieving pots and pans.

If you can't reach to see what's hiding in a high cupboard shelf, hold a hand mirror at arm's length to see what you've stored out of sight.

Using Doors for Storage

Attach small baskets to the inside of kitchen closet doors to hold envelope mixes and small cans.

Hanging a store-bought heavy duty rack on the inside of a pantry door gives plenty of extra can space.

Wall Storage

Place an etagère on an unused wall for lots of handsome storage space.

Install a pegboard near your food preparation area for hanging gadgets, strainers, portable cutting boards.

At Your Fingertips

To add more space to your kitchen, install wire slide-on shelves in your cabinet.

Wooden crates stacked next to a counter can add instant new shelving space for pantry items, dishes, or pots and pans.

Plastic or wire baskets on casters are excellent for pull-to-you storage. Use them for unrefrigerated vegetables or extra storage space for cooking utensils.

To conveniently hold small packages of sauce mixes, seasonings, and packaged cold drink mixes, staple plastic berry baskets to the pantry wall, or to the inside of a cabinet door.

A pair of tweezers can help you get olives and pickles out of narrow jars, and are also useful in placing garnishes on food without hand contact.

Recipe Finders

If you find a recipe that's an improvement over one featured in your cookbook, tape a copy of it right over the book's recipe. The next time you need it, you'll be able to locate it easily by referring to the book's own index.

To keep recipes clipped from newspapers and magazines so they'll be readily available, fold them into an evelope that's fastened to an inside cover of a cookbook.

Chapter 2

GENERAL FOOD STORAGE

A PLACE FOR EVERYTHING AND EVERYTHING IN ITS PLACE—CARRY IT ONE STEP FURTHER WITH THESE CLEVER STORAGE TIPS.

Apples

Store apples in clear plastic rather than a paper bag. You'll be able to spot any that are spoiling and remove them before your whole bag is ruined.

Don't buy more apples than you can use up in 3 weeks. After that length of time, apples begin to spoil quickly.

Apples that haven't ripened on the tree won't ripen at home properly because they've been picked prematurely.

A sure sign of ripeness for apples is a light green color at the bottom of the fruit.

Refrigerate apples to slow down the ripening process. If you don't have room in the refrigerator, keep your apples stored in a cool place, with a wet towel placed over the top of the container to keep the apples moist, but not wet. Keep the container covered to protect the apples from freezing, at which point they spoil.

Bread

Put a celery stalk into the bag with a loaf of bread; its moisture will help keep the bread fresh longer.

Grains and Cereal

If you sift flour directly into your canister when filling it, you won't have to sift it again when you use it for baking. Simply measure what you need.

Flour keeps very well frozen, so go ahead and stock up when it's on sale.

Whole-grain cereals stay fresh longer if they're refrigerated, whether the container is open or unopened.

Hot Foods

To avoid contaminating foods with bacteria, don't cool hot foods before refrigerating them.

To keep your cooking oil fresh, store it tightly sealed in a dark glass or plastic container in a cool place.

Pasta

To preserve the freshness of the unused portion of an opened pasta box, store the remaining pasta in a glass container with a tight cover.

Vegetables

Store root vegetables such as potatoes and carrots in a cool, moist place, so they won't lose their vitamin content.

Let unripe tomatoes ripen at room temperature, but away from direct sunlight. Store them at cool temperatures or in the refrigerator to retain vitamin C.

Seal leafy vegetables in plastic bags before storing them in the vegetable crisper. They'll retain their moisture and stay cold longer.

Coffee

You'll keep ground coffee or coffee beans fresh indefinitely if you freeze or refrigerate the coffee.

Frozen Foods

When buying frozen foods at the supermarket, be careful to choose packages stacked below a freezer cabinet's freeze line, and stay away from those with ice on the package. Ice means the package probably has thawed and been refrozen.

Keep frozen foods stored at 0° F or lower, but not longer than 1 year. Vegetables such as beans, cauliflower, and spinach lose their vitamin content after that time.

Honey

Should honey become granulated, you can restore its smooth texture by dropping the grains in a jar and placing the jar in boiling water. This works for syrup or jelly as well.

To store honey for long periods, freeze it in ice cube trays.

Sugar

To keep brown sugar from drying out, store it in a jar, and throw in a piece of apple or a lettuce leaf.

If brown sugar gets hard, grate it or run it through the blender to make it powdery.

Peanut Butter

When you buy peanut butter that isn't homogenized, storing it upside down will prevent its oil from rising to the top. Stir before using.

Crackers and Marshmallows

If humid weather is making your crackers soggy, store them in the freezer.

Store marshmallows in the freezer. They're easier to cut for cooking and they won't stick to your scissors.

Getting the Last Drop

When a jar of jam, mustard, or mayonnaise is almost empty, place the container on its side when storing it. This makes it easier to scrape out the last bit.

Freezing Foods

When you wrap food in aluminum foil and freeze it, it's a good idea to label each package to avoid future guess work. Just indicate the contents of each package on a plastic bandage you apply to the foil.

When you freeze food in a plastic bag, it's best to remove as much air from the bag as you can. One way to do this is to use a soda straw. Push as much air out of the bag as you can, and then hold the bag shut around the straw. Suck out the last bit of air, extract the straw, and seal the bag.

Because freezing expands liquids and foods, be sure to leave about a half-inch space at the top of each package before putting it in your freezer. Otherwise, the lid might pop off, or the container might crack or burst.

You can freeze extra quantities of homemade soup by storing it in clean half-gallon milk cartons and stapling the tops closed.

Freeze pastry shells unfilled. They won't become soggy when thawed.

Freeze fresh dill in season, so you'll have it on hand for pickling time.

Thaw frozen foods by placing the container under cold running water for a few minutes. Then place it in a pan of lukewarm water until the food slips easily from the container.

Freezing Don'ts

Don't freeze overripe foods. They'll have no flavor or color after you defrost them.

Before freezing, don't let vegetables or fruits sit in water for any length of time. Rinse them quickly with water, and drain well.

To prevent home-frozen vegetables from changing in flavor or color, blanch them with boiling water or steam before packaging and freezing.

Refresh Your Memory

If you indicate the purchase date on your groceries before putting them away, you'll know which foods to cook or eat first.

To keep a running inventory of your freezer's contents, have a write-on/ wipe-off memo pad handy.

Chapter **3**

ENERGY EFFICIENCY

USE LESS ENERGY TO COOK AND STORE YOUR FAMILY'S FOOD. YOUR BILL WILL SHOW THE DIFFERENCE!

Stovetop Cooking

To save on heat costs, don't activate an element or burner until the pot or pan is on the stove. If you're going to simmer, turn down the heat as soon as the liquid reaches the boiling stage. Adjust the setting to just keep the contents boiling, since a higher setting wastes energy. (In most cases, copper and stainless steel cookware require lower heat settings than aluminum cookware.)

Proper use of pots and pans can help your range save on energy. Fit the pot or pan to the burner, since a small pot or pan on a large element wastes heat, and a large pot on a small element is inefficient.

To conserve stovetop energy even more, use small cooking appliances, such as electric frying pans, instead of your range whenever practical. These small units consume less energy and throw less heat into your kitchen.

You'll use less energy when cooking if you cook with as little water as possible since small amounts heat more quickly.

Put a lid on the pan you're using because water boils faster when covered, saving up to 20 percent of the energy that otherwise would be consumed.

To conserve energy with an electric range's stovetop units, turn off burners slightly prematurely. With electric burners, the cooking process often continues for as long as 5 minutes after turn off.

It's important to keep pan bottoms clean because a layer of soot decreases heating efficiency on any type of stove. Shiny pans are particularly efficient in electric cooking.

Oven Baking

To save energy when using your oven, don't preheat it unless required. If you must preheat, put the food in the oven as soon as it reaches the desired temperature. Even then, cook as many things as possible at one time. Also, if you have a double oven, use the smaller one whenever feasible.

Since a great deal of heat escapes each time you open the oven to examine what's cooking, you can conserve energy by minimizing the number of times you "peek" at the food inside. *Note:* During the summer, that extra heat also puts a strain on your air conditioner.

Try cooking food items in the oven-usable paperboard containers in which they're packaged. You'll save from 10 to 20 percent of the oven energy normally required. The containers withstand temperatures up to 400° F. Don't, however, try to reuse them.

A self-cleaning oven will use less energy if you start the cleaning cycle right after cooking since the oven already will be on its way to the high temperature needed for cleaning.

Refrigerator and Freezer

To conserve refrigerator and/or freezer energy by minimizing loss of cold air, plan ahead and insert or remove as many items as possible at each opening. This makes it much easier on the unit, especially in summer.

Make sure your refrigerator is level since if it isn't, it may be working harder than necessary.

If you notice water standing in the bottom of your refrigerator, there may be an air leak around the door. To test the gasket, close the door on a dollar bill. If it pulls out easily, the gasket needs replacing.

A good way to keep your freezer from expending too much energy is to put it at the lowest setting that keeps ice cream firm. If your ice cream is rock hard, the setting is unnecessarily high.

If you have a frostfree freezer, it's best to keep all liquids tightly covered. Uncovered liquids evaporate, form frost, and cause a frostfree system to work harder.

Chapter 4

GENERAL KITCHEN HINTS

QUICK WAYS TO SMOOTH OUT ALL THE STICKY, SQUEAKY, INCONVENIENT PROBLEMS THAT ARE SO COMMON IN THE KITCHEN.

Cooking and Eating

If you need extra counter space when cooking for a crowd or doing holiday baking, create it by placing trays or cookie sheets across pulled out drawers.

Chewing several parsley leaves after you've eaten a garlicky meal will take away the garlic odor.

You'll ingest more iron if you cook in cast-iron pots because foods absorb iron from the pots. For example, stew simmered for several hours in an iron pot contains at least 25 times as much iron as stew simmered in an aluminum pot.

If you put marbles or a jar lid in the bottom of a double boiler, their rattling will alert you if the water boils away.

Ice Cubes

Want to make ice cubes quickly? Use cooled boiled water rather than tap water. It contains less oxygen.

Another way to make a fresh tray of ice cubes more quickly is to leave three or four cubes in the tray when you refill it. The already frozen cubes help cool the fresh water.

To prevent ice cube trays from sticking to the freezer shelf, line it with waxed paper.

The Gas Stove

To be sure that cake tins are completely dry before you store them, place them in a warm oven for a few minutes.

The warmth of a gas range pilot light makes an oven a perfect food dehydrator. Chop the food you want to dry, spread it on aluminum foil, and place it on the broiler rack for a day or two.

To avoid burning your fingers when lighting a pilot light with a regular-size match, clamp the match with kitchen tongs that will extend your reach.

Sticky Matters

If one drinking glass is tightly nested inside another, don't try to force them apart. You may crack both. Rather, fill the top glass with cold water and immerse the lower one in hot water. The top glass will contract slightly, and the bottom one expand, so they'll come apart easily.

If you keep plastic wrap in your refrigerator, it won't cling to itself when handled.

If the rubber gloves you're wearing won't come off because you've forgotten to sprinkle powder on your hands, hold your gloved hands under cold tap water. The gloves will slip right off.

Soundproofing Appliances

An electric beater won't seem so loud if you put a damp dishcloth under the bowl to muffle the sound.

A squeaky oven door can be silenced by rubbing the point of a soft lead pencil across the hinges.

Serving and Pouring

If salt pours out of your salt shaker too liberally, plug up some of its holes with clear nail polish.

Put a few grains of rice in your salt shaker; they'll prevent caking.

If you put a dab of butter under a pitcher's spout, the contents won't run down the side after you pour.

To start a fresh bottle of ketchup flowing, push a soda straw to the bottle's bottom. When you remove it, the ketchup will pour easily.

A gravy boat makes a good server for spaghetti sauce.

When you buy an electric coffee maker, look for one with water markings on the *inside*. They're easier to read than markings on the outside.

New drinking glasses sometimes crack when you pour hot liquids into them. They won't if you "season" them this way: Put them in a large pot filled with cold water, bring the water slowly to a boil, and then turn off the heat and let the water cool.

Play It Safe

When driving home from the store, try using seat belts to secure any bags containing items that could be spilled or broken.

Potholders protect against cold as well as heat, so you can protect your hands when rearranging frozen foods in the freezer by wearing your kitchen mitts.

More with Less

You can improvise a sink or tub stopper from a coffee can's plastic cover. Lay it across the drain and suction will hold it firmly in place.

Is the key or tab on a can missing or damaged? Just turn the can over and use an ordinary can opener.

You can do more with toothpaste than brush your teeth or remove spots. It also works as an adhesive, perhaps for hanging lightweight pictures and posters on your kitchen walls. When you eventually remove the pictures or posters, just wipe away the toothpaste with a damp cloth. There'll be no nail holes to repair.

Garbage Disposal

When your garbage disposal jams, insert a broomstick (or bathroom plunger) handle in the opening. Move the handle in the direction opposite that in which the unit normally turns. Remove the stick and push the start button. If the disposal still doesn't work, repeat the process.

You can sharpen garbage disposal blades by running ice cubes through them.

Reading and Writing Labels

Selling your offerings at a bake sale? They'll move faster if you include the recipe. People like to know the ingredients—and how to duplicate your goodies.

Because instructions on bottle labels frequently are in tiny, almost unreadable print, it's a good idea to keep a magnifying glass handy.

Chapter 5

GENERAL COOKING HINTS

BAKING, BROILING, FRYING, MIXING—STREAMLINE EVEN THE MOST FAMILIAR JOBS WITH THESE TIPS.

Frying

If you're going to sauté or fry a food, it's best to dry it thoroughly before placing it in hot oil. Cold wet food may splatter dangerously.

A temperature test for sautéing in butter: It's time to add the vegetables just after the foam on the butter subsides.

To prevent grease splattering when cooking foods that can't be completely covered, turn a metal colander upside down over the skillet.

Is your frying pan splattering? If you don't have a colander to invert over the pan, take a serving fork, punch a lot of holes in an aluminum-foil pie plate, and place it upside down over the pan. The punctured pie plate confines grease but lets steam escape.

Sprinkling a little salt in the frying pan before you start cooking prevents hot fat from splattering.

To be able to use vegetable oil several times, heat it slowly to frying temperature so that it doesn't decompose. Use a thermometer to avoid overheating.

Don't use the same vegetable oil for frying more than a few times. Old oil soaks into fried foods.

Before you save the hot oil in a deep fryer, test it by dropping a piece of white bread into the pan. If dark spots appear on the bread, the oil isn't worth saving.

For an extra-light, delicate crust on fried foods, mix your batter with club soda, and three-quarters of a teaspoon of baking soda.

Broiling

Broiling with gas is different from broiling with electricity. When you broil with gas, you should keep the oven door closed because gas flames absorb moisture and consume smoke. When you broil with electricity, it's best to keep the door slightly open so the oven can expel moisture.

Think twice before lining a broiling pan with foil. Foil causes frying rather than broiling, because it prevents fat from draining away.

Microwave Cooking

Cut meats and vegetables in uniform sizes to make sure they cook evenly.

Reduce cooking liquid by one-fourth, since there's less evaporation of liquid in a microwave oven.

The skins of foods such as potatoes or apples should be pierced with a fork before cooking.

244

Use only ovenproof glass or ceramic cooking pans. Never use metal cooking utensils in a microwave.

Baked goods rise higher in a microwave oven. To avoid spillage, fill cake and bread tins only half full with batter.

To ensure that your food cooks fully and evenly, stir food pieces and turn dishes periodically while they're cooking.

Boiling

Tired of boilovers that take a lot of time to clean up? You can prevent them by inserting a toothpick horizontally between a pot and its lid so excessive steam can escape harmlessly.

You can prevent steam from scalding your wrists and hands when you drain boiling water from a pot of vegetables if you first turn on the cold tap water.

A gentle boil cooks food just as well as a rolling boil, so save on cooking costs by choosing the heat setting that barely keeps the water boiling.

Sugar and Salt

It's much less expensive to buy unsweetened cereals and add your own sugar than it is to buy presweetened varieties.

Different foods require varied uses of salt during cooking. For instance, it's best to cook vegetables in salted water and to salt soups and stews quite early in the cooking process. But salt should be sprinkled on meat just before removing it from the oven or range top.

To prevent unnecessary spills, store your sugar in a plastic container with a handle and a snap-on lid.

In Case of Fire

If there's a fire in your oven, turn off the heat at once and keep the oven door shut. Lack of air will soon suffocate the flames.

Does dripping fat smoke and catch fire while you're broiling meat? Guard against this by placing slices of dry bread in the broiler pan. The bread soaks up the fat.

If your broiler bursts into flames because of ignited grease, squelch the fire by sprinkling salt or baking soda on it. Partially burned meat may still be edible after you've rinsed off the soda. (Don't try to use flour as a fire extinguisher—it's explosive.)

Easy Substitutions

When preparing a recipe that specifies marshmallows, remember that one large marshmallow is equal to ten small ones.

Out of honey for a recipe? Substitute molasses.

When a recipe calls for nuts and you don't have any, you can use coarse bran instead.

You can transform regular granulated sugar into superfine sugar in your blender.

Ordinary wine works as well as the more expensive "cooking wine" when marinating or preparing gourmet recipes. As a bonus, you'll be skipping the added salt of cooking wine.

Favorite Recipes

If you want to serve a recipe to a larger number of people than the serving number indicated, make up the original recipe several times instead of doubling or tripling the ingredients. Doubling isn't always as successful.

To prevent splattering on a cookbook or recipe card while you're mixing ingredients or cooking, cover the paper with a glass plate or pie pan.

To protect a recipe card from cooking splatters, spray it with hair spray. After the spray dries, you can wipe any smudges off the card with a damp cloth.

Do you find it easy to mislay a recipe card while you're cooking? Next time, keep your card handy by slipping it between the tines of a fork and standing the fork in a glass. That way, the card is more apt to stand out on your countertop.

Another way to keep a recipe card from getting lost amid the clutter of utensils and ingredients is this: Cut a slit in the top of a cork that you have glued to the lid of your recipe box. The cork can hold the card as you prepare the recipe.

Slipping and Sliding

Keep a bowl from slipping on a countertop while mixing ingredients by placing it on a folded, damp towel.

If oven racks refuse to slide easily, coat them with a film of petroleum jelly.

To get a good grasp on jar lids and bottle tops, open them by covering the lid with a piece of sandpaper.

Slick as a Whistle

You can give your skillet a nonstick finish by sprinkling the pan with salt and then warming it for 5 minutes. Remove, wipe out the salt, and use as usual.

If you coat a mold with a light film of salad oil before adding gelatin, it will easily release its contents after it's chilled.

When measuring syrup or other sticky liquids, first wet the cup, or oil the measuring cup with cooking oil and then rinse it in hot water so it will release all of the gooey fluids after they're measured. (Just pour into the center of the measuring cup, *not* down the sides.)

Double Duty

If you need a funnel for flour, salt, or sugar, make one in a jiffy by clipping a corner from an envelope.

Teflon-coated pans make quick-release gelatin salad molds.

You can use a baster to remove grease from the frying pan when you're cooking hamburger or other foods.

A potato peeler makes a perfect peach peeler or even cheese or chocolate grater.

If you mix the ingredients for instant gelatin or pudding in a large pitcher, it will be easy to pour the gelatin into individual molds without spilling.

Grating two or more foods for the same dish? If you grate the softest one first, the harder or firmer foods that follow will clean out the grater's openings.

Chapter **6**

FOOD HINTS

EVEN THE BEST CHEFS LOVE TO LEARN A NEW TRICK OR TWO—AND YOU'LL FIND PLENTY OF NEW ONES HERE.

MEAT, FISH, AND POULTRY

Buying and Storing

When purchasing meat, it will help your budget to consider the price per serving, not the price per pound.

It is more economical to buy slab bacon and slice it as you need it. Slab bacon with the rind on is much cheaper than sliced bacon, and it keeps better.

When you're making hamburger patties to freeze, make a nickel-size hole in the center of each patty. You won't have to thaw the hamburger before cooking, and the hole will close during cooking.

When wrapping chops, chicken parts, or hamburgers for your freezer, it's a good idea to sandwich sheets of waxed paper between the pieces of meat. That way the meat will separate easily and defrost faster.

It's best not to freeze cured, smoked, or canned ham, because freezing causes flavor and texture changes. Refrigerate this type of ham instead.

If you're going to freeze a canned ham, it's best to take it out of the can. Expansion during freezing might burst the can.

One way to freeze fish is to put the fillets in clean milk cartons filled with water. When the ice that surrounded the fish thaws in the defrosting process, use the liquid to water your houseplants—it's ideal fertilizer.

Marinating

A mixture of olive oil and vinegar will tenderize meat. Rub the mixture on the meat and let it stand several hours before cooking.

Another way to tenderize meat is to rub baking soda into it, let it stand for several hours, and then wash and cook it.

Meats can be marinated in a plastic bag by putting the chunks in the bag, adding the sauce you prefer, sealing the bag, and turning it a few times during the day.

Freezer to Pan

If you've forgotten to thaw meat but want to cook it anyway, cook it half again as long as you would if it were thawed.

When a recipe specifies thinly sliced meat, it will help to put the meat in the freezer for a short time before cutting it. Meat slices easier if it's slightly frozen.

Roasting

Meat will shrink less during roasting if it's cooked longer at a lower temperature.

Since a roast will thaw more quickly if all sides are exposed to air, elevate it on a cake cooling rack—or use the burner grill from your range. Put newspaper or a plate under the rack to catch the water and other drippings.

A shallow pan is better than a deep one for cooking a roast because it allows heat to circulate around the meat.

A roast slices more easily if you let it stand for about 15 minutes after taking it from the oven.

To eliminate most of the smoke and grease when broiling fatty meats, pour a cup of water into the bottom portion of the broiler pan before putting it in the oven.

For pan drippings that have superb flavor, support poultry or meat on a grid of celery sticks and carrots rather than a metal roasting rack. Roast as usual.

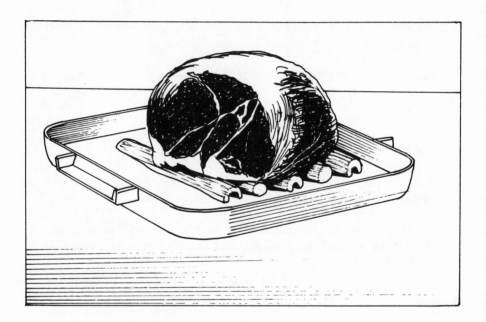

Hamburger and Ground Meats

If you need to defrost frozen ground beef quickly, try sprinkling it with the amount of salt recommended for cooking (salt is a great thawing agent), or heat it in your dishwasher turned to its drying cycle.

Want perfectly rounded, flat meat patties? Press down on a piece of meat with a can and trim off the excess. Choose different cans for varying size patties.

For particularly juicy burgers, put a tablespoon of cottage cheese in the center of each before frying or broiling.

To make relatively greasefree hamburgers with an electric frying pan, securely prop up one of the pan's legs and then fry on the pan's elevated side.

If you're barbecuing hamburgers for a large group of people, you can save on grill time by partially cooking the burgers inside. Line the bottom of a baking pan with foil and lay down a layer of patties; set a piece of foil over this layer, and add another tier of patties. Repeat this procedure till you have four tiers. Place this oversized layer cake in a 350° F oven for about 15 minutes; then finish grilling the patties outside. You can do the same thing with hot dogs, but cook them only a few minutes. Either way, you've solved the problem of too little grill space.

Meat Loaf

A meat loaf can be stretched with raw oatmeal, grated carrots, crushed corn flakes, or instant potato flakes.

If you want to keep your hands clean when mixing meat loaf, place the ingredients in a plastic bag and knead them through the bag. Still using the bag, shape the mixture into the form of a loaf, and gently ease it out of the bag and into a loaf pan.

Meat loaf won't stick to the bottom of the pan if you bake it on top of a few raw bacon slices.

You can cut the cooking time for a meat loaf by apportioning the mixture in muffin tins or cooking it in a flat, shallow pan.

Meatballs

So meatballs won't fall apart when you cook them, chill them first.

An ice cream scoop is useful in shaping perfectly round meatballs.

Beef

Do you like your steaks rare on the inside, but well-done on the outside? If so, grill them straight from the freezer without thawing.

When cooking red meats, it's time to turn the meat over to brown the other side when juices bubble to the surface of the meat.

Plan ahead to have steaks with that unmistakable "outdoor" taste even when you can't grill outside because the weather's nasty. Prepare a quantity of steaks by partially broiling them over charcoal and then remove and store them in your freezer. When it's raining, snowing, or cold outdoors, just finish broiling these steaks in your kitchen and they'll have that wonderful "right from the patio" taste.

Dropping a few tomatoes in the pan will help tenderize a pot roast. Acid from the tomatoes will break down the roast's stringy fibers.

An unopened tin can can be used to pound flour into meat for Swiss steak—but *wash* the can first.

For particularly tender liver, soak it in milk and refrigerate for 2 hours. Then, dry it, sprinkle on bread crumbs, and sauté.

Another tenderizer for liver is to soak it in tomato juice for 3 hours before frying or broiling.

If you partially freeze liver before slicing it, the skin will peel off easily.

Chicken and Other Poultry

If you want a fresh chicken to stay fresh longer, loosely wrap it with waxed paper (not plastic wrap) and refrigerate. Cook it within 3 days.

For pure white breast meat, defrost a chicken by letting it stand for a time in cold water that you've heavily salted. The salt draws out all traces of blood.

A chicken will baste itself if you cover the bird with strips of bacon during roasting.

If you chill a chicken for an hour after flouring it for frying, the coating will adhere better during cooking.

For guaranteed tenderness, marinate chicken breasts in buttermilk, cream, or ordinary milk for 3 hours in the refrigerator before baking.

Unpleasant poultry odors usually can be eliminated by washing the bird with lemon juice and rubbing it with salt.

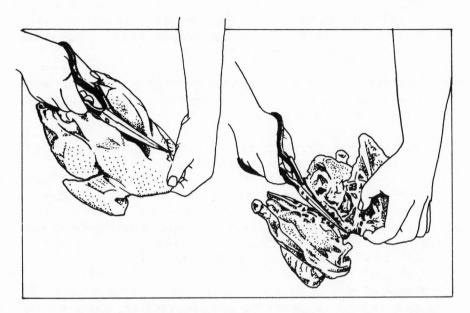

You needn't slam away at a chicken with a knife in order to debone it. Just use kitchen shears to make the job easier.

When frying, broiling, or grilling chicken, always use tongs to turn the pieces. If you use a fork, you're likely to pierce the skin, and natural juices will escape.

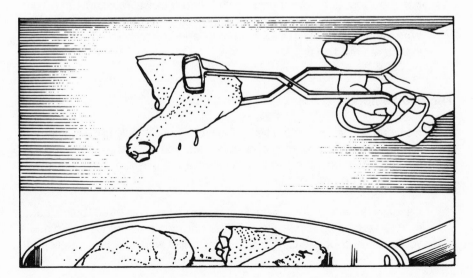

It's best to baste a chicken only during the final 30 minutes of cooking. Sauce won't penetrate during the early cooking stages and may cause the chicken to brown too quickly.

Don't risk having your hands and wrists splattered with hot fat when adding "steaming water" to a browning chicken. Use ice cubes and place the lid on the pan before they melt.

Chicken livers won't splatter during cooking if you first perforate them with a fork. Puncture several holes in each.

To hold in stuffing, truss a turkey with unwaxed dental floss—it's extra strong and doesn't burn. Or, instead of trussing, use two heels of dampened bread to block the cavity and keep dressing in place. Position these so the crusts face out and then overlap each other. One or two raw potatoes also could be used to seal the cavity.

If you don't care for roast poultry dressing, you still can make the bird flavorsome and juicy by pouring a cup of water mixed with one-quarter cup of pineapple juice into the body cavity.

If you want a turkey to be extra juicy, use a basting needle to inject the raw bird with a quarter-pound of melted margarine in six to eight places around its breast and thighs. Then roast as usual.

For the most accurate thermometer reading of a roasting turkey, immerse the thermometer in warm water before sliding it into the turkey. When you insert it, keep it away from fat and bones, both of which render inaccurate readings.

Fish and Seafood

How can you tell whether a fish is fresh or stale? Check its eyes. If they're slightly protruding, bright, and clear, the fish is fresh. If they're pink, sunken, or cloudy, the fish is stale. And if the gills are gray, turn away. They should be red or pink.

It's easy to make your own fish scaler. Just nail three bottle caps, serrated edges up, side by side at the end of a piece of wood. To make your scaling chores easier, rub the entire fish with vinegar to loosen the scales.

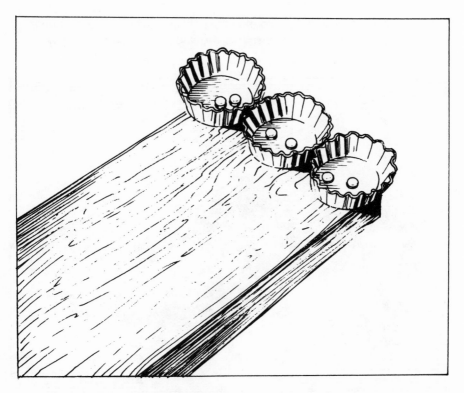

Give frozen fish a desirable fresh flavor by thawing it in milk. The milk eliminates the frozen taste.

You can make any fish taste tender and sweet by soaking it in one-quarter cup of lemon juice and water, or vinegar, or wine before cooking.

To remove most of the salty taste from saltwater fish, soak it in vinegar and rinse under cold water before cooking.

If you like halibut as white as popcorn, add a bit of milk and lemon juice to the seasoned liquid in which you cook it.

After handling fish, you can eliminate the odor on your hands by rubbing them with salt or vinegar.

If you can't get a fishy odor out of a pan used for frying fish, sprinkle the pan with salt, pour hot water in it, let it stand for a while, and then wash as usual.

Fish won't stick to the pan during baking if you lay it on a bed of parsley, celery, and chopped onions. This vegetable bed also adds flavor.

If you chill canned shrimp before adding them to hot mixtures, they'll hold their shape better.

If you don't like the canned taste of canned shrimp, soak it for 15 minutes in a mixture of 1 teaspoon of sherry and 2 tablespoons of vinegar.

If you've put too much mayonnaise in the tuna salad you're making and you have no more tuna to add, substitute bread crumbs.

If you're having a hard time prying clams or oysters from their shells, soak them for a few minutes in club soda to loosen both muscles and shell hinges. Or, wash the shell food in cold water, place in a plastic bag, and freeze for 30 minutes. Or, plunge the plastic bag into boiling water for several minutes. Either freezing or boiling makes shells easy to open with a beer-can opener or a knife.

Pork

To make breaded pork chops that are virtually greaseless, bake them on a wire cake rack in a baking pan. Any grease will drip into the pan.

If you want to tenderize pork chops or chicken pieces before barbecuing, boil them in a saucepan for a quarter hour, drain them and marinate them in barbecue sauce for a half hour. Then position them on the grill and barbecue as usual.

Bacon slices won't stick together if you roll the package into a tube held with a rubber band before refrigerating.

Bacon will curl less during frying if it first has been soaked in cold water.

If you want bacon strips to maintain their shape with minimum shrinkage, start frying them on a cold skillet and periodically prick them with a fork during cooking.

You won't have to clean a greasy frying pan every time you want bacon if you fry a large quantity and freeze it. Place the slices on cookie sheets so they won't stick together, and when they're frozen, repackage them in plastic bags and store. Reheat foil-wrapped slices in the oven for just a few minutes.

Before opening a canned ham, run hot tap water over the container for several minutes. The gelatin will melt and the ham will slide right out.

Frying thin slices of ham for breakfast is more economical than frying bacon.

Here's a way to impart additional tenderness and flavor to both sausage and bun when barbecuing: Immediately after removing a wiener or thuringer sausage from the grill put it in a bun and place the bun in a plastic bag for 60 seconds, temporarily sealing the bag's open end by twisting it. Steam will form in the bag, imparting additional tenderness and flavor to both meat and bun.

Save time and effort when broiling sausages by putting the links on a skewer so you can turn them all with one motion.

FRUITS

Buying and Storing

Though their appearance might not be perfect, standard grades of fruits are as nutritious for you as the more expensive "fancy" grades. Unless appearance is important, you can buy the cheaper grades and save money with no loss in food value.

You can make your own fruit-ripening "bowl" from a perforated plastic bag. The perforations permit air movement, yet the bag will retain the fruit gases that hasten ripening.

To speed up the ripening of pears, tomatoes, or peaches, put them in a brown paper bag and nestle a ripe apple in their midst. Puncture some holes in the bag, and put it in a cool place out of direct sunlight. Or, put the fruit in a box and cover it with a newspaper to seal in the natural gases that promote ripening.

Avocados

To speed up the ripening of avocados, place them in a brown paper bag and store the bag in a warm place. (Once ripe, you can retard spoilage by placing them in your refrigerator.)

You can determine if an avocado is ripe by sticking a toothpick in the stem end. If it slides in and out with ease, the avocado is ready to eat.

To keep an unused avocado half from turning dark, press the pit back into place before refrigerating the uneaten half.

Bananas

To hasten the ripening of green bananas, place them so that they touch overripe ones, or wrap them in a damp cloth and put them in a bag.

If you store bananas in your refrigerator after ripening, they won't go soft as fast. The cold darkens their skins, but it doesn't affect the fruit. The best way to use up overripe bananas is in banana bread.

Berries

When shopping for berries, examine the container bottoms. If they are wet or stained, much of the fruit probably is moldy or mushy, so select only those containers that have dry bottoms and hold fresh fruit. (If you discover one or two bruised and spoiled berries when you get home, discard them because molds quickly spread from berry to berry.)

To keep berries in tip-top condition, wait until you're ready to eat them before you wash them.

Strawberries will stay firm for several days if they are stored in a colander in the refrigerator. (The colander allows cold air to circulate through and around them, keeping them fresh.)

Hull strawberries after you've washed them, or they'll soak up water and turn mushy.

If you want the blueberries you freeze to retain their shape and color, don't wash them. Simply freeze them in their containers, and wash just before using.

To prevent foods such as berries from sticking together when frozen, flashfreeze them first. Here's how: Separate them on a cookie sheet, freeze, remove, and—while still frozen—pack them together in airtight containers before replacing them in the freezer.

Melons

There's an old-fashioned "thumping test" for gauging a watermelon's ripeness. Whack your index finger against it. If you can hear a high plink, the melon isn't ripe. If you hear a low plunk, it is.

How can you tell when a melon is ripe? Hold it to your ear and shake it. It's ripe if you can hear the juice and seeds sloshing around.

Oranges

When selecting oranges, don't be misled by the itensity of their color— most oranges are dyed to make them look more appetizing. Instead, look for brown spots—surprisingly enough, they indicate top quality. And remember: The sweetest oranges have the biggest navel holes.

If oranges seem spongy, light in weight, or puffy, they won't be juicy.

Other Citrus Fruits

To select the juiciest grapefruits, look for those with the thinnest skins. The "yellowness" of grapefruit skin doesn't indicate anything.

To get the juiciest, most flavorsome lemons, pick those with smooth skins and small points at each end.

As soon as you bring lemons home from the store, put them in the refrigerator in a tightly sealed container of water. Doing so encourages them to yield more juice. (You can get the same result by immersing a lemon in hot water for about 15 minutes before squeezing it.)

If you need only a drop or two of fresh lemon juice, you needn't cut into the whole lemon. Just puncture it and squeeze out the desired amount. If you then store the lemon in the refrigerator, its freshness and flavor will be unaffected.

Papayas

Fresh papayas will be soft when you squeeze them.

Dried Fruit

To keep dried fruit fresh, keep it in the freezer.

Preparing and Cooking

If you save the liquids from canned fruits, you'll have instant sauce for cake or pudding just by adding a little cornstarch to the juice.

Juices—that you've frozen and saved—from canned fruits can be combined with flavored or unflavored gelatin for a dessert or salad.

Since carbon steel knives react with fruit and cause discoloration, cut your fruit with stainless steel knives.

Apples

To maintain the crispness of apple slices—and to prevent them from browning—immerse them in salted water for 10 minutes before using them as usual.

So that apples won't shrink when you bake them, remove a horizontal belt of peel from around their middles. And, so that they won't wrinkle during baking, cut random slits in each apple before placing them in the oven.

When dicing several apples to make a large apple salad, mix them with dressing or mayonnaise as you chop. If you wait until you've cut all the apples, the first ones cut may discolor if they are exposed to air; coating them with mayonnaise will prevent that.

You can restore flavor to dried-out apples by slicing them into sections and sprinkling the sections with apple cider.

Grapes

Frozen grapes make cooling warm weather snacks.

A quick way to remove seeds from grapes is to slice the grapes slightly off-center. This exposes the seeds and makes them easy to flick away.

Pineapples

If a fresh pineapple isn't as ripe as it could be, but you're eager to eat it, you can make it taste ripe this way: Prepare it as usual and then put the pieces in a pot, cover them with water, add sugar, and boil for a few minutes. Then drain off the water, let the fruit cool, and store it in the refrigerator till it's ice cold.

The center ring of a doughnut cutter is ideal for removing the core from slices of fresh pineapple. Just press the ring on each pineapple slice.

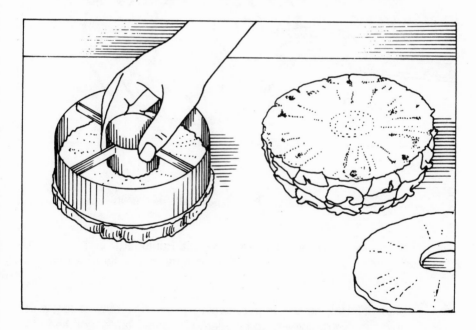

If a recipe calls for gelatin and pineapple, use either canned fruit or fresh pineapple that has been boiled for 5 minutes. There is an enzyme in fresh pineapple that will prevent gelatin from setting unless the fruit is boiled first.

Watermelon

Taking a watermelon on a picnic? If you wrap it in dry newspaper or burlap as soon as you remove it from the refrigerator, it will stay refreshingly cool till you're ready to slice and enjoy it.

Hints to Remember

To peel a thick-skinned fruit, hold it on a fork over a gas flame till the skin cracks, and then slide off the skin.

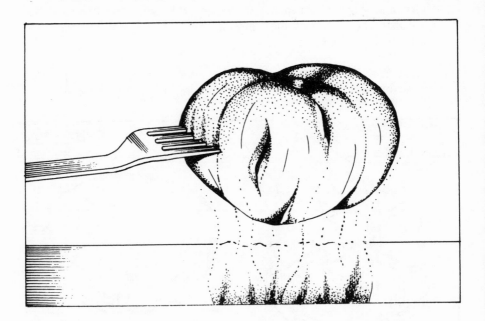

Another trick for peeling thick-skinned fruit: Put the fruit in a bowl, pour boiling water over it, wait 60 seconds and remove, and then peel the skin with a paring knife.

To prevent freshly cut fruit from browning, place it in a bowl of cool water in which you've dissolved two powdered vitamin-C tablets; or, keep the fruit submerged in water to which you've added juice from half a lemon.

To avoid discoloration in fresh fruits you've sliced into, brush the exposed interior surfaces with lemon juice.

VEGETABLES

Buying and Storing

Sometimes day-or-two-old produce offers a better buy than higher priced fresh produce. If older produce merely has a few blemishes that you can cut away, and it's drastically reduced in price, you'll save money by buying it.

Since canned mushrooms cost more than fresh ones, you'll save if you buy fresh ones—especially if they're on sale—and freeze them for future use.

Fresh vegetables in season can be considerably cheaper than the same foods frozen or canned.

To maintain the moisture content that keeps asparagus fresh, store it after cutting a tiny slice off the bottom of each stalk by standing all stalks upright in a container that has an inch of water at the bottom, and then refrigerating.

Artichokes will maintain their freshly picked texture for almost a week if they're wrapped (unwashed) in a damp towel, put in a plastic bag, and stored in the refrigerator.

Because carrot tops can rob the vegetable of moisture during storage, slice off the tops before refrigerating carrots.

Celery and lettuce will stay fresher longer if you add a damp paper towel to their sealed storage container or bag.

Lettuce will rust more slowly if there is no excess moisture in its container. To keep your lettuce bag or refrigerator vegetable compartment relatively dry, put in a few dry paper towels or dry sponges to absorb excess water.

If a head of lettuce won't drop down into a plastic storage bag because it's sticking to the sides, try putting it in the bag this way: Turn the bag inside out, put your hand in the bag, grab the lettuce head through the bag, and pull the bag right-side-out over the lettuce.

Because mushrooms can become slimy if refrigerated in a sealed plastic bag, it's better to refrigerate them in a brown paper bag. Brown paper confines the humidity that keeps mushrooms fresh, yet permits them to breathe.

If you want to freshen blemished or wilted produce, snip off all brown edges, sprinkle the vegetables with cold water, wrap them in toweling, and place them in your refrigerator for an hour or more.

Cooking Vegetables

When slicing raw vegetables, it sometimes helps to cut a small slice off one side to form a steady base.

If you're simmering vegetables and you need to add more water, use *hot* water, not cold. Adding cold water may toughen the vegetable fibers.

Economize on time and fuel by steaming two vegetables simultaneously in the same pot. If you want to serve them separately, loosely wrap each in aluminum foil during cooking.

To make frozen vegetables taste as much as possible like fresh ones, pour boiling water on them before cooking. This flushes away all traces of frozen water.

Artichokes

Cooking artichokes in iron or aluminum pots will turn the pots gray, so use stainless steel or glass pots instead.

Asparagus

To firm uncooked asparagus stalks that have gone limp, position them upright in a deep pot. Add a dash of ice water, and cover the pot with a plastic bag. Put the pot in the refrigerator for an hour, and when you're ready to cook the asparagus, the stalks will be firm.

Fresh asparagus can be cooked to perfection in a coffee percolator. Position the asparagus upright and add an inch or two of water. The stalks will be cooked tender, while the tips will steam to the correct crispness.

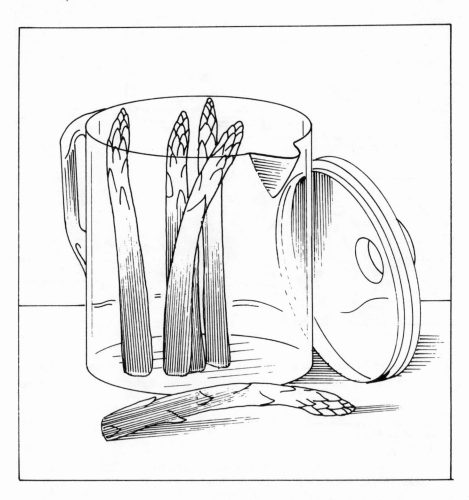

You will avoid damaging the delicate tips of canned asparagus if you open the can from the bottom rather than the top.

If you've purchased asparagus with thick, tough stalks, peel the lower parts of the stalks with a potato peeler till you reach the soft interior. Cook as usual and the stalks will taste as tender as the flowers.

Beets

To prevent beets from fading during cooking, leave an inch or two of stem attached and add a few tablespoons of vinegar to the water.

Broccoli

The pervasive cooking scents of broccoli or cabbage can be reduced by dropping a slice of stale bread into the cooking water. Placing a cup of vinegar (which absorbs odors) on the range, or dropping a lemon wedge into the pot will also lessen the offensive odor.

If you've purchased fresh broccoli, cabbage, or cauliflower, and find live insects in the vegetable, drive them out by soaking the food for 30 minutes in cold water to which you've added a few tablespoons of salt or vinegar.

Brussels Sprouts

You'll speed the cooking time for Brussels sprouts by marking with a knife an "X" on the bottom of each before putting it in the pot.

Cabbage

Cabbage that has been frozen before cooking will not have the characteristic, overpowering odor. (Wash the cabbage and dry with a paper towel before putting it in a plastic bag and freezing it.) After you defrost it, there will be no odor when boiled.

You can prevent red cabbage from turning purple during cooking by adding a tablespoon of vinegar to the cooking water.

Cauliflower

The unappealing scent of cauliflower during cooking will be reduced if you drop unshelled walnuts into the cooking water.

Add a dash of milk during cooking to keep cauliflower snow white.

Carrots

Carrots can be skinned in seconds if they're first dropped into boiling hot water for 5 minutes and then plunged into cold water. The skins will slip right off.

Celery

Out of lettuce for bacon, lettuce, and tomato sandwiches? Use celery-stalk leaves instead.

Corn

For extra succulent corn on the cob, strip green leaves from the cobs and use the tenderest ones to line the bottom of the pot before adding water and cooking.

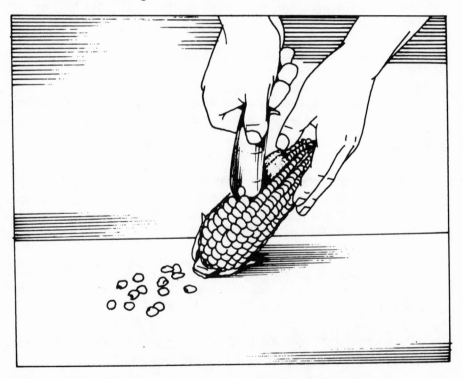

If your preference is corn off the cob, shave off kernels easily with a shoehorn.

A damp paper towel rubbed over corn on the cob easily removes the corn silk.

A dampened toothbrush is effective in brushing the last stubborn strands of corn silk from corn cobs.

If you like to grill corn with the husks on, try it this way next time: First soak the cobs—husks and all—in water for 60 minutes. Then, fasten the ends with wire-twist ties so the husks won't slip off and place the corn on the grill. Turn it every 10 minutes for 40 minutes, remove it from the grill, peel off the husks, and serve.

One way to evenly cover hot corn with butter is to melt the butter and spread it on with a pastry brush.

Eggplant

Occasionally, an eggplant has a slightly bitter taste. You can eliminate possible bitterness by submerging the eggplant in salted water while peeling it. Dry it with a paper towel and cook as usual.

Mushrooms

To cut fresh mushrooms into uniform sections, try using an egg slicer.

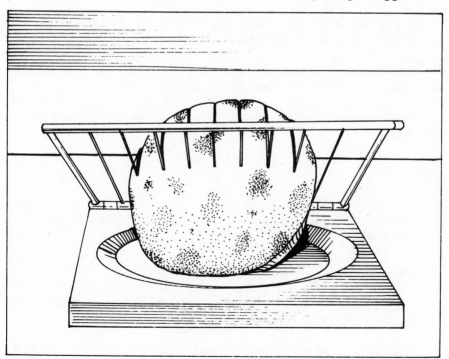

When cleaning mushrooms, try just to brush them clean with your fingers, or rinse them off quickly. Soaking them will make them soggy.

To maintain the whiteness and firmness of mushrooms while sautéing them, add a teaspoon of lemon juice for every quarter-pound of melted butter.

Onions

You can peel fresh white onions in a jiffy if you first immerse them in boiling water for a minute or two.

Your eyes will be less likely to water when you're slicing or chopping onions if you refrigerate the onions before cutting and slice off the root ends last. It also helps to breathe through your nose only and to run the exhaust fan.

If you make an "X" at the root end of an onion with a sharp knife, the onion won't pop apart during cooking.

If you soak onion rings in cold water for one hour, they'll be milder and more suitable for use in salads.

After you cut raw onions, you can get rid of the onion scent on your hands by washing them with baking soda or salt.

If you're out of onions, packaged onion soup mix can be substituted in many recipes.

Peas

Why waste time laboriously shelling peas? Just drop the pods in boiling water. The pods will split open, release the peas, and the pods will float to the surface, where you can skim them off.

Peppers

Peppers and tomatoes will maintain their shape when you bake them if they are supported in greased muffin tins.

Peppers will stay bright green during baking if you coat them with salad oil or olive oil before stuffing and cooking them.

Potatoes

To firm raw potatoes that have gone soft, immerse them in ice water for 30 minutes.

Exposure to air turns peeled potatoes dark, so if you want to peel potatoes ahead of time, cover them with water and refrigerate.

To cook a baked potato in half the normal time required, boil it for 5 minutes before putting it in a hot oven to get the "baked" flavor.

If you need to bake potatoes more quickly than usual, use baking nails to decrease baking time by as much as 15 minutes. Insert a nail lengthwise in each potato; it will heat rapidly and then radiate heat to the inside of the potato.

You can bake potatoes in less time by slicing them in half, lengthwise, and cooking them on a lightly greased baking sheet, cut-side down.

Do the skins crack when you bake potatoes? Keep them smooth by rubbing fat or butter all over the potatoes before putting them in the oven.

You can bake potatoes on *top* of a gas range so you won't have to heat the whole oven. Wrap several medium-size potatoes, side-by-side, in aluminum foil, and place them on a burner set at the lowest possible heat. In 15 minutes, flip the package over. The potatoes should be ready to eat in 30 minutes.

Some people say the very best French fries are made by frying them twice. Here's how: Let potato strips stand in cold water for an hour and wipe them off before an initial, short-duration frying. Drain off the grease, and fry them for the second time till they're golden brown. Drain again and enjoy!

If you prefer your French fries super crisp, immerse them in ice water for 30 minutes before draining and cooking them.

Sprinkle a little flour on potatoes before frying them and they'll be extra crisp and crunchy.

Hash browns that are stuck to the bottom of a pan will lift right out if you nestle the pan in a larger one containing an inch or so of cold water. It will then be easy to loosen the potatoes with a spatula.

You can use unpeeled potatoes when making hash browns. Just run them through the grater, skin and all, and you won't lose the nutrients that are just under the potato skin.

To keep potato pancakes from discoloring, add sour cream to the grated potatoes you use to make them. Or, grate the potatoes into a bowl of ice water.

For extra nutrition, add powdered milk to your mashed potatoes while you're mashing them.

Hungry for a new kind of nutritious snack? Try this: Cut potato skins into strips and season them to taste. Then, bake in a hot oven until crisp.

Sauerkraut

The strong odor of sauerkraut can be eliminated by adding a few celery stalks to the juice.

You can also eliminate the smell of sauerkraut by adding red wine to it before cooking.

String Beans

To test string beans for freshness, snap one in half. If it breaks easily, it's just right.

Sweet Potatoes

The quickest way to peel sweet potatoes is to boil them, and then drop them into cold water. The skins will slough-right off.

Tomatoes

Looking for the ripest tomatoes in a batch? Put all your tomatoes in a large container filled with water. The ripe tomatoes will sink to the bottom, while those that aren't will float to the surface.

You can peel several tomatoes simultaneously by putting them in a net onion or orange bag and submerging them in a pot of boiling water for 1 minute. The skins will drop right off.

For firm tomato slices, cut parallel to the stem axis.

To heighten the flavor when cooking tomatoes, add a pinch of sugar to the cooking water.

You can make a tomato "rose" by removing a continuous peel with potato peeler and twisting this strip in a circular motion before securing with a toothpick.

DAIRY PRODUCTS

Buying and Storing

Dairy products that have almost expired offer good values with little compromise in quality. Ask your store manager about such "unadvertised specials."

If you're going to store unsalted butter in your freezer for a long time, wrap it carefully and seal it airtight. You can be more casual with salted butter you're freezing for a short time, and store it in its original container.

Always store butter in the butter keeper or on the bottom shelf of the refrigerator; otherwise it will absorb flavors from other foods.

It's safe to store milk in the freezer, but be sure to defrost it in the refrigerator, not at room temperature.

Ice cream that's been opened and put back in the freezer may develop a waxlike film on its exposed surface. A film won't form if you press a piece of waxed paper against the exposed surface before resealing the carton and storing it again.

EGGS AND CHEESE

Cooking with Eggs

Large-size eggs should be used in recipes calling for eggs; using small eggs may create a slight imbalance in the ingredients.

Before adding eggs to a yeast mixture, bring them down to room temperature. Cold eggs slow down the yeast's action.

You don't need an eggbeater to beat eggs. Simply break the eggs into a jar, screw the lid on tightly, and shake the jar vigorously.

You can tell whether an egg is fresh or not by putting it in a pan of cool, salted water. If the egg sinks to the bottom, it's fresh. If it rises to the surface, it's not.

You can store egg yolks for up to 3 days by covering them with water in a covered container and refrigerating.

You can freeze egg whites for up to a year, but after you defrost them, remember that 2 tablespoons of egg white that's been frozen equal 1 tablespoon of fresh egg white.

Raw eggs won't slip from your fingers if you moisten your fingertips before picking up the eggs.

Egg yolks won't curdle when poured into a hot mixture if you first add some of the mixture to the yolks to raise their temperature.

Give stability and body to beaten egg whites by adding one-quarter teaspoon of cream of tartar for every two whites.

For maximum volume, let egg whites warm to room temperature before beating and add just under 1 tablespoon of water for each egg white.

Remember that egg whites won't beat properly if any trace of yolk remains. Flecks of yolk can be removed with the tip of a moistened Q-tip.

Hard-Boiled Eggs

To prevent an egg from cracking when placed in boiling water, pierce it with a sharp needle.

If an egg cracks when you boil it, add a little vinegar to the water. The vinegar will prevent the white from streaming out of the shell.

If you want to keep yolks perfectly centered in hard-boiled eggs (perhaps for deviled eggs), stir the water constantly while cooking.

Hard-boiled eggs will be easier to shell if you submerge them for a minute or so after cooking in cold water. Then, when you crack the egg's shell, gently roll the egg between the palms of your hands. The shell should slip right off.

The shell of a hard-boiled egg will slide right off if you crack it against the side of your sink several times and then peel it under cold running water.

When slicing hard-boiled eggs, the yolk will not crumble if you first dip your knife or egg slicer in cold water.

You'll be able to tell the raw eggs from the hard-boiled ones stored in your refrigerator if you hard-boil eggs in water to which you've added food coloring. Or mark hard-boiled eggs with a pencil or crayon before you put them away.

If you haven't marked them, the quickest way to distinguish hard-boiled eggs from uncooked ones is to spin them. A hard-boiled egg will spin; a raw one won't.

If you need a boiled egg for a recipe and the last egg in the carton cracks, don't despair. Just boil the egg in a "shell" fashioned from aluminum foil.

An easy—and neat—way to fill deviled eggs is with a baby spoon.

Omelets

If you rub salt on your omelet pan with paper toweling both before and after cooking, you'll make your own nonstick finish.

If you want an omelet to be extra tender, add a bit of water to the beaten egg mixture, rather than milk or cream. Water slows down yolk coagulation; milk or cream accelerates it.

For extra fluffy omelets add a bit of cornstarch before beating.

When you're preparing to make several omelets, you can still beat all the eggs together if you remember this handy measuring rule: Two large eggs equal one-third cup beaten eggs.

Poached Eggs

A few drops of vinegar in the cooking water will keep a poached egg from running.

Should you make poached eggs and be unable to serve them right away, don't discard them. Simply place them in cool water. Later, when you're ready to serve, if you reheat them slowly in hot water to which you've added salt, the flavor will be unimpaired.

For added flavor, poach eggs in white wine, beer, milk, cream, meat or vegetable stock, tea, or vegetable juice instead of water.

To store boiled and poached egg dishes made a day in advance, cover the eggs with a sauce or aspic, and then refrigerate. Bake or broil the eggs the next day to serve them hot.

Scrambled Eggs

The secret of superb scrambled eggs is to cook the eggs slowly, starting with a cool—not heated—buttered pan. When their texture is almost perfect, mix in 1 tablespoon of evaporated milk or cream per portion. (If you're serving a large group, extend the mixture by stirring in a white sauce.)

If you want to stretch scrambled eggs, just add water and a little baking powder. The taste won't be affected and the eggs will be fluffier.

If you want a soufflè that's so light it practically floats in midair, make a collar with aluminum foil, waxed paper, or brown paper. After buttering it thoroughly, wrap it to a height of 5 inches around a soufflé mold, fasten it with twine, and pour the souffle mixture into this container. Remove the collar before serving.

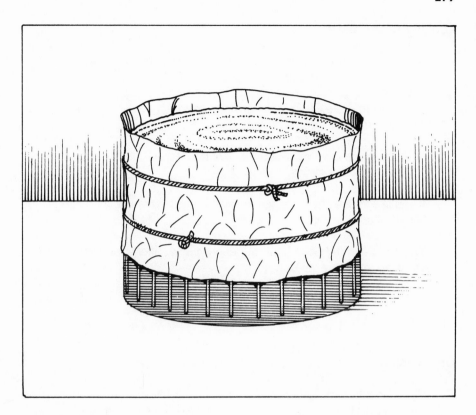

Storing Cheese

Mold won't form on cheese if you store it with a few sugar cubes in a tightly covered container.

If cheese does get moldy, cut or scrape the mold off and then dab the exposed surfaces with vinegar, which retards mold growth.

Cheese will have added freshness and flavor if it's wrapped in a cloth that's been soaked in wine and vinegar and then refrigerated.

Store cottage cheese upside down in the refrigerator to keep it fresh longer.

When cheese gets too hard, you can soften it by soaking it in buttermilk. To prevent cheese from drying out and hardening, apply butter to the cut end, or tightly wrap it in aluminum foil.

Cooking with Cheese

If you don't have a cheese slicer, you can cut cheese easily with extra-strength thread held taut.

It's easier to grate Cheddar or any soft cheese if you chill it in the freezer for a few minutes before grating.

You can make thinner, neater slices of processed cheese if you dip your knife in hot water before cutting.

If you like to use cheese strips in salads and as garnish, try cutting strips with a potato peeler.

Frozen cream cheese that appears grainy after defrosting can be whipped smooth again.

SALADS

Green Salads

If you want to remove the core from a head of lettuce without causing the brown spots that form when you cut out the core with a knife, just smack the core end against a countertop. The core can be twisted right out and the leaves will stay unblemished.

If you put washed salad greens in the freezer about 10 minutes before preparing the salad, the vegetables will be even more crunchy.

You can make soggy lettuce crisp and firm again by submerging it in a bowl of cold water and lemon juice that you place in the refrigerator. After an hour, remove the lettuce from the refrigerator and dip it briefly in hot water, then in ice water to which you've added a dash of apple-cider vinegar. Pat the lettuce dry with a paper towel.

Another way to make lettuce (or celery) crisp is to place it in a pan of cold water to which you've added slices of raw potato.

To make tiny scalloped edges on the cucumber rounds you use in salads, simply run fork tines over a peeled cucumber, then slice as usual.

A soggy salad never garners compliments for the chef. You can keep your salads crisp if you invert a saucer in the bottom of the bowl to allow any liquid to drain and collect under the saucer, away from the greens.

A sticky wooden salad bowl will look and feel smoother if it's washed and dried and then vigorously rubbed, inside and out, with waxed paper.

Seasonings

For instantly cold, well-blended oil-and-vinegar salad dressing, pour the dressing into a screw-top jar, add an ice cube, and shake. Remove the ice cube before pouring the dressing. Here's another twist: Place your greens in a plastic bag, add the dressing, and shake the entire mixture. The greens will be evenly coated on both sides.

For extra-creamy salad dressings, place dressing ingredients in a slow-running blender and slowly add the oil.

If salt is used as a salad seasoning, it's best to add it at the last minute. If you add the salt ahead of time the lettuce will wilt.

A crushed garlic clove rubbed on the inside of a salad bowl will heighten the taste of the salad ingredients.

If you want crumbled Roquefort or blue cheese for your salads, freeze it; then it will crumble easily if scraped with a paring knife. (This does not work well with other cheeses.)

Year-Round Salads

To keep fruit salad, potato salad, or shrimp as cold as possible when serving it, place it in a bowl and put that bowl in a larger one filled to the rim with crushed ice. If you want to make the ice even colder, add coarse kitchen salt to it.

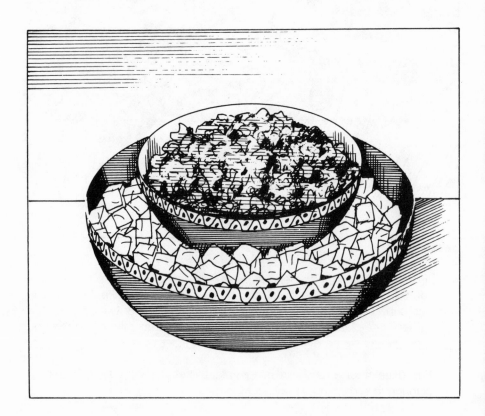

For gourmet-type potato salad, cut your potato slices extra thin with a wire cheese cutter.

When you make a gelatin salad with cream cheese, does the hot gelatin turn it lumpy? It won't if you mix the cheese with dry gelatin before adding liquid.

When cooking cranberries, you'll prevent overboiling and "foaming" if you add a teaspoon of butter to each pound of berries.

Cooking cranberries requires less sugar if you add one-quarter teaspoon of baking soda to the pot.

Cranberries are done cooking when they look as though they're *ready* to burst. If you cook them till they actually pop, they'll taste bitter.

SNACKS AND APPETIZERS

Appetizers

Bacon curls make wonderful hors d'oeuvres. Fry strips short of crispness, then remove them from the skillet and twist them round the tines of a fork. Pierce the curls with wooden toothpicks and broil them under a low flame until they're crisp.

For unusual finger sandwiches, add powdered or liquid vegetable coloring to cream cheese fillings.

You can freeze olives, pickles, and similar condiments if you put them in jars of their own liquid.

One way to remove pits from olives is to place the olives on a paper towel, roll them gently with a rolling pin, and then press them with the heel of your hand. The pits will pop right out.

Buffet Treat

Try this hors d'oeuvre buffet to keep snacks from getting soggy: Put out a plate of empty pastry puffs with an assortment of meat and cheese fillings, and let guests fill their own.

For a delicious pastry-puff glaze, brush puffs right from the oven with mayonnaise, then sprinkle with Parmesan cheese and a dash of paprika.

Snacks

Cracking nuts can be a fun family affair, but the shells tend to mix with the meat. You can separate the meat by dumping both shells and meat into a bowl of water. The meat will sink and the shells will float to the surface, where you can skim them off.

If you run ice cold water over popcorn kernels before tossing them into the popper, there'll be fewer kernels left after popping.

To minimize the number of popcorn kernels that won't pop when heated, keep unpopped popcorn in your freezer.

To restore freshness to potato chips, crisp them under the broiler for a short time.

Halved apples spread with peanut butter are a nutritious after-school treat for youngsters, as are celery slices or bananas spread with peanut butter.

Marshmallows stay soft and fresh when you store them in the freezer.

The prices of solid chocolate Santa Clauses and Easter bunnies are greatly reduced after the holidays are over. That's a good time to stock up and store them in your freezer until needed for a variety of cooking uses.

SOUPS, SAUCES, GRAVIES, AND STUFFINGS

Soups

If you want rich, brown beef stock, add beef bones that have been browned in the broiler (about 6 inches from the heating unit).

Your homemade soup will be fatfree in you make it ahead and then store it in the refrigerator long enough for the fat to solidify. Fat rises to the top of a container, where it's easy to remove.

If fatty soups and stews aren't your dish, render them fatfree by stirring either lettuce leaves or ice cubes into the pot (don't allow the cubes to melt). Fat clings to both substances, which then can be discarded.

Worried about scorching and boil-overs when cooking soup in a large stock pot? You needn't be. Position two or three bricks around the burner so the pot is elevated above the heating coils or the gas flames. Then simmer the pot's contents as long as you want over low heat.

If you want more body for your soups, add bones to the pot; marrow bones and veal bones are especially good. They contribute gelatin, which is a thickening agent.

To maximize flavor when making soup, start heating bones and meat in cold, salted water, instead of dropping them into boiling water.

Soup too thin? Add mashed potatoes or instant rice, stirring until you get the desired consistency.

If the stew or soup you're preparing seems too salty, add sugar or a few slices of raw potato. (Discard the potato slices before serving.)

When saving meat juices for stock, leave the fat in place on the surface. When it solidifies, it'll seal the stock and its flavor as if it were paraffin.

If you want to clear a broth, add a few eggshells to the stock, and simmer it for 10 minutes. The eggshells will attract the "sediment."

For tastier clam chowder, add the minced clams at the last moment and cook just long enough to heat. As a bonus, the clams won't become mushy.

To keep milk from curdling when you prepare tomato soup, add the soup stock to the milk, instead of the milk to the stock.

Gravies and Sauces

If you like rich brown gravy for your roast, and you're out of brown gravy mix, put flour in a pie pan and let it brown in the oven along with the roast. When the meat is done, mix the toasty brown flour with a little cold water and heat it with the meat juice.

If gravy's too salty, add several *pinches* of brown sugar. It'll erase the salty taste without sweetening.

Does your gravy taste burned? It won't if you stir in a teaspoon of peanut butter.

There are two quick ways to darken gravy. The first is to mix a tablespoon of water with a tablespoon of sugar, heating the blend in a pan till the sugar browns and the water evaporates. Pour the gravy into this pan. The second method is to add coffee to the gravy; it will add color without affecting the flavor.

If you want greaseless gravy, let the pan drippings sit for a few minutes. The grease will rise to the top where it can be skimmed off, leaving stock for greasefree gravy.

If an egg-based sauce curdles, it's probably because it's been boiled. Keep the temperature moderate when making egg sauces.

Dressings

Here's a quick way to stuff a turkey: Sprinkle several bread slices with herbs and bits of onion, fold them in half, and push them into the cavity.

You'll be able to remove the dressing from a turkey easily if it's held in a cheesecloth bag that you've pushed into the cavity. When you're ready to serve, pull out the bag and turn the dressing into a bowl.

If you don't have a bowl large enough to hold the turkey dressing you're mixing, try using a plastic garbage-pail bag.

HERBS AND SPICES

Cooking with Herbs and Spices

If you're preparing a slow-cooking dish, it's preferable to use whole spices rather than minced spices. Whole spices impart their flavor gradually, matching the pace of the cooking process.

You can boost the flavor oils in fresh or dried herbs by kneading the herbs between your fingertips to release the oil "bouquet."

If a recipe specifies dried herbs and you have only fresh, triple the amount called for.

If you put a half-teaspoon of whole peppers in your pepper shaker, the pepper will pour better and taste snappier, too.

Using minced parsley (dried or fresh) with other herbs enhances their tastes.

Quick Tips for Use and Storage

The skins will slip right off garlic cloves after they are soaked in warm water.

It's easy to make garlic salt: Sprinkle table salt on a board and cut garlic on it. After the salt absorbs all the garlic juice, store it for future use. Similarly, onion salt can be made by squeezing onion juice over table salt.

You can maintain the freshness and flavor of herbs by soaking them in olive oil and refrigerating them.

You can chop parsley or chives with a grater if you keep both seasonings in your freezer. When you want a small amount of either, remove it from the freezer, use your grater, and put the remainder back "on ice."

Parsley will be easier to chop if you rinse it and refrigerate in a sealed plastic bag or other container until crisp.

If you have a gas stove, you can dry fresh parsley by placing it on a cookie sheet in your oven, where the slight heat from the pilot light will evaporate its moisture in a few days. When the parsley feels appropriately dry to your touch, put it in jars and store in a cool, dry place.

You can make your own celery powder—which makes a good flavoring for stews, soups, and salad dressings—by drying celery leaves and then forcing them through a sieve.

Since chili powder, paprika, and red pepper deteriorate under humid and hot conditions, it's best to store them in dark containers in your refrigerator during the summer.

Since rosemary can be hard and tough, even after cooking, you might want to grind it in a pepper mill before using it.

Seasoned salt is much cheaper to make than to buy. Blend iodized table salt with garlic powder, pepper, paprika, dry mustard, thyme, sesame seeds, and anything else you like. Put the seasoned salt in a shaker and let it stand for a few days to blend the flavors. Use it on salads, vegetables, soups, and casseroles.

Grated citrus fruit rinds make wonderful flavorings for cakes. Store them in a covered jar in the refrigerator until needed.

CEREALS, PASTA, AND RICE

Cereal

If your hot cereal has lumps in it, next time make sure the water is boiling before adding the cereal a little at a time.

You can make chocolate flavored oatmeal—without buying the more expensive packaged kind—by adding cocoa mix to regular oatmeal as you cook it. Mix in enough to please your taste.

Rice and Beans

If you like rice that's snowy white, add some lemon juice to the cooking water.

If the rice you're cooking has burned slightly, you can remove the burned flavor by adding a heel from a loaf of fresh white bread and covering the pot for a few minutes.

When cooking dry beans, a bit of baking soda in the water will prevent mushiness.

Pasta

When buying pasta, make sure it's made from semolina rather than ordinary flour. Pasta made from semolina holds its shape better and doesn't become mushy.

A large strainer or a French fry basket can make it easy to drain pasta. Sit either device inside the cooking pot before you add the pasta, and after cooking, you can simply lift the pasta from the pot.

When boiling water for spaghetti or macaroni, add a teaspoon or so of cooking oil. Then the pasta won't stick together (or to the pot), and you needn't stir it constantly.

There are several ways to prevent pot boil-overs when cooking pasta. You can lay a large spatula across the pot's top; or, before cooking, rub shortening around the pot's rim; or, add several teaspoons of cooking oil or a dab of butter to the cooking water.

For superior pasta, let salted water come to a boil, stir the pasta into the water, put a cover on the pot, and turn off the heat. After it sits for 15 minutes, it will be ready to eat.

To prevent cooked spaghetti strands from becoming sticky, run fresh, *hot* water into the spaghetti pot before draining.

If you've made a pot of spaghetti but can't serve it at once, leave it in water, but make it cool enough to stop the cooking process. To reheat the spaghetti, put it in a strainer and shake it thoroughly as you run it under hot tap water.

If you're going to use pasta in a dish that requires further cooking, reduce the pasta cooking time by one-third.

It is possible to remove ravioli from a can without damaging the "pillows." Open the can; place it on a pan, open-end down; puncture the other end of the can with a can opener, and lift the can straight up off the ravioli. Every pillow will be intact.

One way to dry noodles you make yourself is to drape them over a collapsible wooden clothes hanger.

You can cut a pizza more easily with kitchen scissors than with a knife.

BREAD AND ROLLS

Making Bread

To make yeast bread more moist, use water used for boiling potatoes. As a bonus, the bread will be slightly larger, and it will stay fresh longer, too.

If you find it hard to knead rye, whole wheat, or pumpernickel dough, rub a little oil on your hands. The oil makes the dough more pliable.

Dough rises best in a warm spot. Try putting the dough bowl on a heating pad you've set at medium or on a table in front of a sunny window. Another good place is inside a gas oven where the warmth of the pilot light encourages dough to rise. Or, let your television set do double duty if you're making bread while watching your favorite TV show. Let the dough rise on top of the set, where heat from the picture tube will warm it.

So dough won't form a crust while rising in a bowl, first grease the bowl and press the dough into it. Then, turn over the dough, greased side up, and cover it lightly with a dish towel.

A nonstick cookie sheet is ideal for kneading and shaping bread dough; you won't have to cope with the powdery mess left by a flavored pastry board or cloth.

If your bread dough is not rising properly, try helping it along by putting the bowl on an electric heating pad wrapped in foil. The low-level heat emitted should make the bread rise perfectly.

To check whether bread dough has doubled in size, press two finger tips into the dough; if a dent remains, your dough has doubled in bulk.

To make bread extra crusty, brush the dough with an egg white beaten with a tablespoon of water.

Allow a few extra minutes of baking time to brown bread crust that has been baked in a shiny metal pan.

Home baked bread can be neatly cut into equal-size slices if you cool the bread on a wire rack and then use the wires' slight impressions as your guide.

For round-shaped homemade bread, bake your dough in 2-pound coffee tins—or try a frying pan.

If your bread crust gets too hard while you're baking the loaves, next time place a small pan of water in the oven. Also, when the bread has just been taken from the oven, spread soft butter on the warm crust.

If you allow bread to cool in the baking pan, its bottom and sides will get soggy. It's best to cool bread on a rack instead.

When making muffins, you can prevent burning by filling one of the pan's cups with water rather than batter.

If you want your rolls to have a crystalline glaze, brush them with a mixture of one-quarter cup of milk and 1 tablespoon of sugar before sliding them into the oven. Or brush the dough with a mixture of 1 tablespoon of milk and a beaten egg.

Warm-Ups

To keep dinner rolls piping hot in a straw serving basket, place them on a napkin-covered hot ceramic tile on a trivet. You can heat the tile in the oven at the same time you're heating the rolls.

If you've made and buttered slices of toast, and your youngsters are slow in showing up for breakfast, you can keep the slices warm by wrapping them in aluminum foil.

Leftover rolls that have become wrinkly can be made smooth again by placing them for a few minutes in a 350°F oven.

If you need to thaw a loaf of frozen unsliced bread in a hurry, put it in a brown paper bag in a 325°F oven for about 5 minutes.

Rolls will stay hot longer in a serving basket if you spread aluminum foil under the napkin they're wrapped in.

If leftover rolls have hardened, make them as soft as fresh again by lightly sprinkling them with water, covering them with foil, and heating them in the oven for a few minutes.

Sandwiches

When making a cold-cuts and pickles sandwich, layer the pickle slices between the cold cuts, *not* next to the bread. Doing so prevents the bread from getting soggy.

If you make sandwiches with frozen bread, then peanut butter, cream cheese and other spreads can be smoothed more evenly—and won't be likely to tear the bread.

Crumbs and Croutons

Want to pack additional flavor into bread crumbs? Mix them in your blender with pieces of broken crackers and cookies.

When making croutons for salads or stuffing, frozen bread is easier to cut, especially with an electric knife.

French Toast

Many cooks claim that the most delicious French toast is made with stale bread.

English Muffins

If you separate English muffin halves before freezing them, you'll be able to toast them straight from the freezer.

PANCAKES AND WAFFLES

Pancakes

You can speed up the chore of cutting up pancakes for small children by using a pizza cutter—even a stack is easy to cut this way.

When pancakes stick to a griddle it means they don't contain enough shortening. Mix a little more oil or melted butter into the next batch.

To reheat pancakes without overcooking them, wrap them in a dish towel, and put them in a 250°F oven for a few minutes.

Crepes

Crepes will be lighter if, instead of cream or milk, you use a liquid composed of one part water to three parts skim milk.

For extra delicate and tender crepes, use just enough batter to cover the pan bottom with a paper-thin layer.

The trick in freezing crepes—whether flat or rolled—is to stack them (sandwiched between sheets of waxed paper), cool them, and then wrap them tightly before storing them in the freezer.

Waffles

Replacing the liquid you normally use when making waffles and pancakes with club soda makes them extra light. Don't store any of the club soda batter, because continuing effervescence will alter its texture. Use it all, or discard it.

A toothbrush or pastry brush is helpful in spreading oil evenly on a waffle iron's surfaces. A toothbrush can aid in cleanup, too, brushing batter from the crevices.

PIES AND PASTRY

Making Pie Dough

Opt for lard rather than butter when making pie dough. Butter may taste a mite more flavorsome, but it makes the crust less flaky than lard does.

A wise cook keeps a powder puff in the flour canister. It's perfect for dusting flour on pastry boards and rolling pins.

To prevent pastry dough from clinging to your rolling pin, chill the pin in the freezer before flouring.

When you roll dough on wax paper, dampen the counter before spreading the paper; the wax paper will cling smoothly to the counter.

If you scrape rolling pins and pastry boards clean with a knife rather than washing them, they will be "seasoned" and dough won't stick as much the next time you use them.

No rolling pin handy? Use a full wine bottle or the tube from your vacuum cleaner.

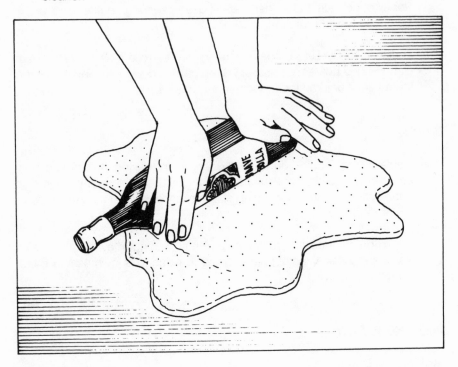

Perfect Pie Crust

Want a tempting brown glaze on your pie? Brush it with milk before sliding it in the oven.

If you love crispy crusts and cherry pie, you can have both. Sprinkle plain bread crumbs over the bottom crust before pouring in the cherry filling.

Frozen pies sometimes have a "dry" taste. You can eliminate this dryness by brushing them with melted butter before baking.

When making a fruit pie, brushing the unbaked lower crust with a beaten egg will keep the crust from soaking up too much juice and turning mushy.

To make an upper pie crust extra flaky, brush its surface with a little cold water before baking.

Before baking a frozen pie, it's difficult to make desired slits in the top crust, since the crust is too hard. Instead, warm the pie in the oven for a few minutes and then make the slits.

When making a pumpkin pie, put a layer of marshmallows on the crust before adding the filling. As the pie bakes, the marshmallows will rise and form a perfect topping.

When making pie shells, double your recipe, and make a few extra. You can store these in the freezer, and they'll be ready in a jiffy at some later date.

Fruit Fillings

Here's a real time- and money-saver. When fresh fruits are in season and on sale, prepare enough pie filling for several pies. Line pie pans with aluminum foil or wax paper, fill with the fruit, cover, and stack in freezer. The next time you want a pie, just slide one of your pie-shaped fillings into a crust and ease it into the oven.

To keep a fruit pie from getting soggy, dust the crust with flour before adding the filling, or sprinkle ground nuts over the bottom crust.

If the fruit filling in a pie you're about to bake is too juicy, you could add a spoonful of tapioca to absorb extra juice.

To thicken juice of a fruit pie so it won't be too runny, add a beaten egg white to the sugar you use when preparing the pie, or add a dash of flour to the fruit itself during preparation.

Meringue

Egg whites refrigerated for up to 2 weeks produce a fuller, more fluffy meringue than fresh egg whites.

Meringues were never easier. Separate the eggs while they're still cold, then let the whites warm up to room temperature before beating them.

Meringue shells won't darken while baking if you grease your baking sheets with a solid vegetable shortening.

To make meringue that's extra high, add a little baking powder to the room-temperature egg whites you beat or whip for the recipe.

To stabilize meringue, add a teaspoon of lemon juice to every three egg whites.

To avoid shrinkage and watery edges in a pie's meringue, spread it all the way to the pie crust's edge.

Your pie's meringue won't split or crack if you cook the pie slowly. Instead of removing the pie from the oven when the meringue turns brown, just shut off your oven, open its doors slightly, and leave the pie for several minutes.

There are several ways to prevent a pie's meringue from sticking to the knife when you cut it. You can dip your knife in boiling water or butter it before slicing the pie, or you can sprinkle a bit of sugar over the top of the meringue before you brown it.

Tips for Baking Pies

The inverted flat top of a 2-quart, ovenproof casserole dish can double as an 8-inch pie plate.

You can avoid oven spills when baking a pie by putting it in a plain paper bag or an oven browning bag that you've cut several slits in. Bake the "bagged" pie 10 minutes longer than called for in the recipe.

So a pie's juice can bubble out harmlessly and in one place, insert a piece of tube-type macaroni in the center of the pie before baking.

When you must cool a pie in a hurry, set the pie pan on top of a larger pan lined with ice cubes.

CAKES

Preparation Hints

To make all-purpose flour as much like cake flour as possible, use seven-eighths of a cup for every cake flour cup listed in the recipe, and sift it twice to make it as light as possible.

You won't have dry pockets of powder on the bottom of a bowl after you've stirred a cake mix if you put the liquid in the bowl before adding the mix.

If you like your cakes more moist than crumbly, mix 2–4 tablespoons of salad oil into the batter.

Fruits, nuts, and raisins often sink to the bottom of cake batter. To keep them evenly dispersed, try heating them before adding them to the batter, or roll them in melted butter first.

For a richer flavor, substitute devil's-food cake mix for cocoa in frostings.

Worried about cholesterol? Substitute two stiffly beaten egg whites for every whole egg that a cake recipe calls for.

Moister Cakes

If you want a chocolate cake that's extra moist and fluffy, add a spoonful of vinegar to the baking soda.

Before you put a cake on a plate, sprinkle sugar on the plate to absorb moisture. Otherwise the cake's bottom may turn gooey and stick to the plate.

Any cake you bake or buy will stay fresh longer if you place half an apple with it in its container. It's the moisture gradually released by the apple that works the magic.

If the top of a cake is browning too quickly, place a pan of warm water on a rack above the cake. The browning will slow down.

When testing a cake for doneness, you can use a stick of uncooked spaghetti if you're out of toothpicks.

Has your fruit cake dried out? It can be freshened if you turn it over, poke some holes in its bottom surface, and place a dab of frozen orange juice in each hole. As the frozen juice melts, it will spread evenly throughout the cake and make it moist. When the cake is thoroughly—but lightly—saturated, flip it over again and enjoy eating it as though you'd just made or purchased it.

Baking Hints

One sure-fire way to prevent a cake from sticking to the bottom of a pan is to position a wax paper cutout on the bottom of the pan before pouring in the batter.

A quick way to cool a cake layer is to place the cake pan on an upside-down colander.

Sometimes when a baked cake is reluctant to come out of its pan, it's because it has cooled too much and the grease used to coat the pan has hardened again. Loosen it—and the cake—by returning the cake to a warm oven just long enough for the pan to become warm to the touch.

Dust the layers of your cake lightly with powdered sugar before spreading on the cake filling. The filling won't soak into the cake.

Frosting the Cake

If you want to make a fancy cake topping in a jiffy, position an open design paper doily on top of the cake. Dust on powdered sugar, which will sift through the doily and create an instant work of art. Lift off the doily and serve.

To decorate white frosting on a cake, you can top it with gum drops shaved paper thin. They'll curl up like tiny flowers.

For an unusual, delectable frosting, add several drops of chocolate syrup to a prepared whipped topping.

If you like fudge frosting but find that it hardens too quickly as you apply it, mix in a teaspoon of cornstarch and keep the bowl in a pan of hot water. Spreading it on the cake will be as easy as buttering a slice of toast.

To frost a very crumbly cake, apply a thin layer of icing and let it harden completely. When this coat is set, spread a second layer of frosting—it will go on easily, with no crumbs.

Powdered sugar icing will stay moist and won't crack or harden, if you add a pinch of baking powder when making it.

Cake icings won't crystallize if you add a bit of salt to the sugar.

If the tiers of a multilayer cake slip as you frost it, try taming them by inserting strands of dry spaghetti. Carefully pull out the spaghetti when you're finished.

If you wrap a cake in wax paper that's been sprinkled with powdered sugar, the frosting won't cling to the paper.

Cake Decorations

You can fashion your own cake decorating tube by rolling an ordinary piece of paper into a cone, open just slightly at the tip. Fill the cone with the icing, fold over the large end, and squeeze, holding the large end closed.

If you want chocolate slivers to decorate a fancy cake, make your own by shaving them from a candy bar with a potato peeler.

Slicing It Right

If you need to cut a cake when it's hot, use unwaxed dental floss. It won't damage the cake as much as a knife would.

You'll be able to slice cleanly through cake icing if you first dip the knife blade in boiling water.

You can slice an angel food cake neatly, with nary a crumb, if you freeze it and then thaw it before cutting.

If you want to cut a cake into decorative party shapes, freeze it first. You'll find it much less messy to handle the frozen cake, and you'll be able to make even the most intricate shapes more easily.

Cheesecake

So that frozen cheesecake won't lose its butter-smooth texture, thaw it slowly in your refrigerator, not at room temperature.

Cupcakes

A spillproof way to pour cupcake batter into muffin tins is to pour it first into a squeaky clean half-gallon milk carton. The carton's spout lets you pour with precision.

COOKIES

Preparing the Cookies

An easy way to cut refrigerated cookie dough is with a wire cheese cutter.

If you want your homemade cookies to retain moisture as long as possible, use honey rather than sugar when mixing the batter.

If you want rolled cookies to have equal thickness so some won't burn before others are fully baked, here's one sure method. Cut a yardstick in half, and place each half flat on the right and left sides of a pastry cloth, close enough to each other so your rolling pin spans them. Roll your dough between the sticks until it can't be flattened further. (The dough will be precisely the thickness of the yardstick—or any other pieces of wood you use.)

Beaten egg yolk thinned with water makes a shiny cookie coating. When it dries, it also forms a good surface for painting with icing designs.

You can give cookies a crisp coating by sprinkling a sugar and flour mixture on a pastry board and rolling the dough on it.

If you want your rolled cookies to be thinner and crisper, put dollops of dough on a baking sheet, and then press on each with the bottom of a water glass you've floured or moistened and dipped in sugar.

Tips to Remember

Need another cookie sheet? Flip a baking pan over and bake your cookies on the pan bottom.

Cookies are more difficult to remove from a baking sheet after they've cooled completely. If you're having trouble lifting them, try using a greased spatula, or reheat the cookie sheet for a moment by running it over a stove burner or briefly returning it to a warm oven.

WHIPPED CREAM AND OTHER GOODIES

Whipped Cream

Before whipping cream, chill the beater, the bowl, and the cream.

To prevent cream whipped ahead of time from separating, add one quarter-teaspoon of unflavored gelatin to each cup of cream during whipping.

If you whip half a pint of cream at a time, rather than a full pint, it'll be much fluffier.

Adding a few drops of lemon juice to cream will speed the whipping process.

If you want whipped cream with good body—and in no time—whip it in a double boiler over salt and ice cubes.

For best results when adding sweetener to cream, wait until the cream has been whipped.

You can maintain whipped cream's shape—and prevent it from getting watery—if you use powdered sugar instead of granulated.

Don't be dismayed if ice crystals remain in heavy cream after you defrost it. The cream whips better in that condition.

Custard

You can delump curdled egg custard by putting the custard in a jar and shaking the jar vigorously.

Doughnuts

To prevent doughnuts from burning, add potato slices to the grease.

For instant bakery treats, deep fry refrigerator biscuit dough. The possibilities are endless—you can pull the biscuits into a long-john shape, twist them like the French twists, or cut holes for doughnuts. Roll the hot biscuits in sugar or frost them; for bismarks, slit them and push in a spoonful of jelly. Served hot, they're delicious!

Pudding

For steamed pudding that's feather light, replace half the flour called for with bread crumbs.

You can prevent "skin" from forming on pudding by resting plastic wrap on its surface before it cools.

Parfaits

Make your own parfaits by spooning different kinds of jelly between ice cream layers. Or, spoon different kinds of sherbet between ice cream layers. Half the fun of a parfait is seeing what you're eating, so make your concoction in a crystal water glass.

DRINKS

Coffee

Keep freshly ground coffee stored in a glass jar in the refrigerator to prevent it from going rancid.

It's annoying when ground coffee spills into the stem opening when you're filling the basket of a percolator pot. You can keep the ground coffee out by holding a fingertip over the stem opening when filling the basket.

Remove coffee grounds immediately after brewing so your coffee won't taste bitter.

If you run out of filters for your drip pot or percolator, simply cut a paper towel to size.

There are several ways to save on coffee. One is to grind beans till they're powdery and use one-third less coffee than usual. Or, use half the ground coffee you normally use, but circulate the water through the grounds twice. Or reuse old coffee grounds. Spread them on a flat pan and put them in the oven for 30 minutes at 350°F. Cool them and mix with half your usual portion of fresh ground coffee.

If your coffee is too bitter because you heated it too long, just toss in a pinch of salt to banish the bitter taste.

If the coffee you've just brewed tastes weak, add a little instant coffee.

You can make café mocha without a special mix by adding an envelope of instant cocoa mix to a cup of black coffee.

Out of cream? Lighten your coffee or tea with beaten egg white.

If your coffee tends to look muddy, next time start with cold water and drop in a few unwashed egg shells after brewing.

If cream curdles in your hot coffee or tea, add a pinch of baking soda to the cream before fixing your next cup.

Hot Chocolate

Does your hot chocolate sometimes have an acid taste? Reduce the acidity by adding a pinch of salt before mixing with boiling water.

To give hot chocolate a butter-smooth texture, add to each potful a pinch of salt and a teaspoon of cornstarch dissolved in water.

Tea

To keep the flavor fresh, store tea bags and loose tea in an airtight tin can.

For tea with intensified flavor and fragrance, store pieces of dried orange blossoms or dried orange rind in the canister.

You'll get a tastier cup of tea if you brew it in a clean china or earthenware pot, using fresh cold water that's been brought quickly to a boil.

Tea won't get cloudy if you add a pinch of baking soda to the pot.

To keep iced tea from clouding over, keep the tea at room temperature. When it's time to serve, just pour it over ice cubes.

The paper tag on your tea bag won't fall into your cup if you tuck it through the cup's handle. Another trick—moisten the string and stick it to the rim of the cup.

To get the last remaining spoonful of honey from the jar, pour in some hot tea, close the lid, and gently shake. Not only is your jar clean, but your tea is sweetened and ready to drink.

When making instant iced tea, the crystals will dissolve better if you add a tiny amount of very hot water before adding cold water.

If you don't have fresh lemon for your iced tea pitcher, you can get the same taste by adding a little lemon gelatin.

Freeze leftover tea, and add the cubes to your next glass of iced tea.

Fruit Juice

When squeezing your own orange juice, press the orange and roll it gently on the table or countertop. You'll get more juice.

The quickest way to thaw frozen orange juice concentrate is to mix it with water in a blender.

A quick way to dissolve frozen orange juice concentrate is to stir it with a potato masher or whisk.

It's easy to make tomato juice into something special, fast. Pour a large can of tomato juice into a large glass jar, and add a chopped-up celery stalk and a chopped green onion. Let the mixture stand for several minutes before serving.

To make fruit soda pop at home, partially fill a glass with a frozen juice concentrate, dissolved in water as per instructions, and top off the glass with club soda.

Carbonated Drinks

If a glass of diet cola doesn't have enough "kick," or seems too artificially sweet, squeeze a lemon wedge into it. It'll taste just right.

You can cut the foam when pouring a carbonated drink over ice cubes if you first rinse the cubes with water.

Beer, Wine, and Other Spirits

It's best to keep bottled beer away from light—particularly sunlight—if you're not storing it in your refrigerator, since light alters the taste detrimentally.

To extend the life of wine remaining in a jug after you and your guests have consumed most of the jug's contents, rebottle what's left in a regular wine bottle or two, leaving a minimum of air space between the cork and the wine. Doing this will help maintain the wine's flavor.

Want to serve drinks with a flair? Freeze cherries, mint leaves, cocktail onions, and green olives in ice cubes. They're a conversation topic when added to martinis, manhattans, or other drinks.

Vodka will be more flavorful if kept in the refrigerator or freezer rather than in the liquor cabinet.

Long, slender slices of peeled cucumber make perfect swizzle sticks for Bloody Marys.

When you chill a champagne bottle in an ice bucket, cover the bottle with ice just up to its neck. If the ice is any higher, you may have a tough time removing the cork.

For maximum champagne flavor, avoid overchilling it in the refrigerator. Champagne lovers know the secret is to chill it briefly in an ice bucket.

Plastic corks sometimes seem impossible to remove from champagne bottles, but if you pour warm water on the bottle's neck, the cork will pop or slide out easily, because the heat will make the bottle's neck expand.

Chapter **7**

GOURMET COOKING HINTS

IF YOU LOVE TO COOK AND BAKE, THESE GOURMET HINTS WILL LIGHT-UP ORDINARY MEALS AND GIVE THE CORDON BLEU TOUCH TO YOUR EXTRA-SPECIAL DISHES.

CHOOSING INGREDIENTS

Only the Best Will Do

Avoid buying prepackaged fruits and vegetables. Such packaging often disguises rotten spots.

Olive oil marked "virgin" or "extra-virgin" has the truest olive flavor because it comes from the first cold pressing of the olives. Pure olive oil comes from a second pressing and doesn't have as intense an olive flavor.

For Oriental dishes, use only sesame oil pressed from roasted sesame seeds (available in Oriental grocery stores). The cold pressed sesame oil found in health food stores doesn't have the same distinctive flavor.

When buying whipping cream, don't choose the ultrapasteurized brands. They whip up poorly and have an unnatural, chalky taste.

Always use unsalted (often labeled sweet) butter for cooking. It's generally fresher than salted butter because salt is a preservative that can mask "off" flavors.

FOOD PREPARATION HINTS

Cutting, Grating, and Peeling

For a picture perfect avocado half, cut the fruit in half, lengthwise. Pull the halves apart, and plunge a very sharp chef's knife into the pit. The pit will pull away cleanly with the knife. Remove the avocado halves from the shell with a spoon, or very gently with your fingers.

A vegetable peeler works well in removing citrus zest (the colored part of the rind). Take care not to remove the bitter white underskin along with the colored zest.

When grating ginger root or citrus zest on the fine side of a vegetable grater, you can remove the little bits that stick to the grater with a pastry brush.

To remove garlic peel easily, lay the clove on a cutting board and smack it sharply with the flat side of a chef's knife or cleaver.

Frozen orange, tangerine, or lemon shells make lovely serving dishes for homemade ices, sherbets, and ice creams. Keep them well wrapped in the freezer. After using them, rinse out the shells and refreeze them for another day.

To separate the cloves of a head of garlic, lay the head on a flat surface, them hit it sharply with the palm of your hand.

Pleasing Pastas

For perfect *al dente* pasta every time, use the old Italian method of testing for doneness. Remove a strand of pasta from the boiling water and throw it against the wall or refrigerator. If it sticks, the pasta is cooked *al dente* and should be drained and served right away.

Homemade egg pastas can be rolled, cut, and partially dried (until still pliable but not sticky), then laid on cloth or heavy paper dusted with semolina flour or cornmeal. Cover the pasta with another towel and store in the refrigerator for up to 24 hours. When cooked, the pasta will have the same flavor as freshly made.

Elegant Vegetables

To keep artichokes from discoloring as you clean them, squeeze a lemon half into a bowl of cold water. As you clean each artichoke, rub it with the other half of the lemon, and then drop it into the acidulated water. Remember to cook the artichokes in a nonaluminum pan.

For a more elegant presentation, remove the seeds from cucumbers before serving them in a salad or as a vegetable side dish. To do so, cut the peeled or unpeeled cucumber in half, lengthwise. Remove the seeds with a melon baller or small spoon.

For extra-crisp cucumber slices, soak them in salted ice water for 30 minutes. Just before serving, drain and rinse well under cold running water. Pat dry and toss with dressing.

Splendid Salads

You can prepare a salad up to 6 hours ahead of time if you place the vinaigrette dressing in the bottom of the bowl and carefully place well-dried salad greens on top. Cover and refrigerate, but don't toss until just before serving.

Be sure that lettuce leaves are well dried before tossing or the salad dressing won't cling.

When dressing a salad with vinegar and oil, remember to pour the vinegar first. If you pour the oil first, the vinegar won't stick to the greens.

Don't pour vinaigrette dressing over salad greens until the moment before serving. Only shredded cabbage or tomatoes can stand a vinaigrette bath for up to an hour before serving without losing firmness.

Don't toss sliced tomatoes into your salad. Their water content will dilute the salad dressing. Add them on top at the last minute, or use cherry tomatoes that aren't cut.

For easy unmolding of gelatin salads or aspics, lightly grease the mold with vegetable oil (or sweet almond oil for desserts) before pouring in the gelatin mixture. Chill until solid. Remove the mold from the refrigerator, and dip it up to the rim in a pan of hot—but not boiling —water. Loosen the edges of the aspic with a wet knife or spatula. Rinse the serving plate with cold water; shake off the excess. Place the serving plate on top of the mold, and, grasping both dishes firmly, invert the mold; lift the mold away from the dish to release the gelatin.

Chef's Secrets

To remove the bitter juices from eggplant before cooking, cut it into slices or cubes as directed in the recipe. Sprinkle the eggplant liberally with coarse or kosher salt, and set the pieces on several layers of paper towels for 30 minutes. Rinse the slices or cubes quickly under cold running water and pat them dry before continuing with the recipe.

The inner layers of leeks are often very dirty. To clean them thoroughly, cut two perpendicular slits, starting about 3 inches from the root end and running all the way through the stem end. Wash the vegetables thoroughly under cold running water to remove all dirt.

To soften and peel whole cabbage leaves for stuffed cabbage effortlessly, core the cabbage head and freeze it for several days. Put the head into a large bowl of hot water, and the leaves will peel right off.

High-Vitamin Vegies

To lock color and flavor into cooked spinach, begin by washing the spinach well in cold water and removing the stems and spines. Lift the spinach leaves from the water, and place them in a heavy, nonaluminum pan (enameled cast iron is excellent). The spinach should fit in tightly. Cover and steam over medium heat, tossing occasionally until the spinach is *just* wilted and very bright green (about 3-4 minutes). Drain and season as desired.

When you want to use cooked spinach in stuffings or molded vegetable dishes, cook it as in the preceeding hint, then drain well. Place the spinach in a cotton or linen towel. Holding it over a bowl or the sink, squeeze the spinach until all excess moisture has been removed.

Oven-Baked "Fries"

To make delicious, fatfree "French fries," cut the potatoes into half-inch thick pieces and soak them in a large bowl of cold water for at least 2 hours. Place the "fries" on a baking sheet with at least 1 inch of space between the pieces. Preheat your oven to 400°F and bake the "fries" about 35 or 40 minutes, until they're nicely puffed and browned.

Some Like It Hot

You can save energy by roasting a lot of red peppers at one time, using the just-lit coals of a barbecue. Char the peppers on all sides, then place them in a heavy plastic bag, and seal for 10 minutes. When the time's up, use a small, sharp knife or your fingers to lift off the skin, stem, and seeds of each pepper. Slice and store the peppers in a jar in the refrigerator. They'll keep for several weeks and can be used in hot vegetable dishes, in salads, or as an antipasto.

When working with hot chilies, it's a good idea to wear rubber gloves. Be careful not to touch your face; the oil from the chilies can irritate your skin.

Whipped Just Right

To make vanilla sugar for flavoring meringues and icings, cut open two vanilla beans, and place them in a quart container. Fill the container with confectioners' sugar and allow the sugar to ripen for a week before using. Keep refilling the container with sugar until the beans are spent (about 2 or 3 months).

For the greatest volume, whip egg whites at room temperature in a greasefree bowl that's been rinsed with warm water, then lemon juice or vinegar, and then dried with paper towels.

If hand- or blender-stirred mayonnaise refuses to emulsify, let the separated mixture sit for 30 minutes at room temperature. Spoon off the oil and add an egg yolk to the mixture. Very gradually add the oil in a thin stream while beating the mixture, and it will emulsify.

Good and Creamy

Skim milk yogurt makes an excellent low calorie substitute for sour cream in many recipes. Take care when adding it to hot foods, however. Too much heat or too vigorous stirring can cause yogurt to become stringy or to separate. Always add it at the last minute and stir gently.

When using ricotta cheese for stuffings or for cheesecake, be sure to dry it thoroughly first. Place the ricotta in a clean cotton or linen towel and, holding it over a large bowl or sink, squeeze the cheese into a tight ball and wring. Keep moving the ricotta to dry parts of the towel and wring until all excess moisture is gone. To remove all ricotta from the towel, use a spatula or pastry scraper.

A *beurre manié* makes a handy sauce thickener. For every tablespoon of softened butter, mix in 1 tablespoon of all purpose flour. The *beurre manié* can be formed into small balls and stored well covered in the refrigerator for several weeks. To thicken a sauce, just break off part of a ball and whisk it into the sauce just before serving. Continue adding pieces of *beurre manié* until the sauce is the desired consistency.

Better Breading and Stuffing

Does the breading sometimes refuse to stick to cutlets? Here's how the pros do it: First dust the cutlet with flour, then brush off the excess. Next, brush the cutlet with an *anglaise* (beaten egg, oil, water, salt, and pepper). Dip it into fine breadcrumbs, pressing the crumbs so they'll adhere, then shake off the excess. For best results, breaded cutlets should be refrigerated 1 or 2 hours before cooking.

Here's how to prepare fresh chestnuts for a stuffing: With a small, sharp knife, slit the flat side of each chestnut; put the nuts in a saucepan; cover them with cold water; and bring to a boil. Cook for several minutes, then remove the pan from the heat. Working quickly with only a few nuts at a time, peel the outer and inner shells. Cook the peeled nuts in a saucepan covered with water or stock. Simmer until tender (about 30 minutes).

New Methods with Meat

If you plan to freeze meat stews like *coq au vin* or *boeuf bourguignonne,* undercook them slightly. When they're thawed and reheated, the stews won't have the muddy flavor and mushy texture of overcooked meat.

When sautéing meats, be careful not to overcrowd the pan. If there are too many pieces in the pan, the meat will steam instead of brown.

Tasty Techniques

For best results when sautéing meats or vegetables, make sure they're completely dry before cooking.

When poaching a whole fish, wrap it in a length of cheesecloth for easy removal from the poaching liquid.

Nutty Ideas

To blanch almonds, place them in boiling water for 1 minute. Then peel off the skins, using either your fingernails or a small, sharp knife.

To toast almonds, place the blanched almonds on a baking sheet in a 200°F oven for 5 minutes, or until dry and lightly toasted.

SAUCES

Through Thick and Thin

Your brown sauce won't thicken if you add acids, such as citrus juice or vinegar, before the sauce has been reduced.

If your brown sauce is too thick, you can thin it with a tablespoon or two of light cream or more meat stock.

Don't cover meat sauces while keeping them warm. Moisture will build up and you'll dilute your sauce.

Richer than Ever

Substitute beef, veal, or pork fat for butter when making a brown sauce for gravies.

To give your sauce an extra-shiny appearance, whip in 2 tablespoons of cold butter just before serving.

With a Little Water

If a sauce begins to separate, add a little cold water. Should the sauce begin to cool too quickly, alternate with hot water.

To skim fat from stock, add a tablespoon of cold water while the stock is simmering, and discard the film that rises to the surface.

Keep It Saucy

You can freeze leftover hollandaise sauce in boilable plastic bags. Thaw as needed by holding the bag under warm running water for 15 minutes.

If you make béarnaise sauce several hours ahead of time, keep it in a tightly closed, preheated vacuum bottle.

MAKE YOUR OWN

Farm Fresh

Homemade *crème fraîche* has a more natural taste and texture than the store bought kind and can be prepared for much less money. Mix 1 teaspoon of buttermilk and 1 pint of heavy cream in a glass jar. Put the covered jar in a warm spot (75–85°F) for about 24 hours, until the cream is a pudding-like consistency. This cream can be refrigerated for several weeks.

The only special equipment needed to make yogurt is a candy thermometer. Use skim milk, whole milk, or half-and-half (for extra-rich yogurt). Heat one quart of milk to 170–180°F. Keep it at that temperature for 3 or 4 minutes, then cool to 110°F. Stir in 1 teaspoon of yogurt culture (available in health food stores) or one teaspoon of plain yogurt, then pour the mixture into a thermos or into a glass jar with a lid. If you're using a jar, wrap it in a blanket or down jacket. Now just let the yogurt set for 24 hours until it reaches a pudding-like consistency. It can be refrigerated for several weeks.

Day-Old Dandies

Save stale French and Italian bread for making your own breadcrumbs. Trim off the crusts and lay the bread on a platter covered with a cloth. Let the bread sit at room temperature for 2 or 3 days or lay the bread pieces on a baking sheet and leave it in a gas oven overnight. Cut the hardened bread into chunks, and process in a food processor with the steel blade or in a blender. For very fine breadcrumbs, pass them through a medium sieve, then store in an airtight container in a cool spot.

To make Melba toast, remove the crust from a loaf of French bread. Slice the bread thin, and bake the slices until crisp and light brown in a 200°F oven. Remove and cool. Store in an airtight container.

A Bumper Crop

There's no need to buy a special jar for making bean sprouts. Just use a canning jar with a screw-on ring top. Place the beans in the jar, and cover the jar top with a double thickness of cheesecloth. Screw on the ring top over the cheesecloth. Rinse with warm water and drain off twice a day until the beans sprout.

SEASONINGS

It's an Art

Any dish that's prepared to be served cold should be slightly over-seasoned, because chilling subdues flavors.

To save money and enjoy fresher flavor, make gourmet mustards and vinegars at home. For mustards: Add freshly ground or cracked spices or fresh, chopped herb leaves to dijon mustard. Flavor to taste. Store in the refrigerator. For herb vinegars: Heat 1 quart of white wine vinegar with 1 cup of minced fresh herbs (or one-quarter cup dried herbs) in a nonaluminum saucepan. Steep at room temperature overnight, then strain through a fine sieve with cheesecloth. Store in airtight glass bottles.

Garlic purée makes an excellent condiment to have on hand for flavoring meats, vegetables, and salad dressings. Wrap at least 10 whole garlic heads in aluminum foil and bake in a 375°F oven for 1 hour. Separate the cloves, and squeeze each one gently to release the garlic. Pass the garlic through a fine sieve. Mix with 1 tablespoon of olive oil for each 10 heads. Season with salt to taste. Store in a jar and cover with a thin layer of olive oil. Remove small amounts as needed. The purée will keep in the refrigerator for several months.

For maximum flavor, buy whole spices and crush or grind them with a mortar and pestle or an electric spice grinder just before using.

Freshly made chili powder has more kick than the store bought kind. Buy dried chilies in a Spanish or Mexican grocery store. Remove the seeds and stems, then grind the chili pods in a blender or a food processor with a steel blade.

A Soupçon of Citrus

A piece of dried or fresh lemon or orange peel makes a tasty, unusual addition to a *bouquet garni* for meat or chicken stews.

To get more juice from a lemon or lime, put it in a bowl of hot water for 1 minute before squeezing.

Gift from the Sea

The best salt is sea salt or coarse kosher salt. Iodized salt adds an unpleasant, harsh taste to foods.

Capture the Flavor

When substituting dried herbs for fresh in a recipe, use one-third to one-half less of the dried.

Herb Delights

In selecting bay leaves, look for leaves that are imported—preferably Turkish. They have better flavor than the California bay leaf, which tends to be stronger and oilier.

For uniform texture in chopped chives, cut the chives at the root end of the plant and bunch them together tightly with one hand. Hold the bunch on a cutting board and chop finely with a sharp knife.

Because fresh basil leaves discolor easily, always use a stainless steel or carbon and stainless knife to cut them. Lay the leaves one on top of the other and roll them into a tight tube. Slice thinly with a sharp knife, then unravel the leaves. This is called a *chiffonade* cut.

Italian or flat leaf parsley has much more flavor than curly parsley, which is best used as a garnish or in recipes requiring little or no cooking. Add the stems to a *bouquet garni* for flavoring long-cooking dishes, such as soups or stews.

Fresh herbs, grown in a summer garden, can be frozen for winter use. Wrap the leaves tightly in plastic and freeze. Some leaves may discolor, but the flavor is still better than most commercially dried herbs.

Herb butters are convenient garnishes for broiled meats, poached fish, or steamed vegetables. For every half-pound of softened butter, mix in the juice of one-half lemon or lime, 2 tablespoons of fresh, chopped herbs, and salt and pepper to taste. Put the butter on a length of waxed paper and roll it all into a tube. The tube can be frozen or refrigerated. To use, cut into small circles, remove the paper, and use as an instant sauce.

FREEZING AND STORING

Fancy Freezing

Pâté à choux puffs that have been stored in a tin for several days benefit from being crisped in a 350°F oven, then cooled before filling.

Pâté à choux puffs freeze well and don't need to be defrosted before serving. Just heat them in a 400°F oven for a few minutes, then cool before filling.

Whole unblanched nuts, purchased in bulk, are generally cheaper than packaged nuts. They can be stored in the freezer and used as needed.

To avoid spoilage after a can of tomato paste has been opened and partially used, freeze the remainder in tablespoon portions. The frozen paste can be dropped into a sauce when needed.

Uncooked soufflés can be successfully frozen. Pour the batter into the soufflé dish, then cover the dish tightly with plastic wrap before placing it on a level spot in the freezer. If using a freezer-to-oven dish, the soufflé can be baked directly from the freezer. If using a china or porcelain soufflé dish, remove it from the freezer 30 minutes before baking. In both cases, bake the soufflé for twice as long as the recipe indicates.

Believe It or Not

Poached eggs can be refrigerated in cold water for several days. To reheat, place the eggs in a strainer, lower into boiling water for about 1 minute, and serve right away.

Fresh ginger root that's been peeled will stay fresh for months if stored in white wine or dry sherry, tightly covered, and refrigerated.

SOUP MAKING

Stocking Up

When cutting a chicken into pieces, save the carcasses, necks, and gizzards. Freeze them, along with roast turkey and chicken carcasses; when you have enough, use the carcasses to make delicious homemade chicken stock.

To save money, trim beef and veal roasts yourself. Store the bones in a heavy bag in the freezer, and use them to make homemade beef stock.

Don't throw out the water leftover from steaming vegetables. Save and freeze it for flavoring the stock of homemade vegetable soups.

Right Every Time

It's easy to make a concentrated stock that will add a chef's touch to your soups. Reduce brown beef or chicken stock to a heavy, syrup-like consistency, being careful not to burn the stock. Store it in the refrigerator or freezer and just break or cut off small pieces as needed to flavor soups or sauces.

When making stock, never allow the liquid to boil. This will result in a cloudy stock.

There's no need to thaw frozen stock before using. Just pop a frozen block of stock into a covered saucepan and heat it until boiling.

Here's how to clarify stock and make aspic in one step: For every quart of stock, sprinkle two envelopes of unflavored gelatin into one-half cup of cold water. Set aside to soften. Beat two egg whites to a froth; crush the shells into the stock in a saucepan; add the egg whites and the softened gelatin to the pan. Over high heat, stir until the mixture boils. Then turn off the heat and let the mixture sit for 10 minutes. Strain it through a fine sieve lined with a wet (wrung dry) kitchen towel. Allow the stock to drip through the sieve without disturbing it. Use the aspic as directed in your recipe.

Overstocked

If freezer space is tight and you want to store homemade stocks, simply cook down the stock until it's reduced by half, then freeze. To use, you can restore the stock to its original volume by adding water.

To avoid having all your plastic containers tied up with frozen stock, line each container with a heavy-duty freezer bag and fill it with stock. Cover and freeze. Slide the bag with the frozen stock from the plastic container. Seal the bag with tape or a twist tie, and return it to the freezer.

COOKING WITH CHOCOLATE

Melt with Pleasure

Chocolate melts more quickly if it's first broken or chopped into small pieces in a food processor fitted with a steel blade or with a chef's knife.

If chocolate contracts into a hard lump while being melted, stir in 1–2 tablespoons of solid vegetable shortening (not butter or oil), and beat vigorously.

If melted chocolate used for dipping becomes too thick to coat evenly, add a tablespoon or two of warm water or brewed coffee to thin it to the proper dipping consistency.

For best results, chocolate should be melted in a double boiler over hot, *not* boiling, water. Working the chocolate back and forth with a spatula helps the chocolate to melt evenly.

Semisweet chocolate with its higher sugar content is best for dipping and icings, because it hardens to a beautiful, glossy sheen.

Once sweet chocolate, milk chocolate, or white chocolate are melted, they must be used immediately in a recipe. Unsweetened and semisweet chocolate will be usable for up to 15 minutes after melting.

Indulging a Sweet Tooth

When you want a pronounced chocolate flavor in your baked goods, it's best to use dark or bitter chocolate in the recipe.

If unsweetened baking chocolate is unavailable for a recipe, substitute 3 tablespoons of cocoa powder (Dutch process is best), plus 1 tablespoon of vegetable shortening or unsalted butter for each ounce of chocolate called for in the recipe.

To make thin chocolate curls for dessert decorations, shave room-temperature chocolate with a vegetable peeler. Refrigerate the chocolate curls after shaving.

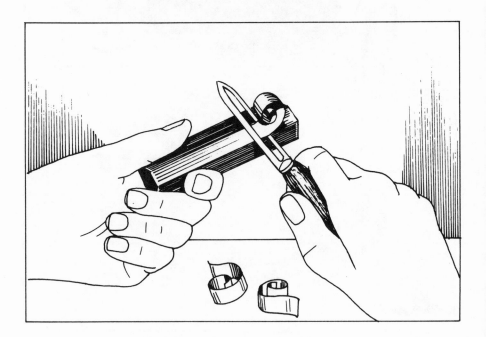

FOOD PROCESSOR HINTS

A Chop off the Old Block

To chop parsley successfully in the food processor, make sure the leaves are very dry by first whirling them in a salad spinner or patting them dry with a heavy towel.

Citrus zest used in a dessert recipe can be chopped in a food processor with a steel blade if some of the sugar from the recipe is placed in the work bowl with the zest.

Slicing It Right

To slice soft cheeses, such as Swiss or mozzarella, in the food processor, place the cheeses in the freezer for about 10–15 minutes before slicing. The firmness of the cheese will make more even slices with less strain on the machine.

When grinding hard cheese, such as Parmesan or Romano, in the food processor, be sure the cheese sits at room temperature for several hours before processing. Then cut the cheese into small cubes, and—with the machine running—drop them through the feed tube.

To slice flank steak, pork tenderloin, or boneless chicken breast in your food processor, partially freeze the meat before slicing. The meat will cut evenly into thin slices.

Use Your Imagination

If unsalted butter is unavailable, you can make your own fresh butter in a food processor fitted with the steel blade. Process some cream until butter forms (about 5 minutes). Drain off the water and dry the butter well in a towel. One pint of heavy cream will make about 7 ounces of butter.

Almost any recipe can be adapted to the food processor. Carry out all the recipe directions involving dry ingredients first and then just wipe the bowl clean with a paper towel. Process the wet ingredients last.

BAKING HINTS

Home Baked Is Best

For best results in baking, always bring eggs to room temperature before adding them to your recipe.

Inaccurate oven gauges often ruin baked goods. Use an oven thermometer to verify the oven temperature, so you can make any adjustments *before* baking begins.

Always use the size baking pan specified in the recipe. If a slightly smaller or larger pan must be substituted, adjust the baking time accordingly.

A baking stone (available in specialty cookware shops) or unglazed red tiles (available at tile supply stores) simulate the old-fashioned brick ovens used by bakers. When bread or pizzas are baked directly on a preheated stone or tiles, the texture of the loaf is light with a superb crisp crust.

For a crisp crust on French or Italian bread, spray the loaves with a fine mist of cold water (use a plant atomizer) at 5 minute intervals during the first 15 minutes of baking.

When brushing puff pastry tarts with an egg wash, don't let the wash drip down the sides of the pastry. If it does, the egg wash will "glue" the puff pastry layers together and they won't rise properly.

Pleasing Pastries

Allow chilled dough to stand at room temperature until it's pliable enough to roll out easily.

For best results, roll out pastry dough on either a marble or a formica countertop. Their cold surface prevents the shortening in the dough from softening.

If you can't roll out your pastry dough on a marble or formica surface, chill your working area by rubbing it with a plastic bag filled with ice cubes. Wipe away any excess moisture.

If you want a tender and flaky pie crust don't overflour your pastry crust as you roll it out.

To prevent pie crust from overbrowning, place a shield of aluminum foil over the edge of your pastry crust when it's baking, and remove it during the last 15 minutes.

To thaw unbaked puff pastry, wrap the frozen dough in a nonterry cloth towel and let it defrost for 24 hours in the refrigerator.

SUBSTITUTIONS

To the Rescue

If fresh herbs are unavailable, dried herbs can be given a fresher flavor for garnishes by chopping them with an equal amount of fresh parsley leaves.

Instead of going through the process of clarifying butter for sautéing foods, add a small amount of vegetable oil to unsalted butter. The vegetable oil will allow the butter to reach a higher temperature without burning.

If salt pork is unavailable for a recipe, substitute bacon that's been blanched in boiling water for 10 minutes to remove the smoked flavor.

Lemon juice, vinegar, sour cream, or milk can be substituted for water in pie crust recipes. Any of these will provide a tender and flavorful crust.

If cilantro (fresh coriander leaves, sometimes called Chinese parsley) is unavailable, substitute by adding 1 teaspoon of finely chopped or grated lemon or lime zest to every 2 tablespoons of chopped parsley leaves.

Boneless chicken or turkey breast can be substituted for veal scallopine or cutlets. The savings will be considerable.

Cooked turkey can be substituted in any recipe calling for cooked chicken, and vice versa.

Making Do

Instead of using expensive cheesecloth to hold a *bouquet garni,* substitute a large, reusable, stainless steel tea ball.

When a recipe calls for meat or fish to be cooked *en papillote* (in a parchment paper casing), aluminum foil can be substituted for the parchment paper.

Use dried beans or rice as inexpensive pie weights; the beans or rice can be cooled and reused many times.

Rings for frying homemade English muffins or eggs can be made by cutting the bottom and top from tuna fish or pet food cans.

Sausage casings can be stuffed using a large pastry bag and a plain tube. Fill the bag with the sausage. Then pull the end of the casing around the pastry tube, and hold it tightly with one hand while squeezing the pastry bag with the other.

If a large spatula is unavailable for folding in beaten egg whites or whipped cream, use the palm of your hand to fold ingredients together gently.

EQUIPMENT

Ready for Anything

Select cooking pans that are durable and made from a good heat conductor, such as copper, cast aluminum, heavy rolled steel, or cast iron. Specially treated aluminum pots and porcelain-lined cast iron pans won't react to acid or cream foods.

Top-quality carbon steel or combination carbon and stainless steel knives are essential to good cooking. Knife edges should be sharpened on a steel or ceramic sharpener before each use. Knives should be reground professionally every 4–6 months, depending on use.

When cooking with a wok on an electric stove, position the ring so that the narrow opening is on the bottom. This will bring the wok closer to the high heat needed for successful stir frying.

An extra set of tweezers makes a handy kitchen tool for removing bones from fish fillets before cooking.

The best type of pastry bag is plastic lined. The canvas makes the bag easy to grip, and the plastic lining makes it easy to clean.

Chapter **8**

HOME CANNING AND PRESERVES

KEEP YOUR GOODIES ON HAND YEAR-ROUND BY PRESERVING WITH THESE TRIED AND TRUE HINTS.

Select Only the Best

When selecting fruit and vegetables for home canning, try to buy them in approximately the same size so they'll cook more evenly before canning.

In order to enjoy canned foods that have a fresh flavor, choose only those foods that are firm, ripe, and fresh, with no bruises that will spoil over time.

Always wash foods thoroughly before canning and discard any rotting sections.

Acid and Low-Acid Foods

Fruits, tomatoes, and pickles are acid foods and can be safely preserved by canning by the boiling water bath method.

Use a pressure canner to prepare low-acid foods such as meats and vegetables.

Jars

Some supermarket jars can be used for canning if you select them very carefully. Jam and jelly jars can be used for canning jams and jellies, and some ketchup bottles can be used for special vinegars.

When you're canning and preserving, match the jar size to the eventual serving size, where possible. This will eliminate a refrigerator full of half-empty jars.

It's a good idea to label all your jars of canned foods with the contents and the date.

Home Canning Techniques

You can process two layers of jars in your canner if you place a small wire rack between them, so that water and steam can circulate evenly around the jars.

To cool hot jars removed from the canner, set them uncovered on a cloth, board, or wire rack, away from any draft.

An easy way to check whether a jar is sealed is to tap the lid with a metal spoon. If you hear a ringing sound, the jar is sealed.

If the seal of a canned jar won't move down when pressed, the jar is properly sealed and ready for storage.

It's easier to fill the jars if you use a wide-neck funnel placed on top of the jar, then spoon the contents into the funnel.

If you work a flexible knife or spatula around the inside of a filled canning jar, you'll eliminate any air bubbles.

Preventing Common Problems

Don't open a processed canned jar to add more liquid. You'll have to reprocess the jar to prevent the contents from spoiling.

To prevent foods from darkening while canned, rinse the foods in a quart of cold water mixed with 1½ teaspoons of salt. Discoloration can also be prevented by adding 50 mg of vitamin C to each quart jar.

To prevent cut fruits from discoloring before preserving, place them in a gallon of water mixed with 3 tablespoons of lemon juice. Drain well before packing in jars.

On the Salty Side

Table salt leaves sediment in the bottom of canning jars, so use canning or pickling salt instead. Vegetables can be canned without salt if you're on a saltfree diet.

Before canning fresh fish, soak it in a solution of brine (one-half pound of salt to 1 gallon water) for 10–60 minutes depending on the size of the fish.

Jelly and Jams

Place several marbles in the kettle when you're making jelly preserves, apple butter, or other foods requiring continuous stirring. The marbles will roll constantly across the kettle bottom and prevent sticking.

When you're mixing homemade jelly, use a potato masher for stirring. The handle is long enough to keep your hand cool and the shape prevents it from slipping into the pot.

To test whether your fruit juice contains enough pectin to jell, mix 2 tablespoons of cooked fruit juice with 2 teaspoons of sugar and 1 tablespoon Epsom salts, and let stand for 20 minutes. The mixture should form into a semisolid if the juice contains enough pectin.

A Real Dilly

For pickling, be sure your vinegar has at least 5 percent acidity, or your pickles may soften and spoil.

To avoid canning hollow or soft pickles, can your cucumbers within 24 hours of harvesting.

A Fresh Approach

Before tasting canned meats, vegetables, poultry, or fish, boil the food in an uncovered pan for 15 minutes to eliminate the risk of botulism.

If canned food smells strange or looks cloudy after opening, discard it immediately without tasting any.

If the lid on a canning jar is bulging, the contents might be spoiled.

To avoid spoilage and explosions, home canned foods should be stored out of direct light and away from direct heat sources.

To prevent explosions should some of your home canned goods spoil, make sure jars with wire bails are stored unlocked.

When you open a canning jar that's been stored for some time, watch for spurting liquid. If any liquid does spirt out, the contents have spoiled.

Keep It Simple

Two of the easiest alternatives to canning are winter storage during cold weather months and dehydration in dry climates. In winter storage, such vegetables as celery, Brussels sprouts, turnips, and winter radishes can be left outdoors if well mulched. Dehydration involves letting the hot sun do all the work, or purchasing an electrically operated dehydrator.

Chapter **9**

WHAT TO DO WITH LEFTOVERS

THESE WINNING WAYS SOLVE THE PERENNIAL PROBLEM. DON'T GIVE UP ON ANYTHING UNTIL YOU READ THESE HINTS!

No-Waste Leftovers

You'll conserve range energy as well as elbow grease when heating small amounts of leftovers if you wrap each type of leftover in a separate aluminum foil "package," place the packages side-by-side in a frying pan containing an inch of water, and boil over a single burner. There's only one pan to clean.

It's best to reheat most foods in a thick, covered pot. A heavy pot and a tight lid prevent drying out.

The vitamin-rich water you've cooked vegetables in can be frozen for later use when making soups.

Roast, steak, and chicken bones enhance the flavor of any soup stock, so freeze them for future use instead of throwing them away.

Leftover vegetables will lend additional flavoring to soup stocks if puréed. If soup isn't on the menu, freeze the purée in ice cube trays and use the vegetable "cubes" later as needed.

Instant beef stock can come from the freezer, too. When you cook a beef roast, save and refrigerate all pan juice. After the fat has risen and hardened, remove and discard it. Pour the remaining juice into an ice cube tray and, when the juice is frozen, individually wrap the cubes in foil and store in the freezer for later use.

Save watermelon rinds from meals or picnics. Keep them in a plastic bag in the refrigerator until you have enough to pickle.

If you have leftover tomatoes, freeze them for later use in stews and soups. The resulting softness won't affect their taste.

Opened tomato paste should be refrigerated. Cover it with a little vegetable oil, which can be poured off when you want to use the paste again.

If you want leftover hot chilies to maintain their "kick" indefinitely, store them in your refrigerator, loosely sealed in a brown paper bag.

To keep a leftover onion slice fresh as long as possible, rub the "open" side with butter.

Instead of discarding leftover spaghetti noodles, cut them into bite-size pieces and store in your freezer. The next time you make spaghetti sauce, just add the noodles to the mixture.

A good way to save leftover dinner wine for cooking is to pour a thin film of vegetable or olive oil over its surface. The film will preserve its flavor by sealing out air.

When you have pieces of leftover cooked bacon, crumple and freeze them for future use as baked potato toppings or salad garnish.

The best way to keep leftover cold cuts fresh, without freezing them, is to roll them up and put them in a covered glass in your refrigerator.

If you have leftover whipped cream, flash freeze dollops of it on a cookie sheet and store it in your freezer in plastic bags. That way you'll have instant cream in an emergency.

If your family can't eat all the waffles or pancakes you make, you can store the extras—keep them flat—in plastic bags in your freezer. These perfectly shaped leftovers can be reheated in your toaster.

It's easy to reheat leftover baked potatoes. Simply run hot water over them, and then bake for 20 minutes in a 350°F oven.

338

If shredded coconut dries out, sprinkle it with milk and let it stand half an hour or so. It'll taste moist and fresh again.

Creative Cooking with Leftovers

Pan-fried slices of leftover meat loaf can be used as a filling for regular or open-faced sandwiches.

Leftover turkey dressing can be baked in muffin tins and served with butter, instead of rolls.

If wine turns sour, you can use it in place of vinegar.

Leftover mashed potatoes make patties that can be coated with flour and fried.

Leftover hot dog and hamburger buns can be deliciously recycled. They taste superb when spread with butter, garlic powder, and Parmesan cheese and them toasted in an oven and crumbled over salads.

When cookies get hard and stale, you can crumble them to use as toppings for pies and coffee cakes.

Have your leftover doughnuts become stale? For a different breakfast treat, just slice them in half, dip them in French-toast batter, and brown them in butter.

Melted ice cream shouldn't be refrozen, but you can refrigerate it and use it on breakfast cereal.

Stale angel food cake can be transformed into wonderful cookies. Cut the cake into half-inch-thick slices, shape them with a cookie cutter if desired, and then toast and frost—and eat!

When the last olive or pickle in a jar is gone, don't pour the remaining juice down the drain. It's ideal for seasoning deviled eggs.

Salvage leftover mixed salad greens by blending them with a can of tomato juice and spices for a quick cup of gazpacho.

Leftover mincemeat can be stirred into rice pudding or vanilla yogurt for a spicy, unusual treat.

Chapter **10**

CLEANING UP

GIVE YOUR KITCHENWARE THE ONCE-OVER WITH THESE QUICK AND EASY TIPS.

To the Rescue

Temporarily out of liquid dishwashing detergent? Just substitute any mild shampoo.

To make an all-purpose soft soap, grate or shave 2 cups of hard bar soap into a large pot or measure 2 cups of powdered soap into the pot. Add 1 gallon of water and heat the mixture to the boiling point over meduim heat, stirring constantly to dissolve the soap. Then, periodically stirring, lower the heat and let the mixture simmer for 10 minutes. Remove the pot from heat and let the soap partially cool before pouring it into a clean container and covering tightly. You now have a gallon of soft soap for general dishwashing use.

If you're using an inexpensive dishwashing detergent to save money but find it leaves dishes spotted, simply put a few tablespoons of vinegar in the rinse water.

Sidelines

Keep a jar of hot, soapy water on the sink when you're cooking, and slip silverware into it when finished. All you'll need is a quick rinse and the utensils will be clean again.

If you don't know how to safeguard your bracelets, watches, and rings when doing dishes, fasten a large cup hook near the kitchen sink and hang them on it.

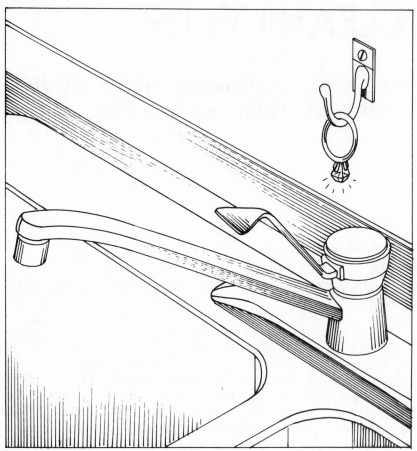

Pots and Pans

A crumpled piece of newspaper will soak up excess grease from a pan before you clean it in the regular manner.

It's usually possible to remove burned-on foods from a pan by generously coating the food with baking soda barely moistened with water. Leave the paste on overnight and then wash the pan as usual.

Another method is to fill the pan with water, drop in one or two fabric softener sheets, and let it stand for an hour or so. The crust will lift right off.

It will be easy to clean a pot in which you boil sweet potatoes if you first rub the pot's interior with margarine or cooking oil.

To rid a teakettle of lime deposits, fill it with a mix of half water and half vinegar and boil the mixture. Let it stand overnight, and then pour the cooled-off liquid—and the lime—down the drain.

If your glass coffee percolator looks dull, make it sparkle again by boiling vinegar in it.

Try removing dark stains from an aluminum pan by filling the pan with water containing 1 tablespoon of cream of tartar per quart and boiling the mixture. Or, white vinegar added to water and boiled is an equally effective solution.

To remove discolorations from an aluminum pot, cook tomatoes or applesauce in it; the acid in the food will brighten up the metal.

A cast iron skillet won't rust if you dry it and then—while it is still warm—rub it with a little cooking oil.

You can remove charred food spots from the interior of a cast iron utensil by sprinkling salt on them, adding enough vinegar to cover, and boiling.

Whenever you wash and towel dry a cast iron skillet, it's best to put it in a warm oven afterward to complete the drying process since moisture makes cast iron deteriorate. It's also a good idea to place paper towels between cast iron pans when you stack them so there's no trapped moisture.

The easiest way to clean the outside of a cast iron skillet is with oven cleaner. Spray it on , let it stand for an hour, and wipe it off with a solution of water and vinegar.

To remove tarnish from a copper pot, rub it with ketchup.

Copper pans can be cleaned with sour milk. Pour some in a flat dish and soak the copper bottom for an hour. Finish cleaning as usual.

A quick, inexpensive way to clean copper cookware is with vinegar. Apply a paste consisting of 1 tablespoon salt, 1 tablespoon white vinegar, and 1 tablespoon flour to clean a discolored skillet. Because vinegar is acid, wash the skillet in hot, soapy water, then rinse it. Finish off the job with a vigorous buffing to restore a desired shine. You can achieve the same results with a paste made of 2 tablespoons vinegar and 1 tablespoon salt.

When stains need to be removed from nonstick coated cookware, mix 2 tablespoons baking soda with 1 cup water and a half-cup liquid bleach. Boil the solution in the pan for several minutes till the stains vanish. After washing the pan, wipe its inner surface with cooking oil to reseason it.

To remove rust stains from tinned kitchenware, simply rub with a peeled potato dipped in a mild abrasive powder and rinse.

To protect your wok from rust when not in use, coat it lightly with cooking oil before storing it away.

Everyday Glassware

Stubborn food spots on glassware will dissolve if rubbed with baking soda.

Greasy glassware will come sparkly clean if washed in an ammonia solution.

If there are stubborn lime and water spots on your glassware, try polishing the spots away with a soft chamois cloth.

Milk glass and woodenware are best washed by hand, because if washed in the dishwasher, the milk glass will yellow and the woodenware will crack and split.

Delicate Stemware

Slip delicate stemware into the wash water edgewise—not bottom first— to prevent cracking. If you want real sparkle, add a little vinegar to the warm rinse water.

Drip dry delicate stemware upside down on a soft towel, or polish it gently with a soft, lintfree cloth.

Use a soft brush to remove dirt from glassware's crevices.

Here's an easy way to remove the cloudiness from your fine crystal: Fill the glasses with ordinary water and drop a denture tablet in each. Wait till the tablets dissolve and rinse—the film will be gone.

Remove stains from crystal glassware by rubbing with a cut lemon, or washing it in vinegar solution.

Cut Glass and Porcelain

You can clean a stained decanter by filling it with water, adding a cup of ammonia or vinegar, and letting it stand overnight. If this doesn't work to your satisfaction, use two packs of powdered denture cleaner dissolved in water.

A good way to clean a glass decanter is to cut a potato into tiny pieces, drop the pieces into the decanter, add warm water, and shake till the decanter's inside surfaces are spotless. Rinse the decanter with clean water after you pour out the potato.

When washing delicate porcelain objects in the sink, you'll minimize breakage if you pad the sink bottom with a towel and wrap another towel around the faucet (secure it with a rubber band).

A vase with a narrow neck appears to be hard to clean, but you can freshen it by dampening the inside with water, sprinkling in some toilet bowl cleanser, and waiting 10 minutes before rinsing. Or fill the vase with hot water, add rice and 2 teaspoons of vinegar, and shake vigorously.

Dishwasher Tips

Always scrape food particles from your dishes before loading them into the dishwasher.

Use special cleaning detergents in your dishwasher. Soap can damage the equipment with suds, and leaves a film on silverware and glasses.

Be sure that plastic dishes are labeled as being dishwasher-safe.

Banishing Kitchen Odors

You can deodorize your kitchen by putting a spoonful of ground coffee in a container and heating it in the oven, or by boiling water containing a little ammonia.

Banish sink odors by washing the sink with a strong salt solution or laundry bleach.

If you can't immediately clean stove or oven spills and boil-overs, sprinkle them with salt to minimize odor.

Refrigerator and freezer odors sometimes can be eliminated by rubbing interior surfaces with a few drops of vanilla extract diluted in a cup of water— some homemakers keep a cotton ball soaked with the extract inside the refrigerator at all times. Or leave an open box of baking soda, a dish of charcoal briquettes, or a lemon half in the unit. If odors still linger, clean all interior surfaces with club soda or a baking soda and water solution.

If pots and pans or other cooking utensils have lingering odors, try washing them with a baking soda and water solution, or boil vinegar in them.

Rubbing salt into a wooden cutting board will eliminate odors as well as lift stains.

You can remove all traces of fish, onion, or other odors on your hands if you wet them and then sprinkle on baking soda. Work the paste over your hands and then rinse away both soda and odor.

Deodorize bottles by filling them with dry mustard diluted in water. Allow the bottles to sit overnight and then clean as usual.

If a plastic container has a strong odor, pack it with crumpled-up newspapers, cover it snugly, and leave it overnight. The next morning, the odor will be gone. Another effective treatment is to wash the container with baking soda and water.

To sweeten a sour-smelling waste disposer, feed it orange, grapefruit, or lemon rinds. A tablespoon of borax or baking soda also does the trick.

Appliances

You'll make defrosting easier if you rub the insides of the freezing compartment with shortening; or, spray them with a commercial coating that prevents food from sticking to pans. Either way, ice will slide right off when you defrost.

If you defrost your refrigerator by letting water drip into a tray beneath the freezer compartment, you can avoid spilling the water on the way to the sink if you leave the tray in position, let its contents refreeze, and then drop the frozen chunk in the sink to melt.

You can speed up defrosting in a manual-defrost refrigerator by placing shallow pans of hot water on the shelves.

A frostfree refrigerator should be cleaned thoroughly every 4–6 months; you should clean a manual-defrost refrigerator when frost is one-half inch thick.

Occasionally remove gas burners and wash them thoroughly. Clean the holes with a fine wire cleaner or a pipe cleaner, then quickly dry the just-washed burners in a warm oven. (Don't try to clean a gas burner's holes with a toothpick. It may break off and clog a hole.)

A cheap, effective way to clean a soiled oven is with ordinary household ammonia. Pour 1 cup of ammonia in a glass or ceramic bowl, place it in the oven, and allow it to sit in the closed oven overnight. Next morning, pour the ammonia into a pail of warm water and use this solution, and a sponge, to wipe out loosened soil. The fumes are strong at first, but they soon dissipate.

After you've cleaned an oven, bake a few orange peels in it at 350°F if you're bothered by "cleaning"odors. The peels will eradicate them.

To clean an electric range's chrome rings, put them in a plastic bag with enough ammonia to cover them. Seal the bag and set it aside half a day. When you remove the rings and rinse them off, they'll be spotless.

Your toaster will gleam if you rub it with a soft cloth dampened with club soda.

Let the blender scrub itself clean. Fill it less than halfway with hot water, add a few drops of dishwashing liquid, and run for 10 seconds. Rinse and dry.

If your automatic dishwasher leaves a film on your dishes, clean it periodically by setting a bowl of white vinegar—about 2 cups—in the bottom rack, and running it through a wash-rinse cycle. If filming persists, change brands of automatic dishwasher detergent.

If you're having trouble cleaning the tiny crevices between appliance push buttons or raised-letter trade names, use a toothbrush dipped in warm soapsuds.

Periodically remove the cutting wheel and lid holder of your electric can opener, and soak them both in a jar of hot, sudsy water. Scrub away caked-on food with an old toothbrush with stiff bristles. Rinse, dry, and replace the parts.

To clean chrome knobs or decorations on an appliance, apply nail polish remover. (First make sure the unit's unplugged, because polish remover is flammable.) Rinse the knobs or decorations with water.

To flush food particles from a meat grinder, run a raw potato or a slice of stale bread through it before washing it.

Stains and Spills

To prevent staining, coat rubber drainboard trays with a thin film of furniture polish. If the trays already have stains on them, remove them with a mixture of bleach and water and then apply the polish.

If your laminated plastic countertop is marred by hard-to-remove stains, don't rub them with steel wool or abrasive cleaners; instead, try a solution of milk, bleach, and water. Let it sit for only a minute and immediately rinse with water.

To remove countertop stains, simply sprinkle with baking soda, rub with a damp cloth or sponge, and rinse with clear water.

A soiled white porcelain sink will gleam like new if you line it with paper towels, spray them until soaked with household bleach, and wait an hour before rinsing.

You can get rid of rust marks in a stainless steel sink by rubbing them with lighter fluid. Afterwards, thoroughly wash your hands and the sink.

Hard lime deposits around faucets can be softened for easy removal by covering with vinegar-soaked paper towels and waiting about an hour before cleaning.

One way to clean porcelain surfaces is to rub them with cream of tartar sprinkled on a damp cloth. You can remove rust spots from metal surfaces the same way.

There are several ways to keep chrome surfaces glistening. You can rub them with dry baking soda sprinkled on a dry cloth, a cloth dampened with hot water and ammonia, or a cloth dampened with rubbing alcohol.

To brighten a plastic laminate countertop surface that's dulled, apply an appliance wax or a light furniture wax.

Coffee or tea stains can be removed by rubbing them with a damp cloth dipped in baking soda.

Tough Little Cleanups

Sweeten a coffemaker's plastic basket by occasionally rubbing it with a paste of baking soda and water.

To remove coffee or tea stains from a thermos bottle's interior, partially fill the container with crushed eggshells, add hot water, and shake well. To remove general stains from a thermos bottle's interior, fill the container with warm water and 1 tablespoon bicarbonate of soda, then let stand for 3 hours, and wash.

Loosen leftover egg and cheese residues on dinnerware by soaking in cool water.

For stains on acrylic kitchen utensils, wipe at once with a damp cloth. If the stains persist, use an all-purpose cleaner or moistened bicarbonate of soda. Always act as quickly as possible and never use harsh abrasives.

Soft cheeses can be cleaned from a grater by rubbing a raw potato over its teeth and openings. (A lemon rind or a toothbrush also do a first-rate cleanup job.)

If you spill cooked rice on the floor, it will be easier to sweep up after it dries.

A rubber window squeegee is ideal for scraping crumbs from tables.

Silverware and Other Metals

You can retard silver tarnishing by placing a piece of alum in the silver-ware drawer. When silver eventually does tarnish, use silver polish and clean it with a sponge rather than a cloth; a sponge squeezes into crevices a cloth can't reach. When you wash silverware, it's best to wash all pieces by hand rather than in the dishwasher; then buff dry to bring up the shine and prevent water spots. The same method should be used for brass and pewter articles.

Using sterling silver flatware regularly slows the tarnishing process and gives the pieces a beautiful patina.

If you do wash sterling silver in the dishwasher, separate it from stainless steel. Contact between the two produces an electrolytic action that pits the stainless steel.

Because contact with rubber darkens silver, you should wear cloth gloves instead of rubber when cleaning it. Also, never fasten pieces of silverware together with rubber bands.

After you've washed or polished sterling silver, it's a good idea to let it air dry for a few hours before putting it away, since even the slightest dampness causes silver to tarnish.

You can keep stainless steel shiny by rubbing it with a lemon peel or a cloth dampened with rubbing alcohol, and then washing as usual.

When black spots appear on carbon steel knives, you can remove them with an old wine bottle cork. Sprinkle cleaner on the side of the blade, wet the cork, and scrub the blade with its flat end; clean the other side the same way.

If you want carving knives to remain sharp, wash them in *cool* water.

To retard tarnish on polished brass, rub it with a cloth moistened with olive oil. When it eventually tarnishes, clean it by rubbing with a lemon wedge dipped in salt. Rinse with water and dry with a soft cloth.

You can minimize scratching on pewter when polishing it if you rub it with cabbage leaves or very fine steel wool. Then, rinse with water and dry with a soft cloth.

Part V

PARTIES, PRESENTS, AND GOOD TIMES

Parties and holiday celebrations can sometimes mean a good time for everyone except the frazzled hosts who are so busy attending to details that they have little time to enjoy the festivities. If that's ever happened to you, it's time you put the fun back into parties, presents, and good times.

Chapter 1, "Entertaining and Parties," shows you how planning pays off. Tips for organizing and executing most of the decorating and cooking *before* the party allows you to be a guest at your own affair. And with the imaginative tips on party themes, menu planning, and place settings, your parties will be the kind that are long remembered by all your friends. Here are ways to make houseguests feel at home, to break the ice among strangers, and to give a special thank you after you've been invited out somewhere.

Creating a convivial party mood with lighting, scents, and decorations transforms even a simple gathering into something special. Whether you're looking for a way to make a pretty centerpiece or how to make a candle dripless, you'll find the solution here in Chapter 2, "Decorations."

If you always find yourself racking your brain for gift ideas or without much time to do a good job of wrapping, Chapter 3 will solve all your future gift and gift-wrapping dilemmas. You'll find clever suggestions for personalizing your gifts as well as ways to do fancy gift wrapping with whatever materials you have at hand.

A blazing fireplace can add just the right note of warmth and hospitality to any party, but fireplaces have their own set of problems, too. Chapter 4 covers the field with tips for starting fires effortlessly, decreasing soot while a fire is burning, making your own economical logs from old newspapers, and keeping most of the heat in the room instead of letting it escape up the flue.

If you find the Christmas season the most hectic holiday of the year, Chapter 5 will banish your woes. There are hints for avoiding the crowds when shopping, trimming the tree, sending cards, decorating your home, and finding just the right gift. Use these festive hints to make your parties more special than ever before—and to have more fun at them yourself!

Chapter 1

ENTERTAINING AND PARTIES

DELIGHT YOUR FRIENDS AND FAMILY WITH SPECIAL PARTY TOUCHES FOR EVERY OCCASION.

Party Planning Tips

If you do a lot of entertaining, keep a record of the parties you've given, including the menu and guests. Next time you need ideas, you'll have lots right at hand.

If you plan a menu of limited courses, everything can be set out on the table or sideboard. That way you'll be able to enjoy the meal along with your guests, instead of running back and forth to serve.

So you won't forget anything that needs to be done at your party, do your planning on paper—including a time schedule.

If possible, do most of your party cooking in advance so you won't be stuck in the kitchen away from your guests.

If you're planning on a houseful of guests for a holiday party, don't forget to rent or borrow an extra coat rack, so you won't have to pile coats on the bed.

For easy party serving and cleanup, use one big platter to hold the entire main course. Arrange meat and vegetables or fish and rice in an attractive manner and serve.

For convenience when preparing for a party, keep all your entertainment equipment in one storage area.

Keep a tray handy between courses and at the end of the meal for clearing the table. It will save you a lot of trips between the table and your kitchen.

Remember to keep plain juices—tomato or orange—on hand for non-drinking guests.

A good substitute for a regular bar can be made by setting out a pretty tray of liquor, glasses, and accessories on a conveniently located table or counter.

Party Themes

Parties are a lot more festive if you carry through with a theme. When serving pasta, for instance, you might want to set the table with a checkered table cloth and lay out a basket of warm bread.

Co-oping a party is a great way to entertain. Ask everyone to bring something, and you provide the ambiance and the wine.

Invite your friends to a make-a-pizza party and see how creative you all can be!

If you're giving a kitchen shower, make a gadget-lady centerpiece. Wrap dish towels around wooden spoons and use them as the body and arms. A scouring pad makes wonderful "hair" and bottle stoppers make darling earrings. Be inventive!

Showing home movies or slides makes great party entertainment, especialy if your guests are the "movie stars!"

One of the easiest and most pleasurable ways to entertain is to invite friends to your home for a relaxing Sunday brunch.

Before a card party, you can make plastic cards spotlessly clean by placing them in a paper bag with a few tablespoons of flour. Shake the bag, remove the cards, and wipe them off with a damp cloth.

For a special occasion party, send balloon invitations. Inflate the balloons and write the information on them with a felt-tip marker. Then, deflate the balloons, put them in envelopes, and mail to your guests.

Children's Party Tips

Create an autograph tablecloth at your child's next birthday party. Have the guests sign their names, then embroider over each signature. Use the cloth at future birthday celebrations, adding new names each year.

Instead of using your best lace tablecloth for a child's party, spread a large, colorful bath towel on the table. It looks festive, absorbs spills easily, and washes quickly.

When giving a party for children, have a stuffed pet-toy contest. Invent enough categories so that every child's toy wins a prize.

Start a holiday tradition by having each child select a special ornament for the Christmas tree each year. Store these in a box for each child, adding new ornaments every year. Once the children have grown, they'll have accumulated a whole set of ornaments to take to their own homes.

Carefree Menus

If you want to serve a new recipe to guests, try it out first on family members or close friends. You'll be sure of the taste and the length of time it takes to prepare.

For an easy party menu, set out different types of lettuce and a lot of toppings so your guests can create their own salads. Add some bread and wine to make the meal complete.

If you're not quite sure how to time different courses, just serve a casserole in an attractive dish.

You can prepare vegetables for a party one or two days ahead of time. Simply cut up the vegetables, wrap them in damp paper towels, put them in plastic bags, and refrigerate.

A creative way of serving vegetables for dips is to line a nice wicker basket with lettuce and then fill the basket with carrots, mushrooms, cauliflower, celery, and other vegetables.

Large green peppers make ideal cups for dips. Slice off their tops, scoop out the seeds, and fill them with your favorite concoction. A loaf of bread sliced in half horizontally, with each half hollowed out, can serve the same purpose.

A hollowed-out half melon makes a perfect container for cut fruit.

An ice bucket can be used as a serving dish, because its insulation keeps foods appropriately hot or cold.

You can make individual butter servings unique if you put pancake-size dollops of softened butter on a cookie sheet, set the sheet in the refrigerator till the butter hardens, and then cut the butter into various shapes with your cookie cutters.

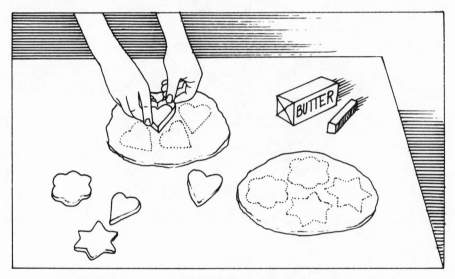

Don't despair if you don't have enough dessert dishes because you can just as easily serve most desserts in wine glasses.

Place Settings

Tumblers and dishes won't slide off serving trays if they sit on damp napkins.

For crisp summer napkins, use men's white linen handkerchiefs.

Get some bagels fresh from the bakery and use them as napkin rings. These are wonderful conversation pieces too.

To help guests at a dinner party get better acquainted, consider having them change chairs between courses of the meal.

Make your buffet convenient for you and your guests by wrapping place settings of silverware in napkins and placing them in a little basket. This saves space on your buffet table, and your guests won't have so much to hold. As an added touch, you can tie decorative ribbon around the napkins.

High Spirits

Aperitifs served before a meal should be dry to stimulate the appetite.

Here's how to measure the amount of liquor you'll need when stocking your bar for a party: A fifth contains 20 straight shots; a bottle of wine serves 6; a bottle of sherry or port serves 13; a bottle of brandy or after dinner liqueur serves 26.

To keep the carbonation in an unfinished bottle of champagne, drop a strainless steel turkey skewer into the bottle, and attach a balloon securely over the bottleneck.

Punch

If you're making any kind of fruit juice punch, freeze some of the juice in a large bowl or container, and use it instead of ice cubes. The punch won't be watered down.

You can keep punch chilled without letting it become diluted by placing a sealed plastic bag of ice cubes in the punch bowl or pitcher.

A pretty party garnish for punch is peppermint sticks poked through the centers of lemon or orange slices. They'll float like tiny boats.

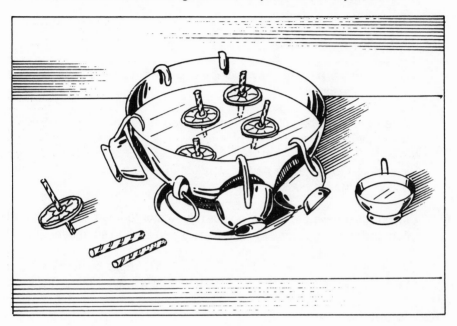

Beer

Before pouring beer into a glass or mug, make sure the container is spotlessly clean. The slightest trace of soap, lint, or grease will cause bubbles to cling to the side. Next, tilt the container and start pouring beer down the side, then quickly straighten the glass or mug, and pour into the center to minimize the foam. If you *prefer* a thick head, simply increase the pouring distance between the beer bottle or can and the glass or mug.

Wine

When you're storing wine for any length of time, keep it in a dark place.

Since wine can be damaged by vibrations, store it away from a staircase or machinery.

If the wine you're serving needs a corkscrew to open the bottle, the wine should be stored on its side. This keeps moisture in the cork and makes opening the bottle easier.

A large copper wash basin filled with ice makes a great wine cooler for a party.

Ice Hints

Freeze a rose petal in individual ice cubes for a beautiful touch when serving refreshments.

When you buy a bag of ice for a party, keep its contents from melting by placing it on dry ice.

Ice will last longer for a party if you first freeze an inch of water in the bottom of the ice bucket.

If you don't have the space in your refrigerator to keep soft drinks and beer cold during a party, fill your bathtub with ice and store drinks there.

If you have leftover tea or coffee from a party, freeze them in ice cube trays. Use the cubes to chill iced tea or coffee without diluting the flavor.

Red Carpet Treatment

Because morning schedules vary from one person to the next, let your holiday house guests know where to find the fixings to make their own breakfasts.

Handtowels for your guests can be rolled up and put in a pretty basket in the bathroom.

When you're entertaining weekend guests, make them feel more at home by sharing a few chores. Write down some simple chores on slips of paper, fill a basket, and let your guests choose one at random. Some chores the guests can help with are emptying the trash, locking windows, cleaning up after breakfast.

If you're having guests, supply the guestroom with books and magazines, an extra robe, and a tray to keep all their personal things in one place.

Your guests will always remember your parties if you send them "picture postcards" of themselves. As each person enters the party, snap a photo. When the pictures are developed, "address" the photo, put a stamp on it, and mail.

A nice way to thank your host and hostess for the time spent as their house guest is to send pictures of your time together pasted into a pretty scrapbook.

Chapter 2

DECORATIONS

SIMPLICITY AND INGENUITY CREATE JUST THE RIGHT PARTY MOOD.

Decorations

An empty wine bottle may be pretty enough to save, but you won't want it if there's a cork stuck inside. If you can't fish out the cork, pour ammonia in the bottle and put it where there's plenty of air circulation. The ammonia will disintegrate the cork in less than a week.

If you want to give your entire house a refreshing scent—perhaps before a party—sprinkle cinnamon on a sheet of aluminum foil, put it in a hot oven, and leave the oven door open.

You can also make your house smell good by placing a solid room deodorizer beside an air-return vent of a forced-air heating system. The air will recirculate and carry the fresh smell to every room.

You can make a room smell pleasant by dabbing perfume on a lamp's cool bulb. As the bulb heats, a sweet scent will permeate the air.

Candles

Lighting a group of birthday candles with a short match can result in burned fingertips. A better idea is to use a lighted strand of uncooked spaghetti. The same trick works for lighting a candle in a long, deep container.

If a candle is too large for a candleholder, shave off some of the excess wax and then hold the candle bottom over a lighted match for a few seconds. When the wax softens, squeeze the candle into the holder.

To make candles burn slowly and evenly, with virtually no dripping, put them in your refrigerator for several hours before your guests arrive.

When a large decorative candle burns down in the middle and becomes hard to light, don't discard it. Instead, drop a small votive candle into the "hole" to make the candle as good as new again.

You can snuff out a candle flame with kitchen scissors.

Chapter 3

GIFTS AND GIFT WRAPPING

OUT OF IDEAS FOR GIFT GIVING? THESE IMAGINATIVE BOOSTS WILL GET YOU OFF TO A FRESH START.

The Right Gift

Need an unusual gift for a friend? Paint a pillow with nontoxic acrylic paints and list your friend's important personal dates and places on it.

When bringing fresh flowers to a friend, put the stems into a balloon filled with a little water and secure with rubber bands. The flowers stay fresh and you have a convenient carrying method.

You'll always have little gifts on hand if you remember to buy doubles of things you need yourself. When you need jam or correspondence notes, for example, buy extra and store the gifts on a special shelf in your house.

Fill a pretty basket with special spices for a friend's gift.

A straw basket filled with special soaps, nail brush, and good face cloths makes a wonderful house gift.

Make a loaf of bread and wrap it up along with a jar of homemade preserves. Your friends will never forget such a hearty present.

Instead of buying a box of note cards as a gift, make up a package of the lovely art reproduction postcards you can buy at museums.

Think big when buying baby shower gifts. Babies are ready for the 6-month size within a couple of months of birth. Also, every mother needs baby shampoo, soap, washcloths, crib sheets, soft towels, disposable diapers, baby sleepwear.

For a practical, yet fun, shower present, buy a laundry basket and attach kitchen gadgets and towels to it by using colored yarn or ribbon.

Suit Them to a "T"

For a friend or boyfriend who dislikes the drudgery of keeping the apartment clean, give a gift certificate for one day's professional cleaning service.

Have a writer on your gift list? He or she will appreciate a supply of legal size, lined, yellow pads in a monogrammed leather case.

For friends who enjoy the beach or have the luxury of their own swimming pool, a set of plush bath towels is a welcome gift.

If you have any artistic talent, put an original ink drawing on the cover and several inside pages of a notebook, and give it to a friend to use as a diary.

Enlarge the cultural horizons of a friend and give a gift of musical recordings from Latin America, Italy, Germany, etc.

Neat and Accurate

Organize your gift-wrapping chores by storing wrapping paper rolls in a narrow wastebasket, along with scissors, tags, Scotch tape, and assorted colors of marking pens.

If you're not sure how much to cut from a large roll of wrapping paper for a particular package, first wrap a string around the package, cut it so there's a slight overlap, and use it as a measuring guide.

Two in One

Wrap a baby gift in a receiving blanket or diaper.

Give gifts in baskets, which eliminates the need for wrapping paper and ribbons and doubles your gift.

If you're mailing cookies, minimize breakage by packing them in fluffy popcorn. The recipient can eat both the cookies and the packing.

A gift for a teen can be wrapped in a colorful bandanna.

Wrap-Ups

If you buy an assortment of colored boxes and bows, you won't need anything more to wrap your presents.

Smooth out wrapping paper from gifts you've received and use again.

Newspaper and brown paper bags are quite good for package wrapping, and surprisingly attractive.

Wrap gifts in color comic strips or bright magazine covers and artwork.

If a paint or wallpaper store will give you old wallpaper sample books, you can use the sample pages as gift-wrapping paper—elegance at no cost at all.

For a unique gift wrap, check out the accessories in a fabric goods store to decorate your package.

Old maps and pieces of sheet music make fine wrapping paper.

All Tied Up

To press wrinkled ribbon flat, pull it through a hot curling iron.

Instead of tying a package with ribbon, glue on dried leaves and flowers to decorate. Or simply paint a ribbon on your gift-wrapped box.

To protect a gift bow on a package from being crushed in transit, keep a plastic berry box taped over it until you arrive at your destination.

Tagalongs

Make small squares of wrapping paper double as a gift tag. Fold a piece in half, punch a hole in the corner, and write your message inside.

Dress up a plainly wrapped package by spelling out a greeting or the recipient's name from letters cut from newspaper or magazine headlines.

Blow up a balloon; paint the recipient's name on it; and tie it to your gift.

Chapter **4**

THE FIREPLACE

GATHER ROUND THE BURNING LOGS FOR A PERFECT WINTER FIESTA.

Hearth Ideas

Empty cardboard milk cartons make wonderful kindling for fires. (This also is true of candle stubs.)

To make a wood fire start and burn like magic, immerse an unglazed brick in kerosene for 24 hours. Then, nestle it in the wood and touch a lighted match to it. Even damp logs will snap, crackle, and pop without kindling, thanks to this miraculous brick. You can reuse the same brick by immersing it in kerosene again.

A starter for wood fires can be created by slowly adding 1 cup of kerosene to 4 cups of sawdust in a large can, stirring steadily. (Stay away from heat and make sure there's adequate ventilation because kerosene is flammable.) When the kerosene is completely and evenly absorbed, cover the can tightly and store it in a closed metal container. Use one-quarter to one-half cup of sawdust to start each fire.

When burning fireplace logs, you can reduce soot by two-thirds by periodically sprinkling salt on them.

To make newspaper logs, coat a 3-foot dowel, or section of broomstick, with paste wax. When the wax dries, buff it to a slick, smooth finish. Next, place a newspaper—open to full-page size—on a large flat surface, and, while holding the dowel firmly at each end, roll sheets of paper onto the dowel as tightly as you can. (Tightly rolled logs burn much longer than loosely rolled ones.) Continue to roll paper onto the dowel till the roll is 3–3½ inches in diameter (log size). Carefully holding the paper in place, fasten the log firmly at each end and in the center with thin wire. Slide the dowel out of the roll, and repeat to make as many logs as needed. (Two to three thick newspaper sections make one log.)

To make a dry fire extinguisher, pour 6 pounds of fine sand into a large container and add 2 pounds of baking soda. Stir the mixture thoroughly. Keep the container in your shop or garage, or pour the mixture into smaller containers for storage elsewhere. This mixture can be sprinkled directly on small oil, grease, and petroleum product fires.

Drawing More Heat

Add a curved-tube convection heater to your fireplace to draw more heat from the fire into the room, instead of letting it escape up the flue.

A curved-tube heater that has a blower unit can double the amount of heat thrown into a room from your fireplace.

When buying a curved-tube heater for your fireplace, be sure to select one that's big enough to fill the opening.

370

Leave the glass doors on a fireplace partially open, or you'll reduce room heat from the fire by as much as 70 percent.

Special Effects

Dried orange peel tossed into a log fire will produce a pleasing and exotic fragrance.

Clean fire-stained brass andirons by dipping fine (00) steel wool in cooking oil and rubbing gently. Then apply a polish to bring up the shine.

Chapter 5

HOLIDAYS

CHRISTMAS, EASTER, VALENTINES, AND EVERY OTHER SPECIAL DAY BRING OUT THESE CREATIVE IDEAS.

The Christmas Tree

You can fireproof a Christmas tree by spraying it with a half-gallon of lukewarm water to which you've added 1 cup of alum, 4 ounces of boric acid, and 2 tablespoons of borax, thoroughly mixing all ingredients. If there's any solution left, pour it into the water in the tree stand.

Make your fresh tree last longer by cutting the trunk by 1 inch on the diagonal after you purchase it. Stand it in a water base, and replenish the water daily.

To keep small children and animals from toppling the Christmas tree, place the tree in a playpen "fence."

If you're going to plant a "living Christmas tree" on your property, do it long before the ground hardens. Dig a hole big enough to accommodate the burlap-covered roots of the tree, then cover the surrounding ground's surface with a thick layer of mulch. When snow begins to fall, the tree should be well established, and it will look spectacular when garnished with lights.

Tree Trimming

Gingerbread men are not just for eating. Hang the cookies as ornaments on the Christmas tree or string them across the room. Before you bake them, punch holes in the head with a straw, so you can thread yarn through them for hanging.

A safe way for storing your Christmas ornaments is to pack them away in divided egg cartons.

When it's time to put away the Christmas ornaments, buy an extra box of hooks and pack them away too. Next year you'll have extra hooks for the new ornaments.

Season's Greetings

Postage stamps stuck together? Put them in the freezer for a while. They'll usually come apart with no damage to the glue.

If you're sentimental about greeting cards you've received and want to preserve them, lightly coat them with hair spray. The hardened spray prevents colors from fading.

Instead of boxed Christmas cards, send personalized season's greetings on note paper trimmed in red or green. Decorate the envelope with seals or stickers.

Be different: Send out New Year's greetings instead of Christmas cards this year.

Make up next year's Christmas card list from the return addresses on the envelopes of this year's cards.

To get into the holiday spirit, tie jingle bells to the knobs of doors you open often, such as clothes closets, and the front and back doors of the house.

Consolidate your Christmas greetings to friends by placing an ad in your local newspaper as a community Christmas card.

Deck the Halls

In lieu of a Christmas tree, decorate the branches of any large house plant with garlands, tiny flashing lights, and red bows.

For a smart-looking table decoration, stack shiny red apples atop a bed of pine branches tied with a red satin bow.

Keep candles standing tall and upright by putting a dab of florist's clay in the bottom of the holder.

To make yuletide candles look new again, spray and wipe them thoroughly with furniture polish.

To make decorative, inexpensive holiday tablecloths, dye white bed sheets red or green in your washing machine. After ironing them, store the cloths wrapped around a broomstick handle to prevent wrinkles.

To display your Christmas cards attractively, cut out a large tree or bell from a piece of felt, paste it to the wall or door, and pin your cards to it.

Display your Christmas cards by stringing them up against a staircase banister or pasting them around a large wall mirror as a decorative border.

Dress up and decorate wooden clothespins to resemble storybook characters, and use them as tree ornaments or gift-package decorations.

Save assorted cartons and boxes throughout the year, and assemble them into a holiday castle. Spray paint with gold or silver, and sprinkle with red and green glitter.

When using candles in a table centerpiece, keep them short, so they won't obstruct your guests' view of one another across the table.

Merrymaking

Host a tree-trimming party for neighbors and friends. Ask them to bring decorations on themes other than Christmas, such as travel, cooking, animals, etc.

Encourage neighborliness by planning a caroling party—and making it an annual event.

Your garage can be transformed into a rest station for neighborhood carolers. Offer pots of hot chocolate and cookies fresh from the oven.

For a festive holiday treat, have a Christmas cookie exchange. Invite neighbors and friends and ask them to bring one or two dozen of their favorite cookies.

Party Clothes

Wear your most attractive and comfortable outfit to every holiday party, and let it be your "signature" dress. It'll eliminate having to shop—and spend—for more than one outfit.

Sew a variety of colored ribbons together to make a holiday apron.

Breeze through Gift Shopping

Holiday shopping won't seem a hassle if you schedule your shopping excursions at off hours, right after the stores open or in midafternoon (2:30–4:40 P.M.) Avoid the crowds on weekends, lunch hours, and at quitting time too.

Team shopping with a friend who has similar needs and interests can save time and money. You'll give each other helpful advice on making the right purchases.

If you're short on time and patience, ask your favorite department store if they have a shopping service. You tell them what you want in any given price range, and they'll shop, gift wrap, and deliver for you, often free of charge or for a small service fee.

If you procrastinate and need a few last-minute gifts, investigate smaller stores that specialize in hardware, health food, lingerie, etc., for some nice items.

Consolidate your gift shopping by buying all your gifts in one department of the store.

Don't start on your shopping trip without an organized list of who you're buying for, their color preferences, and sizes.

To keep track of children when you're shopping in crowded holiday stores, dress them in bright colors, especially a brightly colored cap.

Holiday Helpers

Before the Christmas season begins, keep a file of gift ideas clipped from mail order catalogs and newspaper ads to spur your thinking once you begin to shop.

Hire a neighborhood teenager with a driver's license to hand deliver your gift packages.

Take a photo of your children, opening the gift package from a relative or grandparent, then send the picture to the giver as a thank you note.

If you're the sole guardian of the car keys at your house, the trunk of the car is a great hiding place to stash gifts until Christmas morning.

Hide children's gifts right in their own rooms, out of reach in a closet, or in the bottom of a clothes hamper.

Fill an old mason jar with pretty pebbles and sea shells collected at the beach, tie on a ribbon, and give as a decorative doorstop.

To lighten your luggage at holiday time, have your gifts mailed ahead to their recipients directly from the store.

Gift Ideas

Get into the holiday mood by making festive barrettes. Glue decorative strands of ribbon to the top side of the barrette. At the ends of the ribbons tie pine cones, feathers, or jingle bells.

To wrap an oversize Christmas gift, why not use a paper Christmas tablecloth? It handles easier than several sheets of ordinary wrapping paper.

So that your children have a chance to buy Christmas presents (without your finding out what they're choosing for you), have a neighbor or a friend take them shopping. You, in turn, can return the favor with your neighbor's children.

Use recycled old lace and pretty fabrics to make beautiful Christmas stockings.

Avoid embarrassment at the last moment when you've forgotten to buy a Christmas gift. Just wrap up an issue of a popular magazine and attach a tag saying a subscription is on the way.

Christmas Dinner

For a memorable holiday meal, invite family and friends over to help cook the meal! With everyone in the kitchen, the preparations will be great fun!

Filling a hurricane lamp with glass ball ornaments makes a lovely centerpiece for your holiday table.

Easter

Natural dyes can be put to work at Easter time. You'll have green eggs if you boil them with grass; red if they're boiled with beets; and yellow if onion skins are in the pot.

Valentine's Day

It's easy to make a heart-shaped cake to serve on Valentine's Day. Just bake a round cake and a square one. Face the square one toward you, point forward like a playing card diamond. Slice the round cake in half and position the two halves against the diamond's uppermost sides. Frost and serve.

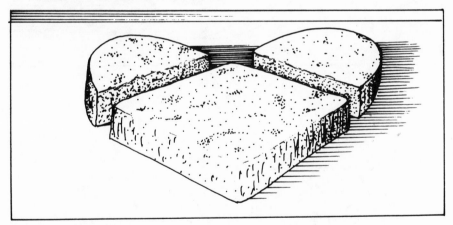

Mother's Day

On Mother's Day, use an oven mitt as the wrapping for a small gift.

Halloween

If you're proud of your carved Halloween pumpkins and want to keep them in firm shape indefinitely, simply spray their inside and outside with an antiseptic, repeating periodically as necessary. The antiseptic destroys the bacteria that normally devour (and thereby soften) pumpkins.

Don't throw out the pumpkin seeds when you're through carving a Halloween pumpkin. Salt the seeds and dry them in the oven for a tasty, nutritious snack the whole family will love.

Part **VI**

DECORATING

The most important element of successful home decorating doesn't cost a thing—it's imagination. For those who are a little reluctant to rely on their own inspiration, this section is a passport to the exciting world of do-it-yourself home beautification. Even if you're one of those people who has a knack for just the right decorating touch, you'll find dozens of fresh ideas to start you off in new directions.

In Chapter 1, "General Decorating Techniques," you'll learn such professional tricks as how to make a room look larger with color and pattern, how to create visual excitement with imaginative, inexpensive window and floor treatments, how to use small spaces creatively and make all your spaces shine. Chapter 2, "Special Decorations," gives you hints on quickly executed chair covers, coffee tables, and decorative accents that will give your rooms a lift.

With these hints and all the others in Chapter 3, "Improvising," and Chapter 4, "Special Projects," you'll be able to reclaim wasted space, making it both functional and attractive, personalize your decorative touches—something no professional decorator can do quite as well as you—and use your home's furnishings originally. These hint-inspired decorating ideas will be the beginning of a whole new enjoyment of your home.

Chapter **1**

GENERAL DECORATING TECHNIQUES

EVEN IF YOU'RE SHORT ON TIME AND MONEY, THESE DECORATING HINTS WILL TAKE YOU A LONG WAY.

Room Magic

A room will appear larger if you paint an oversized piece of furniture the same color as the walls.

Your small rooms can be made to look large by putting mirrors on one wall to reflect the rest of the room.

For a soft room glow, light objects in a room instead of the whole room. Spotlight a piece of art or a bookcase, for example.

Curtains

Lots of hanging plants are a great substitute for curtains.

For a summery, airy window treatment, stretch chiffon or gauze between two dowels and hang them inside the window frame.

For an unusual window covering, attach wooden rings to an antique quilt and hang it from a wide, wooden rod.

If you have an Indian print bedspread not in use, hang it full-width across a window. Open it diagonally across half the window and secure with a tieback.

You can make a curtain panel from a bedsheet by knotting the top corners around a bamboo pole.

Blinds and Shades

Your old wooden blinds can be renovated. If the slats are removable, spread them outdoors on newspaper and finish with high-gloss spray paint or brush-on enamel.

Hang shiny, metallic blinds vertically or horizontally to help reflect summer sun attractively. This works especially well in south and west windows of apartments where you can't construct awnings.

There is no need to invest in drapes if you don't want to. You can brighten up shades by decorating them with colored tape or by gluing fabric on them.

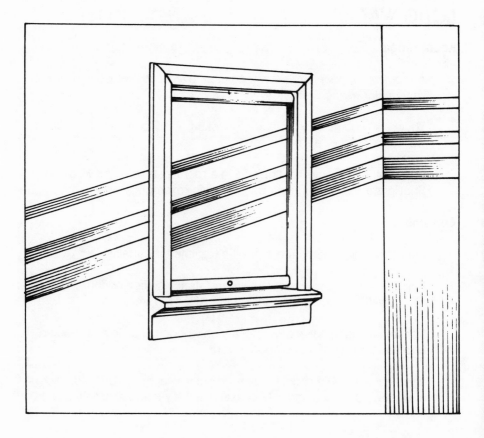

To add color to matchstick blinds, weave rows of colored ribbon through them.

Fancy Floors

Give your floor an exciting new look: Paint it a bright color or paint on a stencil design.

To make a quick floor covering in a beach house, stretch natural-colored painter's canvas from wall to wall, stapling it to the baseboards.

Extra high-gloss vinyl flooring like that used on submarines and naval ship's decks makes the finest flooring for lofts, darkrooms, and photo studios. Inquire at your nearest army surplus.

Sofas and Chairs

For a quick, easy, and inexpensive way to recover a chair, drape a twin-size sheet over the chair, and tie or pin the corners to fit. You can use the same trick to add interest to a small table.

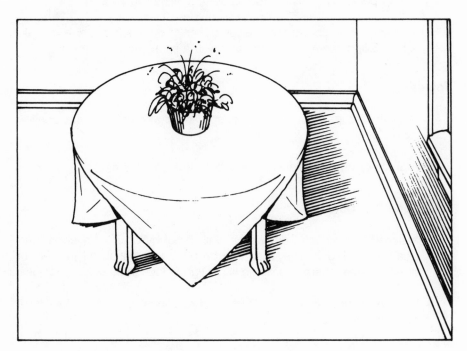

If you have a conversation-pit sofa grouping but no room for a coffee table, just use one of the ottomans and top it with a decorative tray.

If you use the same fabric on two different chairs, it will tie the decor of the room together.

Papering It Over

If you want to make a large room seem smaller or cozier, choose a wallpaper with a large, bold pattern. Don't, however, use it in a small room because it will make the available space seem crowded.

A mural-pattern wallpaper makes a small room appear larger.

When selecting a wallpaper for a particular room, keep in mind the dominant colors already present in that room. One or more of those colors should be present in the wallpaper to tie everything together.

Wallpapers now come in mix-and-match patterns, simplifying the problem of papering adjoining rooms without visual clashes.

To make a high ceiling seem lower, paper it with a bold pattern. To make a low ceiling seem higher, paper it with a small print or a texture.

Tables

Mexican serapes and Indian bedspreads make colorful, inexpensive table cloths.

A pretty or unusual blanket can substitute as a table cloth.

Doors and Partitions

Matchstick blinds can disguise a wall of hobby or utility shelves for a clean, unified look. They also can be used to partition off a closet or dressing area where you would like a lighter look than a door provides.

In a beach house, use roll-down window blinds to make a door for a doorless room.

Office

No shelf space? Hang slatted boxes for storage of scissors, envelopes, even a cassette recorder. Drape a shade-loving ivy in the topmost box.

Fasten bright and colorful paper shopping bags to the wall for storage of art supplies and other lightweight items.

For office brighteners, put pencils and pens in a flowerpot and use a music stand for a magazine rack.

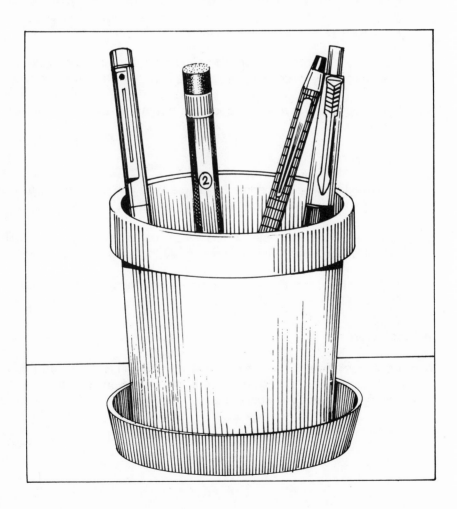

386

Hardware

You'll never have trouble tightening screws and bolts if you remember that for most, right is tight and left is loose.

For an easy way to give a room a facelift, update hardware, such as doorknobs, drawer pulls, and curtain rods.

Baskets

Place baskets of shells on a low table or show them off in glass canisters.

A basketful of pinecones in front of the fireplace is especially lovely.

Storing your needlework or mending in a pretty basket under a side table or in the foyer is decorative and adds a feeling of warmth to the area.

Keep your decorative baskets looking healthy by placing them away from dry heat.

No Wasted Space

A nonworking fireplace, primed and freshened with paint, makes a cozy niche for a sewing machine table or an aquarium.

A stairway landing is the perfect place for an armoire. Line it with attractive fabric and fill it with linens, coats, or out-of-season clothes.

Turn your bathroom into a miniature gallery by hanging your old pictures that don't fit on other walls.

A Last Resort

If you don't want to buy furniture just yet, you can rent it at surprisingly reasonable rates. Furniture for rent includes everything from sofas, carpets, and lamps to works of art.

Chapter **2**

SPECIAL DECORATIONS

GIVE ANY ROOM A BRIGHT NEW FACE WITH THESE UNUSUAL TOUCHES.

Special Decorations

A silver goblet is perfect for holding cigarettes on a coffee table.

Replace a drab string cord or light-bulb chain with a piece of satin piping or silver cord. Put a pretty ceramic bead at the end of the cord for a finishing touch.

Add a miniature hammock to a corner in a child's room to make a place for all his or her stuffed animals.

A branch cut from any blossoming tree or bush makes an unusual centerpiece on a dining or coffee table.

Display flowers in unusual "vases" such as a crystal ice bucket or fluted champagne glasses.

Buy gourds in the fall at the supermarket. Use them for a month or so in an arrangement, then put them someplace warm and dry for a while. The gourds become very light as they dry, and the colors mute beautifully with age.

Use leftover dining room wallpaper to make matching place mats. Paste the paper onto sturdy cardboard and coat each mat with a plastic spray.

When drying flowers or vegetables, most have to be hung upside down in small bundles in a dark, dry place for a few weeks. Try hanging branches by strings of different lengths from coat hangers. This allows for good air circulation.

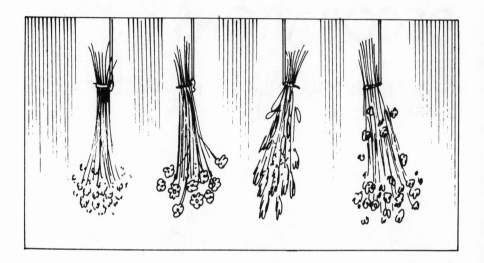

To keep drying flowers dust-free, cover them with plastic bags punched with air holes. When the flowers have dried, spray them with hairspray to get a clear matte finish, to keep them from shedding, to keep insects away, and to protect them from moisture.

Some flowers and foliage can be placed in a vase without water and dried upright. Pussy willows, wild grasses, and grains and flowers with large composite heads and sturdy stalks such as Queen Anne's lace and cockscomb are perfect.

Layer seeds and nuts in attractive apothecary bottles.

Glue corn pads to the rough bottoms of vases and art objects to keep them from scratching tables.

Hot peppers threaded on long string make a beautiful kitchen decoration while drying. Why not try artichokes, garlic, broccoli, brussels sprouts, onions—even cauliflower or cabbage, too?

Chapter **3**

IMPROVISING

FIND NEW USES FOR OLD ITEMS, OR GIVE A DOUBLE IDENTITY TO OLD FAVORITES.

Hot Pads

A decorative hot pad for the table or kitchen counter can be made from one or more attractive ceramic tiles.

Shower Curtain Rod

Suspend a hula hoop over the bathtub to make a shower curtain rod.

Curtains

You can make small window curtains from pretty dish towels.

Window Curtain Rod

Old, carved door knobs, attached to each end of a dowel, make an attractive curtain rod. Paint or stain the knobs to match your furniture.

Lampshade

A basket turned upside down makes a wonderful lampshade.

Scented Rooms

A handy deodorizer for wastebaskets in your house: Place a sheet of fabric softener inside the bottom of each wastepaper can.

Throw Pillows

Dimestore bandannas make pretty, inexpensive pillow covers. Buy assorted colors for a colorful effect.

Use old pantyhose to stuff pillows and toys.

Centerpiece

Any combination of fruits in a bowl can double as both centerpiece and dessert.

For those who can't get to the woods, use a basket of Italian onions for a lovely centerpiece when serving an Italian dinner. Pomegranates are also beautiful in bowls.

You can make unusual centerpieces in no time by floating one or two flowers in clear glass dessert dishes. Fill the dishes—half-way—with water, cut the stem from the flowers, and place them in the dishes.

Arrange beet lettuce in vases by day and use it in your salads by night.

Place a pineapple top in a plain little sugar bowl and insert feathers into the leaves to make a centerpiece.

Wall Decoration

An old kimono can be draped on a wall for an elegant splash of texture and color.

A bicycle hanging on a wall becomes a piece of art as well as functional.

Chapter 4

SPECIAL PROJECTS

SOME FANCIFUL DECORATING IDEAS THAT ARE WORTH THE EXTRA BIT OF TIME AND EFFORT.

A Tropical Touch

With an old-fashioned ceiling fan, avoid using a light dimmer switch as a variable speed control. A light dimmer switch can't handle the load involved. Use only a speed control and lighting-fixture outlet designed for your specific brand of fan.

Don't install an old-fashioned ceiling fan too close to curtains, or the blades may rip them away from the window. And if you install one in your bedroom, be careful when raising your arms to remove clothing. A whirling blade can give your wrists a nasty crack.

Never install an old-fashioned ceiling fan on a ceiling that's less than 8 feet high, since the blades twirl about a foot lower. If the ceiling is too low, the blades are close enough to head level to be dangerous.

Special Projects

An old dining table found at a flea market makes a great sofa-height coffee table. Just cut the legs to the height you need.

There's no need to invest in wallpaper to give your walls new life. A super graphic on the wall can make a room exciting!

Change the look of an old formica table by laminating it with colorful fabric.

Make an extra closet into a cozy book nook for quiet reading. Simply remove the door, install a wall lamp, shelves, and a comfy chair.

You can make cheap floor rugs by stenciling canvas with nontoxic acrylic paints.

You can make inexpensive book cases out of flue tiles or conduit pipes. And the cubbyhole effect is perfect for storing wine!

Part VII

HEALTH AND DIET

Sound nutrition and good health are two essential keys for a long and happy life. By giving your body the best food to keep it well fueled and regular exercise to keep it well tuned, you can look forward to vitality and energy in every phase of your life.

Chapter 1, "Healthy Eating," brings you suggestions and information on creating a well-balanced and nutritious diet. With these tips, you can increase your intake of fresh, unprocessed foods and begin to moderate the amount of fat, sugar, and salt in your family's diet. Also included are imaginative flavor substitutions for salt and fat in cooking and hints on good nutrition for the special needs of growing children, pregnant women, and senior citizens. If you've got to eat on the run, you'll want to try all the suggestions for delicious, healthful, and money-saving brown-bag lunches, too.

When you or someone in your family is trying to lose weight, look into Chapter 2 for guidance and good ideas. You won't find gimmicky instant-weight-loss tricks, but you will find down-to-earth suggestions to help you cut down on calories through cooking know-how and yummy low-calorie food substitutions. There are even tips for the traveling dieter.

Whether or not you're trying to lose weight, exercise and fitness make you feel better and look better. The tips in Chapter 3 are a handbook for exercising and warm-up techniques; there are even suggestions to spur nonathletic, never-exercise folks into action. And if you just want to work on one or two problem areas, you'll find dozens of exercises from which to choose, from the top of your head to the tip of your toes. A very special section also deals with the fitness needs of pregnant women and senior citizens.

The best ways for coping with stress are covered in Chapter 4. Natural methods, including exercise, deep breathing, and relaxation techniques, can help you manage the million and one little frustrations that often leave you feeling tense and full of stress. There are even hints to make driving your car a stress-free experience.

Chapter 5, "Medical Matters," tells you how to choose a good doctor and how to evaluate his or her services. And when the sickness or injury is minor, you'll want to turn to the pages on home remedies, often saving a costly visit to the doctor. Or, in case of an accident or emergency, there are a variety of first-aid techniques that could save the day.

Good health is one of the precious gifts of life—learn to maintain it with these healthful, helpful hints.

Chapter 1

HEALTHY EATING

GOOD SENSE COMBINES WITH GOOD TASTE IN THESE POINTERS ON HOW TO EAT FOR HEALTH.

A WELL BALANCED DIET

Good Changes

Take a positive approach when making healthy changes in your diet and lifestyle. Instead of thinking of what you're giving up, think of all the wonderful new things you're getting.

You can improve your chances for a long and healthy life simply by cutting down on the fat, salt, caffeine, and sugar in your diet. The average American eats four times more fat, forty times more salt and caffeine, and one hundred times more sugar than the body needs.

Eating a nutritious breakfast every morning and avoiding snacks between meals are two of the easiest ways to improve your eating habits.

Smoking destroys your body's supply of Vitamin C. Drink a glass of orange juice in the morning instead of lighting up a cigarette.

Eating between meals upsets the proper functioning of your metabolism. If you must snack, try raisins, nuts, apples, or crunchy vegetables instead of sugary foods.

Moderation in All Things

A balanced diet is a varied diet. It's best to eat many kinds of foods in order to ensure that your body gets all the proteins, carbohydrates, fats, vitamins, and minerals it needs. Most people really don't need to take vitamin and mineral supplements. A well-balanced diet should provide you with all the vitamins and minerals required for good health.

Foods closest to their natural state are the best for you. Vegetables you've grown in your own backyard are far superior to commercial frozen, canned, or dehydrated products. But you can also home-can, freeze, and dry your garden's surplus without any of the preservatives or additives usually found in the supermarket versions.

High-fiber vegetables, fruits, and whole grains are natural intestinal cleansers and also help to keep down the levels of cholesterol in the blood by binding up cholesterol and fats. Studies also show that a daily dose of bran in your breakfast cereal reduces the risk of bowel cancer.

Drink at least seven to eight glasses of water daily. Water cleanses your system and promotes healthy-looking skin.

The Sweet and Sour of It

Sugar is a culprit in the development of tooth decay, obesity, diabetes, and cardiovascular disease. If you do nothing else to improve your diet, at least cut down on your intake of sugar.

Cookies, cakes, and candies made with sugar provide only "empty calories"—that is, they have no nutritional value.

Put natural sugar in your diet by replacing baked goods and other fattening desserts with fresh fruits.

When you need a pick-me-up, try drinking a glass of fruit juice or fresh, cold water instead of a sweetened soft drink or chewing gum.

Substitute dark molasses in place of sugar whenever possible. Molasses has a natural laxative effect.

Sugar is sugar, no matter what form it takes. Don't be misled by "sugarless" products that contain corn syrup, honey, molasses, maltose, glucose, dextrose, and invert sugar. These are just other names for sugar. If you must avoid sugar for medical reasons, read labels carefully.

Don't Salt It Away

Your body needs no more than a teaspoon of salt a day under normal circumstances. Too much salt in the diet can lead to high blood pressure, overweight, and heart and circulatory problems.

You can cut down on salt painlessly by leaving it out of your cooking, by removing the salt shaker from the table, and by using salt substitutes if you really miss the taste.

Substitute herbs, spices, and pepper in place of salt when seasoning foods.

Use lemon and lime wedges and juices to flavor vegetables in place of salt.

Eating licorice can help your body to retain salt and water, thus reducing your craving for salt. Licorice can also raise your blood pressure.

Reduce the salt content of instant broth by using twice as much water as the package directions indicate.

Most commercial canned foods are swimming in salt. Canned soups are especially high, containing one gram of salt (half the amount you need for a whole day). Read labels carefully.

Remember Jack Sprat?

A high-fat diet can be dangerous to your health. When cooking, use polyunsaturated fats such as corn, soybean, and sunflower oil instead of saturated fats such as lard, butter, chicken fat, coconut oil, or hydrogenated vegetable oils.

Low-fat skim milk is a healthier choice than whole milk. Skim milk cheeses and low-fat cottage cheese and yogurt are also to be preferred.

When buying meats, look for the leanest cuts. Trim off any visible fat before cooking, and choose broiling over any other preparation method. Broiling can reduce the fat content of meat by up to one-half.

You can improve your whole family's diet by beginning to replace some meat dishes with fish and poultry. You'll be eating less fat, earning high marks for nutritional value—and getting all that for less calories.

Begin to experiment with meatless meals to cut down on your fat intake and to increase the amount of good sources of fiber. The choice is almost endless, and your family will enjoy meatless spaghetti sauce, chili, and vegetable soup as much as the meaty versions.

The News about Protein

Legumes, especially peas and beans, are an excellent source of protein and should be included in your weekly menus.

Whole-grain bread, pasta, potatoes, rice, and other grains are good energy foods and sources of protein.

Avoid eating too much of preserved meats such as ham, hot dogs, and corned beef. Processed meats contain chemical additives.

Cook Right to Eat Right

Don't toss away the darker outer leaves of your lettuce head. They're higher in nutrients than the leaves found closer to the core.

Scrub vegetables with a vegetable brush to remove any surface dirt before cooking. Don't remove the skins, because you'll also be throwing out most of the vitamins and minerals.

Cook your vegetables briefly by steaming them. Overcooked vegetables lose their Vitamin C and mineral content.

Fry your foods in a nonstick pan, which requires no additional oil for frying.

Although broiling is best, you can also substantially reduce the fat and calorie content of meat by boiling or pot-roasting it.

If you're allergic to wheat, use any of the following substitutes for one cup of wheat flour: 1¼ cups rye flour, ¾ cup rice flour, 1⅓ cups oat flour; 1 cup corn flour; ¾ cup coarse cornmeal; 1 cup fine cornmeal; or ⅝ cup potato starch flour.

Let's Have Healthy Children

Be sure your child's diet contains lots of milk and milk products, as well as enriched breads and green, leafy vegetables. These foods are high in calcium, which is essential to building strong bones and healthy teeth.

Begin to wean your children away from sugar treats by preparing their breakfasts with unsweetened cereals. Sweeten with raw honey, sliced bananas, chopped apples, or raisins. Though kids may still eat sugary foods away from home, at least you'll be helping them to cut back on the total intake.

In place of candy, potato chips, and pretzels, give your youngsters snacks that are rich in vitamins: sunflower seeds, raw almonds or cashews, roasted soy nuts, or dried fruits.

Flavored milk and milk shakes are healthier drinks for children's teeth than soft drinks. If children do drink soft drinks, buy the artificially sweetened varieties.

404

Summer Thoughts

Cut out as much sugar as possible from your diet in the summer. Mosquitoes are attracted to people with high sugar consumption.

If you're often out in the sun, stay away from caffeine drinks such as coffee, tea, or cola. Caffeine makes your skin more sensitive.

Eat smaller meals more often in summer. Your body will have to work less to digest the foods, and you'll feel cooler.

Use more salt in your foods during the summer months. You'll need to replace the salt your body loses due to heavy perspiration.

Eating Right During Pregnancy

To control weight gain during pregnancy, cut down on sweets but not on whole-grain bread and potatoes. You need their nutrients and protein for energy.

To reduce feelings of nausea, try eating only cold foods.

If you can't tolerate any other foods in the morning, at least eat bread or dry toast with milk.

To ensure that your diet contains a good supply of Vitamins A and D, eat liver or an oily fish such as herring, sardines, or mackerel once a week.

To prevent constipation, eat fiber-rich foods such as whole-grain breads and lots of fresh fruits and vegetables.

To control nausea, take small sips of cola or bites of bland food, such as custard, gelatin, or mashed potatoes, throughout the day.

Nibbling on nuts, cheese, or other high-protein foods can help relieve feelings of nausea in early pregnancy if done every two to three hours. Substitute these frequent nutritious snacks for three heavy meals a day.

Eating a cracker with a glass of milk before bedtime helps reduce heartburn and ensures a sound sleep.

Good Eating Tips for Seniors

If you're susceptible to colds, fortify your diet with extra Vitamin C by drinking lots of fruit juice or rose-hip tea.

To keep your bones from getting brittle, be sure that your diet is rich in calcium (milk products) and Vitamins A, C, and D (citrus and vegetable juices).

A tablespoon of brewer's yeast added to a glass of fruit or vegetable juice or of milk acts as a natural laxative.

Substitute honey for sugar as a sweetener. It serves as a natural laxative.

To calm an upset stomach, drink a glass of buttermilk or skim milk mixed with a tablespoon of cider vinegar.

EATING ON THE RUN

Easy Lunch Box Fix-Ups

Freeze a carton of yogurt overnight. The yogurt will be thawed by lunchtime the next day, and you'll have a delicious, low-calorie lunch ready.

You can fix lunches for the entire week on Sunday night. Hard-boil a dozen eggs and fry two chickens. Then wrap each piece securely in plastic wrap and divide into lunch bags, with a different piece of fruit and cheese for each day of the week. Store the bags in the refrigerator and take one out each morning on your way to work.

You can make and freeze sandwiches up to two weeks ahead of time, provided you use no jelly, mayonnaise, eggs, lettuce, or tomato in the filling. Butter your bread, add the sandwich filling, and wrap your sandwiches tightly in plastic wrap before storing in the freezer. A sandwich removed from the freezer in the morning will be ready to eat by lunchtime.

During hot weather, you can freeze sandwiches containing mayonnaise or salad dressing the night before, even though mayonnaise separates when it's frozen. If you can't keep your lunch refrigerated before eating, the sandwiches will thaw nicely without spoiling from the heat.

Plan box lunches that are a well-balanced meal. Include a protein-rich food, something crispy, a beverage or soup, and a treat.

Make extra servings of chili and stews to use in your lunch box. Pour them hot into vacuum containers for eating the next day, or freeze in serving-size portions for later in the week.

Freeze cartons of prepared shrimp or crab cocktail. They'll thaw out but still be cold by the time you're ready to eat lunch.

Sandwiches to Go

Pita bread makes a perfect pocket to hold your favorite filling for an easy sandwich. Fill pita with grated cheese, cottage cheese mixed with tomatoes, onions, and cucumbers, a spread made from chick–pea, or pâté. Add plain yogurt and shredded lettuce just before eating.

To prevent soggy sandwiches, moistureproof your sandwich bread by spreading on a thin layer of margarine or butter before adding the filling.

For more energy and nutrition from your lunch, make sandwiches from whole-grain breads and buns instead of white bread.

You can cut down on calories at lunch by eating hamburgers and sandwiches open faced, with only one slice of bread or bun.

Light Lunches

A 40-ounce plastic freezer container provides the perfect lunch box for carrying salad fixings to the office. Add a low-calorie dressing of lemon juice and herbs just before eating so your salad won't be limp.

Fill little plastic bags with an assortment of fresh vegetable sticks for a light vegetarian lunch.

You can avoid that mid-afternoon slump that usually follows close on the heels of a heavy lunch by choosing salad instead.

In a Hurry

Eat your lunch while you work so you can use your lunch hour to visit a museum, do some shopping, or take a lunchtime exercise class.

A packet of powdered skim milk provides a quick, vitamin-packed, liquid lunch. It's also a great source of protein, calcium, and Vitamin B_2 for energy.

Make a batch of energy cookies to keep in your desk for days when you miss lunch. Here's how: Cream ½ cup butter and ¾ cup sugar. Beat in 1 egg. Combine with 1 cup flour and ¼ teaspoon baking soda, then stir in ½ pound crisp crumbled bacon, 2 cups cornflakes, and ½ cup raisins. Bake at 350°F for 15 to 18 minutes. Cool.

For an eat-on-the-run energy lunch, mix one fresh egg yolk into a glass of orange juice. Add a teaspoon of honey to sweeten.

Get a supply of protein tablets from your health food store and keep them in your desk to boost your energy when meetings run late and you miss lunch.

Even if you're in a hurry, don't gulp down your lunch. You'll only suffer indigestion later. Set aside at least 15 minutes and eat slowly, chewing your food well.

Instead of taking a coffee and doughnut break, take an exercise break instead. Treat yourself to a handful of raw seeds or nuts afterward.

Perking Up Those Brown Bags

To keep brown bag lunches from getting blah, trade parts of your lunch with other brown baggers in the office.

Several ice cubes sealed with a twist tie in a plastic bag is an easy ice bag for keeping your lunch cold.

Keep a mouthwash concentrate in your purse or desk to mask the scent of any onions or garlic eaten at lunch.

Chapter **2**

WATCHING YOUR WEIGHT

TRYING TO LOSE WEIGHT? USE THESE HINTS TO TIP THE SCALES IN YOUR FAVOR.

The Bare Facts

Gaining or losing weight is basically a matter of addition or subtraction. Each pound on your body is worth 3,500 calories. In order to lose one pound, you must cut back by 3,500 calories. In order to gain one pound, you must increase your food intake by 3,500 calories.

Don't expect to lose weight by exercising. It will take you forever to shed a significant number of pounds. Dieting is much more effective. Exercise will tone you while you're shedding those extra pounds.

Despite extravagant claims by certain advertisers and certain health clubs, vibrating machines, body massages, saunas, and steam baths won't really reduce your weight. True, you'll lose a lot of body fluid because of perspiration, but the fluid will return as soon as you drink water.

Make It Easy on Yourself

Instead of spending extra money on diet foods or low-calorie items, eat what you normally do but cut the amount in half.

Drink eight glasses of water a day and you'll feel full between meals with no calorie intake.

Break the habit of always eating while you're busy doing something else, such as watching TV or reading. Making just a single change in your snacking habits can help you shed unwanted pounds.

If you're having trouble losing weight, don't keep foods that can be eaten without extensive preparation around the house. The thought of having to spend time preparing goodies may deter you from eating them.

Cutting down on alcohol will also significantly reduce the amount of calories you take in. Some people lose weight simply by eliminating alcohol from their diet altogether.

Friendly Persuasion

Keep a record of everything you eat, and it'll be easier to reinforce your goals for weight loss.

If you eat your meals with someone whose company you enjoy, you'll probably talk more and eat less.

If you feel you want seconds of some food, tell yourself you can have it in five minutes. During that time, keep busy doing something else and you'll probably forget about the extra food.

For a super dieting trick, always leave a bit of food on the plate.

Use smaller plates for your diet-size meals. Portions look more satisfying on a smaller plate, and you won't feel "cheated." The same strategy applies to wine glasses and dessert dishes: use small ones.

When you're on a diet, foods that take longer to eat can be more satisfying than easy-to-eat foods. For example, corn on the cob seems like more than the same amount of cut corn, and lobster in the shell will keep you busy longer than a boneless steak, allowing you time to reach a "full" feeling.

If you're on a diet, it might help to turn after-meal clean-up over to somebody else. That way you won't be tempted to munch on leftovers as you're putting them away.

Information for Dieters

It's best to look for specific calorie information on "dietetic" foods, because a "dietetic" product doesn't always contain fewer calories; it may simply be salt-free. For example, some "dietetic" candies made for diabetics have just as many calories as regular candy.

If you're drinking one sugar-sweetened cola per day, you could lose nearly 15 pounds in one year by substituting a diet drink—or by eliminating the cola altogether.

Lean Canadian bacon is a better choice for dieters than regular bacon, which is more than half fat even after it's been broiled or fried and well drained. Canadian bacon contains only 45 calories an ounce compared with 200 for regular bacon.

Dips made from packaged mixes pack a weighty wallop of calories, but it isn't the mix that makes them fattening—it's what they're mixed with.

Most packaged mixes add only 50 calories, but the directions call for a base of sour cream (485 calories per cup) or cream cheese (850 calories in an 8-ounce package). You can cut calories dramatically by substituting plain, unsweetened yogurt for sour cream—only 130 calories—or the low calorie, low-fat "imitation" cream cheese—only 416 calories.

If you check the nutritional label panels of competing products and choose one with the lowest calorie count, you can save calories the same way a cost-conscious shopper saves money.

The lower the fat content in dairy products, the fewer calories they contain. For example, cottage cheese that's labeled 99 percent fat-free is only 160 to 180 calories a cup, while regular creamed cottage cheese is 240 to 260 calories.

The word "imitation" on low-calorie, low-sugar, or low-fat products doesn't necessarily mean that the product is made up of chemicals, only that the lower sugar or fat content keeps the product from conforming to standard recipes. Often the imitations are more nutritious than the real thing. For example, low-sugar jams and preserves contain more fruit and less sugar, and the so-called imitation low-fat cheeses have a higher protein content.

Fat-Free Forever

When making stews and other dishes containing grease or fats, prepare them ahead and then store them in the refrigerator. The fat will rise to the surface, where you can easily lift it off.

Substitute yogurt for whipped cream or artificial dessert toppings.

Substitute club soda or mineral water for that evening cocktail. Eat fresh vegetables from the relish tray instead of fattening hors d'oeuvres.

To cut down on calories, season your vegetables with lemon juice and your favorite herbs instead of butter.

Dieters can snack, too, if their diet allows for it. There are many snacks that fall under 100 calories. Try 5 ounces of ginger ale over a peeled and separated orange. Or add a spritz of orange and lemon to tomato juice, then blend with ice cubes. And enjoy lots of raw vegetables along with ⅓ cup of plain yogurt splashed with herbs for dipping.

A cup of plain herbal tea (no cream or sugar) is your best bet for a no-calorie, no-caffeine, low-cost beverage.

In place of two slices of bread, roll your sandwich filling into lettuce leaves for a low-calorie lunch.

A low-calorie substitute for sour cream: Mix cottage cheese in your blender until smooth and flavor it with herbs.

The Traveling Diet

When traveling by car while you're on a diet pack some dietetic meals that won't spoil, such as tuna, fruit, and diet drinks.

If you're on a special diet and are taking a plane trip, call the airline 24 hours in advance to ask them to serve you one of their low-calorie diet meals.

The Party-Goer's Diet

To avoid gorging yourself at holiday parties, drink a glass of skim milk or eat a piece of fruit before you go. You won't feel like devouring everything in sight once you get there.

Don't waste party leftovers but don't let them go to your waist. Offer guests the option of taking a doggie bag home with them.

Chapter 3

EXERCISE AND FITNESS

STAYING IN SHAPE BRINGS YOU HEALTH AND BEAUTY DIVIDENDS TO LAST A LIFETIME.

YOUR EXERCISE PROGRAM

Use It or Lose It

Vigorous exercise brings both mental and physical benefits. Not only does it send more blood to the heart and improve the heart's pumping activity, but it makes you feel good and less likely to crave cigarettes, alcohol, and junk foods.

Walking, biking, swimming, or jogging are among the best forms of aerobic exercise. Whichever you choose, it should be something you enjoy. Otherwise, you won't get the mental benefits—and you probably won't stick with it very long, either.

If you take in more calories than you burn up, you'll soon find yourself overweight. In order to lose weight, you must combine sound nutrition with vigorous exercise—at least 20 minutes of aerobic exercise, three times a week. Exercising strenuously one day a week can do more harm than good and won't make up for not exercising on a steady basis during the rest of the week.

Design an exercise program for yourself that helps to tone each part of the body: arms, chest, waistline, legs, and abdomen. Always do warm-up and cool-down exercises as part of your daily regimen.

Take the pinch test for fatness: If you can pinch more than an inch of fat in the fold of skin just above your hipbone, you're out of shape and in need of an exercise program.

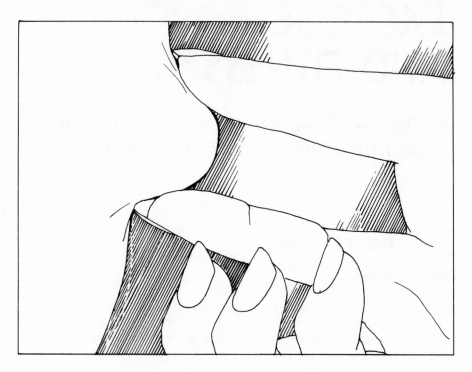

Carry a sweater or sweatshirt to wear after exercising, but *don't* put it on immediately after you finish. Wait until you've cooled down a bit, or you may actually interfere with the body's normal efforts to eliminate excess heat.

If jogging, swimming, bicycling, or dancing just aren't your cup of tea, you can still add lots of exercise to your life. Try getting off the bus or train a few blocks ahead of your stop, and then walk briskly the rest of the way. Or walk up and down stairs instead of riding an elevator. You might also get up a little earlier each morning and take a good 15-minute walk before breakfast.

Exercise is a good preventive measure against heart disease. Sedentary people are twice as prone to heart attack as those who exercise regularly.

Get Off to a Good Start

Exercise will benefit most people—no matter what their age. However, if you're over 35 and have been sedentary until now, be sure to check with a knowledgeable doctor before starting a gradual exercise program.

Exercise anytime during the day that suits your schedule, except the hour after eating a meal.

Plan to exercise at the same time every day so that exercising becomes a habit.

It's a good idea to drink an 8-ounce glass of water before you exercise. If you're a runner, you should also drink on the run: A glass of water for every five miles you cover.

Wear comfortable clothing that doesn't restrict your body movements while you're exercising. Also, wear clothing made of a natural fiber like cotton, which breathes and lets your perspiration evaporate.

Using Good Sense

Avoid the "weekend athlete" pattern. To be sedentary from Monday through Friday, and then frantically active on Saturday and Sunday, can put a heart-damaging strain on your body.

Also avoid the "vacation athlete" pattern. To be sedentary for 50 weeks out of the year, and overly energetic for 2 successive weeks, can land you in the hospital. It's far better to exercise regularly.

Don't Forget to Warm Up

Always warm up and cool down your body before and after exercising to lessen the chance of injury or muscle strain. Sit-ups and leg-stretches should be included in any series of warm-up stretches. You can cool down nicely by finishing off your exercise period with some walking.

Try this deep-breathing routine to warm up for exercising: Standing straight with your arms at your sides, rise up on your toes while making small circles with your arms as you raise them over your head. Inhale deeply while doing this movement. Then, exhale slowly as you lower your arms to your sides and lower your heels.

Another good warm-up is to stand with your hands on your hips, feet together, then jump from side to side for a minute to get your circulation going and to loosen your muscles.

You'll get the most benefit from your exercise movements if you do them on the floor, softening it a bit with a mat or large bath towel.

To condition your body for skiing, practice the following exercise: Hold on to the edge of a chair and extend your right leg in front of you at least one foot off the floor. Lower your body to a squatting position without letting your leg touch the floor. Come up again to your original standing position and repeat this sequence with your left leg extended. Alternate five times with each leg.

Fit as a Fiddle

If you get regular exercise in the form of physical work or vigorous work-outs, you'll be fit as a fiddle—and you'll also sleep like a baby every night.

When doing any aerobic exercise, use the "talk test" to determine whether you're working at the proper rate. If you can't talk normally while exercising, it means you're working too hard and too fast.

Walking briskly is excellent exercise for your heart, lungs, and general muscle tone. Walking at a good clip burns off 360 calories an hour.

Whenever you drop a piece of paper during the day, do either a deep knee bend or a toe-touch while retrieving it.

Buy a heavyweight rope at the hardware store and skip rope while you watch the nightly news or your favorite television program. To benefit your heart and circulation, keep up nonstop for five minutes. Or try running in place for five minutes.

To tone your entire body and increase your circulation, stand up straight with your elbows bent at shoulder level. Pump your arms as you gently jump your legs up to your chest. Alternate and lift each leg at least five times.

Bicycling is a good overall body conditioner and benefits both your respiration and your leg muscles.

Swimming will strengthen your leg, arm, back, and abdominal muscles.

Have Fun with It

Go slowly when you first begin any exercise program. It's best to build up your stamina gradually.

Don't jog immediately after eating a meal or in very hot or cold weather. Running tracks and grass are the safest surfaces for your feet. Avoid running on concrete whenever possible.

Exercising in any extremes of humidity and temperature can cause strain. Remember to take it easy and take frequent rest periods. On very hot and humid or on very cold days, it may be best to skip exercising.

Stop exercising if you feel chest pain or shortness of breath. If either condition continues longer than five minutes, get medical attention.

Don't continue to exercise if you suffer a strain or a sprain. Give your body a chance to recuperate by taking a rest from physical activity for a few days.

Good Jogging Gear

Sneakers don't provide your feet with enough support when jogging, and wearing them could result in injury. Outfit your feet with comfortable running shoes that have firm soles, a good arch support, and flexibility. It's worth the investment.

Women should wear specially designed sports bras for added support and protection when jogging.

When jogging, wear cotton clothes that allow perspiration to evaporate. Rubberized or plastic garments will make you sweat more initially, but will eventually produce chills.

In cold weather, insulate your feet by wearing two pairs of socks. Wear a nylon or rayon pair next to your feet, and cover these with a heavy cotton or wool pair.

ALL-OVER EXERCISES

First Thing in the Morning

Take a tip from cats, who are among the most supple, athletic creatures alive, and stretch when you get out of bed every morning. Stretching loosens the muscles and lengthens the spine, both of which aid in good posture.

Sitting on the edge of the bed, drop your upper body between your legs, then slowly raise your arms up toward the ceiling as you arch your back and hold for five seconds. Stretching early in the morning will revitalize all the muscles in your body.

While lying on the edge of the bed, raise your left leg and swing it over your right leg while trying to touch your toes to the floor. Move to the opposite edge of the bed and repeat by swinging your right leg over your left.

Stand on one foot without any extra support while you put on your shoes and socks. This will strengthen your leg muscles and improve your balance.

To stretch tense back muscles, extend your leg onto the back of a chair or a window sill at waist height. Reach for your ankle with both hands and stretch as far as possible while you bend your knee slightly. Hold for five seconds, then repeat with your other leg.

To stretch and strengthen your back and legs, sit on the edge of the bed and pull the knee of your right leg up to the chest, clasping both arms around the back of the leg. Slowly extend your leg forward, keeping it as straight as possible, then slowly lower it back down to the floor. Repeat with your left leg, alternating leg stretches six times.

Sit on the edge of the bed with your feet flat on the floor. Take a deep breath while you raise your shoulders up to your ears. Exhale slowly while you lower your shoulders and relax. Repeat three times.

Keep Your Balance

To improve overall balance and muscle tone, stand up straight and bring your right knee up to your chest, grasping your lower right leg with both hands. Pull your thighs as tight to your chest as you can, keeping your back straight. Hold this position for ten seconds, and then repeat with your left leg.

Anytime Is a Good Time

After your shower or bath, vigorously rub your body with a bath towel. This not only increases the circulation, but also improves your skin tone by sloughing off dead skin cells.

If you tend to sit all day at your job, stand every once in a while to make your phone calls. It's good for your circulation and bone structure.

Your Face Needs Exercise, Too

To strengthen and tighten your neck muscles, break into a wide grin as you tense your neck muscles. Repeat ten times.

To firm up your cheek muscles, open your mouth wide and act as if you're about to scream. Hold this position for several seconds, then relax and repeat several times.

To strengthen eye muscles and smooth the skin surrounding your eyes, open your eyes as widely as possible and hold them open. Look to the right, the left, then up and down for several seconds each. Close your eyes to relax, then repeat the movements five times.

To reduce laugh lines around your mouth, pucker up as if you're about to whistle and hold this position for a few seconds, then relax. Pucker up ten times.

To exercise your jaw muscles, put your lips into a pucker and move them in a circular direction for five seconds.

Smile often during the day. It's a great and easy way to exercise your facial muscles.

To prevent age lines around your mouth, fill your cheeks with air and press your fists against your cheeks without releasing any of the air. Count to ten, then blow out the air slowly. Repeat the sequence ten times.

The Natural Facelift

To slim that double chin, stick out your chin and pull your lower teeth over your upper teeth. Turn your head as far as it will go to the right, then as far as it will go to the left.

You can lift your facial muscles by holding your cheeks tightly with your hands, then moving your mouth from side to side as far as it will go.

Exercise your facial muscles by opening your mouth and eyes as wide as you can, then holding this position for ten seconds. Next, squeeze your face as tightly as you can for five seconds, then relax.

Yawning is one of the best exercises of all for your facial muscles, and it also forces you to get more fresh air into your lungs.

Trimming Your Waist

Standing straight with your feet wide apart, stretch your arms at shoulder level and twist your upper torso to the right and then to the left, going back and forth for a total of 20 counts. The twisting motion in this exercise is guaranteed to slim your waistline.

You can trim a thick waist by practicing this simple exercise daily. Scatter matches on the floor and pick them up one by one without bending at the knees.

Stand with your feet slightly apart and your arms straight out at shoulder level. Touch your right hand to your left toe, then touch your left hand to your right toe, alternating ten times for each hand.

Stand up straight with your feet slightly apart. Place your right hand on your hip and stretch your left hand over your head, bending your upper body over your right arm. Alternate with your left hand on your hip and bending to the right, repeating ten times on each side.

Waistline bulge will disappear if you stand with your hands on your hips and bend as far as possible to the right, then as far as possible to the left, alternating sides at least ten times.

With your left hand on your hip and your right hand straight up in the air, stand with your weight on your left leg and raise your right leg to waist-high level. Bend over and try to touch your toes with your right hand. Return to your original position and repeat with your opposite arm and leg, raising and lowering each leg ten times.

When doing toe-touching exercises, you'll become quickly winded unless you breathe properly. Do it this way: Inhale then exhale as you bend forward. As you straighten up, breathe in again.

How to Flatten Your Stomach

Exercises to firm your stomach create a natural girdle by strengthening the muscles that criss-cross your abdomen. When you strengthen your stomach muscles, you may find it also helps to ease problems with a bad back. If your stomach muscles have been too slack, the back muscles have been carrying the extra load.

Work on keeping your tummy in shape while you're watching TV; tighten the muscles of your diaphragm, relax, and repeat several times.

Sitting on the floor with your feet spread apart in front of you, lift your legs several inches off the floor and cross them in a scissors kicking motion several times. This exercise does wonders for flabby stomach muscles.

Sit with your hands behind you on the floor and your legs bent at the knees in front of you. Extend your legs, pointing your toes toward the ceiling, then return to your original position. Repeat this movement six times.

Lie on a slant board, with your head down and your feet elevated 12 to 15 inches. Draw in your stomach while you count to ten, then relax.

Lie on your back with knees bent, then come up to a sitting position. Lie back down and repeat the sit-ups at least ten times. You can vary this by doing the whole exercise with arms folded across your chest.

Here's a quick tummy-toner while sitting. Start with your feet flat on the floor, then lift your knees to waist level and extend your legs straight forward. Lower both feet slowly back to the floor. Repeat ten times.

Tried and True Thigh-Slimmers

To trim your inner thighs, hold on to the kitchen counter and swing your left foot out to the side as high as it will go. Repeat this movement several times, alternating left and right legs.

Lie on your back and support your hips with your arms. Move your legs in a pedaling motion as if riding a bicycle, and continue for two to three minutes.

From a standing position, bend your knees to a 45° angle, keeping your feet flat on the floor, then return to a standing position. Repeat 20 times.

Sit up straight in a chair with your hands holding onto the sides. Lift your left leg waist high and hold it straight in front of you for five seconds. Lower your leg, then repeat with the right leg. Alternate right and left legs at least five times each.

Lie on your left side with your legs straight and your arms stretched out above your head on the floor. Lift your right leg as high as possible, and lower it slowly back down to the floor, to a count of five. Roll over and lie on your right side and repeat the sequence with your left leg. Alternate sides so that you raise and lower each leg at least five times.

Inches off the Hips

Holding on to the back of a kitchen chair, bend your knees slightly and keep your hips tucked under. Push your right leg behind you until you feel the muscles in your leg pulling, tightening your fanny muscles as you push back each leg.

This exercise is so easy you can do it either standing or sitting and just about anywhere. Tighten your fanny muscles and hold for three seconds, then relax. Repeat ten times.

To trim excess fat from flabby hips, get on your hands and knees and extend your left legs sideways as high as it will go. Then repeat the same motion with your right leg. Alternate legs and repeat ten times.

To firm your buttocks, lie on your stomach with your legs together and your arms close to your sides. As you inhale, raise both your legs as high as possible and hold for five seconds. Lower them slowly while exhaling. (Don't do this one if you've had lower back problems.)

Lie on your stomach with your hands placed comfortably under your chin. Raise each leg as high as possible, moving it in a small circle. Then roll over onto your back and repeat the sequence with each leg.

Tender, Loving Care for Your Spine

Good posture in both standing and sitting can help avoid back strain and tiredness. If your chair is uncomfortable, prop a cushion behind your lower back to support your spine.

Proper posture while sitting will help prevent back and neck pains at the end of the day. You'll discover how to sit properly if you balance yourself with a rolling pin under your bottom while sitting crosslegged on the floor.

To increase flexibility in your lower back, stand with your feet slightly apart and your arms raised overhead. Bend forward from the hips and swing your arms downward between your legs. Repeat five times.

If your job requires you to stand all day, shoes with heels over two inches high will throw your pelvis out of line and cause a backache by the end of the day. Stick to lower heels and be comfortable.

To relieve back tension and strengthen back muscles, get down on all fours, then slowly round your back like a cat. Hold for a few seconds and then relax your back completely.

When carrying luggage or packages, try to arrange your things in two smaller parcels rather than one heavy one to help balance the weight and prevent back strain.

Million-Dollar Legs

To tone and firm your calves, place your toes on the edge of a stair step and push down against your heel, pushing up and down rapidly ten times, then repeat with your opposite foot. It's best to do this on a bottom stair so you won't tumble too far if you lose your balance for a moment.

To exercise your leg muscles after sitting for a long period of time, cross your right foot over the left, pressing the right heel against your left instep. Cross your legs in the opposite direction and repeat.

To exercise your leg muscles and increase circulation to the legs, climb the stairs two at a time.

To refresh your legs after prolonged sitting, hold on to a countertop or the back of a chair and quickly bounce from heel to toe 25 times.

Strengthening Chest and Shoulder Muscles

You can firm your breasts by practicing this exercise daily. Place your hands at eye level against a doorjamb and draw your hands together as hard as you can, lowering your hands down to waist level as you push.

To strengthen chest and arm muscles, clasp your hands together close to your chest and push your palms together as hard as you can. Hold for five seconds.

Lie face down on the floor with your palms facing down at shoulder level. Pushing off against your hands, raise your body off the floor, keeping your elbows straight. Lower yourself back to the floor and repeat as many times as you can to strengthen arm, chest, and shoulder muscles.

Tone your chest and arm muscles by vigorously polishing something such as your car, a glass table, all the mirrors in your house.

To firm the bust, sit with your feet flat on the floor, with your arms folded across your chest. Raise your arms to chest height and press your arms as far to the right and then to the left as possible, repeating 25 times in each direction.

Your arms and shoulders will get a good workout if you sit in a chair with your hands grasping the sides. Push yourself up and out of the chair with your arms, then lower your body back down into the chair. Repeat three times.

Toning Your Upper Arms

Extending your arms with clenched fists over your head, make tiny circles in the air, keeping your arms rigid. Widen the circle gradually to hip level. Stretch your arms out in front of you and relax.

Lying face down on the floor with arms tucked under your chest, push your upper torso up off the floor. It's important to keep your hips on the floor. Lower yourself back down and repeat six times.

Scrubbing pots and pans using a vigorous circular motion helps to firm your upper arms.

Digging and hoeing in the garden or raking leaves are good activities to strengthen and firm your upper arms.

To firm flabby upper arms, raise your elbows to shoulder level, then swing your arms back and forth like a pendulum.

Stand with your arms extended straight out to the sides, palms open toward the ceiling. Make a tight fist, hold for three seconds, then relax.

Strengthen arm muscles by extending your arm over your head, bending your elbow, then stretching down toward the middle of your back as if to pull up a zipper.

Wake Up Your Ankles and Feet

To strengthen and slim your ankles, sit in a chair and move your feet in an arc while keeping your heels on the floor. Do ten arcs, then relax.

Exercise your feet and strengthen the arch of your foot by kneeling with your toes bent forward. Then sit back on your heels for five seconds.

To revive tired feet at the end of the day, stand on your toes and roll onto the outer edges of your feet, back onto your heels, then onto the inner edges, ending up on tiptoe. Repeat ten times.

To strengthen foot muscles, alternately walk on your toes, on your heels, on the outsides of your feet, and on the insides of your feet.

To increase the amount of circulation to your feet while you're seated, circle your foot at the ankle, making five complete circles in each direction.

To give your feet a quick pick-me-up after sitting for a while, remove your shoes and place the weight of your leg on the heels and raise your toes. Move your feet in a circular motion from the ankle for a count of fifteen, then change the direction of the circle.

To strengthen tired ankles and feet, stand with your knees slightly bent and your head and back rounded forward. Roll onto the outside arches of your feet and hold this position for five seconds before returning to your original position. Repeat five times.

Read the Fine Print

Keep in mind that a health-club membership is a long-term commitment. You won't get your money's worth unless you work out two or three times weekly.

Don't join a health club that's a long way from your office or home. If it's more than 20 minutes away, you'll waste time and your gasoline expenses will soar.

If there isn't a health club in your vicinity, join the local YMCA or YWCA. The equipment isn't as extensive, but the work-outs can be just as beneficial. You'll save money too.

When checking out a health club, visit it during the hours you'd normally be attending. If the facilities are packed wall-to-wall with people, turn elsewhere. Overcrowding means you'll have to wait in line to use any equipment.

Don't sign a health-club contract without examining it with a jaundiced eye. It should contain a proviso about a refund in the event you decide to quit. If there's no such stipulation, keep your money in your pocket.

SPECIAL EXERCISE NEEDS

For the Mother-to-Be

Remember to walk tall and maintain good posture during pregnancy. It will help to evenly distribute the weight of your body, and you'll feel less tired.

When sitting support your back and elevate your legs whenever this is possible.

To prevent varicose veins, put on support stockings first thing in the morning and elevate your legs as often as possible during the day.

To ease leg cramps, wear low-heeled shoes during pregnancy and walk in bare feet whenever possible.

Lie down, pressing your back against the floor. Pull your knees up to your chest and tighten your fanny muscles, then relax. Repeat five times.

Lying on your back with your hands above your head, press your back against the floor and raise your pelvis. Relax and repeat five times.

Lying on your back with your knees bent toward your stomach, roll your knees to the right and then to the left, rolling to each side five times.

Fitness after Fifty

To improve your overall flexibility, sit in a chair and place a scarf firmly under your foot and pull up on your toes several times. Repeat with the other foot.

To keep your waist flexible, sit in a chair and swivel your upper torso to the right and then to the left, keeping your hands at your side.

To reduce swelling in your ankles, cross your right leg over your left leg. Press your toes up, down, in, and out, then move them in a circular motion. Uncross your legs and repeat with your left leg crossed over the right.

To strengthen your back and spine, sit upright in a chair. Then draw your back up against the chair, throwing your chest out and keeping your head up. Hold for a few seconds, then relax and repeat.

To flex your neck muscles, let your head fall forward, then lift it up and lean it first to the right and then to the left side.

Chapter **4**

COPING WITH TENSION AND STRESS

DON'T LET STRESS GET THE BETTER OF YOU. NEXT TIME, TRY COPING CREATIVELY IN SOME OF THESE WAYS INSTEAD.

TENSION RELIEVERS

Take a Break

While you can't eliminate stress, you can learn to manage it before it creates serious physical or emotional problems. Exercise is a good tension reliever. Deep breathing and meditative relaxation can also help you cope.

Any exercise you do for 30 minutes or more will calm your nerves and reduce whatever stress you feel.

Take an exercise break the next time you feel tension and stress mounting, whether at work or at home. Shoulder rolls, head rolls, shaking the wrists, arm circles, and taking several deep breaths are some of the easiest and most effective stress relievers.

Been Sitting Too Long?

Stand with feet apart and raise your arms up over your head. Bend from the waist and try to touch your palms first to your right foot and then to the left foot. Raise your arms back over your head and relax.

To relax tense shoulder and neck muscles, lie on your back and arch your chest and shoulders until the top of your head is resting on the floor. Hold for five seconds and then relax.

Traveler's Special

Hunch your shoulders up toward your ears, keeping your muscles tense for a few seconds. Relax and repeat several times.

To reduce the tension that collects in your neck, arms, and shoulders after prolonged sitting, clasp your hands behind your chair and raise them as high as possible. Lower and repeat five times.

Stress-Free Driving

To help reduce shoulder tension while driving, grip the steering wheel tightly and raise your elbows as high as possible to the side, raising and lowering them ten times, then relax.

To relieve back tension while driving, try this exercise while waiting at a stoplight. Grip the steering wheel and round your back, then slowly arch your back as far as possible, holding this position for five seconds before you relax. Keep repeating this movement until the light changes.

Unkink Your Shoulders and Neck

To relax a stiff neck, stand with knees bent slightly. Lean your right ear toward your right shoulder, then roll your head back toward your left shoulder, coming full circle and dropping your chin on your chest. Repeat five times.

To reduce tension in the head, neck, and shoulder region, stand or sit with hands resting in your lap. Drop your chin onto your chest as you raise your elbows as high as possible. Lower your elbows and lift your head to the starting position. Repeat five times.

To loosen stiff neck muscles, clasp your hands behind your neck and push as hard as you can. Repeat this contraction five times.

Eliminate neck tension caused by overconcentration by doing this quick neck roll: Let your head fall forward, then roll it clockwise and counter-clockwise several times.

To relax tense shoulders, sit up straight and rest your fingertips on your shoulders. Then pull your elbows back as far as possible. Repeat several times.

Utterly Relaxed

The yoga slant can help relax tense muscles and straighten your spine. Elevate a 1½-inch wide by 6-foot long board by propping the lower end 12 to 15 inches off the floor. Recline with your feet in the elevated position for 15 minutes daily.

For an overall relaxer after exercising, lie on your back with arms relaxed at your sides. Working from your toes up to your scalp, concentrate on making each part of your body go limp.

To relax your entire body, lie on your stomach with your legs bent, your feet resting on your fanny. Grasp your ankles with your hands, then raise your head and chest up as you pull your legs toward the top of your head. Hold this position for ten seconds, then relax.

Be Kind to Weary Legs

To relax tired leg muscles and to trim ankles and calves, sit in a chair and extend your right leg out in front of you, flexing your foot inward. Bounce your leg up and down 15 times, then repeat with the left leg.

Tense and Tired?

Suffering from a pounding tension headache? Relax in a very warm bath and soak away all your tenseness. Warm water draws blood away from the head and helps reduce the pressure causing your headache.

If you wake up feeling tense and tired, rub some rose oil purchased from the druggist on your arms and neck during a warm shower. You'll feel the tenseness in your muscles melt away.

If you feel tired at mid-afternoon during the workday, slump forward in your chair and sit with your head between your knees for a minute or two.

A GOOD NIGHT'S SLEEP

Before Bedtime

Getting a good night's sleep does wonders for your mental attitude and sense of physical well-being. Budget your time to get your full ration of sleep every day.

Engaging in some physical activity during the day will help you to sleep better at night. Exercise acts as a natural tranquilizer, provided you don't work to the point of exhaustion.

Before bedtime, avoid eating any rich, spicy foods or taking caffeine drinks such as coffee, cola, or tea. Drink a cup of warm milk instead.

Reading before bedtime will help make you drowsy enough to sleep. It's also a good idea to keep a book on your night table so you can read yourself to sleep again if you awaken in the middle of the night. Make it a boring one—you'l fall asleep even faster.

Under the Covers

Don't smoke in bed. Not only is it a dangerous habit, but smoke fumes lingering in the air may prevent you from getting a restful sleep.

If you're bothered by street light coming in at the windows, buy blackout shades. You won't be disturbed by the dawn's early light the next morning, either.

Cold feet can keep you awake. Wear bedsocks or put a hot water bottle to good use.

Tense and relax each of your muscles, working from your feet all the way up to your face. This will help to relax your body, and you'll drift off to sleep easily.

If you awaken in the middle of the night and feel restless, drink a cup of warm milk mixed with a spoonful of brandy or sherry. Calcium tablets are also a natural tranquilizer.

Place a board under your mattress for a firmer sleep foundation.

HOT TUBS

Do's and Don'ts

Have a local building inspector double-check your hot tub's installation. You don't want to suffer from electrical shocks.

Whatever you do, use a tested, reliable thermostat in a hot tub. Defective thermostats are sometimes off by as much as four degrees.

Keep hot tubs as clean as possible, and avoid immersing your head. Diseases can be easily transmitted in your hot tub through the nose and mouth.

Keep an eye on a hot tub's temperature. If it rises two degrees above 104°F, heat stroke could set in. The maximum temperature for adults should be 100°F, and 98°F for children under age five.

To be on the safe side, never enter a hot tub alone. This is particularly important for those who have a health problem such as epilepsy, high blood pressure, or diabetes.

Don't enter a hot tub if you've had an alcoholic drink or two, or a tranquilizer. There have been cases of people who've become so drowsy and relaxed that they slid under the surface of the water and drowned.

When you're pregnant, don't soak in a hot tub whose temperature is over 100°F. You may damage your unborn child.

Don't overstay in a hot tub. After more than 15 minutes, your body may overheat and your blood pressure drop to a dangerous low.

After sitting in a hot tub, don't shock your system by going directly into cold water such as that of a swimming pool.

Chapter 5

MEDICAL MATTERS

HERE ARE TIME-HONORED TECHNIQUES AND COMMON-SENSE REMEDIES TO TAKE CARE OF WHAT AILS YOU.

YOU AND YOUR DOCTOR

Choosing a Doctor

If you need to find a family doctor, poll your friends, neighbors, and relatives for recommendations. Perhaps the strongest recommendation of all is one given by a hospital nurse, intern, or resident who's actually observed a doctor on the job.

Although you may be impressed by a doctor who's on the staff of several hospitals, remember that such a physician may not always be available as promptly as one who isn't so heavily committed.

You can usually assume that a doctor affiliated with a university teaching hospital is top-notch. However, be sure that the time your doctor must spend in teaching and lecturing doesn't take away from the amount of time he or she can spend discussing health matters with you.

Be Informed

Don't be shy about asking your doctor for clarification or explanation of your health problem or the prescribed treatment. It's true that a doctor's time is valuable, but the better informed you are, the better able you'll be to follow the doctor's orders.

Be sure to ask your doctor whether generic drugs can be used to fill your prescription as generics can save you money. Also ask your doctor for any booklets or other literature on the use and possible side effects of prescribed drugs.

If you're scheduled for surgery, find out if all the required lab tests can be done prior to your admittance. You can save hundreds of dollars by cutting even one day off a hospital stay.

Office Visits

Avoid going to a hospital emergency room for treatment, unless it's a serious emergency. You'll pay two or three times more than you'd be charged for a visit to your doctor's office.

Mornings and early afternoons are the best times for scheduling a doctor's appointment. At those times appointments are more likely to be running closer to schedule.

When making an appointment with your doctor, try to avoid scheduling the visit for a Monday or a Friday. These are often the busiest days, as both doctor and staff try to catch up after the weekend or try to get a lot done right before the weekend.

Be sure to keep accurate records of your medical and prescription bills so that at tax-time you can take all the medical deductions for which you're eligible.

COPING WITH SICKNESS AND INJURY

Allergies

Many people are allergic to pollens, molds, and house dust. Air-conditioning can lessen your contact with pollen. Keeping your kitchen, laundry, and bathroom areas spotlessly clean helps prevent the spread of molds. Regular dusting and vacuuming will keep down the house dust too, particularly if your vacuum cleaner has a filter. And the new air cleaners can work wonders for the sneezers in the house.

To combat allergies, cover box springs, mattresses, and pillows with plastic covers.

Taking Aspirin

Avoid taking an aspirin before or after drinking orange juice. The combination can be damaging to the stomach.

Coughs and Sore Throat

You can make your own cough syrup by mixing one teaspoon of honey with one teaspoon of lemon juice.

Hoarseness can be helped by wrapping a warm towel around the neck.

Unless your sore throat is severe, you can often treat it at home. Gargle every couple of hours with a glassful of warm water mixed with ½ teaspoon of table salt. Keep warm, drink plenty of fluids, and rest.

Dishpan Hands

Wearing rings when you have your hands in dishwater can lead to irritation when soap becomes trapped under your rings. Take your rings off before you start the cleanup.

If you've got dishpan hands, begin to wear protective rubber or vinyl gloves whenever you have to put your hands in water. When cleansing your hands, use vegetable or mineral oil instead of soap.

Expert Bandaging

Keep your adhesive bandages in the refrigerator. The cold makes the backing peel off in a jiffy.

After putting a bandage in place, don't disturb it for the next 24 hours. If the cut or wound needs to be bandaged longer than that, you can change the dressing as often as needed after the first 24 hours.

When removing a bandage, lift it off lengthwise, rather than horizontally, to keep from reopening the cut or wound.

Calming a Heat Rash

You can treat heat rash by keeping the area dry and applying calamine lotion. Wear light, loose clothing that won't further irritate the skin.

Eye Irritation

If you're puzzled about a change in your child's eyes, consider this: Eye allergies cause itching and tearing, but never pain or pus. Viruses cause pain and tearing, but not pus. Foreign bodies cause pain, sensitivity to light, and tearing, but there'll be no pus and the redness will be confined to one part of the eye.

Toothache Relief

Cold—not heat—will help relieve a toothache.

Boils

Constant soaking in warm Epsom salts solutions (½ cup per quart of water) can bring a boil under control.

A Trick for Tired Feet

When feet swell in the summer heat, bathe them in tepid water and rinse with cool. Splash with bracing cologne and dust on talc. Sprinkle talc inside your shoes, too.

Soak exhausted feet in warm water and Epsom salts. Then lie down with feet elevated for ten or fifteen minutes.

Splinter Removal

If you pat the skin around a splinter with baby oil or olive oil, it will slide out more easily.

Mite Infection

If you feel movement on your skin, but can't see anything, you may have a mite infection. Moisten a piece of sterile cotton with rubbing alcohol and press it to the skin for a minute or two. Have a dermatologist examine the cotton to reach a diagnosis. If you do have mites, call an exterminator too—the presence of mites usually indicates that there are mice in the house.

Lower-Back Ache?

To protect your back, always bend your knees when reaching down to pick up an object.

FIRST AID

Fast Action

If you have a special health problem, wear a tag identifying your health problem, in addition to carrying an identification card in your wallet. Even if you're unconscious, people will be alerted to a medical emergency.

You can probably drive an ill person to the hospital quicker than an ambulance could—since there's no waiting for the ambulance to arrive. Calling an ambulance or rescue squad should be reserved for life threatening situations or when no other transportation is available.

Fast action is important if a harmful liquid or powder gets in the eye. Hold the eye open and flush it with cold water. See a doctor immediately for further care.

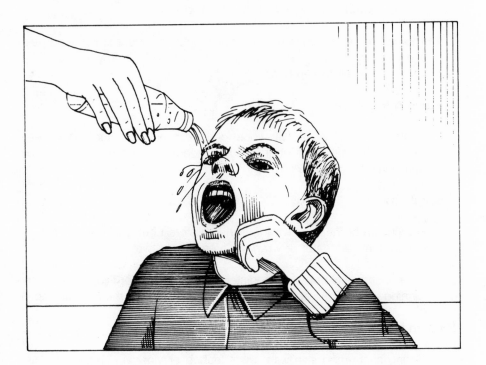

Take the Sting Out

Bees are attracted to hair spray, bright colors, and perfume. If you are stung, remove the stinger and wash the spot. Then dissolve one tea- spoon of meat tenderizer in two tablespoons of water. Rub this mixture on and around the stung area as soon as possible. Another way to get relief from an insect bite is to dampen a cotton swab with aromatic spirits of ammonia, patting the bite area with the swab. If the swelling is severe or the victim suffers other symptoms, get medical attention immediately.

Juice from a broken rhubarb stalk helps relieve the pain of an insect bite.

You can take the sting out of an insect bite by applying cold for a few minutes and then calamine lotion.

Cuts and Bruises

To stop a cut from bleeding, press the wound hard with a clean compress. After the bleeding has completely stopped, you can wash the cut gently under running water with a mild soap.

You can minimize bruising if you apply cold compresses soon after an injury has occurred. After 24 hours, a bruise will tolerate warm applications, which will hasten healing.

Treating a Nosebleed

To stop a nosebleed, sit with your head tilted back and pinch your nose, while breathing through your mouth. If bleeding is heavy, tuck pieces of gauze into the nostrils.

Nasty Burns

For kitchen burns in which the skin is blistered but unbroken, immerse the burn in cold water or wrap the area in cold, wet towels.

To treat chemical burns, immediately wash the area for five minutes with running water. Then apply a clean dressing and seek medical attention.

Sunburn Pain

Patting sunburned skin with a wet teabag or vinegar-dampened cloth provides relief. Or, tie six to eight teabags together and add them to a tepid bath for all-over sunburn relief.

If you've overdone the sun, cool off burned skin by bathing in a lukewarm bath to which you've added bicarbonate of soda.

Treating Animal Bites

If you're bitten by an animal, wash the area with soap and water and have the injury checked by a doctor. If you can, capture the animal alive to have it checked for rabies.

Electric Shock

If someone has suffered an electric shock, locate the source of power and shut it off before touching the victim. If you can't break electrical contact, pull the person away from the source of power by using a dry rope, wooden pole, or a loop made from clothing or fabric.

Sunstroke

To remedy sunstroke, take the person immediately into a cool, shady spot. Give the victim a glass of water and place an ice pack on his or her head. If the victim's temperature is below normal, keep the person warm and call a doctor.

The Best First Aid

Most people don't realize that accidents are most likely to occur in their own homes. Nip accidents in the bud by taking a good look around your house or apartment to identify any health hazards you've never noticed before. Eliminate or correct these danger zones.

Part **VIII**

GROOMING AND PERSONAL CARE

Most of us prefer to look our best at all times—and in professional and personal situations, our appearance can often mean the difference between success and failure. It pays to look sharp, attractive, and in style without being faddish. In Part VIII, you'll find the kind of grooming and personal care hints that can make a difference.

Both men and women will want to experiment with the many suggestions for complete personal care. Chapter 1, on skin care, includes suggestions for proper cleansing and facials, as well as special sections on seasonal skin care and overall body care. With the expert tips in Chapter 2, you'll learn how to create a beautiful head of hair. There are hints for concocting your own conditioning shampoos from inexpensive ingredients at home, as well as remedies for common hair problems such as dandruff and split ends. Eyes and teeth are not only cosmetically important, they're essential to good health. Taking good care of them is an important part of your personal grooming, and the hints included in Chapter 3 are your guide.

Every woman can enhance her best features through the magic of cosmetics. Chapter 4 offers a fascinating variety of highlighting and contouring techniques borrowed from the pros. Effective and easy to follow, there are dozens of tips for making up your eyes, lips, and face.

Because beauty doesn't stop at the neck, you'll want to garner some new ideas from Chapter 5, "Hand and Foot Care." Soft, well cared for hands and feet make your life more comfortable, as well as being elements of good personal grooming. Finally, our tips on fragrance, in Chapter 6, will keep you smelling as good as you look.

Whatever you want to change or enhance in your appearance, you'll find plenty of ideas here. Start right now to create a new you from head to toe.

Chapter 1

SKIN CARE

LOVING CARE PLUS THESE SUPER HINTS WILL KEEP YOUR SKIN YOUNG AND RADIANT.

YOUR FACE

Let It Breathe

Unclog your pores with an easy weekly facial sauna. First, boil a few tablespoons of your favorite herbs in water for several minutes. Remove the pot from the heat. Using a bath towel as a tent, cover your head over the pot and let the steam rise to your face for three to five minutes. Then rinse your face with very cold water to close the pores. Your skin will feel super-clean and smooth.

Once a week, go completely without makeup to give your skin a chance to breathe.

Nature Does the Rest

To promote healthy, blemish-free skin, always remove your makeup before retiring. Leaving makeup on your face while you sleep clogs the pores and invites blemishes.

A good night's rest does wonders for your complexion. If you're a poor sleeper, try this nightcap before bedtime: Mix one teaspoon of instant powdered milk into a cup of hot skim milk. Then add a teaspoon of honey or molasses. Sip it slowly and expect pleasant dreams.

Deep Cleansing

Real grains of bran and oatmeal make the finest cleansing grains. Soak bran in buttermilk till softened or mash colloidal oatmeal (from a drugstore) into a paste with warm water or buttermilk.

Massage your face with a combination of sesame and olive oils. Leave the mixture on your face for a few minutes, then scrape it away using a popsicle stick or tongue depressor. You'll be peeling away dull dead skin cells in the process, leaving your skin glowing.

Classic Skin Treatments

Cucumber masks and lotions are among the most time-honored beauty treatments. Pulverize half a cucumber in the blender, skin and all. Strain through a piece of cheesecloth, and you've got cucumber lotion, a good skin "milk." Keep this refrigerated to last for several days.

Mildly acid products like yogurt or buttermilk make good clarifying masks. Any acid fruit, sliced thin and applied to skin, also has a mild astringent effect.

To make a drying cucumber/yogurt mask, wash one cucumber, and, leaving on the peel, slice it into your blender. Purée to a smooth consistency, add one tablespoon of yogurt, and purée again. Apply to your face. Let the mixture dry for 20 minutes before washing your face with warm water and rinsing with cool.

Large facial pores can't be eliminated, but a good astringent can temporarily camouflage them. For best results, apply astringent shortly before going out. When it starts to tingle, you'll know it's doing its job.

An excellent astringent for oily skin can be made from ½ cup of witch hazel and ¼ cup of lemon juice.

The classic skin-tightening mask is whipped egg white applied to the face and allowed to dry. Rinse off after 20 minutes. This excellent mask is not for dry skin, however.

Bringing Out Your Natural Glow

Peel and core a large slice of pineapple, then whip it to a pulp in the blender. Drain off the juice and apply to your skin for 15 minutes. Every kind of skin will benefit from this wash.

Normal and oily skin get a healthy lift from this easy, papaya toning mask: Mix ½ of a small papaya, one egg white, and a ½ teaspoon of lemon juice in the blender until creamy. Apply to your face, and leave on for 20 minutes. When the time is up, rinse your face well with cold water.

To make an oatmeal toning/cleansing mask for normal-to-oily skin: Put three tablespoons of finely ground oatmeal in a small bowl. Add three tablespoons of witch hazel, and stir the mixture till it's a smooth paste. Apply to your face, and let it dry for 20 to 30 minutes before rinsing off the mask with warm water.

To make an egg/mayonnaise mask for dry skin: Separate the yolk from one egg and mix it in a small bowl with 2 teaspoons of mayonnaise. Blend in ½ teaspoon of lemon juice. Apply to your face, and let it dry for 20 minutes. Wash off with warm water.

Emergency Treatment

Here's a lifesaver that comes in handy, especially just before a date. To eliminate pimples and prevent new skin blemishes, apply a mixture of calamine lotion and 1 percent phenol (available from your druggist).

Banish Dry Skin

Natural vegetable oils make the best cleansing creams. Use them to remove makeup, and follow with an astringent to be sure all the oil is removed.

Should you run out of your favorite brand of moisturizer, your skin will benefit just as much from a thin film of cold-pressed soy oil or almond oil.

"Laugh wrinkles" around the eyes are due to dryness, not to laughing. Pat eye cream lightly around the outside corners, under the eyes, and on the eyelids. Never rub the delicate eye area, even when applying cream.

You can treat dry skin with a fruit mask. Cut a banana in half, peeling one half, but not the other. Slice both halves. Then cut an avocado in two, setting one half aside for some other use. Peel the other half, cut it into pieces, and put it in a blender with the sliced banana halves. Puree till smooth; add one tablespoon of honey, and puree again. Apply to your face and let it dry for 20 minutes. Wash it off with warm water, and then rinse your face with cool water.

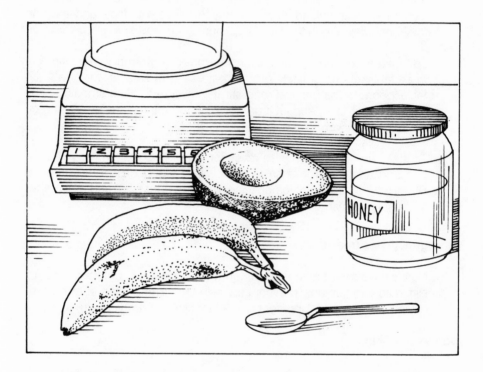

Wake Up Your Skin

Keep skin freshener, astringent, and cotton pads for your eyelids in the fridge if you suffer from facial puffiness upon rising in the morning. This offers a wonderful pickup to the skin in the summer, too.

Special Winter Care

To lessen the drying effects of indoor heat on skin, lower your thermostat to 68°F or less. When sleeping, place a humidifier or basin of water in a heated room.

Dry air at home or in the office isn't healthy for your skin. Lots of plants, placed on trayfuls of pebbles and water, can add moisture to the air if no humidifier is available.

To guard against cold, dry, winter air, wear makeup that is oil- rather than water-based. This helps to moisturize and protect your skin in winter.

Here's a great winter skin treatment. Soak a cloth in natural cider vinegar and lay it against your skin for 15 minutes. Remove the cloth and gently rub the skin with avocado oil, then rinse with warm water and apply a moisturing lotion.

If you're in the habit of licking your lips to moisturize them in cold weather, you're actually helping to chap and crack the skin. Wear a lip balm or lip gloss instead. Always remove lipstick with creamy lotions or oil, use a humidifier in the house, and wear a face mask when skiing, ice skating, or otherwise spending a lot of time outdoors.

If you're a skiier or a snow-sport enthusiast, wear a sunscreen with moisturizer whenever outdoors. The sun's rays can still burn you even if the air feels cool. Sun reflected off the whiteness of snow can be particularly powerful.

Summer Skin Care

Use a water-based foundation to help moisturize your skin, but use waterproof makeup for lips, eyes, and lashes to prevent running and smearing in the heat.

Be sure to moisturize your skin well after it's been exposed to the drying effects of the sun.

To soothe sunburned skin, keep an aloe plant on your dresser table. Break off a leaf as needed and squeeze the plant's aloe gel onto red skin to soften and heal it.

Sunbathers Beware

Your skin can suffer the most damage from the sun between the hours of 11:00 A.M. and 2:00 P.M. Always be sure to wear a sunscreen if you're outdoors during those times—and especially while swimming. The sun's rays easily penetrate water, and you could get a nasty burn.

The color of your eyes can usually tell you how much sun protection you need—the lighter your eyes, the easier you'll burn. No matter what your skin type, use a high-protection lotion the first time you plan to be in the sun. Use a total sunscreen on your face and the backs of your hands, since these will be constantly exposed.

When sunbathing, start with no more than 15 minutes' exposure. Work up gradually over a few weeks' time to an hour. Never stay out in the sun for longer than that.

Whenever your body is tanning, it uses up more of the B-complex vitamins. If you start to lack these vitamins, you'll feel tired and draggy. Supplement your diet with more B vitamins.

BATHING

Time It Right

Take a shower instead of a bath if you'll be heading outdoors immediately afterward. A shower is quicker and less drying to your skin.

Try to schedule your daily bath for the evenings so you won't have to expose your skin immediately to outdoor air. Skin needs at least eight hours to replenish its natural oils after bathing.

Add several handfuls of Epsom salts to your bathwater to help revive tired muscles.

Bathe Away Dry Skin

Toss two or three teaspoons of baking soda into a tub to make skin-softening bath salts.

Make your own bath oil by adding two to three tablespoons of vegetable oil to your bath. For foaming oil, add a teaspoon of plain shampoo. Never use special dandruff, coloring, or other treatment shampoos (including herbal types) for this purpose.

Before drawing your bath, mix equal parts of peanut, camphor, and castor oils for a soothing and fragrant skin massage.

To get rid of flaky skin or the remnants of last summer's tan, add a cup of natural cider vinegar or the juice of three fresh lemons to your bathwater. Slough away the dead skin cells with a dry sponge or brush.

Adding instant powdered milk to your bathwater does wonders for dry skin in cold weather. It not only softens the water, it makes your skin feel silky-smooth without leaving a sticky film.

Sweet-Smelling Baths

Cornstarch sprayed with your favorite scent makes an excellent bath powder.

When you buy fragrant bath soaps, unwrap them and tuck the bars into your linen closet or your lingerie drawers before using them. They'll dry out and last longer in the tub when needed.

ALL-OVER BODY CARE

Baby oil can be made at home by combining 1 cup of light mineral oil and ¼ cup of vegetable oil. Mix thoroughly, adding 1 or 2 drops of oil-based perfume if desired. Pour into a clean bottle and cover tightly.

To make a rough-skin softener, mix one tablespoon of finely ground oatmeal and one tablespoon of cold cream in a small bowl, stirring till the mixture is a smooth paste. Several times a week, apply the paste to any rough areas of your feet, knees, and elbows, and wash it off with warm water while rubbing gently.

One way to remove rough skin is with a combination of ¼ cup of table salt and ¼ cup of Epsom salts. Add to this ¼ cup of vegetable oil while stirring constantly. Massage this mixture into rough skin for several minutes, removing the mixture by bathing or showering as usual.

Massage your neck nightly for three or four minutes with the same cream you use on your face. Massage with upward strokes, then blot off any excess.

For a smoother, softer finish when removing leg hair, rub moisturizing lotion on your legs before applying shaving foam.

Rub callouses on feet and ankles with a pumice stone while you shower or bathe.

Chapter **2**

HAIR CARE

GIVE YOUR CROWNING GLORY THE ROYAL TREATMENT WITH THESE ELEGANT IDEAS.

Keep It Healthy

To prevent hair loss and promote growth, bend over and brush your scalp and hair from back to front until the scalp tingles. Then massage the scalp with your fingertips. Do this every day to stimulate and distribute your hair's natural oils.

Dull, lifeless hair can be a sign of poor diet. Keep your protein intake high, but your calories, cholesterol, and fat intake low. Your hair will reflect the added protein.

To keep your hair in shape, you need a trim every six to eight weeks to eliminate split ends.

Salon Shampooing at Home

Spread shampoo evenly onto the palms of your hands instead of putting it directly onto your head in order to get better coverage and to keep from wasting shampoo.

After a shampooing, your hair needs a cool-water rinse to seal in the moisture in the hair shafts.

Enrich plain, inexpensive shampoo by adding an egg or a pinch of unflavored gelatin to a cupful of shampoo. This mixture can't be stored, however.

Before shampooing, improve the circulation to your hair roots by bending over and massaging your head and scalp gently until it tingles.

Rub out the excess water from your hair before using your blow dryer. You'll save time and avoid damaging your hair with too much heat exposure. If you blow-dry your hair often, you should condition it after every shampooing.

Nature's Own Rinses

To make your hair bouncy and oil-free longer, macerate a handful of watercress in the blender with a cup of water, then boil 10 minutes. Strain out the water and let it cool. Apply to your hair for 20 minutes, then rinse out.

Add a packet of unflavored gelatin to a quart of water for an economical protein hair rinse.

To make your own lemon rinse, blend ½ cup of strained lemon juice and

1 cup of distilled water in a bottle. Comb the liquid through your hair after each shampooing.

Let It Shine

Mayonnaise is a fine hair conditioning treatment. Scoop out the cream with a spoon, spread it on your hair, then wrap your head in a warm towel. Wait half an hour before shampooing thoroughly.

Make your own egg conditioner by separating the yolk from an egg and beating it till it's thick. Beat and blend in one teaspoon of vegetable oil. Add ½ cup of water to the egg-oil mixture. Work this into your hair after you shampoo, leave it on for one to two minutes, and rinse thoroughly.

In summer, comb some conditioner through your hair after swimming, and let it air-dry. The sun makes a natural heat cap.

Down with Static

To reduce static electricity, massage warm, polyunsaturated oil into your hair. Then wrap your head in a hot, damp towel for several hours before shampooing.

To cut down on static electricity, dampen your hairbrush before brushing dry hair.

Never brush hair when it's wet since wet hair is elastic and subject to easy breakage.

Got a Cold?

Baby powder makes a good dry shampoo. Brush it out thoroughly for best cleaning results.

Remedies for Dandruff

To make your own dandruff remover, mix ½ cup of white vinegar and ½ cup of water in a bottle. Shake vigorously to blend the ingredients, and then dab the solution directly on your scalp with absorbent pads before each shampoo.

If you suffer from a flaky scalp, try the following treatment every two

456

weeks: Section your hair and rub the scalp with a cotton pad saturated with plain rubbing alcohol. Let the alcohol dry, then brush your hair and rinse thoroughly with warm water, but don't shampoo.

Quick Setting Tips

Flat beer makes an excellent setting lotion for your hair and gives your curls extra body.

Before going out for the evening, set your hair before your bath or shower. The steam will help set your curls, and the added moisture is good for your hair.

To perk up permed hair between shampoos, lightly mist your hair with fresh water and arrange curls into place with your fingers.

You can save your hairstyle if you sleep on a satin pillowcase.

Do It with Style

Your hairstyle can alter the shape of your face. Height at the crown of the head can lengthen a round face. Bangs can shorten a long face or add softness to an angular face.

To get a fuller look to your hairstyle, bend over so your hair falls forward and blow dry it upside down.

To give long hair the illusion of a shorter style, set your hair tightly on small rollers and comb the set into a pageboy style.

For a chic holiday hairstyle, wear your hair loose, secured with a thin gold or silver ribbon at the hairline.

For a romantic evening hairstyle, roll your hair up on top of your head and secure it in place with a wide golden cord, anchored by hairpins.

Change with the Seasons

During humid summer weather, use a few pretty combs to hold your hair up and away from your face. You'll look and feel a lot cooler.

When temperatures dip below freezing, hair gets brittle and can split easily. Always wear a hat in cold weather.

In cold weather, your hair needs more moisture. Use the mist setting on your electric rollers.

Hair Care Utensils

When cleaning combs and hair brushes, add shampoo to the water. It cuts through and removes hair oil.

Use divided cutlery trays for storing bobby pins, curlers, and combs.

No Surprises

Carry a waterproof scarf in your purse on overcast days in case you're caught in a sudden rain shower.

Chapter 3

EYE AND TOOTH CARE

BRIGHT EYES AND A BRIGHT SMILE ARE ASSETS WORTH THEIR WEIGHT IN GOLD.

EYES

Put Back the Sparkle

Give tired eyes a quick pickup by applying cotton pads moistened with witch hazel over your closed eyelids for a few minutes.

If your eyes are puffy, cover them with cotton pads soaked in milk, and relax for ten minutes. Your eyes will sparkle again.

Another treatment for puffy eyes: Dip two tea bags in boiling water for two minutes, and then let the water cool slightly. Meanwhile, heat ½ teaspoon of olive oil till it's warm (not hot). Using an absorbent pad, carefully dab the oil around your eyes and on your eyelids. Lie down, and cover each eye for ten minutes with a still-warm tea bag. Remove the tea bags and gently wipe the oil from your skin with tissue.

To exercise and strengthen your eye muscles after an extended period of close reading or work, hold a pencil about ten inches from your face and look at its tip, then into the distance. Repeat ten times.

At Bedtime

To moisturize the skin around your eyes while you sleep, apply odorless castor oil at bedtime.

Sun Protection

Limit your use of eye drops during the summer. Too many drops can prove harmful. Rinse chlorine and salt water from irritated eyes with pure mineral water instead.

Be sure to protect your eyes from the sun's glare by wearing sunglasses. If you can see your eyes clearly through the lens of the glasses, they aren't dark enough to give you adequate protection.

Place thin slices of freshly cut cucumbers over closed eyelids to help reduce swelling caused by overexposure to the sun.

Contact Lenses

To wear contact lenses with comfort, you must clean and disinfect them daily. If you don't have the time or inclination to care for contacts properly, you're better off with glasses.

Hard contact lenses are easier to take care of than soft contact lenses.

Searching for a contact lens lost in carpeting is painstaking, but you can retrieve the lens quickly by vacuuming with the vacuum tube covered with a nylon stocking. The lens will cling to the stocking without being sucked through the tube.

TEETH

An easy trick to increase circulation to gums for healthier teeth—especially when your toothbrush isn't handy—is to chew a handful of pumpkin, sunflower, or melon seeds vigorously. They're nutritious too.

Use dental floss in addition to your toothbrush. Flossing removes plaque that causes decay and ensures good circulation to the gums.

Baking soda, when used as a tooth powder, can help whiten and brighten your teeth. Make it taste good, too, by adding two tablespoons of powdered cinnamon and two tablespoons of oil of cinnamon to two tablespoons of baking soda.

Chapter **4**

MAKEUP

BRING OUT YOUR STRONG POINTS BY TUNING IN TO THESE TIPS FROM THE EXPERTS.

FACIAL MAKEUP

A Shade of Difference

When shopping for foundation makeup, test its color by applying a bit to your face or neck, rather than to the back of your hand. If possible, step over to a window in order to check the color in natural light.

To emphasize facial contours, select a foundation that's a shade lighter than your tan during summer months.

There's an Art to It

When applying your makeup, always use a mirror in which you can see your whole face, not just one section of it.

To apply foundation like a professional, use a damp sea sponge. It makes blending a snap and gives you the most natural coverage.

Before reapplying makeup or simply to remove excess oil or shine any time, pat your face gently with a tissue or with a damp paper towel.

Always be sure to blend your makeup well so that the highlights and contours don't look artificial.

Once you've applied your makeup, use a large makeup brush to dust your whole face lightly with translucent powder. You can further set your makeup with a light spray of mineral or ordinary water. A plant mister is just fine for this purpose.

Moisturize First

Using a moisturizer underneath your makeup foundation helps to prevent caking and splotching.

Your makeup foundation will last longer and give better coverage if you mix it with an equal portion of skin freshener.

Smooth and Relaxed

After your morning cup of tea, pat the wet teabags against your face and let the moist film air-dry. Rinse with cool water before applying makeup.

To relieve facial tension, hold a cork between your teeth and lie down for ten minutes. Biting down gently on the cork will help you unclench those tight facial muscles.

Before applying your evening makeup, soak cotton balls in chamomile tea, and place them over your closed eyes for ten minutes. Lie down with your feet elevated to get the most from this technique. You'll feel really relaxed and refreshed afterward—and your face will show it.

Powder Plus

If the powder in your compact has developed a hard surface, gently rub it with a piece of fine sandpaper to make it powdery again.

Use plain talcum powder (or any vegetable starch to which you aren't allergic) to take the shine off nose or forehead.

The Blush of Youth

A rose-colored blusher brushed onto the sides of your throat will give your skin a healthy glow.

For a great, do-it-yourself blusher, blend a dab of lipstick with a bit of cream foundation onto your cheek area.

When you'll be going out for the evening, highlight bare shoulders by brushing on a shiny blusher.

If you'll be wearing sequins or shiny materials, avoid wearing glows, cheek tints, and frosted powders. Your face will look too shiny. Stick to matte powders, shadows, and creams, which will absorb the reflected light from your outfit.

Bleach It Away

To camouflage light facial hair above the lip line, use a facial bleach regularly to lighten the hair. Or, the hair can be removed professionally through electrolysis.

Watch Those Lights

When you'll be in fluorescent light at the office, avoid purple or blue eyeshadows and blue-red lipcolors. In candlelight, counteract the yellow glow from the candles by wearing rose, mauve, and grape tones on your face.

Avoid tan, gold, or beige makeup when wearing black. Moisturize your face well, and apply a porcelain or ivory foundation to complement and enhance your skin color and clothing.

Winter weather makes your skin look sallow, so it's best to avoid makeup with gold or brown tints. Use reds and pinks instead to highlight and brighten your face, along with gray or brown eye shadows.

Makeup Tricks for Round Faces

To help camouflage a double chin, use a bit of blusher under the chin, then blend it upward to the bone and across, toward the edges of the jaw.

If your face is too full, apply foundation a shade darker than your normal shade to the outer contours of your face.

You can slim down a round face by applying blusher in a triangular shape, with the tip of the triangle pointing toward the center of the eye. Apply a bit of blusher on your chin as well.

Bring Out Your Best

If your facial features are small and petite, highlight them with a light foundation. Use a darker foundation if you want to minimize large features.

Undercover-Up

To hide bags under your eyes, cover the area with a foundation darker than what you use for the rest of your face.

Create Your Own Effects

To shorten a long nose, blend dark foundation under the tip of your nose.

To straighten a crooked nose, place a line of light-colored foundation down the center of your nose, blending well at the tip.

To slim down a broad nose, put dark foundation on either side of your nose and blend well.

Filling It All Out

To help widen a long face, apply your blusher in a rectangular area at the cheekbone, centered under the eye, brushing up and out toward the temples.

Choker necklaces and beads have a foreshortening effect on long faces.

Long strands of neck jewelry lengthen a round face.

On Top of It All

Apply a dark shade of blusher from the top of your brow to your hairline to make a high forehead appear more narrow.

Summer Specials

In hot weather, switch to a matte makeup to reduce the amount of extra oil you put on your face.

A quick rule of thumb regarding the amount of makeup to wear in summer: Accentuate your eyes with color, but keep your face understated.

Keeping It Together

A tackle box is a great place for organizing and storing your cosmetics.

For travel or just a day at the beach or on a picnic, carry trial-size tubes or bottles of all your necessary grooming items.

EYE MAKEUP

Thick, Long Lashes

For the thickest-looking lashes, apply mascara and let it set for a few minutes. After curling the lashes, add a little more mascara to the lash tips to give the illusion of length.

Applying fresh mascara over the old will make your lashes brittle. Always remove your eye makeup before bedtime. Sleep with a little petroleum jelly on lashes for conditioning as well as darkening.

A good substitute for mascara: Glue on a few single, false eyelashes to make your lashes look fuller and thicker.

When your mascara begins to dry out, don't throw it away. Run hot water over the tube for a minute and the mascara will again be easy to apply.

Eyebrow Magic

To make your eyebrows look darker, use an old toothbrush to brush eyebrows up toward your temples. Your eyes will look wider and brighter, too, even without using eye makeup.

Using two shades of eyebrow pencil can help make your brow color more natural.

Best Ways with Eyeliner

Eyeliner pencil will flow more smoothly and apply more easily if you gently heat the tip of the pencil over a match stick for ten seconds (without putting the pencil point directly into the flame).

After applying eyeliner pencil, always smudge the line gently with your pinky finger to reduce the harshness of a solid line around the eyes.

To make the whites of your eyes appear whiter, line your lower lashes with a deep blue color stick.

For party makeup, line your eyelids with a metallic powder to make them sparkle.

Foolproof Eye Enhancers

To bring out deep-set eyes, apply a light, frosted shadow on both your lids and brow bone, using a darker shade in the eyelid crease.

Small eyes can be made to look larger by applying a bit of eye shadow under your lower lashes, starting at the center of the eye and blending to the outer corner. Sweep the color along the brow bone out to the side of the eye.

If your eyes are too closely set, pluck eyebrows to start farther apart.

If your hair is dark, your eyes will actually appear bigger if you lighten your eyebrows by brushing them lightly with your makeup foundation.

You can achieve a deep-set look for your eyes by applying lots of dark color in the crease of the eyelid. Pale or frosted eye shadow will work against this effect.

Don't match the color of your eye shadow to the exact shade of your eyes. The colors will cancel each other out, making your eyes look drab instead of exciting. Choose eye shadow colors in the same family as that of your eye color.

The Summery Look

In summertime, highlight your eyes by drawing a thin line of brown cake shadow in the crease and blending it into the crease.

During the hot, muggy days of summer, use only powder blusher and eye shadows; creams tend to stick and smudge. Also, powders help absorb excess oil and moisture from your face.

Sunlight bleaches and splits delicate eyelash hairs. Always lubricate your lashes by wearing a thin coat of waterproof mascara whenever you're outdoors.

Look Good in Glasses

If you wear eyeglasses, a frosty eye shadow and an extra coat of mascara will help enhance your eyes behind the lenses.

Select eyeglass frames that complement your facial structure. Round frames help shorten a long face. Round faces benefit from angular frames.

LIP MAKEUP

Don't Forget to Moisturize

Your lips have few natural oil glands and chap easily. Protect them with a thin coating of colorless lip balm whenever you aren't wearing lip gloss or lip color.

All-Day Lipstick

For long-lasting lipstick, apply a generous coat, then let it set for about two minutes. Blot with a tissue, puff on some powder, then apply another generous coat of lipstick. Wait again and blot.

To brighten your makeup at midday, outline your lips with a soft brown pencil and smudge slightly with your finger tips until the line is barely visible.

Fluorescent lighting gives a garish cast to blues and reds, so choose warm, tawny lip colors for office light.

You Can Fix It

Mend a broken lipstick by holding the two ends over a gas burner, a match, or a lighter flame until the two pieces melt enough to adhere when pressed together. Let the lipstick cool and set before using.

Instant Lip Tricks

If your upper and lower lips are uneven, apply makeup foundation over your lips; then fashion a completely new lip line with a pencil a shade darker than your lip color.

To make thin lips appear fuller, draw a lip line outside your natural lip line. Fill in with a lighter shade of lipstick.

To make full lips appear slimmer, draw a lip line inside your natural lip line. Fill in with darker shade of lip color.

Chapter **5**

HAND AND FOOT CARE

HANDS AND FEET NEED PAMPERING, TOO. TRY ON THESE HINTS FOR STYLE.

HANDS

Baby-Soft Hands

Cream your hands with lanolin before bedtime during the winter. Once a week, put on white cotton gloves after moisturizing, and sleep with the gloves on for smooth, soft hands when you awaken.

Apply hand cream before putting on rubber gloves to do dishes.

Keep a container of hand lotion next to the kitchen sink. Use some lotion on your hands after every time they're in the water.

The acids in lemon and vegetable juices are bad for your fingernails. When cooking, rinse your hands often under cool running water.

Emergency treatment for dry, chapped hands: Once a week, soak your hands in a bath of warm baby oil mixed with sesame oil.

Jiffy Cuticle Cure

To soften cuticles, soak hands in a solution of one cup warm water and a teaspoon of dishwashing liquid.

Always push back your cuticles with a towel after each handwashing.

If you're in the habit of biting your nails or chewing your cuticles, carry a tube of cuticle cream with you. Whenever you get the urge to start chewing, rub the cream on your nails instead. You'll break yourself of a bad habit at the same time you promote healthy nail growth.

Five-Finger Exercise

Any activity that requires fingers to be nimble—needlepoint, typing, embroidery, or playing the piano—is good for nail circulation and helps your fingernails to grow.

Doing Your Nails Better

Cut metal nail files are too harsh for your nails. Use a diamond-dust file or an emery board instead, and file your nails in one direction only.

A light color nail polish gives your hands the illusion of being longer and more graceful.

To quick-dry your nail polish, plunge your hands into a bowl of ice water while the polish is still wet, or place your hands into the freezer compartment of the refrigerator for a few seconds.

Your hands and feet will be ready for a holiday party if you coat both fingernails and toenails with several coats of golden polish.

Save That Manicure

When cleaning around the house, wear white cotton gloves to protect your manicure. Remove the gloves every few hours and rinse your hands under warm water to remove any perspiration.

Save your manicure by using the blunt end of a pen or pencil to dial the telephone.

When nails chip excessively, it's often due to the use of polish remover. Leave polish off for a few days and watch your nails revive.

Don't Throw It Out!

Don't toss away nail polish which has become hardened or gummy. Place the bottle into a pan of boiling water for a few seconds, and the polish will flow smoothly again.

To prevent nail polish bottletops from sticking, rub the inside of the cap and the neck of the bottle lightly with petroleum jelly.

Keep nail polish in the refrigerator to keep it from becoming thick and hard to apply.

Budget Polish Remover

Make your own nail polish remover by buying two ounces of acetone from your druggist. This makes a two-month supply.

FEET

Liberated Feet

Hopping on one foot 20 to 30 times while wearing exercise sandals helps to increase the leg muscle tone and strengthen the feet.

Go barefoot around the house as often as possible. Your feet contain 26 separate bones, all of which need freedom of movement and exercise away from heavy shoes and high heels.

Rest for the Weary

After standing on your feet all day or after a lengthy walk, soak away the tiredness in a footbath of Epsom salts and warm water.

Sleeping with several pillows tucked under your lower legs can help prevent varicose veins.

Help for Common Woes

To prevent ingrown toenails, cut the nails straight across, leaving no jagged edges.

To prevent foot perspiration—especially in summer—dust your feet lightly with baby powder before putting on your socks and shoes.

Chapter 6

PERFUMES AND COLOGNES

SOME LIKE IT FLOWERY, SOME LIKE IT SPICY. WHICHEVER YOU PREFER, LEARN TO USE FRAGRANCES TO YOUR BEST ADVANTAGE WITH THESE TIPS.

Get Your Money's Worth

For fragrance that lasts all day, saturate a cotton pad with your favorite perfume and tuck it into your cleavage. Your body's heat will help intensify the scent.

Don't spray perfume just anywhere on your body. Apply it directly to pulse points such as the throat, wrist, inside the elbow, the back of the knee, and the groin area, for a longer-lasting scent.

The scent of perfumes, colognes, or body oils will last longer if you apply them while you're still warm and damp from a shower or bath.

Dab petroleum jelly on your pulse points before applying your perfume. The scent will last longer.

Hidden Scent

Spray the inner hem of your skirt and inside your gloves with your favorite perfume.

Spray your favorite cologne on your bathroom and bedroom light bulbs. When they're lit, the heat from the bulbs will release a pleasant fragrance throughout the room.

Special Instructions

Apply perfumes and colognes before putting on your jewelry. The alcohol and oils in your favorite scent can cause a cloudy film on both real gold and costume jewelry.

If you're allergic to the perfumes in commercial deodorants, dust yourself with baking soda for an effective, fragrance-free substitute.

Keep an Eye on the Calendar

Don't stick to one fragrance all year long. Temperatures affect the intensity of fragrance. Heavy scents and oils are perfect for winter, but hot weather calls for lighter, floral fragrances in smaller doses.

Keep a mister of cologne in the refrigerator during the summer. After your shower, spray it all over for a cool, tingly refresher.

Part IX

DRESSING AND WARDROBE

The average clothes closet these days represents a considerable expense in both time and money: Time spent in selecting the right clothes and money spent in buying them. With clothing costs rising every year, we must all learn to select quality garments and to take good care of them. You'll be able to make your special clothes last for a long time with the neat tricks in this part.

Everything a man or woman needs to know about dressing well is included in Chapter 1. How to evaluate fit, correct figure defects, coordinate a wardrobe, and many more aspects of wardrobe planning are fully covered.

Chapter 2, "Buying Clothes," is a guide to the importance of planned buying to avoid those disastrous impulse purchases, as well as how to take advantage of special sales all year long.

No matter how fine your wardrobe, it won't stay that way without proper storage. Chapter 3, "Organization and Storage," provides the right storage methods for every kind of garment, as well as tips on organizing your closets and bureau drawers so you'll be able to dress without losing time or motion. You can extend the life of your garments by following the general care hints in Chapter 4. Annoying chores like removing lint and fuzz balls are a snap with these on-the spot tips.

Since shoes and boots also represent a considerable cash outlay, be sure to try on some of the smart tips in Chapter 5 for size. Learn to care properly for leather, suede, and fabric shoes, how to waterproof boots, and how to remove stains from all your shoes. With the hints from the section on stockings, you can lengthen the life of your hose, repair runs, and mix and match stockings to make new pairs.

Whether your jewelry is made from precious gems or costume imitations, you'll sparkle along with it if you follow the advice in Chapter 6, "Jewelry and Accessories." And if you've invested in a fur coat, you need to give it special care and special storage. Take a cue from the hints in Chapter 7, and your fine furs will remain as beautiful as the day you bought them.

If it's true that clothes make the man, then it's also true that our dressing and wardrobe hints will make that man's (or woman's) clothes look better and last longer.

Chapter 1

DRESSING WELL

NOTHING SUCCEEDS LIKE SELF-CONFIDENCE— ESPECIALLY WHEN YOU KNOW THE ART OF DRESSING FOR SUCCESS.

HINTS FOR WOMEN

The Importance of Fit

Your shirtsleeves should reach to the end of your wristbones, and your jacket or coat sleeves should cover the tops of your wristbones. If not, sleeves will look too short and your arms too long.

Never purchase a size smaller than you wear, hoping to alter the garment to fit. A smaller size cannot be altered to a larger size.

Ill-fitting clothes, especially those that are too tight, can actually make you feel tired.

Posture Pointers

No matter how expensive your clothes, they won't fit properly if you slouch. Remember to walk and sit tall during the day. You'll appear taller as well as slimmer, and your clothes will hang properly.

Jackets and suits will fit better if you remember to keep your shoulders back and your stomach tucked in.

Get Organized

Decide tonight what you're going to wear tomorrow. You'll feel better organized first thing in the morning and won't be surprised by missing buttons, stains, or ripped hemlines.

Always try on a garment you're planning to pack for a trip. The morning of an important business meeting isn't the time to discover something needs cleaning or mending.

The Hidden Factors

Always dress in front of a full-length mirror in the morning to see the total look you'll be presenting to others during the day.

Be sure you have the proper bra to wear under any new outfit. Low-cut and backless dresses require special foundations.

The Light and Dark of It

As a general rule, it's best to choose dark colors for the outer layers of dress, such as a coat or jacket. Save bright colors for your tie, blouse, or shirt.

Lighten the too-severe look of a dark-colored outfit by wearing a bright scarf next to your face.

To create the illusion of more height, dress all in one color. Stick with solids or small prints.

Dark colors tend to slim your figure; bright colors enlarge it.

Solid, neutral colors such as navy, black, gray, or beige are the most acceptable colors for a business wardrobe.

Coordination Is the Key

Try to purchase separates from the same designer line of clothing. They're color-coordinated and intended to be worn together for a "put-together" look.

Your belt color can help to lengthen or shorten your torso. Match your belt to your shirt or sweater if you're short-waisted; match the color of your belt to your skirt or slacks if you're long-waisted.

Wearing a scarf with a color that matches your eyes will highlight and intensify their color.

Cool and Calm

White cotton is the best fabric for summer wear. White reflects the sun's rays and keeps you cool. Cotton also lets your skin breathe.

If you perspire heavily, stick to a cotton wardrobe, especially in the summer. Cotton blends will not wrinkle as easily as pure cotton fabrics.

In Winter Weather

In cold weather, you're smarter to dress in layers of lightweight, loose clothing than in one heavy piece. Air trapped between the layers of clothing is warmed by your body's heat and provides excellent insulation.

Clothing made with natural fibers such as wool and cotton is actually warmer in cold weather than synthetics. Because natural fabrics breathe, they allow body perspiration to evaporate and you won't feel wet and chilled.

When the temperature dips below freezing, wear turtlenecks, long sleeves and slacks, and other clothing to cover as much of your body as possible.

Up to one-third of your body heat can escape through your head. Always wear a hat or scarf in cold, windy weather.

Dressing Slim

A vertically striped suit and a vest with waist points give the illusion of slimness and added height.

If you're a bit overweight, wearing undersized clothes will accentuate the problem. Wear looser clothing to give the illusion of a slimmer figure.

Never wear a short coat over a full-length gown. An ankle-length coat in a neutral color is slimming.

Vertically worked skins on a fur coat will have a slimming effect.

Wear layers of lightweight sweaters instead of a bulky sweater. You'll look thinner and actually feel warmer.

Walking Tall

To create the illusion of tallness, cover the entire instep of your shoes to give an unbroken look from hipline to toes.

To lengthen a short torso, wear belts loosely so they fall below your natural waistline. Avoid wearing skirts or pants with wide waistbands.

If your legs are short, you'll look best in trousers that are straight, narrow, and uncuffed.

To de-emphasize a short, stocky figure, avoid horizontal stripes, large prints, plaids, and clingy fabrics.

A short figure is most flattered by a V-, U-, or collarless neckline, or a shirt with a pointed collar.

To Minimize Height

Extra-tall women should avoid clothing with ruffles and extra detail. Longer jackets and tops, as well as cuffed pants, will help minimize height.

A three-quarter-length coat will also minimize your height.

Tall, full figures carry large prints well.

Collar Matters

If you're broad shouldered, avoid oversized collars.

Open-collared shirts and sweaters with oval, square, or V-necks will help to elongate a short neck.

To make your neck look longer, wear an open-collared shirt with a neck chain falling just below the collarbone.

To shorten a long neck, wear turtlenecks, fur collars, and mufflers.

A Soft Touch

A fresh flower at the neckline is a nice, light touch when wearing silk and chiffon fabrics. Avoid heavy, chunky jewelry.

You can soften a tailored look by tucking in a scarf at the neckline of a suit.

If the Shoe Fits

Select shoes with heels in proportion to your height. Heels that are too high will make a short-legged person look awkward, not taller.

Shoe color should be the same color as, or darker than, your outfit.

Wear slingback shoes to lengthen the look of your legs.

Shoes with wide straps that cut across the instep of your foot will make your legs look heavier and clumsy.

A Perfect Pair

Always match the tone of your stocking color to your shoe. It helps create an unbroken line from the tip of your skirt hem to your toe, and that makes you look taller and slimmer.

When wearing a black shirt and black shoes, wear a stocking with a tint of black. Nude stockings make your legs look harsh against the black.

With brightly colored evening shoes or slippers, wear a neutral stocking so you won't detract from the shoe color.

When wearing open-toed sandals, be sure that you're wearing sandal-foot stockings.

To select the proper color hose, pull the stocking over your forearm, not the back of your hand. Your hand is likely to be more tanned and therefore will alter the color of the hose. Keep in mind that hosiery will look different in natural light than it does in the store's fluorescent light.

Leg Slimmers

Heavy legs can be camouflaged with sheer stockings or stockings with a thin vertical rib.

Dark shades of stockings will help slenderize your legs.

The Shoulders Have It

Coats and suits with broad shoulder lines can help to camouflage a bulging stomach.

If you have large hips, draw attention to your upper torso with scarves and jewelry.

To rectify the problem of sloping shoulders, wear padded jackets and coats.

Play It Down

If you have an ample bosom, avoid wearing balloon sleeves and frilly necklines—or other styles that draw attention to your upper torso.

Women who want to play down an ample bosom should avoid double-breasted coats and shirts with detailing such as breastpockets.

If you're big-breasted, avoid wearing rib-knit pullovers. They tend to emphasize your bosom and make you look top-heavy.

The Right Length

Dark-colored skirts or those made from weighty fabrics can be worn shorter. Lightweight fabrics can be worn much longer.

The Finishing Touch

No matter how stylishly you dress, you still won't get noticed if you have a scratchy, weak, or monotone voice. Practice improving your vocal quality by reading poetry aloud or talking and singing into a tape recorder.

HINTS FOR MEN

A Smart Dresser

Keep a sport coat in your office closet, even if your normal attire is casual and you go coatless. You'll always be prepared for an unexpected luncheon or dinner invitation. Most good restaurants require male patrons to wear a jacket.

The best choice of dress for a job interview is a conservative, single-breasted, American-cut, dark blue suit. To complete the outfit, wear a white dress shirt, black or blue socks, and laced shoes.

Stick with the tried and true. Fashion fads go out of style too quickly to be a good clothing investment.

When wearing jewelry, try to wear fewer and more expensive pieces for the most tasteful effect.

A Sense of Proportion

Always coordinate the width of your tie with the width of your coat lapel or collar.

Your coat should be long enough to cover your hips. A slightly shorter coat will make a short man look taller; a longer coat can make a tall man appear a bit shorter.

If you have a short, stocky figure, don't wear suits with wide lapels. They emphasize your shortness.

A heavy or short build looks best in dark colors and pinstripes. A tall or thin build can carry plaids well.

If you're broad shouldered, choose dark, plain coats with a brighter, patterned fabric for the slacks. If you're very thin, you'll look best in brighter-colored or patterned coats with dark, plain slacks.

Say It with Color

Coordinate the color of your wardrobe to complement your skin tone, eyes, and hair color. Dark complexions looks best in blues and grays. Light complexions look best in browns and light greens.

In selecting your tie for the day, make sure its color goes well with your jacket or suit coat.

Remember that darker-colored clothing lends an air of authority; lighter colors are appropriate for a softer, casual look.

For the best effect, emphasize your shirt, tie, or jacket, and play the rest of your outfit down. Your good shirt or tie, or the fabric of your new suit, will stand out much better without competition from other strong colors, textures, or patterns.

Suit Yourself

A man's wardrobe needs at least three basic suits: A navy suit, a gray or brown suit, and a blue jacket with gray slacks (or a brown jacket with tan slacks).

Look for quality of workmanship when selecting a suit, and stick to natural fibers such as wool. Wool molds itself to the shape of the body and will always hang well on you. Also, wool lasts five to ten years longer than a synthetic fabric.

It's better to invest in several well-fitting, less-expensive suits than in one very expensive outfit. You'll have the flexibility of changing your outfit more often, and your wardrobe will have a fresher look.

Have a change of suit for every day of the business week. Never wear the same suit two days in a row.

486

Is It Suitable?

A black suit tends to make you look old—whether or not you are.

A vest can dress up your suit and also make it appear especially businesslike.

Choose a suit with a lapel width of no more than three and a half inches. The suit will stay in fashion for a long time.

Shirting the Issue

White dress shirts or those of a soft pastel color or subdued stripe are most appropriate for business wear. Never wear a loud-colored or print shirt with a business suit.

In addition to white shirts, your wardrobe should include several different colors of dress shirts. That way, you can vary your appearance from day to day, even when wearing the same suit or jacket.

Even in hot summer months, always wear a long-sleeved business shirt to the office. A short-sleeved shirt is more appropriate for blue-collar work.

Starch the collar, cuffs, and upper front area of your shirts to give them a fresh, crisp look.

Never wear a patterned shirt and tie together. Also avoid the combination of checks and stripes in the same outfit.

Starting Off on the Right Foot

Brown shoes should be worn only with a brown suit. Brown shoes worn with blue or black slacks look very mismatched.

Your socks should match the color of your shoes and slacks. White socks aren't appropriate for business wear. Wear white only with tennis or running shoes.

Always wear calf-length socks with good elastic bands which will hold your socks up firmly. There should never be any skin exposed when you sit down or cross your legs.

Chapter **2**

BUYING CLOTHES

LEARN HOW TO SHOP FOR BEST BUYS IN CLOTHING AND TO CARE FOR YOUR FAVORITES THROUGH MANY YEARS' WEAR.

BUILDING A WARDROBE

Save Time and Money

You'll save money if you buy clothing that coordinates with accessories already in your wardrobe.

Factory outlets and fashion discount stores offer considerable savings on good-quality clothing. If you're able to make small repairs, you also might consider buying seconds.

"Dry clean only" garments are often more costly in the long run, because of their monthly or bimonthly cleaning bills. If you choose washable clothing—even if it's initially more expensive—you'll come out ahead.

Buying clothes out of season allows you to save as much as 50 percent. Store-wide clearance sales usually are held after Easter, Independence Day, and Christmas and offer values on off-season garments.

When dividing your clothing budget, apportion the most money to items you'll wear frequently. An expensive winter coat is a more sensible expenditure, for example, than a costly evening dress.

Buy hosiery, underwear, shirts, and handkerchiefs in multiple packs to save time and money.

Beware Those Impulses

Go through your closets annually to discard any garments not worn in the past twelve months. Make a mental note of any color or styling mistakes, and avoid repeating these on your next shopping trip.

Keep a "grocery list" of clothing needs inside your closet door. If an item keeps showing up, you'll know it's legitimate.

Don't buy a garment with ornate or unusual buttons unless an extra button comes with the purchase. Otherwise, the garment will become unwearable if you should lose a button. You may find it both troublesome and expensive to replace all the buttons.

Be Creative

Substituting a leotard for a bathing suit will save some money.

A long skirt can be worn high as a strapless dress.

If you're a junk-shop addict or simply a saver, you probably have a collection of old ties, out of style but too good to throw away. Sew them together to make a skirt.

A bandanna can also become a scarf, headband, or halter.

A shawl or sarong can be improvised from any large piece of fabric.

A poncho or strapless sundress pushed down to the waist makes a skirt.

Add modish belts, bracelets, scarves, and earrings for an instant update of last year's styles.

Buy four large, cotton bandannas in the dimestore. Sew them together, leaving room for neck and arm openings, and wear over your jeans as a poncho.

Buy long, narrow scarves to double on occasion as pants belts.

Buy gold or silver bedroom slippers to wear with your holiday evening dress. They look delicate and cost less than shoes.

Dress up an old knit beret for the holidays by sewing on sequins or metallic beads.

Dress up a plain or pastel-colored shirt by tying a ribbon at the collar into a small bow and clipping on a cameo pin.

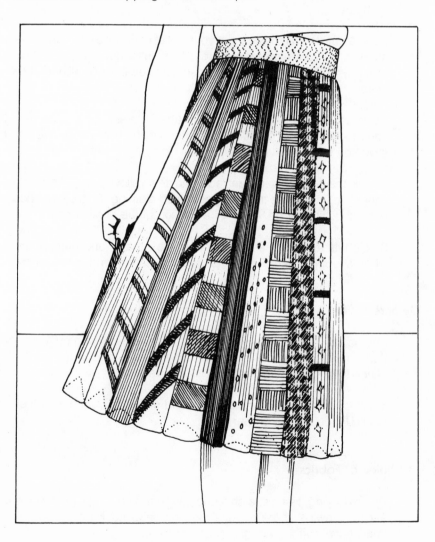

SHOPPING HINTS

Be Prepared

Before heading off on a shopping trip, make sure you're wearing the kind of clothes and accessories you'd wear with the item for which you're shopping. For example, if you're looking for a jacket, wear a shirt and tie. This takes the guesswork out of how the item will look once you get it home.

Keep an updated index card in your wallet noting the sizes and measurements of all your family members. While out shopping, you'll always be prepared to take advantage of an unexpected bargain without having to guess.

Before shopping for clothes, phone ahead to see if the store has what you're looking for. You often get better service over the phone and can save yourself the time and trouble of going from store to store.

Check the newspaper want ads and the yellow pages under "resale shops" to find stores that sell good used clothing. A little-used designer original outfit may be yours for a fraction of the original cost.

Staple bits from skirt and pants hems to a card, and carry it with you when shopping for coordinated shirts, sweaters, and accessories.

Be Sure It Fits

Always look at yourself in a three-way mirror when trying on a new outfit. See how the garment fits in front, on the side, and in the back. Also, check to see how it looks when you move about.

Shop for a new pair of shoes at the end of the day when your feet have swelled. You'll get a proper fit.

A Choice of Fabrics

Before buying, test a stretch fabric garment by pulling it gently crosswise and lengthwise. If the material doesn't snap back into shape quickly, you'll have trouble with bagging after wear.

When buying permanent-press garments, remember that you won't be able to lengthen the hemline without showing an unsightly crease.

Check the labels of children's cotton pajamas to ensure that the material is flame resistant. Although cotton is strong, durable, and cool, it's very flammable unless specially treated.

Keep It New

When you buy a new garment, dab the center of each button with clear polish to seal the threads. Buttons with sealed threads stay on longer.

Coating the edges of pockets with clear nail polish also helps resist wear. The polish lasts through many washings. When it wears off, apply another coat.

When getting dressed, slip on a skirt or dress over the head. Stepping into a skirt has resulted in many a broken zipper and ripped hem.

Chapter **3**

ORGANIZATION AND STORAGE

A WELL-KEPT WARDROBE MAKES THE BEST IMPRESSION—KEEP YOUR CLOTHES IN SHAPE THE EASY WAY WITH THESE CLOSET TIPS.

CLOSET SMARTS

Eliminate Wrinkles and Creases

Hang up a suit or dress immediately after wearing. Since the material retains body heat, the wrinkles fall out more easily.

For longer wear and a better fit, cashmere and wool clothing should be briskly shaken after each wearing, and then hung to air out before being put away in the closet.

Hang your clothes on wooden or plastic hangers, being sure to close zippers and buttons. Make sure that shoulders, sleeves, and creases are straight and that collars are lying flat in place. The next time you search for that item in the closet you won't be disappointed to find a wrinkled, misshapen garment.

To prevent a horizontal trouser crease midway up the trouser leg, put newspaper over a hanger rod, then fold the trousers over that.

Fortify Your Hangers

Slip rubber bands on the ends of wire hangers to keep clothes from falling to the closet floor.

To prevent sleeveless garments from slipping off wire hangers, bend up both ends of the hanger.

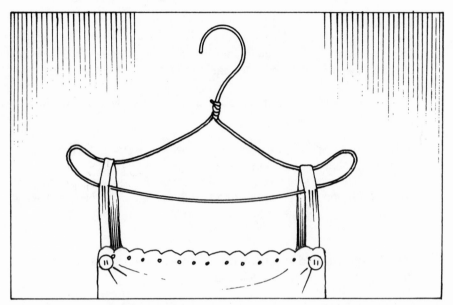

Wind cellophane tape around wire hangers to prevent them from leaving rust stains on clothing.

Double the strength of wire hangers by taping two together with adhesive or cellophane. The hangers won't cave in under heavy garments.

Down with Dust

When storing a hanging garment in a plastic bag from the cleaners, use a twist tie to seal any openings against dust.

STORAGE

Fending Off Moths

Moths love grease spots as much as they love wool. Dry clean or launder woolen articles before storing.

Moth preventives should be hung as high as possible in the closet because the fumes filter downward. Otherwise, you get only partial protection.

Folded or Flat?

To store sweaters, fold them in your bureau drawer. Hangers can distort the shoulder shape of a sweater and stretch the garment unnecessarily.

To reduce wrinkles, lay a panel of tissue paper over the back of a garment before folding it.

When folding clothes to be packed in a suitcase or stored for the season, lay the garment out flat, and place a piece of tissue paper over it. For skirts, fold the garment twice on the horizontal. For dresses, position the sleeves over the tissue paper, then fold the dress in thirds, horizontally. Fold a coat or a sweater just as you would a dress, but fold it over only once.

Heavily embroidered or sequined clothing should be stored flat. Hanging these garments will distort their shape.

Quick-Change Artist

Keep one foolproof outfit, complete with belt and scarf, up front in your closet. It's a lifesaver for rushed mornings.

Rummaging through shoeboxes to find a certain pair of shoes is time-consuming and inconvenient. If you cut one end off each box, then stack the boxes on a shelf beside or on top of each other, you'll be able to select a pair at a glance.

Hang up your hats, scarves, belts, and bags for display and easy access. Put up two lattice strips on the wall and add hooks.

The Bureau of Inventions

Line your bureau drawers with tissue paper to prevent clothing from catching and snagging on any rough edges.

For an instant jewelry chest, line a drawer with foam rubber to keep things from skidding around.

Here's a way to make several sweet-smelling sachets. Melt ½ cup of paraffin in a double boiler over low heat. Remove from heat, let cool slightly, and then stir in six drops of lavender or other perfumed oil. Lightly coat, with petroleum jelly, the inner surfaces of the caps from small jars. Pour the paraffin/oil mixture into the jar-cap molds and let it cool and solidify overnight. In the morning, tap the cooled cakes out of their molds.

If your boots are topsy-turvy in the closet, use the cardboard tubing from giftwrap or paper towels to keep them neatly upright during nonwinter months.

Chapter 4

GENERAL CLOTHING CARE

GET OUT THE SPOTS AND THE WRINKLES, THE LINT AND THE CREASES, BY FOLLOWING THESE SIMPLE STEPS.

Keeping Up with Wool

When brushing clothes, brush with the nap, rather than against it, to remove the most dirt and lint.

Loose dust and dirt won't harden and cut heavy fabrics if you clean them with the small brush attachment from your vacuum cleaner. The dirt is sucked out of tweeds and heavy woolens, and the texture is revived. Be sure the brush is clean before you start, however.

To remove the shine from wool clothes, sponge the garment with a solution of one teaspoon ammonia to a quart of water. Press on the wrong side.

Pesky Fuzz Balls

To remove knots and fuzz balls from a sweater, gently rub them with sandpaper.

Slip a clean blade in your safety razor and run it over a shirt collar to remove fuzz balls. You'll be able to scrape away the balls without ruining the shirt fabric.

The Last of Lint

For a do-it-yourself lint remover, roll up a magazine and wrap wide adhesive tape on it (sticky side out), then pass over lint, threads, and hairs.

Wrap adhesive or cellophane tape around your finger with the sticky side out to remove lint from a small area quickly.

Prevention First

If you're annoyed by clinging dresses, starch your slips.

Rub zipper teeth occasionally with wax for smooth working.

To prevent mildew from forming in a leather-lined purse during storage, fill the purse with crumpled newspaper and leave it unfastened.

It's best to apply perfume to your skin, instead of to your clothing. Chemicals in the perfume may weaken a fabric or change its color.

Keep angora sweaters, gloves, and scarves from shedding by keeping them in the refrigerator between wearings.

Keep your lips pressed together while dressing or undressing in order to avoid staining tight pullover garments with lipstick.

Wrinkle Removers

You can de-wrinkle clothing in a hurry by running hot water into the bathtub and hanging clothes on the shower rod. The steam will remove the wrinkles in no time.

Overloading clothes in the dryer not only causes wrinkling but reduces heat efficiency and prolongs drying time.

Just-Right Jeans

Take your jeans out of the dryer while they're still damp, and wear them for a few hours. They'll mold perfectly to your shape once they're dry.

If you've let down the hem on a pair of old jeans, eliminate the old hemline by coloring it in with a permanent ink marker.

You can brighten up old jeans by washing them with a brand new pair. Some of the dye from the new pair will inevitably run out—and right into the faded jeans.

Before Spot Cleaning

Before trying a chemical stain or spot remover, test the liquid on a hem, seam, or other hidden part of the garment. If the liquid discolors or stains the cloth, you won't have ruined the entire garment by trying to clean it yourself. Head for professional help from the nearest dry cleaners instead.

If you use a cleaning fluid on an item of clothing, don't use water on it as well.

Emergency Cleaning

Club soda, either straight from the bottle or flat, is a great emergency cleaner with a damp cloth and soap and water.

Leather look-alike fabrics such as vinyl or polyurethane are easily cleaned with a damp cloth and soap and water.

Let Them Know

When taking soiled garments to the dry cleaner, be sure no spots or stains are overlooked. Pin a note to each spot explaining what the substance is to call it to the dry cleaner's attention. Always have belts and accessories cleaned along with the main garment to be sure the whole outfit remains the same color.

Chapter 5

SHOES AND STOCKINGS

SHOES AND STOCKINGS TAKE A BEATING THROUGH EVERYDAY WEAR, BUT YOU CAN MAKE THEM LAST LONGER WITH THESE TIMELY HINTS.

SHOES

Shoe Sense

Change shoes daily to double their life. Airing them out between wearings prevents perspiration from rotting the leather.

Consider buying summer shoes a half-size larger for extra room, since your feet swell in the heat.

The best investment is a pair of shoes in a neutral color like peanut, butterscotch, or caramel—colors which complement any color of clothing.

Avoid wearing either very flat or very high-heeled shoes. Neither is designed to provide good arch support for your feet.

A Brand-New Pair

When buying shoes you'll be wearing a lot, choose a pair made of leather or woven fabric. Since these materials breathe, the shoes will be much more comfortable to wear than synthetics.

Sandpaper the soles of new shoes to keep from slipping on them. Or rub the shoes against a cement step or sidewalk.

Between Wearings

Insert shoe trees immediately after removing shoes, since they're still warm and pliable.

Never store leather shoes in plastic bags. The plastic keeps the leather from breathing.

Shake baking soda into shoes to help banish perspiration odors.

Wet Feet?

Place strips of adhesive tape around the inside of boot tops to keep them from leaving dark rings on your stockings during rainy weather.

To waterproof leather, apply silicone-based waterproofer and rub it in well with your hands.

A quick way to dry shoes is to hang them by their heels on a chair rung. Since they're off the floor, air can circulate on all sides.

Rain-soaked shoes sometimes stiffen up when they dry. Avoid stiffness by rubbing saddle soap into them before they dry completely.

If leather or vinyl shoes get wet, stuff them with paper to hold their shape and let them air-dry. To preserve the finish, redampen with warm water, and apply glycerine with a soft cloth.

A Spit-and-Polish Shine

Weatherproof and cream-polish new leather shoes and handbags before the first wearing to give them protection and shine. Keep them well polished to prolong their life span and to make it easier to remove surface dirt.

Remove water stains on leather shoes by rubbing with a cloth dipped in a vinegar/water solution.

Lemon juice is an excellent polish for black or tan leather shoes. Follow by buffing with a soft cloth.

Paste floor wax doubles as shoe polish in a pinch.

Whiter Than Ever

If you rub your white shoes with a slice of raw potato before applying polish, the polish will go on more smoothly. After the polish dries, spray the shoes with hair spray for extra protection and longer life.

If white shoes have dark heels, apply a coat of colorless nail polish to the heels. This prevents white polish from rubbing off on the heels later on. You can just wipe off any leaks with a damp cloth.

Scuff marks on white or pastel shoes can be removed by rubbing the spot with nail polish remover.

Patent Leather Care

A dab of petroleum jelly rubbed into patent leather shoes gives them a glistening shine. It also keeps them from cracking in winter.

To keep patent leather shoes from cracking, treat them periodically with a leather conditioner or preservative. Don't wear them in cold temperatures because cold causes them to crack.

Simple Suede Cleaning

Suede and napped leather shoes can be easily cleaned with a bristle brush to remove any surface dirt.

Remove rain spots from suede shoes, bags, and hats by rubbing them gently with an emery board.

You can rub dirt marks off suede shoes with an art-gum eraser; then buff with sandpaper.

To clean stained suede shoes, first brush them, then hold them over the steam from a kettle or an iron just long enough to raise the nap but not wet the shoes. Brush the nap with a soft brush.

Give black suede shoes a facelift by applying a sponge slightly moistened with cool, black coffee. Rub in the coffee gently.

Befriend Your Boots

Weatherproof your boots against rain and snow by applying a silicone spray, especially at the seams.

A good cleaning with saddle soap will help remove road salt and other chemicals from leather boots. Check your boots daily for signs of salt stains; salt can eat away the leather if not removed promptly.

To find a pinhole leak in rubber boots, hang them up and fill with water. Mark the resulting leak and patch it.

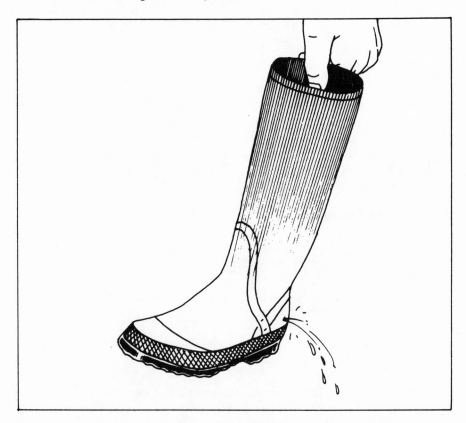

When wearing boots, put on two pair of thin cotton socks instead of one pair of thick socks. The air trapped between the two layers of thin socks will not only insulate the feet, but will allow moisture to evaporate more quickly, keeping feet dry. Moisture doesn't evaporate readily from thick socks.

Fabric Shoes

Lift off a fresh grease spot from a nonwashable fabric shoe by sprinkling the spot with cornstarch. Let the cornstarch soak up the grease for several minutes, then brush it away.

Cleaning Synthetics and Shoe Brushes

Lighter fluid can remove tar and asphalt marks on synthetic shoe materials. Be extremely careful to keep fluid away from flames; always work in a well-ventilated area.

To clean shoe brushes, soak them in warm, sudsy water to which a few drops of turpentine have been added.

Lost Something?

Misplaced your shoehorn? Try using a tablespoon instead.

When metal tips come off shoe laces, harden the tip ends with a little nail polish.

STOCKINGS

More for Your Money

A proper fit in pantyhose is essential for long, comfortable wear. A size too small will run easily because of no elasticity; a size too big or long will wrinkle and bag at the knees and ankles.

Your pantyhose will last longer if you give it the following treatment before the first wearing. Immerse the hose in water, wring it out, put it in a plastic bag, and place the bag in the freezer. Once frozen, remove it from the freezer and hang it up to dry. Sounds silly, but it really works.

Buy two or three identical pairs of pantyhose. If you get a snag or run in one leg, you can cut it off and match it with a second pair which also has one good leg.

Those Home Runs

Wear a pair of white cotton or rubber gloves while putting on or removing your hose to reduce the chance of snagging the stockings with your fingernails.

If a stocking runs, repair it with colorless nail polish or hair spray.

Instant Twins

If you have mismatched stockings left over from various pairs, you can dye them all the same color by boiling them in water along with two tea bags. Let them sit in the water until it cools, and then rinse and dry your newly matched hose.

Chapter **6**

JEWELRY AND ACCESSORIES

WHETHER YOUR JEWELS ARE FAKE OR REAL, IT'S EASY TO KEEP THEM SHINY, NEW-LOOKING, AND ALWAYS READY TO WEAR.

Earrings

If you lose a post-type pierced earring, you can give its double new use as a push pin for a home bulletin board.

Because pierced earrings are easy to lose in a suitcase, hold them together on an index card.

Winning against Tarnish

A piece of chalk in your jewelry box will prevent costume jewelry from tarnishing.

Belts and Bags

To keep belts and handbags neatly in place, hang them on large shower curtain hooks on your clothes rod.

Put an old towel to use by making it into a beach bag.

Glue a piece of foam rubber to the underside of a shoulder bag or schoolbag straps, and the bags won't slip when you carry them.

Tangle-Free

When restringing a broken necklace, use fishing line. It's easy to handle and extremely sturdy.

Bracelets and necklaces will stay tangle-free if they're stored on cup hooks attached to the inside of your closet door.

To untangle a knot in your necklace, lay the chain on a piece of wax paper and put a tiny drop of salad oil on the knot. Working with two straight pins, carefully loosen the knot.

To keep necklaces and fine chains from tangling together in your jewelry box, cut a plastic drinking straw in half and slip one end of the chain through the straw; fasten the clasp closed. Slip each chain through a separate straw.

Storing Valuable Jewelry

Storing jewelry in plastic bags will reduce tarnish by protecting it from dust, lint, and moisture. Don't store pearls this way, they need to breathe.

Separate jewelry in a jewel box so the harder stones won't scratch the softer stones and metals.

If you wear silver jewelry frequently, it won't tarnish as quickly and your skin oils will give the silver a protective satiny finish over time.

Protect pearls from dust, cosmetics, and perfume because these can dull them.

Cleaning Jewelry

To clean around the settings of precious stones, use a cotton swab dipped in alcohol.

If you want to wear gloves when polishing silver, choose plastic instead of rubber, which promotes tarnishing.

Chapter 7

FUR CARE

WHEN YOU PROTECT YOUR FURS WITH INTELLIGENT CARE, YOU'RE PROTECTING YOUR INVESTMENT, TOO.

When You Take It Off

Furs and down need breathing space when hung in a closet, so give them plenty of room between other garments.

After you wear a fur, just shake it gently, rather than combing or brushing the garment.

To prevent your fur from losing its shape, always store it on a heavy wooden or plastic hanger designed to support the weight of the garment.

Never store your fur coat in a bag, whether it be plastic, cloth, or paper. Furs should be stored with no covering, as they need good air circulation to prevent the hairs from drying and breaking.

If It Gets Wet

If snow or rain dampens your fur, hang it to dry in a cool place where there's plenty of air circulation, perhaps on a shower curtain rod.

The Shape of Things

Remove your fur coat whenever sitting for long periods or sliding in and out of car seats. Excessive friction causes the fur to wear down.

Don't carry a shoulder bag when wearing a fur coat. The constant friction of the strap against the fur will wear down the hair.

Let the Pros Handle It

Keeping your fur coat at home year-round in a cedar closet will damage the fur. Fur needs to be stored at cold temperatures and with proper ventilation to keep its natural sheen and luster. At the first sign of spring weather, put your fur coat into cold storage; this guarantees a constant, even temperature and proper humidity and air circulation. Your coat will last much longer.

Dust and grime on fur cannot be safely removed through dry cleaning or regular laundry methods. These cleaning techniques will strip the fur of its natural oils, causing drying and shedding of the hairs. Always have your fur professionally cleaned by a furrier.

Part **X**

SEWING AND NEEDLEWORK

Whether your stitching efforts are a relaxing hobby or a budgetary necessity, knowledge of professional techniques and shortcuts can make any project more fun. With the hints in this section, you'll enjoy quicker results and avoid some of the most frustrating common mistakes. Chapter 1 offers a variety of hints for organizing your sewing and sewing equipment in ways that help you work with less wasted motion. Use these shortcuts to cut sewing time dramatically. Even mending need no longer be the bane of your existence if you follow our darn good tips. When sewing garments from scratch, it's often the small, detailed jobs that frustrate and sometimes discourage the home sewer; our tips for advance planning can help you through some of these problem areas. You'll also find tips for tailoring techniques, special sewing methods for difficult fabrics, and perfect finishing touches to give the garments you make a truly professional look. Finally, to keep your sewing machine humming, use the suggestions for maintaining your trusty machine.

Chapter 2, "Needlework," is a potpourri of knitting, crocheting, embroidery, needlepoint, and quilting tips. Among the hints included in the section on knitting and crocheting are a foolproof test to determine if a forgotten skein is wool or synthetic, an ingenious method for ironing kinks out of previously knitted yarns, and tricks for keeping knitted items in shape. If you like to stitch, you'll find the section on embroidery full of easy ways to prevent floss from tangling and safe needlework projects for kids. The needlepoint section includes hints for designing a needlepoint pattern on canvas and for blocking designs made from noncolorfast yarns. Quilters will be enthusiastic about the many quilting tips including suggestions for filing patchwork pieces so they won't become mixed up or lost while you work.

These imaginative hints are guaranteed to keep you sew happy.

Chapter **1**

SEWING

WHETHER YOU'RE SEWING *HAUTE COUTURE* OR SIMPLY MENDING A SOCK, THESE HINTS ARE TAILOR-MADE TO DO IT BETTER.

GENERAL SEWING HINTS

Bull's Eye

To help you thread a needle, keep a magnifying glass in your sewing basket.

It's easy to thread a needle if you spray your fingertips with hair spray, and then stiffen the tip of the thread by rolling it back and forth in your fingers.

Cut Your Losses

Attach your tape measure to the sewing table, and you'll never again have to rummage through all your equipment to find it.

Safety pins can be neatly stored on a pipe cleaner. Thread the pins on the cleaner, bend it into a circle, and twist the two ends together.

Keep a small magnet in your sewing basket. When needles and pins drop on the carpet while you're sewing, retrieve them quickly with the magnet.

Getting to the Point

Sewing needles can get rusty and dull. Rub off any rust with an abrasive soap pad or steel wool. A dull needle or pin can be livened up by rubbing it over your hair (with its natural oils).

A bar of soap makes a perfect pincushion for pins and needles, as well as lubricating their tips to slide easily through stiff fabrics.

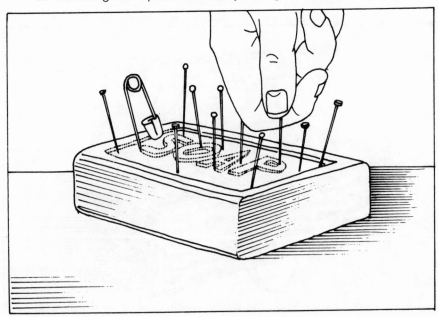

To keep your scissors from damaging other items in your sewing basket, cover the points with the same rubber protectors sold for knitting needles.

All Together Now

If you aren't satisfied with your sewing basket or box, try making this hang-up sewing center. Insert wood screws or nails across and down a bread board with a handle, then hang up all your spools of thread on it. If you want to hang scissors and other sewing utensils, add a row of cup hooks along the bottom.

The spongy filter tip from a cigarette makes a convenient pincushion. Slip it right into the hole of a spool of thread, and then stick it full of needles.

Sequins and tiny beads are often used together to decorate sweaters and other garments. If the two have gotten all mixed up in your sewing box, here's a nifty trick for separating them. Drop both sequins and beads into a colander. The beads will fall through, and the sequins won't.

Clean out all the cream from an old lipstick case, and you'll have a purse-size container for pins and needles.

For Aching Fingers

If you've got "sewer's cramp" from a long bout of stitching, flap and shake your hands gently to relieve the ache. Another good circulation booster is to hold out your arms and wiggle your fingers like mad.

SEWING BUTTONS

Fall-Out Protection

For extra-strong stitching when sewing on buttons, double the thread before threading the needle. You'll have four strands of thread for each stitch.

To keep a four-hole button in place longer, sew through only two holes at a time, using separate threads for each set. If one thread breaks loose, the other will hold the button securely.

Ingenious Solutions

When you use elastic thread to sew on buttons at the waistband of a skirt or pants, the garment will expand to fit even if you put on a few pounds.

When sewing buttons on children's clothing, consider using dental floss. It's much stronger than thread.

Having trouble removing a button? Slide a comb under it, and slice through the lifted thread with a razor blade.

Puzzled about how to store tiny buttons? Put them in empty pill bottles.

MENDING

Darn It!

When you're mending the finger of a glove, a glass marble can serve as a darning egg.

Slip a light bulb into the toe of a sock to be mended, and your darning will be easier.

Seams Like New

Here's a quick way to mend a garment when appearance is nonessential. Put a piece of paper under the hole, then darn back and forth with the sewing machine. When you wash the garment, the paper will get soggy and wash away.

It's easier to repair seams on lingerie or nylon jackets if you slide a sheet of paper under the section that needs mending. Stitch through both the fabric and the paper, and then carefully rip away the paper.

Natty Patches

Repair worn and frayed elbows of jackets and sweaters by sewing on leather patches.

Cover a hole in a blouse or dress with a pretty bit of embroidery design or a fancy appliqué.

RECYCLING

Inspired Ideas

When discarding clothing you no longer wear, first stock up on notions by saving any usable zippers, buttons, or decorative trim.

Thrift-store clothes are sometimes worth buying for the buttons alone. Good buttons are hard to find these days, and you can often find real pearl ones on old clothes.

Gather all that fluffy lint from the basket of your clothes dryer. It's the cleanest and cheapest stuffing you'll ever find for making small Christmas decorations, dollhouse furnishings, etc.

Change a used full-length slip into a half-slip by cutting off the bodice and inserting a narrow elastic band at the waist.

Unlimited Uses

Save men's old dress shirts, cut off the collars and cuffs, hem the sleeves, and use the shirts as beach or pool coverups.

Make tunic tops from your old mini-dresses, and wear them with matching pants.

You can lengthen a very short skirt by adding a lace border or a wide band of ribbon.

Magic Changes

Transform a pair of regular pants into maternity pants by removing the zipper and replacing it with a panel of stretch fabric.

Transform old slacks into knickers. Cut them below the knee and insert an elastic band into the hem.

MAKING CLOTHES

Thinking Ahead

In order to sew accurately for yourself, you must know your body measurements to a "T". Ask a friend to help you, and take measurements over your usual undergarments (not over dresses, blouses, or slacks) using a nonstretch tape measure.

Sewing projects will proceed more quickly if you complete each phase before starting another. For example, if you cut out all garment, interfacing, and lining pieces at one time, you won't have to stop to do pattern-cutting during garment construction.

Before sewing in a zipper, shrink it: Set the zipper in very hot water for a couple of minutes, then let it dry. Repeat the whole process once more before sewing in the zipper.

If you're sewing a woman's blouse, sweater, or dress that will button down the front, make the buttonholes horizontal instead of vertical. The buttons will always stay firmly shut.

Play It Again, Sam

If you have a pattern you want to use again and again, it's a good idea to preserve it with some kind of backing. Patterns can wear out after repeated use.

You can smooth wrinkled pattern pieces by pressing them with a warm, dry iron. Don't use steam, as it will distort the pattern size.

Make a file of your dress patterns by storing them upright in an old shoe box.

The Cutting Edge

Cutting a pattern on heavy fabrics, such as quilts or coatings, will be more accurate if you pin through only one layer of fabric. If you pin all the way through, the pattern will pucker, making it difficult to cut around.

Dressmaker's carbon and a fork make a great do-it-yourself tracing wheel for marking out darts on a pattern.

Cut through fake fur and other deep-pile fabric with a razor blade. Work from the wrong side, and cut through only the backing, since you want the furry side or pile to remain intact.

Glue It Instead

You can use a glue stick instead of pins and/or basting when making lapped seams. Apply the glue to the underside of the overlapping section. Press in place, allow to dry a minute or two, and topstitch.

You can hold nonfusible interfacing in place temporarily with adhesive from a glue stick. This eliminates the need to baste interfacing to the garment piece, and makes sewing faster.

When sewing an emblem on a uniform, first position and hold it in place with several dabs of white glue. After the glue sets, stitch the emblem by hand or machine. The glue will wash out with the first laundering.

Darts and Seams

Before pressing, sew as many seams and darts as you can. You'll minimize the number of trips to the ironing board and find the project going much faster than if you sewed and pressed each seam individually.

It's easier to stitch darts from the widest portion toward the narrowest.

You can make a facing lie down by stitching it to the seam allowance— not the fabric that will show—just inside the seam. Or, simply tack it at the seams. If you tack it all around its edge, the stitching will show on the right side of the fabric.

You'll probably be happier with the look of a plaid garment if it's made from fabric that has a woven, rather than printed, design. Woven plaids are easier to match at seamlines than printed plaids, which often are not printed perfectly straight with the grain of the fabric.

Tailor-Made

To prevent heavy materials from dragging on the floor while you're sewing, support them next to the sewing machine table by propping them onto an ironing board placed next to your machine.

When you're machine sewing delicate or hard-to-handle fabrics, tissue paper can save the day. Lay it under nylon fabric to keep it from slipping. When sewing lace, placing tissue between the fabric and the machine will keep the lace from snagging in the feed dog.

Some fabrics tend to pucker slightly when sewn. This usually can be prevented if the fabric layers are held taut as they go under the presser foot. Hold the fabric in front of and behind the presser foot, keeping it taut but not stretching it or pulling it through the machine.

When stitching a fabric for gathering, it's a good idea to test-gather a scrap of your fabric to see if you're getting the desired look. A long stitch length generally gives the best appearance for heavy fabrics, while a shorter stitch length is more suitable for fine fabrics.

When making an elastic waistband, it might be useful to fasten the ends of the elastic with a safety pin for the first few wearings and washings to make sure the elastic length is comfortable. Elastic sometimes shrinks or relaxes after the first washings. After the final length of elastic has been determined, you can tuck in the ends and permanently stitch the waistband.

Cuffs and Collars

Shortening the stitch length when stitching around collar curves reinforces the seam and makes the curves smoother. On collar corners, shorten the stitch length and sew one or more diagonal stitches to reinforce the corners and make room for the seam allowances when the collar is turned.

When sewing cuffs, you'll have more room for seam allowance when they're turned inside the cuff if you take one or more diagonal stitches across the points of square corners. The heavier the fabric, the longer the diagonal needs to be.

It's a Snap

It's not so hard to sew snaps into place. Stitch in the top half of one, and rub a little chalk over its tip. Press it against the other side of the garment to mark the exact spot where you should sew in the rest of your snap fastener.

Snaps can be unmanageable at times, slipping around because they're so tiny. Before sewing one on, fasten it down with invisible tape. When the snap is sewn, lift off the tape.

Finishing Touches

Before you hem a skirt, dress, or pants, let the garment hang for a day. The fabric will settle, and you'll get a more accurate hem.

You can make your own hem gauge from any lightweight cardboard, including a postcard or index card. Just notch the card at the depth you've planned for your hem, then pin it up in a jiffy.

To hold a hem in place while you sew it, you may find clip-type clothespins more convenient than pins.

You can usually steam out small amounts of fullness at the top edge of a hem. So don't redo a slightly puckered hem until you've tried to press out the pucker.

Winding Things Up

Thread is like paint: It looks darker on the spool than it will on fabric. Choose a shade somewhat darker than the material you'll be sewing.

Keep old plastic egg cartons for storing spools of thread in your sewing room.

Loose Ends

To save time spent on sewing clean-up chores, tape a plastic garbage bag underneath your sewing machine table to discard thread ends and scraps as you work.

After ripping out a seam, pick up all those loose threads with a pencil eraser.

For a handy pincushion, glue a small sponge to the corner of your sewing machine.

SEWING MACHINE CARE

You can sharpen a sewing-machine needle by stitching through a piece of sandpaper.

A small paintbrush is a helpful tool for cleaning dust and loose threads from your sewing machine.

Does the foot control of your portable sewing machine creep on the floor when you sew? It won't if you glue a piece of foam rubber to its bottom.

After you've oiled your sewing machine, stitch through a blotter to soak up any excess lubricant that might damage fabrics.

Chapter **2**

NEEDLEWORK

WHEN YOU'RE KNITTING, QUILTING, EMBROIDERING, OR DOING NEEDLEPOINT, YOUR FINGERS WILL FEEL MORE NIMBLE IF YOU STITCH WITH THESE HINTS.

KNITTING AND CROCHETING

There's a Lot to It

When buying yarn, check the labels to be sure it's all from the same dye lot, or you could end up with yarn of slightly different shades. Keep a note of the dye lot, even if you've bought all the yarn for a project in advance. You may run short unexpectedly.

Rather than settle for yarn of a different dye lot in an emergency, finish up your sweater, scarf, or socks with a stripe of yarn whose color contrasts nicely with the rest.

All Things Considered

Before buying yarn, consider the advantages and disadvantages of both wool and synthetics. Although wool will keep you warm even when wet, it may shrink when laundered, unless you give it special handling. Most synthetic yarns can be machine washed, but some synthetics may gradually stretch out of shape. Wool may be irritating or allergenic to some people; synthetics are less likely to cause an allergic reaction.

There's an easy test that will tell you whether a long-forgotten skein of yarn that's just turned up is wool or synthetic. Put a small piece of the yarn in an ash tray, and set a match to it. If the yarn burns to ashes, it's wool. Synthetics will harden into a dark lump when burned.

Roundup Time

Here are two of the best ways to wind a hank of yarn into a manageable ball. Have a friend hold the hank taut between two hands while you wind the ball. If no help is available, a ladder-backed chair works just as well. Always wind the ball loosely to keep from stretching the yarn out of shape.

You can recycle yarn from knitted items you no longer use. After the yarn's been unravelled, wind it loosely around a cake rack, dip the rack into water, and then let the whole thing dry out. All the kinks will be "ironed out" of the yarn, and you can then rewind it.

Metallic yarns have a tendency to unravel. To prevent that from happening, dip the ends in clear fingernail polish to keep the strands together while you work.

Knowing Your Place

You can make markers for your knitting from the little plastic price tags used to fasten bread wrappers. Or, if you're working with fine yarns, tie a piece of yarn into a circle for use as a marker—but don't use yarn of the same color.

When teaching a beginner how to knit, use a red needle to mark the purl row and a white needle for the plain row.

Attach a paper clip to the page of your knitting book, and move the clip up or down the page to keep your place when following detailed instructions.

It's easy to pick up the wrong directions for size when working with a knitting pattern. Before you begin, use a black magic marker to circle the numbers of the directions that apply to your size. If you decide to make the same pattern in a *different* size later on, just use a bright-red, pink, or green ink to circle the new numbered steps.

Sizing Things Up

You can test your knitting pattern for gauge size by doing a test run. Using the needles and yarn suitable for the pattern, knit a sample piece of about four inches. When you measure this, you'll have a good idea of any adjustments that may be necessary.

The plastic hairpins that come with brush hair rollers are better than straight pins for pinning seams. The plastic pins are longer and stay firmly in place. They'll never rust either!

To make sure knitted sleeves are identical, knit them on the needle at the same time.

It's Knot a Problem

For a smoother look, try splicing the ends of your knitting, instead of knotting them. Unravel about an inch of each yarn end, then loosely weave the strands together. You can finish off with a twist that matches the twist of your yarn.

It's easier to camouflage the place where you've knotted two lengths of yarn if you do it at the edge rather than in the middle of an item. At the edge, you can cover the knot with a seam or edging; in the middle, the spot may stick out like a sore thumb.

Carrying Case

If you want to transport your knitting around with you, you can make a carrier from a plastic bleach bottle that's been well rinsed. Cut off about two inches from the top of the handle and spout, and drop in the ball of yarn. Draw up the end of the skein through the spout as you work. No more tangles!

Here's a foolproof way for keeping your yarn spotlessly clean while you knit or crochet. Put the ball of yarn into a plastic bag, and poke a hole in the bottom of the bag. Thread the end of the skein through the hole, then draw out the yarn a little at a time as you work.

Looking for a good place to store skeins of yarn? You can tuck them neatly into the slots of a wine rack.

Happy Endings

If you break a knitting needle, it can be used to prop up a houseplant in need of staking.

You can make a double-pointed knitting needle from a broken plastic one. Just put the broken end of the needle into a pencil sharpener to make a new point.

A knitting needle can do double duty as a ruler. Starting from the top down, mark off every inch with a bit of nail polish or a waterproof marking pen.

Shape-Ups

Knitted cuffs have a tendency to lose shape. You can interweave elastic thread through the cuffs to help them keep their shape, or you cn knit sewing silk of the same color into the first couple of rows.

Knitted cuffs and other ribbed edges will keep their shape better if you use needles a size or two smaller than those used for the rest of the garment.

Ribbed edges should never be ironed with steam. This causes the ribbing to flatten out and lose its flexibility.

You can prevent the strap of a knitted or crocheted shoulder bag from curling up or stretching out of shape. When making the strap, use two separate knitted or crocheted pieces, and bind them together with fusible web.

Flying Fingers

When your hands feel stiff from too much knitting, powder them with a bit of talc. The yarn will glide easily again over your fingers.

Stop the Itch

Many people are sensitive to wool clothing. To make a wool sweater less scratchy, rinse it in cool water to which a tiny bit of glycerine has been added. Or, you can line the sleeves of a wool sweater by tacking in the legs from an old pair of nylon hose.

Knitted Gifts

If you want to make a baby sweater for a friend who's expecting, make buttonholes down both sides of the front opening of the garment. It'll be easy enough to sew buttons on the right side—and close the extra openings—for either a boy or a girl after the baby is born.

If you plan to give something you've knitted or crocheted as a gift, use a bit of the leftover yarn to wrap the gift. Your recipient can use this remnant for any future mending. Slip the washing instructions from the yarn label into the package, too.

Crochet Hooks

Treat your crochet hooks to a paraffin rub from time to time to keep them in good working condition.

Use plastic toothbrush tubes for storing your crochet hooks.

EMBROIDERY AND NEEDLEPOINT

No-Fuss Floss

Embroidery floss has a tendency to tangle. You can eliminate the problem by winding it onto knitting bobbins.

When you need to separate embroidery floss, it can be done without a lot of fuss. Cut the length of thread you'll need, then moisten it with a damp sponge. You'll be amazed at how easily the moist strands separate—and then dry again in a flash.

Use a somewhat larger needle when embroidering with metallic floss. Because the eye of the needle is larger, the thread won't catch and fray as easily.

For Kids Only

Instead of using buttons or beads, it's safer to embroider the eyes, mouth, and nose onto stuffed animals you create for a child. Colorful embroidery is prettier, too.

Styrofoam meat trays make good sewing cards for children. Punch out a design with a paper puncher, and let the children sew in the design with colorful yarn. To make a safe needle substitute, wrap cellophane tape around the tip of the yarn.

You can make tiny buttons for doll clothes by punching out holes from an empty plastic dish-soap bottle. Gather up the little plastic circles, and pierce buttonholes into them with a hot needle.

Taking Precautions

Some domestic and many imported yarns aren't colorfast. When in doubt, dampen some particularly bright threads, and rub them against a scrap of white cloth. If the colors run, it means you can't wash or otherwise wet the needlework in which the thread is used.

Crewel work can collect a lot of dust and grime. Spray it with fabric waterproofing or guard to keep it dust-free.

Down to Basics

Ordinary tea can be used to dye white cotton or linen needlepoint canvas. The stronger the tea, the darker the color you'll get. Use one to three teabags to a cup of hot water (depending on how deep a color you want). Brush the tea on your canvas, then simply block it and let dry.

When doing needlepoint, cover the rough edges of your canvas with masking tape. This prevents the yarn from catching and fraying. (Bind the top of the canvas with colored tape, so you'll know which end is up.)

Never fold up a needlepoint canvas when you're not working on it. To keep the canvas sturdy, roll it up instead.

Designer Colors

You'll be able to draw designs on needlepoint canvas with greater ease if you pull, rather than push, the pencil.

You can waterproof paints you've used on your needlepoint design by spraying the canvas with acrylic spray.

Holding Fast

When blocking needlepoint whose yarn isn't colorfast, douse it liberally with salt before wetting it down with cold water. Then just let it dry.

Another way to block non-colorfast yarn is to combine two tablespoons of white vinegar with a cup of cold water, and use it to thoroughly moisten both sides of the finished canvas. Be careful not to saturate the needlepoint, however. This technique will also keep the underlying inks of the design from bleeding.

Quality Control

You can check for any stitches you may have missed by holding a finished needlepoint canvas up to the light.

QUILTING

Invisible Ink

If you prefer not to mark up your quilt face with a pencil, "draw" in the straight lines with strips of masking tape.

For interesting markings that won't show on the finished quilt, put your cookie cutters to use. Dip each cutter into cocoa or cinnamon, and stamp the spice design on the quilt top. No marks—and it smells great, too.

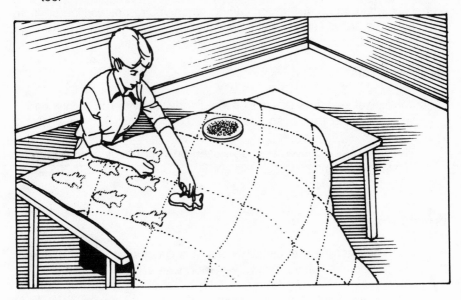

The Master Plan

Cardboard templates become quickly worn. Put tape around their edges so repeated use won't appreciably change the size of the pattern.

You can make a sturdy master pattern for patchwork pieces from an iron-on mending patch. If won't slip or fray, and it will hold its shape for a long time.

Iron on some fusible bond to the backs of lightweight quilting appliqués. They'll stay flat and keep their shape. You can get the same effect by treating them with spray starch and then ironing.

Taking Charge of Things

After sorting your patchwork pieces, slip a doubled thread through a pile, leaving the knotted end of the thread at the bottom of the stack. With the top end left unknotted, you can peel off each square as it's needed.

You can keep track of your patchwork squares by storing the pieces in large-size coffee cans. Count the pieces carefully, and note the number on the lid.

Part **XI**

KIDS

These days the members of many families live great distances from one another, and it's not as easy as it once was to turn to Mother or Grandma for experienced child care advice. If you're relying on guesswork when making important child care decisions, you may find just the hint you need in this part.

Care of babies and small children is covered in Chapter 1, which surveys everything from safety, bathing, and high-chair hints to teething, traveling with small children, and diapering. These are the kind of tips guaranteed to make life easier for both parent and child. You'll find hints for dressing a small child, as well as ways to make a pair of jeans wear longer or extend the life of a jacket your child is quickly outgrowing. You'll also want to try out some of the imaginative, inexpensive ideas for toys, entertainments and amusements, and to look into the sections on sleeping, health, and safety. Training your infant to sleep with a reasonable amount of background noise will result in a child who can doze off almost anywhere, a blessing for most parents. And, knowing that you can command the attention of a screaming child with a whisper instead of a raised voice means you'll also prevent an embarrassing public scene.

As children grow and their needs change, so must parental tactics. Chapter 2, "Older Children," covers the special problems of raising school-aged youngsters. There are smart ideas such as organizing a neighborhood baby-sitting co-op, as well as ways for painlessly removing adhesive tape from a child's sensitive skin and removing gum from a kid's hair. You'll find it easy to keep your children entertained with our trunkful of ideas on party activities, homemade toys and games, and travel hints that are guaranteed to drive boredom away.

Parenting becomes really creative when you've got these tried and true child-raising hints at hand.

Chapter **1**

BABIES AND SMALL CHILDREN

SOUND AND SENSIBLE TIPS FOR THE BEST POSSIBLE CARE OF YOUR CHILD.

Bathing Babies

If there are children in your house, it's a good idea to set the water heater below 115°F, which is scalding, so they won't harm themselves at the sink or tub.

You'll have a better grip on a soapy baby if you wear a soft cotton glove on one hand.

A baby won't be as slippery in the tub or sink if you line it with a towel or diaper.

Use soap sparingly to preserve baby's own protective skin oils.

You'll stay dry even if baby splashes by clipping a towel around you like a bib. As a bonus, the towel will be ready at hand when the bath is over.

Powder won't go into baby's face if you carefully put it on your hand first and then apply.

If your infant doesn't like to take baths, try bathing him with you to give him a secure feeling.

To keep soap or shampoo out of an infant's eyes, gently rub petroleum jelly on his eyelids and eyebrows. The jelly will make the shampoo run sideways rather than downward. (Let an older child wear a small diving mask, turning bathing into an adventure.)

Bathing Toddlers

If you're nervous about bathing a small child in the tub, try setting a clean plastic clothes basket in the tub. Add water and set the child into the basket—there's no danger that the little one can slide too far.

You can give your toddler a better footing with decorative, nonslip tape or cutouts in your tub or shower.

Toddlers find bars of soap too slippery to control, yet many insist on washing themselves. Solution: Stuff a sock with small chunks of soap and fasten the open end. A child will be able to work up a lather, but the sock won't frustrate him by sliding out of his grasp.

To avoid scarring when bathing a child who has chicken pox, gently pat him dry so you won't disturb the blisters or scabs.

High Chair Hints

To prevent an overactive baby from tipping over his high chair, latch the chair to a wall with a childproof hook and eye. (If a persistent child tries to slide out from under the high chair's tray, make the chair less slippery by fastening a rubber sink mat to the chair's seat.)

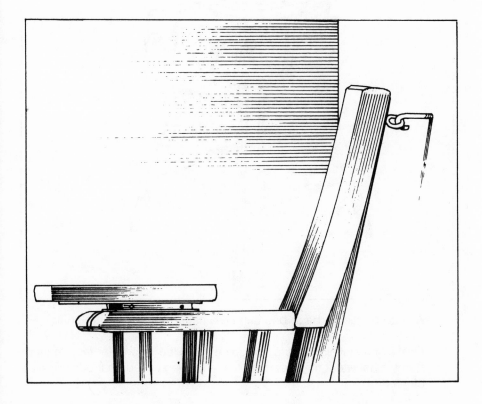

Baby's plate or bowl won't slip on his high chair tray if you put it on a rubber suction soap holder.

If you attach a towel bar to the back of a high chair, you'll have a convenient place to hang a washcloth and bib.

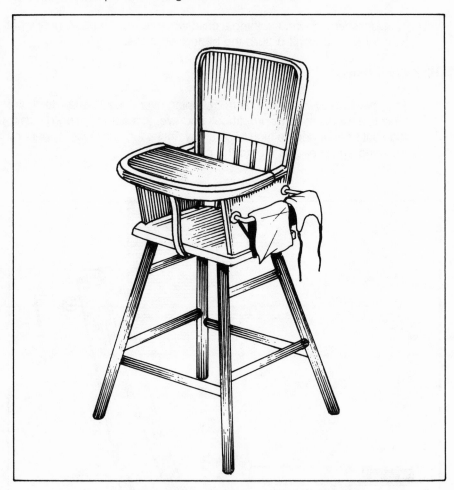

A large plastic garbage bag can be a catchall under a high chair.

Plastic or metal high chairs can go right into the shower for fast cleanup. Run the hot water for a few minutes, and even caked-on foods will wipe off easily.

Just-Right Formula Milk

If you sometimes make baby's formula too warm for him to tolerate, keep extra formula on hand in your refrigerator. Add the appropriate cold amount to the too-warm formula to cool it off.

To warm an 8-ounce bottle in a microwave oven, use high power for 15 to 30 seconds if it's at room temperature and for 30 to 60 seconds if it's cold from the refrigerator. Test the milk on the inside of your wrist before feeding the baby.

If you're nursing but need to give supplemental bottles occasionally, consider using powdered formula. That way you can mix just the amount you need, instead of opening an entire can for just one bottle.

Baby's Bottle

You can regulate the flow of liquids by loosening the bottle collar if the flow is too slow or tightening if the flow is too fast.

If you mark the ounces on baby's bottle with nail polish, you'll be able to read them even in a dimly lit room at night.

If the holes in a baby bottle nipple are too small, you can enlarge them by boiling the nipple for about five minutes and then allowing it to cool for about three minutes with toothpicks lodged in the holes. If the holes are too large, reboil the nipple.

Baby bottles won't tip over in the refrigerator if you stand them in a soft-drink carton.

You can keep nipples from deteriorating as quickly by occasionally brushing them with a salt solution.

Bottle nipples stored in a cool, dry place will last longer.

Baby can be weaned gradually from a bottle by letting him drink directly from the familiar container, but with the nipple removed or replaced by a soda straw.

Sterilizing Baby's Bottle

If you have a dishwasher, set your water temperature at 180°F, to sterilize baby utensils along with family dishes.

If you put glass marbles in a sterilizer, they will attract water minerals and help keep baby bottles clear of deposits.

You can clean bottle nipples in the microwave by boiling them in water in a glass jar. If you add a teaspoonful of vinegar to the water, mineral deposits won't collect on the jar.

Feeding Comfort

Your baby is less likely to suffer the pain of trapped gas if you feed him in as nearly an upright position as possible. (The bubble at the bottom of his stomach then can rise and be burped easily.)

You'll be more comfortable when nursing if you sit in a cushioned rocker, armchair, or sofa that has low arms.

A heating pad can keep an infant's crib warm while he's feeding. The bed will be comfortably warm when baby returns for a nap.

Teething Pains

When your child is teething, you can soothe the pain—and give him Vitamin C—with frozen orange sections. Baby will love both the coolness and the sweet taste.

You don't have teething foods handy, and baby is fussing? Try hardened bread, biscuits, or stale bagels.

Traveling Tot

If you take baby on a prolonged trip, regular formula or milk in baby bottles may spoil. Instead, put powdered formula or milk—in correctly measured amounts—in the bottles he normally uses. When it's feeding time, just add water to a bottle and shake it.

Baby Food

For lump-free baby food, you'll need to put enough food in the blender to cover the blades one inch.

An ice-cube tray can be used to freeze blocks of baby food.

If the lid of a baby food jar simply will not budge when you try to unscrew it, punch a small hole in the lid to break the vacuum seal. The lid should twist right off.

A small, wet cloth can be put in a baby food jar or other small jar with a screw-on cap for cleanups on the road.

The Little Gourmet

When a child is first trying to drink from a cup or glass, you can make the utensil easier to hold by putting several wide rubber bands or strips of tape around it.

If your kids are picky eaters, try them on miniature meat loaves, made in muffin tins.

For a picky toddler, put different bits of food into compartments of a muffin tin and lunch becomes a game. The same works for a child sick in bed, the compartments holding various foods and a tiny drinking glass.

An ice cream cone makes an edible "fun" container for tuna, egg salad, cottage cheese, or yogurt.

You can make sloppy joes more manageable for your children if you start with unsliced hamburger buns. Cut a quarter-inch-thick layer off the top of each bun and scoop out just enough bread to leave a bowl with sturdy walls. Lightly fill the hole with sloppy joe mix and then press the removed top firmly back in place.

Diapering

Hang a shoebag near baby's changing table to hold diaper pins and ointments you repeatedly reach for.

Cornstarch mixed with powder gives you the fresh baby powder odor plus extra protection from wetness. However, cornstarch alone is a good substitute.

It's best to use fabric softener sparingly because some babies are sensitive to softener buildup, and overuse makes diapers less absorbent. A handful of baking soda in the next-to-last rinse will keep diapers soft and fresh smelling.

Masking tape can be used to mend torn tabs on disposable diapers.

You'll always have diaper pins handy away from home if you pin a few to your key chain.

A bar of soap makes a good pincushion for diaper pins and also lubricates them so they slip through cloth diapers more easily.

If baby's plastic pants are becoming dry and brittle, rub a little baby oil into them—or put the oil into the rinse water.

Clothes and Dressing

If you offer your child a choice of outfits, he may be happier about getting dressed. Choosing also gives practice in decision making.

You can buy a child's clothing without bringing him along if you trace paper patterns of clothing that already fits.

Children will be more likely to hang up their clothes themselves if they can reach the hooks.

Iron-on patches on the insides of the knees of new jeans will help the jeans last longer.

A child offered a raisin or piece of dry cereal will close his hand around it and make it easier for you to get his hand through a sleeve.

It will be easier to put shoes on a wiggly toddler if he's "trapped" in a high chair.

Zippers, rather than buttons, make it easier to dress a toddler.

It will be easier for both you and your child if his clothes have front fasteners.

Most youngsters have a tough time telling right from left, especially when putting on shoes. You can help by putting a distinctive mark (such as a square of red tape) on the right shoe.

Shoelaces will stay tied if you dampen them before tying.

If you cut two tiny parallel slits in the tongue of a child's shoe and pull the laces through the slots to tie as usual, the tongue won't slip down out of place.

If you dip the ends of frayed shoelaces in clear fingernail polish, they'll be easier to poke through eyelets.

If your child is outgrowing his winter jacket and you need to make it last the season, just add knitted cuffs to the jacket's sleeves. (You can buy knitted cuffs at department store notion counters.) As a bonus, the cuffs act to keep out cold air.

If your toddler has figured out how to take off mitten clips, attach his mittens to a long string that goes across his back and down both coat sleeves.

Mitten clasps can help hold overall straps so they don't slide off a toddler's shoulder—or, sew Velcro tabs on straps where they cross.

When a child will be playing in snow, cover his mittens with plastic bags so they'll stay dry.

So your child won't lose his snow boots in the jumble of other boots at school, put colored tape on them.

If your youngsters' boots are wet inside, you can dry them quickly and thoroughly with a portable hair dryer.

An inexpensive inner tube repair kit, available at a hardware store, is useful in repairing rubber boots.

Toys, Entertainments, and Amusements

Any door or wall can be made into a blackboard with chalkboard paint (available at paint stores).

A large household sponge can double as a washable blackboard eraser.

Sandbox and Swings

Make an indoor sandbox from an old plastic dishpan. Spread newspa-

544

per and plastic bags underneath to handle the overflow.

An old tractor or truck tire makes a great outdoor sandbox. Just be sure there are no sharp metal edges.

If you cover the edges of swing seats with slit sections of garden hosing, you'll soften the blow if a seat swings into a child.

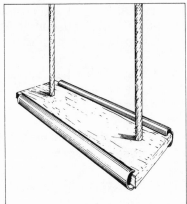

Toys

You can extend the life of cardboard games, paper dolls, and jigsaw puzzles by spraying them with shellac.

Stuffed toys that are not washable can be cleaned with dry cornstarch. Rub it in, let it stand for a bit, and then brush it off.

Snap-on plastic shower curtain hooks can hold toys and rattles on baby's crib, in view and off the floor.

If you gather beach toys in a mesh vegetable bag, you can easily rinse them of sand.

If you store your child's bike outdoors, consider protecting the seat with a shower cap.

If a youngster complains that his sled doesn't zip down a hill fast enough, you can speed things up by spraying the bottoms of the sled's runners with vegetable oil.

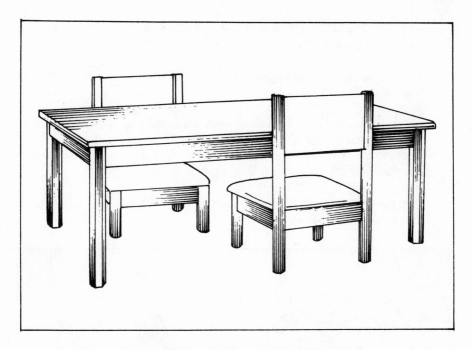

Cutting off the legs of an old, adult-size table makes a play table just the right height for children.

Kiddie Artwork

Save money by making your own fingerpaints for your youngsters. Mix ¼ cup of cornstarch with 2 cups of cold water and boil the mixture till it thickens. Pour it into suitable size containers, and add harmless food colorings.

Another method for making fingerpaint or decorative play plaster: Mix two cups of soap flakes and two cups of liquid laundry starch in a large bowl. Blend with a wire whisk or an electric beater set at high speed till the mixture has the consistency of whipped cream. If you want the mixture to be colorful, add four to six drops of food coloring and beat the mixture again. Mix a fresh batch for each play period.

Children love to squeeze play dough into imaginative shapes, and you can always have it handy if you mix it yourself as needed. All that's required are two cups of flour, one cup of salt, and just enough water to make the mixture rubbery and soft. So that it doesn't dry out, keep it tightly sealed when not in use.

If you wrap crayons with masking tape, a child will be less likely to snap them in half accidentally.

Junior Picassos can leave a mess when dabbling with paint, but you can keep the mess manageable by inserting the paint container into an opening cut in a sponge. The container can't tip over, thanks to the sponge, and the sponge will soak up any drips.

Add glitter to the soap flakes you use as decorative "snowy" covering for children's holiday art projects.

A flip-top bandage container can make a good storage container for crayons.

Proud of your child's intitial attempts at artwork? You can preserve the freshness of the colors by coating each creation with hair spray.

If your little girl wants to dress up like a lady, let her make her own necklaces. The ingredients? Dry macaroni dipped in a variety of liquid food colors. After the macaroni is colored, drain it and let it dry before stringing it with needle and thread.

Orange juice cans are good items for preschoolers to decorate as pencil holder gifts for parents. They can be decorated with string, noodles, stars, etc.

Sleeping

If you try to keep baby's surroundings totally quiet during naps, he'll soon require silence for sleeping. It's better to maintain a reasonable noise level so he'll learn to sleep just about anywhere.

A small inflatable plastic pool makes an ideal bed or playpen for an infant when you're traveling. Just inflate it and line it with a sheet or blanket. There are no hard edges on which the baby can hurt himself, and he can't roll out either.

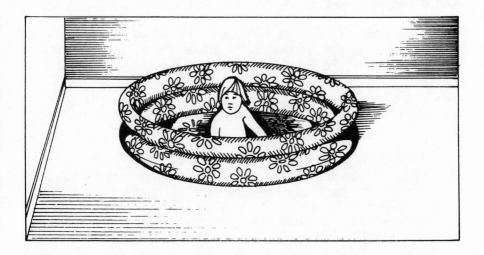

A rubber sheet under the regular bedsheet will protect mattresses from staining.

If your infant doesn't yet know how to roll over easily, it's best to lay him on his stomach. That way, he is less likely to choke if he vomits.

Since the sound of running water simulates intra-uterine sounds, you might be able to lull baby to sleep with a tape recording of water filling the tub.

A padded laundry basket or padded dresser drawer makes a good bed for a visiting infant.

A large bed sheet provides a clean infant play area on a motel floor or on a grassy area outdoors.

Health and Safety

Since a child under three could choke to death on a large pill, it's best to use liquid medication. If a liquid form is not available, mash the tablets and combine with juice or food.

If you use a medicine dropper to give your child oral, liquid medicines, release the liquid slowly into a cheek; be careful not to point the dropper into the throat, forcing medicine down the windpipe.

Out of Reach

If a youngster is at the creeping stage, he's likely to seize lamp cords and pull lamps from table tops. You can prevent this by tightly wrapping all light cords around table legs. Reinforce the windings with transparent tape, if necessary.

You can prevent electrical burns to children by blocking electrical outlets with plastic plugs.

If the knobs on your range are within your toddler's reach, consider removing them to thwart his curiosity—and keep him safe. If you store them nearby, you'll have the knobs when you need them.

To prevent a curious toddler from opening kitchen cabinets and drawers, slide a yardstick through the handles of adjacent drawers and cabinets.

Small children sometimes can't remember which is the hot water tap and which is the cold water tap. You'll make it easier for them by marking the hot tap with red tape.

If you have a piano in your home, a toddler may accidentally drop the lid over the keys and hurt his fingers. Guard against this by fastening an upright cork at each end of the keyboard.

Keeping telephones out of reach of toddlers will prevent mysterious charges from appearing on your phone bill.

If a child is angry and crying, the normal tendency is to raise your voice so he'll pay attention to you. However, if you whisper instead, a child will stop crying so he can hear what you're saying.

To prevent a child from accidentally locking himself in the bathroom, drape a towel over the top of the bathroom door.

If you fasten bells (out of a child's reach) on exterior doors, you'll know when your toddler is headed outdoors unsupervised. Or you might sew bells on an elastic bracelet which a child can wear to keep you advised of his whereabouts in the house.

For peace of mind—and safety—when taking small children to a zoo, circus, or fair, attach a stick-on label to each youngster's clothing. The label should list the child's name, address, and telephone number. In case a child gets lost, you'll be notified immediately over a loudspeaker system.

Make it easy for small children to go up and down your stairs. Add a temporary hand rail at child-height on the wall opposite the permanent hand rail.

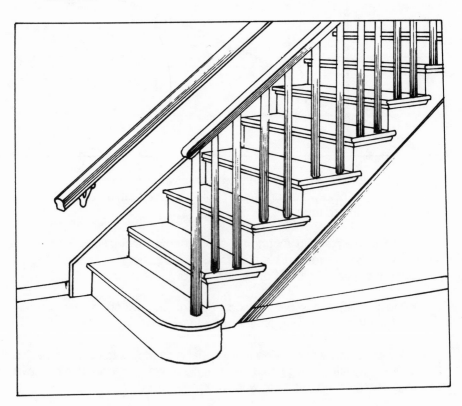

A toddler may find it difficult to walk on a hard surface with his first pair of hard-soled shoes. You can make it easier for him by glueing thin strips of foam rubber to the shoe's soles. Or, put strips of masking tape on the bottoms of his shoes.

If an adult sits next to a restrained toddler while traveling in a car, the child will be happier and the trip will be more pleasant.

Chapter **2**

OLDER CHILDREN

FROM GROWING PAINS TO INDOOR GAMES, THESE TIPS ARE ON TARGET FOR THE OLDER CHILD.

A Little Help

If there are enough young children in your neighborhood, you can set up a baby-sitting co-op.

Carry a powder puff and a box of cornstarch to the beach for dusting sand from your child when it's time to leave.

Clothes and Dressing

A man's shirt, with the collar and sleeves removed, makes a shortie nightgown for a grade-school girl. A big t-shirt also makes a good nightshirt for a child.

Sew buttons on children's clothing with dental floss or fishing line instead of thread in places where the clothing gets most wear and tear.

If you use elastic thread to sew on the cuff buttons of your child's shirts, you'll never have to continually button and unbutton the cuffs. The elastic provides just enough stretch so that your child can slip his or her hand through the cuff even when it's buttoned.

Put a plastic bag around your child's foot before slipping on galoshes. This makes fitting easier and keeps his feet warmer, too.

Spray children's raincoats with silicone furniture polish to keep them looking new.

The kids will be more eager to help clean up their rooms if you make the chore into a game, offering points for each item picked up and put in its place. Award a prize to the child with the most points.

Happy Birthday

At a birthday party, cover the party table with shelf paper and let each guest decorate his or her own place with nontoxic magic markers. They can decorate their white paper plates too.

Have an undecorated frosted birthday cake ready, as well as a big dish of sugar cookies. Let the birthday child decorate the cake from jars of instant frosting while the rest of the kids decorate cookies with jelly beans, candy hearts, gumdrops, chocolate pieces, etc.

Sometimes birthday candles drip wax into the frosting and discolor it. You can prevent this by securing each candle with a small marshmallow.

If you keep old wallpaper books or wrapping paper, you'll have a great activity for a birthday party; each child can make his or her own hat. Provide scissors, yarn for the ties, newspaper for making streamers, and a stapler.

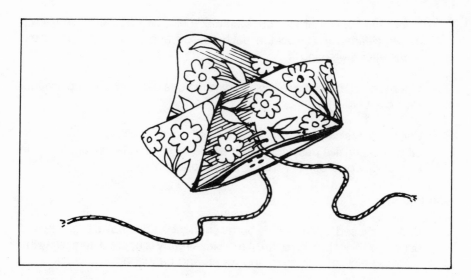

Health and Safety

Keep the following houseplants out of the reach of children. They're pretty to look at but poisonous if swallowed or chewed: poinsettia, mistletoe, rhubarb, laurel, rhododendron, azalea, cherry boughs, and daphne berries.

For your child's safety when bicycling, make out an index card listing his or her name, address, and phone number. Tape this card securely to the bicycle handlebars.

A child who is choking and can't clear the obstruction by himself can be helped by putting his head down over your lap and pounding on his back.

A dehydrated child should be given commercially prepared liquids containing needed salts and sugar (such as lytren and Pedialyte mineral and electrolyte mixtures). Other good liquids are gelatin desserts (liquid or jellied), fruit juices, weak tea with sugar, ginger ale, colas, or other carbonated drinks.

If you're having trouble depressing a child's tongue to check for a sore throat, try using a small lollipop.

If your child has a history of "swimmer's ear," it's best to have his ear canals cleaned (by a doctor) each season and to use preventive ear drops after swimming.

When a child balks at swallowing a vitamin or a pill, bury it in applesauce. He'll eat it willingly.

Cheer up a sick child with a bagful of books, coloring materials, and other inexpensive pastimes. Wrap all the items, and label each with the time of day or order in which it can be opened.

Bandaging

Blisters caused by friction or burns should be covered with gauze and bandages—not broken open. If a blister already is opened, trim away the loose skin, clean with soap and water, and bandage.

If your child's fingers or toes are cut, they will heal better if kept immobile. Try splinting the fingers or bandaging toes together.

Children hate to have adhesive tape removed from their skin, but they won't complain if you first rub the tape with a wad of cotton soaked with baby oil. The tape will come off painlessly.

Instead of throwing out the old white socks your children have outgrown, recycle them as bandages for skinned elbows and knees. If you cut off the toe, the socks can slip over an elbow, the heel portion covering the joint. The cuffs of the socks are great for an injured knee.

Slick Tricks

You can remove gum from a child's hair with cold cream. Massage the cream into the gummy area, and then pull down on hair strands with a dry towel.

It might be more fun for your children to brush their teeth if you have them "race" a minute-glass you keep on the back of the bathroom sink. After each meal, have each youngster vigorously brush his or her teeth till the top section of the glass empties.

Growing Pains

You'll know your child's aches as growing pains if they occur only at rest, at night, or during naps. A disease or abnormality is indicated if the child is in pain when he is active, too.

If growing pains are frequent and severe, sturdier shoes might alleviate the problem.

Shoes that are too small or too pointed could be the culprit if your child repeatedly develops ingrown toenails.

If your three- to six-year-old is flat-footed, it will help if he tiptoes bare-footed five to ten minutes per day. A child six to eight years of age will benefit from walking barefooted on the outer edge of his foot with his toes clenched for ten minutes daily.

Homemade Toys and Games

A tire hung from a tree branch makes a great swing.

To make a hobby horse, stuff a sock, insert a broomstick all the way into the heel and tie the sock on tightly. Decorate it with a face and mane.

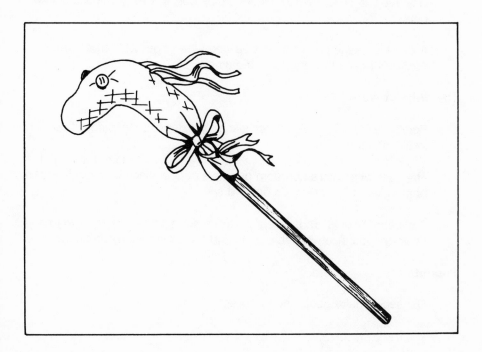

Mount greeting cards, magazine scenes, Christmas cards, etc. on cardboard. Then cut them out in irregular patterns for do-it-yourself puzzles.

To make stilt walkers, remove the lids from two tin cans. Punch two holes in the bottom of each can near the edges. Thread strong string through the holes and tie a knot to secure. The child can slip his elbows through the looped string. Really small children can start with tuna cans.

Fill your little ones' Christmas stockings with dimestore items—crayons, bags of gold stars, magic markers, colored chalk, etc.—which will keep them occupied all winter long.

If you lack space for storing a toy train, devise a simple pulley and rope system to raise the train board to the ceiling of a child's room. If you paint the underside the color of the ceiling, the board can hang camouflaged.

You can make a child's ball from an old sock stuffed with panty hose. This is one ball that won't break either heads or windows.

Save the plastic caps from empty toothpaste tubes, and fill them with clay. Kids can use them to decorate their doll houses as miniature flower pots.

A piece of tissue paper placed between the pages of a child's coloring book will prevent colors from smearing.

The Written Work

Reinforce the spines of children's school textbooks with strips of colored insulation tape.

The back of a child's bedroom door is a perfect place for a cork bulletin board. And if it's messy no one will see it!

A sheet of flexible, transparent plastic is perfect for children to write and draw on. Just use washable pens and the plastic will wipe clean.

Puppets

Old socks make good hand puppets.

Make finger puppets from leaky rubber gloves by cutting off the fingers.

You can turn a closet into a puppet theater if the door has three large horizontal panels. Remove the middle panel and hang a rod with a curtain from the inside of the closet. Replace the doorknob with a latchless wire pull so your child can't get locked inside.

Music-Making

Make a flute from a paper tube by punching it with holes an inch apart. Cover one end with waxed paper and it's ready to be played.

Cut a hole in the cover of a shoebox and stretch five rubber bands across it lengthwise to make a splendid banjo.

For maracas, fill yogurt cups, bottles, tin cans, or margarine tubs with uncooked rice, dried beans, stones, or buttons.

Crafts

Children can make place mats by arranging leaves on burlap and covering them with clear plastic wrap.

Take a day trip to the woods with your children. Collect seeds and pods of all kinds for decorating the house and gift packages during the holidays.

Buttons or pasta can be strung into necklaces just as well as can beads.

You can use screw-on earrings as miniature clamps for model building.

Travel Hints

While traveling, kids can color and play games on a lap tray—or even on a cookie sheet.

At camp, a teenager can use a shoebag hung next to her bunk for storing books, brush, comb. It saves climbing up and down when she's got the top bunk.

Car traveling with children can be enjoyable if you plan ahead. Take along a plastic shopping bag filled with paper and pens, crayons and coloring books, some books, and even a favorite toy or game.

Part **XII**

PETS

Pets add so much pleasure and affection to our lives, but they also need lots of attention to keep them properly fed, groomed, disciplined and doctored. The many hints in this part maximize the pleasure and minimize the problems of owning an animal.

Chapter 1 deals with our most popular four-legged friends, dogs and cats. The hints for feeding will save you money at the grocery checkout as well as fortify your pet's diet. Did you know that higher-priced hamburger look-alike is made to appeal to the owner, not the dog? The dog can't tell the difference in color, and the food is no more nutritious than lower-priced alternatives.

Keeping pets clean and sweet smelling is an especially important part of good care—for both you and your pet. Our tips on bathing finicky cats can save a lot of time and fuss, and the tips on dry baths for dogs and on keeping their hair from shedding all over furniture will be a boon for dog owners.

Pet owners will find the health and first-aid sections especially valuable, especially since an animal can't tell you where it hurts. You'll learn to watch for warning signs that indicate sickness or injury and how to deal with them effectively. Also included are first-aid hints on how to make a pet stretcher, how to make a splint for an injured animal and how to handle a pet that's in shock or has eaten a poisonous plant. And if it's fleas you and your pet are battling, try out some of our innovative combat techniques.

Less common pets call for different types of care, and our hints in Chapter 2 offer valuable guidance. There are hints for choosing and caring for birds such as parakeets, canaries, parrots, and budgerigars. You'll also find care hints for pets such as rabbits, hamsters, opossums, snakes, salamanders, and crocodiles! And if a land tortoise is your best friend, keep him happy by letting him have the run of your house or apartment instead of confining him to a cage. He'll find cozy places to sleep and warm spots to sun himself. The final section includes tips on dealing with wild and exotic creatures. Although these animals don't make very good pets, you never know when you may need a hint or two for dealing with one.

Pet care becomes purr-fectly easy with our grrrr-eat hints.

Chapter **1**

DOGS AND CATS

WHEN PET PROBLEMS START RAINING CATS AND DOGS, CHECK OUT THESE EVER-READY HINTS.

CARE

Better Safe Than Sorry

Don't leave your pet in a car in summer, even if the windows are open—the heat could cause collapse or even death.

On a hot day, be vigilant about an animal's water supply. Fill your pet's bowl with cold tap water and freshen it often.

To avoid colds, keep your pet inside for several hours after a bath.

Never give a child under three years of age a kitten or puppy (or any small animal) as a pet. The child may lovingly—but unintentionally—maul it to death or seriously injure it because of rough handling.

Keep a kitten or puppy away from live electrical connections. The animal may electrocute itself by licking them out of curiosity.

If your dog or cat is allowed to run free after dark, you can make your pet more visible to motorists by wrapping reflective tape around his collar.

Don't turn to pet-store owners for advice on how to care for pets. They're in business to sell small animals and pet food. They really know very little about nutrition, disease, and pet problems.

Comfy Cats and Dogs

It's foolish to waste money on an expensive pillow for a dog or cat's sleeping basket. Two or three old towels will do just as well.

Carpet scraps make a perfect lining for a pet's bed or basket.

A wooden barrel, turned on its side and appointed with a pallet filled with wood shavings, makes a cozy dog house.

Dog Care

Before buying a puppy, check out its parents, if at all possible. The parents should be friendly and outgoing. If they're vicious or shy, the puppy will probably be the same.

To wipe away the daily rheum that gathers at the corners of your dog's eyes, use a dab of cotton dipped in a boric-acid solution.

It's best to exercise your dog early in the morning and late at night. Midday heat could be dangerous to him.

Remove the leash from your dog when in the car. A leash can get caught in door handles or other projections and cause injury to your pet.

If you have to leave your dog alone at home for several hours, also leave your radio on. The accustomed sounds will reassure your pet and make him feel less abandoned. (A radio that's on also deters would-be housebreakers. They're likely to assume that someone's home.)

If the pads of your dog's feet become dry or cracked, rub a little petroleum jelly into them.

If your dog has just been clipped, make sure you don't walk him in strong sun, to avoid the chance he could get burned.

If washing your dog normally leaves you soaked with suds, try making a coverall apron for yourself by cutting holes for your head and arms in a plastic trash bag.

It's important to wash off your dog's feet in the winter since he will probably pick up salt and chemical deicer when outdoors. This can injure your dog's feet, especially if the pads are cracked.

If you have to give up your dog, bathe and groom him before taking him to an animal shelter. This vastly increases the odds that he'll be adopted quickly.

Cat Care

Contrary to traditional advice, cats should not be given petroleum jelly to treat hair balls. Ingesting petroleum jelly or mineral oil prevents the absorption of certain B vitamins. Ask your vet for a malt lubricant instead.

When petting your cat, always stroke in the direction in which its fur lies. Otherwise you'll irritate rather than soothe your pet.

Cats prefer to be talked to in a high voice; they associate lower voices with scolding.

Discourage your cat from leaping to your stove's surface, particularly if it's a smooth-top electric stove. Because cats are heat-seekers by nature, they may burn themselves severely by stepping on or lying down on one of the active elements.

It isn't an unkindness to keep your cat indoors, particularly if it has the companionship of another cat. It's less likely to get into fights with other cats, be attacked by dogs, or be hit by cars—especially when you're gone.

If you let your cat roam free, attach a bell to its collar as a warning to neighborhood birds. Make sure its tags are on, too.

When a cat gives birth to kittens, don't handle the newborn yourself. This may upset the mother, and she may reject them.

Guard your cat from drinking from pools of antifreeze which gather under cars—it's poisonous.

Disciplining Your Pet

Whenever you give a command to your dog or cat, first establish eye contact. Eye contact means you mean business.

When disciplining an animal, never call its name and then administer a punishment. Calling his name should be reserved for good things.

Start training your puppy at seven weeks. Only one family member should do the training, and it should be someone with patience who will also be spending a lot of time with the animal.

In training a dog, use one-word commands because they're clear and easy to understand. Don't expect a dog to comprehend full-fledged sentences.

It isn't wise to have your dog attack-trained. Instead of guarding you, he may jeopardize your safety. If you have youngsters who roughhouse together, he may attack *them*.

If you have to slap your dog, rap him upward under the chin. Raising your arm and hand is a threatening gesture of aggression.

If you want to keep your pets off the furniture, tuck moth balls in under the cushions.

Traveling

Before traveling with a pet, accustom the animal to its pet carrier. Leave the carrier out where he can smell it, explore it, and sleep in it.

If you want to take your cat on a car trip, first take it for short rides; increase the time each trip so it gets used to the car.

If you pet is traveling in a case, put some of his favorite toys inside so he'll feel more secure.

Don't feed your pet for six hours prior to a car trip. If he has a tendency to car sickness, try to avoid giving him water for two hours before.

If possible, carry water from home for your pet. The different mineral content of water in a new location could give him diarrhea.

When traveling with a dog, put a leash on him before both of you exit from the car at your destination. Excited by the prospect of no longer being confined, he may impulsively leap onto the street and be hit by another auto.

When you travel with your dog in a car, bring along a plastic freezer container of frozen water. As you travel, the water will thaw, and your dog will have a drink right at hand.

FEEDING

Safe and Nutritious

Never offer your pet any food that's spoiled or moldy. Anything unsafe for humans is also unsafe for pets.

If moist pet food, leftovers, etc. aren't eaten within two hours, refrigerate them. Dry food and biscuits are the only foods that can be left out for any length of time.

Don't be misled into buying packaged food for dogs that is higher-priced because it looks appetizingly red, like hamburger. A dog can't discern the difference between red and gray or brown. It's what's *in* the food that counts, not what it looks like.

In general, "dry" dog food is more nutritious than "wet" dog food. This also applies to cat food. (However, don't feed a dog or cat an exclusive diet of dry or wet food.)

A teaspoon or so of oil mixed into your pet's food every day will make its coat glossy, and stop dry-skin scratching.

It's best not to feed your dog immediately before or after exercising.

If your pet always knocks over its water dish outside, you can solve the problem by substituting an angel food cake pan for the dish. Put a sturdy stake through the pan's center hole and into the ground, and even a frisky dog won't be able to knock it over.

No More Fights

If you have both a cat and a dog, put the cat's food on platforms out of the dog's reach or behind a barrier the dog can't squeeze his nose through.

If you have more than one cat, give each one its own food bowl. Separate the bowls by at least a foot at feeding time to prevent fights.

Don't Rock the Boat

If you're going to change your pet's diet, do it gradually. A too sudden change may be a distressful shock to its system. Cats and dogs—just like their wild ancestors—like monotony in their foods.

Animals like sameness in their home surroundings. If you extensively redecorate your home or apartment, your cat or dog may lose its appetite for a few days. Don't be upset. When the animal gets used to the new decor, its desire for food and water will return.

What about Bones?

If you give your dog a bone, use only marrow or knuckle bones that have first been boiled in order to remove diarrhea-causing fat and grease. Take the bone away as soon as it starts to splinter.

Never offer your dog or cat pork chop bones, chicken bones, or fish bones. These can splinter into sharp pieces and catch in your pet's throat.

Fussy Cats

Your cat may crave red tuna fish, but don't feed it to him exclusively. Too much of it can cause yellow fat disease.

Sometimes—just to get attention—a cat, no matter how hungry, will refuse to eat any food you give it. It wants to be petted more than it wants to eat. Pet the cat at sufficient intervals and it will resume eating normally.

When your cat gets old, feed it more frequently than when it was young, but give it smaller portions.

Cook raw meat thoroughly before feeding it to a cat. It may contain parasites.

GROOMING

Clean and Sleek

When you bathe a dog or cat, make certain the water temperature is roughly 100°F. Warmer or cooler water will cause your pet distress and make him difficult to handle.

When your dog or cat starts to shed hair, usually after the cold-weather months, massage its coat with your hands, then stroke the animal from head to tail with your palms. It's better to get rid of loose hair this way than to have it decorate your furniture.

Your pet's ears should be cleaned once a month. Clean only that part of the ear canal that you can see, using a cotton swab soaked in mineral oil or alcohol. Wax protects the ear canal, so a small amount left behind is beneficial.

The Pampered Cat

Groom your cat regularly to help keep it free of hairballs. Brush short-haired cats daily. Long-hairs should be combed. Grooming is especially important in hot weather when cats are shedding old fur.

If you encounter matted or tangled fur when combing a long-hair, use your fingers to separate the tangles, not the comb.

When brushing short-haired cats, be sure to brush between the shoulders where the cat can't reach.

Your cat's claws will be easier to trim if you press the paw to better expose the nails.

Cats normally don't need bathing, but if your cat does need a bath, get a friend to assist. If you don't have help, place a small washable rug or turkish towel over the side of the basin or tub, to which the cat can cling steadfastly while you hold it with one hand and lather quickly with the other.

A double kitchen sink is best for giving cat baths—one side for soaping, the other for rinsing. Two plastic dishpans are also good, but the bathroom sink is usually too shallow.

Bathing a cat is never easy, but to make it a little less traumatic, place an angled window screen in the tub so your friend can hold on and steady himself on it.

Rinse your cat with water and a little vinegar for the second rinse. Blot its fur with a towel, but let the cat finish drying off with a tongue-wash.

It's better to towel-dry a bathed cat than to use a hair dryer. The humming, buzzing sounds of hair dryers frighten cats.

The Pampered Dog

If your dog smells bad but there's no time for a bath, just rub baking soda into his coat and brush it off.

When you bathe a dog, wash its head, ears, and neck first. If you don't, its fleas will take refuge there while you clean the rest of its body.

Groom short-haired dogs once or twice a week with a grooming comb. Long-haired coats need bristle, wire, or card brushes and pet combs with rounded teeth. Comb out long-haired dogs before a bath.

Burrs will be easier to comb from your dog's coat if you first crush them with a pair of pliers.

Vacuum your dog's coat when he starts shedding in spring. Once he gets used to it, he'll love it.

If a skunk sprays your dog, it will help to wash the dog with tomato juice, then with shampoo and water. (Do this in a well-ventilated area.)

When washing your dog in the bathtub, prevent clogged drains by placing a piece of nylon netting over the drain to collect doggie hairs.

HEALTH AND FIRST AID

General Precautions

Many early health problems can be caught and treated before they become serious. Have your pet examined fully once or twice a year.

Don't neglect annual booster shots for rabies and distemper, and any annual medication—like heartworm medicine for dogs—that your vet recommends.

Keep your cat or dog away from dieffenbachia; it's poisonous. And at Christmas, watch out for mistletoe berries and poinsettia; they're both poisonous too.

Animals' appetites lessen in warm weather. If you have a kitten, give it small amounts of food frequently on hot days. Don't let it fast too long.

If you give your cat vegetable oil for constipation, never put the oil directly into your pet's mouth. It may trickle into the breathing tubes and lungs before the cat can cough. Instead, mix the oil with his food.

All worming medications can be dangerous if used incorrectly. Never worm your cat or dog with any medication not prescribed by your vet.

Don't worry if your cat or dog eats grass; many animals actually graze. They like their daily salad, too.

Lameness, stiff neck, reluctance to get up or lie down, or tense abdominal muscles are indicators that your pet is in pain. Get to a vet!

When walking a puppy, keep it away from the droppings of other dogs. A disease known as parvovirus kills 75 percent of the young dogs under five months of age who contract it. (Older dogs are more or less immune.) Most puppies contract it through contact with infected feces.

Handling Injured Animals

Always physically restrain an animal you're examining for injuries because it will inevitably try to break free. Be gentle but firm. If he breaks free, it will cause any injury to intensify. (Remember that the animal has no idea you're restraining it for its own good.)

When approaching *any* injured animal, speak calmly in a soothing tone. It isn't the words that matter, it's the tone. Whatever you do, don't shout or cry out. That will only upset the animal more.

In case of small burns to your pet, apply commercial burn ointment or soak a cloth in strong tea and apply. But get to a vet fast with serious burns.

If your pet appears to have broken a limb, wrap it firmly (but not so tight as to cut off circulation) in a towel, newspaper, or magazine as a temporary splint; then get to the vet.

If you have to carry a large dog who is unable to walk, place a rug or blanket behind the animal and slide him onto it to make a stretcher.

Doctoring Your Cat

If your cat is feeling under par, take its temperature with a rectal thermometer greased with petroleum jelly. A temperature of 101.5°F is normal for a cat.

To give a cat a pill, hold your pet firmly on your lap or between your knees. Grasp the cat on either side of the jaws to force its mouth open, and quickly pop the pill down its throat; it has no choice but to swallow.

If your cat has a fever, don't give it an aspirin without a veterinarian's recommendation. Your cat will have trouble detoxifying and excreting it.

When you give a cat medicine orally, gently rub its throat to stimulate swallowing.

Raw liver is a natural laxative for a constipated cat. Give small servings no more than twice weekly. Adding a little milk to cat food might also work.

If your cat has diarrhea, cooked liver might help.

If your cat has an eye irritation which it keeps scratching, you can prevent him from doing so by fitting a piece of round cardboard around his neck in the shape of an Elizabethan-type collar.

To control a cat's movement when doctoring it, place it on a bath mat or small rug so it can dig its claws in. Better yet, put the cat on the floor and squat down with your pet between your knees.

If you have two cats, and one suddenly reacts with hostility when the other returns from a trip to the vet, it's because the cat that visited the vet has picked up strange smells. The stay-at-home cat will soon become friendly again.

If a cat is too sick to clean itself, keep it brushed and rubbed down. Wipe runny eyes often.

Cats are prone to become diabetic. If yours comes down with diabetes, have your vet show you how to give it the required insulin injections. If you do this faithfully, diabetes will not shorten your cat's life.

First Aid for Cats

If an injured cat is bleeding, stop the blood by applying a pressure bandage over the wound. Use a large handkerchief, towel, or other clean cloth.

Cats go into shock easily after an injury. Keep the animal warm but not hot while you call the vet.

If a cat has chewed on a poisonous plant, you can induce vomiting by making it swallow one teaspoon of 3 percent hydrogen peroxide every ten minutes.

Use heavy leather gloves if an injured cat is out of control and liable to hurt you; restrain it in a towel, blanket, or pillowcase. However, if it isn't absolutely necessary to handle the animal, wait for professional help.

When trying to restrain an injured cat, don't use a leash. A cat will struggle to free itself from a leash and possibly strangle.

576

If your cat has a convulsion that has nothing to do with poison ingestion, don't panic. Convulsions last only a few minutes and very few are fatal. Just pull it away from walls and furniture, so it won't injure itself, and wrap it in a blanket until it calms down. Then get it to a vet—it probably needs professional help.

Telltale Symptoms

If a cat appears malnourished even though well fed, has frequent loose stools, a lackluster coat and bloated stomach, you should suspect worms. Get it to a vet quickly.

If the cat's membranous eyelids half-cover its eyes, it's a sign of illness—generally intestinal. Consult the vet immediately.

If you note constant discharge from your cat's eye, it can be a symptom of either local infection or systemic disease. This is another case for the vet.

If one of your kittens dies suddenly with no outward sign of illness, it probably had feline distemper. You should have your other cats vaccinated immediately.

Preventing Cat Problems

Prefer home-raised kittens to those found in pet stores. The latter have a tendency to be unhealthy.

Keep an eye on your cat's litter box to make sure your pet is urinating normally. If a cat has trouble urinating, get it to the vet fast; a cat that hasn't urinated regularly needs immediate attention.

Cats have dental problems too. A little dry food in his diet helps prevent tartar buildup, but doesn't replace an annual dental checkup by the vet.

Don't let a cat eat a dead rat or dead mouse. Not only does the rodent have internal parasites that will be transmitted to the cat, it may have been poisoned. The poison that killed the rodent may similarly kill the cat.

To Neuter or Not

Even a neutered male cat will sometimes "spray" in the house, particularly if it perceives a threat to the status of its environment (such as the appearance of a new baby). Such spraying normally stops after the cat has adjusted to the change.

Neutering a cat doesn't cause laziness and obesity—overeating and getting too little exercise do.

If a female cat isn't either spayed or bred, she will come into heat for two or three weeks twice a year. If you don't want your cat to periodically act like she's insane, either have her spayed or let her have kittens.

Healthy Dogs

If you want a dog that will live for a long time, pick one of the smaller breeds. Generally, the larger the dog, the shorter its life span.

A dog's normal temperature is between 101.0° and 102.5°F. Anything higher indicates a problem.

No Cause for Alarm

If a puppy is only a few months old and has "garlic breath," don't worry. This is normal and shows the presence of "good" bacteria in his mouth. The odor will disappear in a few months.

If your dog or cat drinks from the toilet (and most dogs do), don't be upset. Water in a flushed toilet bowl won't harm your pet in any way. But don't let a pet drink from a toilet that has a cleaner or freshener in the tank or bowl—the chemicals are toxic.

Don't be alarmed if your dog twitches or jerks spasmodically when asleep. He isn't having convulsions; he's just dreaming.

When Your Dog Is Sick

If nausea is present in your dog, remove all food and water for 24 hours. Give the dog ice cubes to lick, as these will supply water in small amounts so dehydration won't occur.

Worms are not caused by candy and cannot be cured by garlic. Never treat a dog on your own with store-bought worm medicine; get to a vet instead. Dogs do not transmit pinworm to children.

If your dog tries to urinate and can't, take him to the vet at once. A dog that hasn't urinated for 24 hours may die of uremia.

Don't feed a dog milk under the mistaken impression that it's good for his teeth. It will probably give him diarrhea.

If a dog shows the signs of shock, keep him warm. Never change his position too suddenly. A fast lift or rotation can cause shock to move to the irreversible stage.

To prevent your dog from straining with impacted feces, add a teaspoon of cooking oil to each plateful of food. The oil will also give a sheen to his coat.

If you must gather an outdoor stool sample from your dog, try not to include any soil in the sample. Dirt can contain harmless soil worms that may confuse the examiner.

Down the Hatch

If you must administer liquid to a dog, put him in the tub to help avoid a mess.

After inserting a pill in your dog's mouth, close the mouth quickly and tap his nose with your finger. This causes the dog to lick and then swallow.

When your dog hesitates to swallow a pill, bury it in a piece of cream cheese, which most dogs will eat willingly.

Fleas

Check carefully for fleas when brushing or combing your pet, especially around the ears, face, and tail.

Fleas spend more time off your dog or cat than on. Vacuum weekly (especially in dark corners and crevices) and then throw out the vacuum bag. Spray commercial insecticide around the house periodically for a few months.

An overwhelming reason to keep your cat or dog free of fleas is that children have been known to get tapeworms from swallowing infected fleas. (Fleas sometimes carry tapeworm eggs in their stomachs.)

Always air out a flea collar for several days before putting it on your dog or cat. Otherwise, its potency may irritate his skin. But keep the airing collar away from both people and pets.

Avoid applying excessive amounts of flea powder to a dog or cat's coat, and brush off all excess within 30 minutes of application. Otherwise your pet may try to lick off the residue and become ill in the process.

A bit of brewer's yeast added to their food makes some animals distasteful to fleas.

To eliminate fleas, restrict your cat's hunting; wild animals are often flea-infested and the fleas can carry dangerous tapeworms. Empty the cat's litter pans frequently, and wash them with a disinfectant periodically.

Never combine a flea collar with the use of flea powder or flea sprays. This constitutes a harmful overdose.

A handful of naphthalene flakes in the vacuum cleaner bag will kill fleas in the carpet. Be sure to throw out the vacuum bag afterward.

Mixing onion or garlic salt with your pet's food may repel fleas. Also try mixing cedar shavings with your pet's bedding.

If you scatter fresh pine needles under your dog's sleeping pad, fleas will keep their distance. If he sleeps in a doghouse, wash it periodically with salt water; fleas are also repelled by salt.

Ticks

Ticks can be firmly pulled out with a tweezer. Don't try to burn them out with a match; you could hurt your pet.

Ear Mites

Ear mites are an ornery problem with cats. If you notice black, brown, or gray waxy material in the ear instead of the usual clean pink surface, it's probably mites. When giving medicine prescribed for mites, add some to the cat's tail too. Since a cat often sleeps with its tail curved around the body, the mites can infest its tail, thus reinfecting the cat's ears.

If you have more than one cat and one gets ear mites, chances are the others will too. Have them all checked by the vet.

Chapter **2**

OTHER PETS

PETS THAT SWIM, FLY, CRAWL, AND HOP NEED EXTRA-SPECIAL CARE.

BIRDS

Easy Does It

When holding a pet bird, be very gentle. Bird bones are so fragile that even the slightest pressure on the wrong spot can cause a fracture.

You won't be doing a pet bird a favor by putting it outside in its cage to enjoy fresh air. Wild birds will flutter around, attracted by the food in the cage, and your pet bird may pick up some of the parasites and diseases they carry.

Never let a pet bird loose in the kitchen. It's likely to land on a hot pan or burner. And don't let a bird loose in a room where an electric fan is operating. Many birds fly into twirling fans and damage or destroy themselves.

If a pet bird breathes through its open mouth, you know it's sick. Buy a bird antibiotic at the pet store, pulverize it, and add it to your bird's drinking water. If this doesn't help, get it to the vet.

Parakeets and Canaries

When you buy a parakeet, buy a young one. Older birds are less likely to become attached to you.

A parakeet becomes bored almost as quickly as a small child does. Be sure there are plenty of playthings in its cage. Otherwise it may sit there as if it were comatose.

If you want a parakeet to regard *you* fondly, buy only one. If you buy two, they'll turn to each other for affection rather than to you.

If a parakeet's beak becomes soft, add a few drops of cod-liver oil to its diet.

If you have a pet canary, be sure to protect it from drafts and from direct sunlight. Either can be fatal.

Hesitate to buy a canary between the months of July and October, which is the canary's molting season. A sudden environmental change during that period may send it into a state of shock.

Polly Want a Cracker?

Planning to buy a parrot? Purchase one born and raised in this country, rather than one that's been imported. Domestically bred birds are likely to be much healthier.

If you have a parrot, resign yourself to a lifetime relationship. (It may live longer than you do.) Never sell it to someone else because it will probably die of heartbreak if you do. Parrots become extremely attached to their owners.

If you want a parrot whose imitative speech most closely resembles that of a human, purchase the rather drab-looking African Grey.

Not every bird of the same species relishes the same type of food. For example, some parrots love spinach leaves and apple slices. Others turn up their beaks at such tidbits and prefer eggs, cheese, or tiny chunks of meat. You have to experiment with your pet's food preferences.

Busy Budgies

If you want a truly affectionate budgerigar, pick a male. They're friendlier than females.

It's easier for a girl or woman to train a budgerigar to speak because their higher-pitched voices are more like the budgie's than a boy's or man's.

Should a budgerigar regurgitate, don't worry about it. It's normal for healthy adult birds to do it periodically, since this is the way they feed their young. The habit is programmed into them.

Should your budgerigar escape from its cage and be difficult to catch, wait until dark. It can't see in the dusk as well as you can, and will make no attempt to avoid you.

GOLDFISH

When you buy a goldfish at a pet shop and bring it home in a small plastic bag partially filled with water, float the bag in your home aquarium for 30 minutes before releasing the fish. This helps the fish adjust to the tank's water temperature.

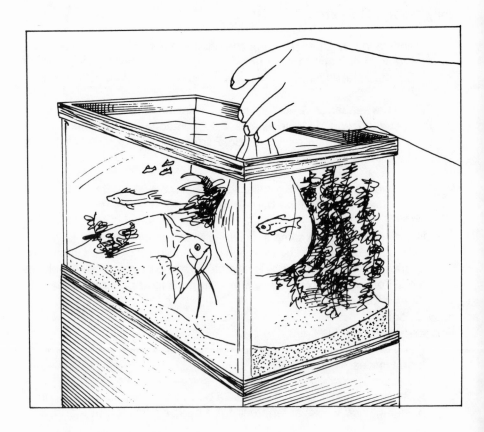

SMALL MAMMALS

Cautious Moves

Be careful about moving a small animal's cage from one location to another. An animal has a strong sense of territory, and you may upset it very much by relocating it.

Avoid sudden gestures when handling small mammals. They're easily frightened and—no matter how cuddly—may bite you.

Rabbit Tales

Don't turn up your nose in disgust if a pet rabbit eats some of its own droppings. The droppings contain B vitamins necessary for its health.

If you have rabbits, don't keep two males (known as bucks) together in the same cage or hutch. They'll fight like gladiators.

If you have a pet rabbit (and no cat or dog), don't be afraid to let it loose in the house. It can be housebroken to use a kitty-litter pan filled with paper shreds. Keep an eye on it, however, so it doesn't nibble on furniture legs.

Never lift a rabbit by its ears. Doing so may damage the musculature around its head and make its ears floppy.

Mice

When picking up a pet mouse, lift it by the root of its tail, not the tip. The skin at the tail's tip is likely to slide right off.

If you have pet mice, make sure they have a piece of unpainted hardwood to gnaw on. If they don't gnaw on something hard, their front teeth will grow so long they'll have difficulty eating.

Hamsters and Gerbils

It's best not to expose a hamster to direct sunlight for a prolonged period. If you do, it may die of heatstroke. Hamsters are, by nature, nocturnal animals and prefer subdued light.

Gerbils make better pets for children than hamsters because they're less likely to bite.

Chipmunks and Opossums

Pet chipmunks are happy with a diet of peanut butter and sunflower seeds.

If you have a pet opossum, feed it raw eggs right in the shells, plus canned dog or cat food. Pet raccoons thrive on the same diet.

REPTILES

Snakes, Salamanders, and Crocodiles

If you have a reptile or amphibian as a pet, don't be hurt if it doesn't recognize you, even if you're the one who feeds it. These creatures can't tell humans apart.

If you have a pet reptile, such as a lizard or snake, and decide to clean its terrarium home, have a duplicate (empty) terrarium handy in which you can place your pet while touching up its quarters. Otherwise it may escape, and you could spend hours trying to track it down.

If you catch a garter snake or some other small harmless snake for your terrarium, the best way to bring it home is in an empty pillowcase, the opening of which has been closed with a sturdy rubber band.

If you have a pet snake that likes to eat live mice, but you can't stand the thought of it, you can trick it into eating other meat. Have a pet mouse (in another cage) sniff or scramble around on a piece of raw hamburger. Its scent will permeate the raw hamburger and the snake will then swallow the scented meat, unaware of the difference.

You can keep a pet salamander happy and well fed on a diet of canned dog or cat food.

Handle a pet salamander or newt with wet hands. The rough texture of dry skin may injure it.

If you have a baby alligator or crocodile and it won't eat, check the temperature in its cage or tank. These reptiles won't eat unless the temperature is 70°F or above.

Turtles

If you have an adult land tortoise as a pet, you needn't confine it in an enclosure. Give it the run of your house or apartment. It will discover cozy places to sleep in and warm places to sun itself. Feed it slices of ripe fruit and pieces of leafy vegetables, and provide it with a nontippable pan of water to drink from.

If you keep aquatic turtles in an artfully appointed tank, feed them in another tank that you can empty with a minimum of fuss, because they're very messy eaters.

WILD AND EXOTIC ANIMALS

Never touch a wild animal that approaches you and seems tame. The odds are that it has a disease and will bite you. If an opossum stands on your driveway and just stares at you, call the local animal control unit.

If a squirrel or any other animal gets into your house or garage, don't try to deal with it—call the animal shelter.

Never try to raise wild animals as pets. They can't really be tamed and their behavior is unpredictable—and it's not fair to the animal to keep it in captivity.

Monkeys are inadvisable as pets. They tend to be destructive, ill tempered, and prone to bite the hand that feeds them. What's more, a solitary monkey is always unhappy. Simians crave to be with their own kind.

When an exotic-type pet gets sick or acts strangely, call the nearest zoo or nature center. Their trained personnel can advise you regarding what to do.

Part **XIII**

YARD, GARDEN, PATIO

Want to make the most of outdoor living around your home? Part XIII brings you outstanding ideas for your yard, garden, and patio. Chapter 1, on lawn care, teaches you to lay sod and achieve professional results. You'll also learn how to use your lawn mower to help early grass get a good start—or what to plant so you never have to mow the grass at all! There are also fence and wall tips that will help you screen out your surroundings or paint a chain link fence in a snap.

With the picnic and barbecue hints in Chapter 2, you'll be nominated the dandiest backyard chef in your neighborhood. Save your old paper egg cartons—they make great charcoal lighters when packed with coals. And if you want to handle flare-ups from dripping fat, simply put lettuce on the coals to subdue the scorching flames.

If you don't have a patio—but wish you did—Chapter 3 tells you how to lay a patio, as well as how to maintain it and how to choose and care for patio furniture.

Chapter 4, "Outdoor Gardening," covers all aspects of backyard agriculture. You'll learn to study the sun conditions of your plot in order to know what to plant and where to plant it. You'll be able to start a compost pile for your garden, and you'll find hints on how to store, germinate, and plant the seeds you've chosen for your garden. This chapter also includes old-fashioned but effective tips on pest control, such as planting basil near tomato plants to keep the tomatoes free of worms and flies. And you'll keep your green things in good health with our hints on watering and weeding, while also keeping your hands clean and your knees comfortable.

Indoor-plant fans can count on getting the full lowdown in Chapter 5 on indoor gardening. The recipes for creating your own potting soil will save you money and allow you to adjust the soil to what you're growing. Among the potting tips, you'll find facts on proper drainage and what kind of cast-off household items can be recycled to become attractive plant pots. Watering hints include ways to water hanging plants without deluging the floor below and what kinds of cooking water your plants would love you to give them. And whether you grow them indoors or out, the hints in Chapter 6, "Enjoying and Arranging Flowers," will let you get the most from all your garden endeavors.

With these hints, your yard, garden, and patio—and your whole house—will bloom with great ideas.

Chapter **1**

ALL AROUND THE YARD

CARING FOR YOUR LAWN, FENCES, AND WALKS IS A SNAP WHEN YOU HEED THESE HINTS.

Lawn Care

When laying sod, set succeeding rows of strips with staggered joints, as if you were laying brick.

As hot weather approaches, set your lawn mower blades higher so that the longer grass will provide shade protection for the roots.

A wooden coat hanger is great for storing a garden hose. Wrap the hose around the hanger and hang it on a hook in the garage.

Fix a small leak in a plastic hose by just barely touching it with the tip of a hot ice pick. The plastic will melt and seal the hole.

Plant ivy instead of grass, and eliminate grass cutting forever.

Just before the leaves start falling, apply a nitrogen-rich fertilizer to your lawn. Then give the soil a good soaking, down to a depth of three or four inches.

Don't turn your back on your lawn in the fall. Autumn is the best time to remove the accumulated debris of spring and summer—debris that acts as a barrier between the root zone and needed water and air. Do a thorough job, as if you were combing and cleaning your lawn's green hair.

Fences and Walls

When setting a fence post in concrete, mount the concrete around the post so water won't collect on top of it. Otherwise, the concrete might form a shallow basin to retain water, and even a post treated with a chemical preservative will suffer eventual decay.

If you are erecting fence posts and don't have a carpenter's level, make sure they're vertical by visually aligning them with the edge of the nearest building.

The quickest way to paint a wire or chain link fence is with a sponge. (Protect your hands with rubber gloves.)

If you use a roller when painting long, flat surfaces on a fence, the work will go much faster than if you use just a brush.

When you're building a stone retaining wall, make sure you dig below the frost line for your footing, otherwise the wall could fall apart.

To screen off neighbors, plant trees or shrubs in staggered rows, instead of single file.

Using and Storing Tools

Unless you're experienced, it's best to use a chain saw to cut only wood that is smaller than the length of the guide bar. If you bury the saw nose in wood, it is likely to kick back, making the saw difficult to control.

Old car tires make firm anchors for outdoor garbage cans.

To prevent outdoor padlocks from freezing during winter months, fasten plastic sandwich bags over them.

A metal garbage can is perfect for storing long-handled yard tools. Hooks can also be attached to the outside of the can for hanging up smaller tools. When it's time to do some gardening work, just lift up the whole can and take it to the yard.

Walks and Drives

Small cracks in blacktop can be patched with sand and liquid blacktop sealer. Pour sand along the crack to fill it part way. Then, pour the blacktop sealer into the crack over the sand, which will absorb the sealer quickly. Repeat, if necessary, till the surface is smooth.

Instead of using conventional stepping-stones, you could make your walk a trip down memory lane. Have each family member put his hand prints, name, and birth date in a square of wet cement. Mark other important dates in remaining squares.

So you won't have to install new light bulbs outdoors in the winter cold in northern areas, try replacing all outdoor bulbs at the end of the fall with new ones. You probably won't need to do it again till spring. Should the bulbs you remove still have life, install them indoors, or save them for warm-weather reinstallation outdoors.

To help repel moisture on outdoor light bulbs and make the bulbs easy to remove after they burn out, rub a light coat of petroleum jelly on the bulbs' threads.

To increase the light from portable lamps used during summer in the backyard or on camping trips, place a piece of aluminum foil behind the bulb.

Enhance a carport with lattice work and hanging baskets. Close off the back of the carport with a trellis that will enclose the backyard seating area.

For the Birds

Save lint from your clothes dryer, and put it into a box or a tin can. Attach the container to a tree in your yard to provide the birds with nesting material.

Pine cones covered with bacon grease or meat fat, and then rolled in bread crumbs, make a treat for the birds in your garden during the winter months.

Birds will flock to your birdbath if you throw a few colored marbles into the water.

Chapter 2

OUTDOOR FUN

PICNICS AND COOKOUTS IN FINE WEATHER ARE A PLEASURE THE WHOLE FAMILY SAVORS.

Picnics

When you pack a picnic , keep the salt and pepper from spilling out of shakers by wrapping wax paper or plastic wrap around them.

When organizing your picnic basket, be sure to include a cutting board, knife, plastic bags, and twisties.

Give an old picnic table a new lease on life by covering the top with a pretty sheet. Staple the sheet in place and you have a permanent table cloth. A junior-size bedsheet also works well—and the gustiest wind can't blow it off.

If you use thumb tacks to secure paper plates to a picnic table, you won't have to worry about them blowing away in the wind.

A plastic window shade makes a wonderful tablecloth for a picnic. When the picnic's over, just wipe off the shade, roll it up, and store it.

If you need a cutting board for a picnic, use scrap wood meant for the campfire, or fashion a "board" by covering a hefty magazine with extra thick aluminum foil.

Keep dessert foods covered when picnicking outdoors. Insects are attracted to the sweet smell of sugar.

Protect soft foods and fruits from being crushed while on their way to a picnic by placing them in old egg cartons.

Barbecues

Just before the barbecue season starts, fill several brown paper bags with just enough briquettes for a cookout. Fold over the tops of the bags, and when ready to use, just place a bag in the grill and touch a match to it. Heat from the burning paper will light the briquettes in a jiffy, and your hands will be spotless. An alternative is to pack briquettes in empty egg cartons with the covers closed. You'll still have a quick fire and clean hands.

An empty plastic squeeze bottle makes a handy bellows for barbecue coals.

When you barbecue juicy meat, fat dripping on the hot coals can cause flame flare-ups. These can be squelched by putting lettuce leaves on the coals, or by squirting water on the coals with a spray bottle or turkey baster.

A proven way to spice up the flavor of food on the barbecue is to sprinkle the coals with fresh herbs you've soaked in water.

You can cook an entire meal—not just meat, baked potatoes, and ears of corn—on an outdoor grill. Put vegetables and appetizers in covered kettles, and place these on the grill. You'll save on household energy and keep the kitchen cool.

A beer-can opener makes a great scraper for cleaning barbecue grills if you file a notch in the end of the opener opposite its sharp point.

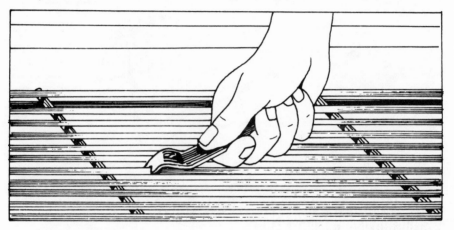

There are several ways to make grill cleaning less of a chore. A grill will steam-clean itself if wrapped in wet newspapers or sprayed with window cleaner while it's still hot. Or, you can wipe it with crumpled aluminum foil while it's still warm. To coat it protectively before cooking, use vegetable oil and wipe off the grill as soon as it's cool enough to touch.

Campfire Cooking

Cooking with pots and pans over an open fire can leave metalware bottoms with black scorch marks. However, permanent scorching can be prevented by coating the bottoms of pots and pans with bar soap or shaving cream—or painting on liquid detergent with a pastry brush—before subjecting the pan to an open flame. When the metalware cools, you'll be able to remove black marks with a minimum of elbow grease.

A disposable pie pan can help you protect yourself against burns when roasting marshmallows or hot dogs on sticks. Make a hole in the center of a pan, slide the stick through the hole, and let the pan serve as a heat shield.

Picnic Coolers

If your picnic cooler leaks, try plugging the leaks, inside and out, with melted paraffin wax.

Dust talcum powder on the edge of your ice cooler to give longer life and keep it from sticking in hot weather.

When you're outdoors, consider storing ice in a sugar bag, rather than in a plastic bag; its thickness offers better insulation.

If you accidentally jab a hole in the cooler when breaking ice in a plastic-lined model, dab the hole with fingernail polish and fill it in. Don't use household glues as some can attack liner.

Backyard Pools

A wading pool can double as a foot washer for your backyard swimming pool, keeping the pool water clean longer.

Use plastic fruit-and-vegetable bags for stuffing beach and pool pillows.

Chapter **3**

PATIO

NO MATTER HOW SIMPLE THE DESIGN OR FURNISHINGS, THERE IS ALWAYS AN ELEGANCE ABOUT PATIO LIVING.

Patio Projects

Before constructing a curved patio, you can easily determine the precise contours you want by maneuvering a garden hose on the grass.

When laying a brick patio, start from a corner of the patio near the house and work outward toward the edges in an expanding wedge pattern.

Laying a dry brick patio is quite simple. Dig out the area needed, edge the excavation with weather-resistant boards staked into place, and spread out a sand base 2¼ inches deep. Spray it gently with water, let it dry, and tamp it down until it's at a 2-inch level. Position the bricks, fitting them tightly and making sure they're level. Pour sand on the bricks, sweep it into the crevices, sprinkle with water, and repeat as necessary to fill any gaps.

Maintenance

Keep weeds from growing in the cracks of your walks, patio, or driveway by dousing the cracks with salt or boiling salted water.

You can conserve a lot of personal energy by using a power blower to blast leaves out of places that are hard to reach with a rake, and by blowing light snow from driveways and walks. A blower is also ideal for removing leaves from gutters.

Patio Furniture

Transform an old barbecue grill into a conversation piece by painting it, filling it with soil, and planting flowers or vines in it.

Nail kegs make good extra stools for a rustic deck or patio. All you have to do is stain the kegs and make cushions for the seats.

If you wax the leg bottoms of wooden patio furniture, you'll help protect against moisture that might be sponged up from standing rain water.

The metal edges of tubular patio chairs won't be able to cut through the rubber cups on the leg bottoms if metal washers are first inserted in the protective cups.

It's a good idea to drill holes in the seats of solid metal patio furniture so rain water will drain. Otherwise, if water is allowed to collect, the seats will rust prematurely.

When storing folding patio chairs, old pillow cases can serve as protective covers. Slip a case over each chair end and pin it together. The fabric guards against scratches and dirt but doesn't trap moisture, as plastic bags might.

Chapter 4

OUTDOOR GARDENING

GROW YOUR OWN—BE IT VEGETABLES, GERANIUMS, OR GARLIC.

Have It Both Ways

If your garden is really tiny, you can still have both flowers and vegetables if you organize properly. Try planting beans with sweet peas, tomatoes behind the marigolds, and put in peppers with petunias.

Good Soil

When cultivating your soil, remember that good soil is slightly lumpy. If you work it till it's too fine, it will pack hard in rains or blow away.

Start a compost pile in fall with dried leaves from the yard. Keep kitchen scraps in plastic bags and empty them onto the pile when full. Kick more leaves over the food scraps. Never start a compost pile when there is the danger of attracting rats.

The Right Light

If you can, it's best to position your tall-growing plants on the north and northeast side of your garden so that, as they grow, they won't shade the rest of the bed.

In planting a vegetable garden in the city and on small lots, try to avoid the shade from buildings and large trees. Besides blocking sun from your garden bed, large trees will compete for the available soil nutrients and moisture. Remember that a tree's root system can reach beyond the span of its branches.

Because vegetables grown for their fruits need at least six hours of direct sun each day—sometimes as much as eight to ten hours—don't frustrate yourself by trying to grow tomatoes, peppers, or eggplant in the shade. They'll often produce a good green plant without giving you anything to eat.

Seeds and Seedlings

If the seeds you're planting should be set in rows, you can use a broom handle to form the trenches. Press the broom handle into the dirt—about ¼ inch deep—with your foot. You'll have a perfect row at the right depth.

Seeds need only enough soil to cover them and to supply even moisture for germination, so don't plant them deep unless the weather is uncertain or the plants will need to be firmly anchored when they sprout. In small areas, sprinkle seeds with soil so they're covered up to four times their smallest diameter; then keep the ground moist, but not wet. You can simply press fine seed into the soil's surface.

If you want to speed up seed germination, place seed trays on top of your refrigerator, where the 72° F to 75° F heat emitted will promote steady growth.

Use an egg carton for a seedling nursery. Place half an eggshell in each compartment, then fill with loam and your plant seed. When the seedlings are ready to be transferred, plant the shell and the plant. The eggshell will decompose and enrich the soil.

If you have plants that need to be brought in and potted for the winter, line the pots with plastic from cleaner's bags. Leave some excess plastic over the ledge of the pot, and punch a couple of holes in the bottom for drainage. In spring, when it's time for transplanting, lift the dirt and plant out of the pot by the plastic.

Keep seed packets in the refrigerator till you're ready to plant them.

Poisonous Plants

A number of common plants are poisonous, so it's best to keep children away from them. These include holly, yew, and privet berries; rhubarb and lily of the valley leaves; and the whole of larkspur and oleander plants.

Fruits and Vegetables

When buying tomato plants for the garden, look for plants that are short, stocky, and have a bright green color. Be sure not to plant your tomatoes until the soil is warm and the danger of frost has passed.

To make a garden for strawberries, fill an old gutter spout with soil, and attach it to a fence.

Because of the space it occupies, corn is impractical in a small garden. But consider growing corn in a washtub. Usually the results are better if you grow a small variety and water feed it more frequently.

Growing Herbs

Because thyme, marjoram, and parsley don't grow higher than a few inches, position them at a garden's perimeter so they aren't overshadowed by other plants.

Since coriander, tarragon, and dill grow to a height of two feet or more, position them in a garden's center if it's a walk-around type of display, or toward a garden's rear if it's a three-sided setup.

Grow rosemary and bay in clay pots buried just beneath the surface of your garden's soil. Doing so facilitates moving them indoors when the weather gets cold, since they're temperature-sensitive and may perish if you don't protect them.

Certain herbs spread so fast when planted outdoors that they must be contained or they'll take over. For example, wild marjoram, tarragon, and mint—being perennials—flare out in all directions from season to season. You can restrict them with a sunken section of stovepipe that confines their roots.

After growing herbs, you can store them by putting them in oil or vinegar, by freezing them, or by drying them. Do this just before they flower, when their oils are most abundant. The best time to cut them for storage is at midmorning on a sunny day.

Planting Flowers

The best time to plant peonies is in September and October. Be careful not to position the crowns deeper than two inches beneath the surface. If you push them down farther, they won't bloom.

Unless the outdoor temperature is almost Arctic, you can plant new roses as late as November.

Plant tulip bulbs late in the fall. Plant all other bulbs before then, with their pointed ends up.

Dig up gladiolus corms in the autumn, dry them in the sun for seven days, then store them during the winter in a dark, dry, cool place.

Grow a Willow

A two-foot-long branch, the size of your little finger in diameter, can be cut from a willow tree and planted in moist soil to start a new tree.

Window Boxes

Replace the bottom of a wooden box with chicken wire to make a colander for garden vegetables. Place your vegetables into the box and spray with the garden hose to wash off dirt and bugs before you bring them inside the house.

To prevent the rain from splattering window-box dirt onto your picture windows, secure the soil with a top layer of gravel.

Outdoor Planters

The trunk of a hollowed-out tree makes a great planter. Just line the trunk with plastic, fill with rocks and soil, and plant something special!

A plastic paint pan makes a perfect planter when decoratively wrapped with aluminum foil.

Container gardening helps you plant more than you have ground space for. Items that can be recycled into planting containers are tin cans, old washtubs, plastic bottles, peach baskets (though these rot out quickly), old tires, sewer pipes, plastic bags, wire screens, and little red wagons.

Pest Control

If you want your garden to be relatively pest-free in the spring, scrupulously clean out all vines, stalks, stems, and rotten fruit in the fall.

Chives are resistant to both pests and virus attacks. Bequeath their immunity to the rest of your plants by feeding them chive tea. Chop the leaves finely and cover with boiling water (½ cup chive leaves to a pint of water). Infuse the tea for 15 minutes and cool. Spray this preventative on your garden.

If you want to keep potato beetles away from the potatoes in your garden, plant horseradish nearby.

Plant onions next to beets and carrots to keep bugs away.

If you plant basil near your tomatoes, worms and flies will be repelled.

Rhubarb, which contains poisonous oxalic acid, is effective against aphids and red spider mites. Pour two pints of boiling water over a pound of chopped rhubarb leaves and let it set overnight. Next day strain and add a tablespoon of detergent to the liquid. Spray on vegetable crops, but not within a week of harvesting. Keep your kids and pets away, too.

Before resorting to pesticides, remember that a strong jet of water from a garden hose will dislodge aphids, mealy bugs, cabbage worms, spider mites, and young scale.

During the early stages of pest infestation (when you note chewed deformed foilage), you can often hand-pick the larger insects and their eggs from the leaves or brush them into a jar coated with detergent.

Another insecticide is made by mixing ½ cup detergent (or 1 tablespoon of the biodegradable kind) to a pint of water and using it to spray both sides of the plant leaves. After an hour, spray or hose down with clear water.

If tiny worms infest the soil in which your ferns are growing, you can get rid of them by pushing matches in the soil, sulphur ends down.

Shoo-Fly

Flies that swarm around garbage cans will be repelled if you wash the cans thoroughly, let them dry in the sun, and then sprinkle dry soap into them. The flies will take one whiff and head for your neighbors' cans.

To control flies and gnats, make sure garbage cans have tight-fitting lids. In addition, attach impregnated resin strips to the can lids.

Snails and Slugs

Pestered by slugs and snails in your garden? It will help if you get rid of their hiding places. Put scratchy sand or cinders around each plant, or arrange cool shady spots they can crawl under so you can collect them in the morning.

Annual Pests

To keep squirrels, mice, rats, and rabbits out of your garden, spread moth crystals (paradichlorobenzene) along the garden's edges. (Because moth crystals are toxic and harmful to eyes, make sure that children and pets can't get near them, and wash your hands thoroughly after handling the crystals.)

Dogs and cats will be repelled by a mix of two cups of isopropyl rubbing alcohol (70 percent) and one teaspoon of lemon grass oil. Brush or spray the liquid on areas you want dogs and cats to avoid.

Dogs, raccoons, or opossums will leave your trash cans alone if you sprinkle ammonia around each can. Soak your garbage bags with full-strength ammonia for double protection.

Tending the Garden

The best time to water gardens and lawns is early in the morning. Early-morning watering lets the sun dry the leaves quickly, preventing the spread of spore and fungus diseases, which thrive in moist conditions.

Always soak the soil thoroughly when watering. A light sprinkling can do more harm than no water at all because it stimulates roots to come to the surface, where they're killed when the sun bakes down on them. Never water from above, because many diseases are encouraged by wet leaves. Direct water at the soil, but do it gently so the soil won't be washed away or the roots exposed.

Be kind to your knees when working in the garden. Use plastic foam meat trays as kneeler pads.

If you dislike getting your fingernails dirty when gardening, yet find gardening gloves clumsy, dig your nails into a bar of soap, or coat their undersides with nail whitening pencil. Your hands will wash clean easily.

Crushed eggshells scattered on your garden will boost plant growth.

If you want your garden vegetables to ripen outdoors at a faster pace, place aluminum foil beneath them to reflect extra sunlight.

To avoid bruising tomato plant stems when staking, fasten them to stakes with strips of pantyhose.

To encourage ivy or myrtle to root, pin vines to the ground with hairpins.

When rinsing dirty vegetables just pulled from the earth, collect the dirty water to pour back on your garden. It is rich in nutrients that can help the other plants grow.

You'll avoid getting pricked when you're pruning thorny tree branches and bushes if you use a big pliers to grab the branches.

It's best to finish pruning by August so any new growth can harden before winter. When you prune, always cut flush, leaving no stubs to decay.

An apple corer from the kitchen makes a handy garden tool to remove thistles and dandelions from your lawn.

Watering Cans

Select a watering can made of a lightweight material. Remember that you'll have to carry and lift it when it's filled with water.

Buy a watering can that's short enough to fit under the kitchen tap so it can be easily filled with water.

Harvesting and Storing

It's best to harvest radishes when they're one inch in diameter; larger radishes are tough.

Because peas respond negatively to warm weather, harvest them before summer.

If you raise sweet corn in your garden, it will taste the best if you cook it promptly after picking.

The best place to store leftover garden seeds is in your refrigerator. Put them in a glass jar with a bit of silica gel and screw the cap on tightly.

Because grapes don't continue to ripen after they've been picked, leave them on the vine till the first light frost.

Leave Nothing to Chance

Don't allow a carpet of autumn leaves to remain on your lawn over the winter, telling yourself you'll rake them up in the spring. If you leave them in place, they'll gradually mat, then smother the grass beneath them. Rake them up promptly on dry days. On a wet day, the leaves will weigh twice as much.

There's a trick to spreading mulch around newly planted shrubs and trees during cold-weather months. Don't pile it up too high until after the ground freezes. If you pile it up high when the temperature is above freezing, you may prevent delicate roots from going into the desired dormancy state.

Chapter 5

INDOOR GARDENING

PAMPER YOUR PLANTS WITH ANY OR ALL OF THESE TECHNIQUES FOR POTTING, FEEDING, AND TENDING.

Potting Soil

To make your own potting soil for most houseplants, mix the following ingredients in a large baking pan: 4 cups of black dirt or potting soil; 4 cups of leaf mold, peat moss, or sphagnum moss; 4 cups of coarse sand; 2–4 cups of activated charcoal; and 1 tablespoon of steamed bone meal. Spread this mixture evenly in the pan and cover with aluminum foil, shiny side down. Replacing the foil each time, stir the ingredients periodically while you bake the mixture for 30 minutes at 200°F. (The soil will give off an unpleasant odor during "cooking.") Remove the baked soil from the oven and cool it completely before pouring it into a clean, covered container. When using, first put a layer of charcoal in each flower pot, then fill the pot with soil.

To make your own potting soil for plants with hairlike roots, decrease the black dirt and sand to 3 cups each, and increase the peat or sphagnum moss to 6 cups.

To make your own potting soil for cacti, decrease the black dirt and leaf mold or moss to 2 cups each, and increase the sand to 6 cups.

Light on the Matter

Because houseplants lean toward the brightest sunlight, it's a good idea to periodically rotate them a quarter-turn so they'll grow straight.

You can use the "paper test" to determine whether the spot on which you'd like to have a plant gets enough light. On a sunny day, place an ordinary sheet of typing paper where the plant might be, and hold one of your hands a foot above the sheet. If there's a sharp, well-defined shadow of your hand, you have bright light. If the result is a fuzzy, but recognizable, shadow-hand, you have filtered light. If all you get is a blur on the paper, your light condition is shady, and you'll have to consider abandoning that spot or adding a periodic or permanent light.

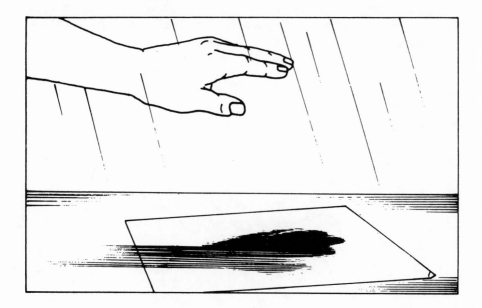

If your plants are ailing, try moving them to sunnier spots. In most indoor situations, plants need more, not less, light.

If you like the look of plants, but not the fuss, invest in large, mature, well-established plants since they need less care than young plants. Your plants also will be easier to care for if you select plants that have similar water and light requirements.

Give newly potted plants a little less light for the first few days.

Potting

Repot only when needed. Spring is the best time because it favors new growth.

When reusing old pots, wash them in hot water and then soak overnight in a solution of one part chlorine bleach and eight parts water. Rinse off the pot next day. It's free of former pests or disease.

If you haven't any clay shards for drainage in pots, recycle tin tops from cans. Bend them slightly so that, when they cover the hole, concave side down, there's plenty of room for the water to drain out.

If you have to transport your plants from one location to another, here's a sure way to prevent the soil from spilling. Crumple balls of dry newspaper and pack them around the base of the plant. Lay strips of masking tape around the top of the balls of paper and stick them into the sides of the pot. This creates a "tape net" to keep the paper and soil in place.

Old sponges—cut into squares—are great for covering drainage holes in flowerpots.

You can make hanging mini-planters from egg-shaped pantyhose containers. Puncture holes in the sides and insert string or fish wire for hanging.

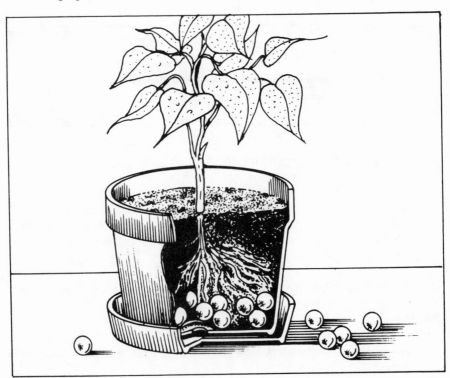

Watering and Drainage

Use an old knitting needle to test when your houseplants need water. If the needle inserted into the soil comes out dry, get out your watering can.

Group plants together rather than scattering them sparsely. When clustered, they create their own moist environment.

When you go on vacation, set all your houseplants on old towels folded once or twice in a few inches of water in the bathtub. The plants will drink when they're thirsty.

During cold weather months, a room filled with houseplants will benefit from the moisture provided by a portable vaporizer.

A freestanding stepladder makes a good display stand for plants.

Plant Treats

If you have opened bottles of club soda left after a party, feed the contents to your house plants or outdoor plants. Flat soda is beneficial to green, growing things.

Cool the water leftover from cooking spaghetti or potatoes. Your plants will love the starch.

After you boil eggs, use the cooled water on your houseplants. "Egg" water is packed with growth-stimulating minerals.

Old aquarium water is perfect for fertilizing houseplants, as is water in which fish has been frozen.

Melted snow contains minerals that make it good for watering your plants.

Put your plant watering can under the shower before you step in. The first spray is enough for a dozen plants, and helps conserve water.

Save the rinse water from dishwashing. Mist plants with it, as the invisible soap film kills some pests such as mites and scale. This occasional misting won't hurt plants.

Periodically water ferns with tea, or mix soggy tea leaves into the potting soil because it's one of their favorites.

You can "water" a terrarium by simply patting the inside of the glass with a wet paper towel.

Wise Watering

An ordinary basting syringe is useful for watering a terrarium.

Water houseplants with room-temperature water. Cold water injures them.

When you water a houseplant, it's best to water slowly and thoroughly till the water runs out the bottom of the pot. If you have the plant in a saucer, empty the saucer after the plant finishes draining.

If you're not sure whether a houseplant needs watering or not, poke your index finger an inch into the topsoil. If the soil there is moist, don't water. If it's dry, do.

Chlorine in water can give houseplants brown tips. To avoid this, let tap water stand for a full day so its chlorine evaporates.

Let newly potted soil dry a little longer before watering.

Water newly planted seeds from the bottom—so as not to dislodge them—by placing the containers in saucers of water.

It's best to water bulb houseplants from the bottom also. Fill a pie pan with water and let the bulbs sit in it for awhile.

Ice cubes will water plants in hanging baskets without making a mess. Because they'll melt slowly, they won't overflow.

Drainage Hints

Any container must have drainage holes. If you're using a recycled one such as a paper food tub, be sure to make holes.

Cracked walnut shells, marbles, stones, or fruit pits can be used to provide drainage at the bottom of a houseplant pot.

For a lightweight drainage layer in the bottom of a hanging planter, use pieces of Styrofoam.

Set potted plants on pebble trays filled with water. The moisture from pebble trays cuts down the plant's transpiration loss, and you save water.

Some smart green-thumbers slip shower caps over the bottoms of their hanging planters to catch the overflow when watering. The caps can be removed after an hour or so.

Desert Plants

When handling cactus plants, use ice tongs to protect your fingers.

If your dish garden contains any cactus, place a newspaper strip around the cactus to protect your fingers while transplanting.

Plants originating in deserts and dry areas like to be drenched and then permitted to dry out. Do this by soaking the plant and its pot in a bucket or sink filled with tepid water till no more air bubbles emerge. Then, remove the pot from the water and let it dry completely before drenching again.

Nurturing Your Plants

When one of your houseplants appears "sick," attach a pest strip, then cover the plant for a few days with a plastic bag. By the time you remove the bag, the plant should have perked up nicely.

Want to put a gloss on your houseplant's leaves? Swab them with a soft cloth dipped in glycerine. Unlike other gloss-producing substances, glycerine won't collect dust.

One of the quickest ways to clean a houseplant's leaves is with a feather duster.

If a growing houseplant needs support, you can use an adjustable curtain rod.

An ailing houseplant can be treated with a tablespoon of castor oil dribbled on its soil, followed by a thorough watering.

A plant will last longer if you don't let it go to seed. As blossoms begin to fade, it's best to cut them off.

If you pinch the tiny new shoots at the growing points, you'll encourage branching, which produces more growth for flowering.

Though most plants benefit from pinching, never pinch back palms. It's fatal to them.

Spring is an excellent time for pinching back.

If your cat digs in the soft soil around your plants, you can put an end to it by putting sharp white stones on top of the soil.

Pest Control

To keep all types of pests away from a houseplant, plant a garlic clove beside it.

Sometimes people unwittingly bring bugs into a house by taking house-plants outside for extra sun and then returning them to their places indoors. If you want to take plants outdoors, keep them isolated from other houseplants for three or four weeks after you bring them back in. If you detect bugs on the plants, wipe the stems and leaves with a mild soap-and-water solution.

If you think there may be root-damaging worms in the soil of your potted plants, place a slice of raw potato on the surface of each. The worms will crawl out to get at the potatoes, and you can capture and destroy the worms.

Indoor Vegetable Gardening

If you have the space, you can grow vegetables indoors in artificial light. Lettuce does especially well when grown under fluorescent lights. Plant your lettuce garden in the basement, the attic, or anywhere the temperature stays between 65°F and 70°F during the day, and drops about ten degrees at night.

Here's a novel—but effective—way to grow parsley in your kitchen or on your sun porch: Slice sponges in half and sprinkle them with parsley seeds. Arrange the sponges on dishes in a sunny location, keep them moist, and watch your parsley grow.

Chapter 6

ENJOYING AND ARRANGING FLOWERS

HOW DOES YOUR GARDEN GROW? GATHER FLOWERS TO GRACE YOUR HOME INDOORS AS WELL AS OUT.

Garden Bouquets

When you're cutting flowers from your garden, carry a bucket of water in which to place them.

It's best to cut flowers in the early morning when they're holding the most moisture from the previous night.

If you want flower buds to open faster, put the stems in a container of warm water.

Florist Flowers

When you receive a box of cut flowers from a florist, it's best to recut the stems to encourage maximum water intake.

Droopy cut flowers will stand upright if you push floral wires through their stems.

One way to stretch your cut-flower dollar is to use interesting foliage. Foliage is generally more long-lasting than flowers. With luck and good care, some foliage material can be kept attractive for months. The same material can be used in a number of successive arrangements, so flowers can be added or replaced as desired.

To encourage carnations to last longer, add a touch of boric acid to the vase water.

If you refrigerate a vase of flowers each night, they'll last longer.

Arranging Flowers

There are several ways to quickly patch holes in a leaky vase or flower bowl. (If you have difficulty locating holes or cracks so you can patch them, turn the container upside down over a light. The light will shine through any openings.) If a hole isn't large, drip melted candle wax over it from the inside of the container and allow the wax to harden. Or patch a crack by dripping epoxy glue on it and letting it harden. Quicker still is to use a plastic bag as a liner; the weight of the container's contents will keep the bag in place.

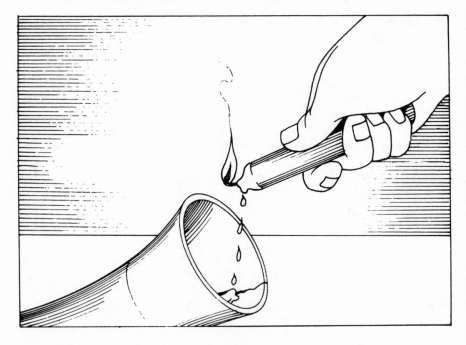

Long-stemmed flowers will stand erect in a wide-mouthed vase if you make a lattice across its top with transparent tape.

Hair rollers tied together and stood on end at the bottom of a vase will help hold flowers securely in place.

Cut flowers last longer if you cut their stems at an angle. To avoid mashing, use a very sharp knife or pair of scissors. Also, always cut the stems under water so air bubbles won't form.

Loosely arranging flowers in a vase also lengthens their lives.

If you want to give short-stemmed flowers more length, slide them into soda straws before putting them in a vase.

After you put cut flowers in a vase, it's best to remove any leaves that are below the waterline. If they decay, they'll pollute the water.

If you want cut tulips to stand straight and not open up like inverted umbrellas, put a penny in the vase.

You can change the colors of cut flowers by putting the stems in warm water containing food coloring. You'll end up with some interesting rainbow blends.

Since cloudy water is not attractive in a clear vase, prevent water from clouding by adding a teaspoon of liquid bleach to each quart of vase water.

Artificial Flowers

Perk up slightly wilted fabric flowers by holding them over steam from a teakettle or steam iron.

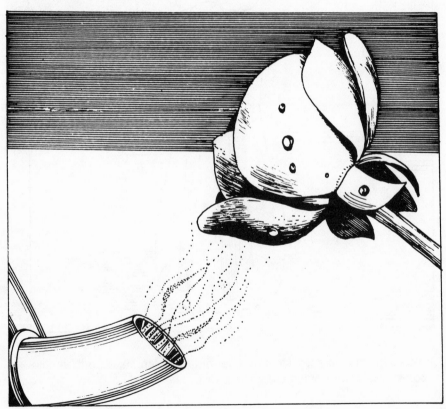

Artificial flowers can be cleaned by placing them in a large paper bag containing a handful of cornmeal or salt. Shake gently. The cornmeal or salt will remove the dust by acting as an abrasive.

If you want to remove stubborn dust from fabric flowers, gently wipe each petal with a soft toothbrush.

Potted Flowers

Potted geraniums thrive on rinsed coffee grounds.

Part **XIV**

YOUR CAR

Whether you start out with a new car or a used car, eventually you'll end up with numerous and sundry expenses for minor repairs and problems. Many of these little expenses can be reduced or even eliminated by following the hints in this part.

Tired of pouring dollars into your gas tank? Energy efficiency hints in Chapter 1 will save you big dollars in fuel costs. You'll learn the best way to warm up your car, what time of day to buy gas, the secret of gas-efficient acceleration, the best cruising speed to save gas, and even how to choose streets that will save gas for you.

When buying a car, the hints in Chapter 2 will help you decide how to choose the size and model best suited for your needs. And the special advice on smart shopping for a used car can save you dollars and headaches. Once you've made a selection, the hints in Chapter 3, "Body Work," will keep your car looking new and increase its resale value. You'll also be amazed at how our easy maintenance tips in Chapter 4, "Engine Work," will keep your car away from expensive mechanics while still keeping it in top running order. Finally, the safety hints in Chapter 5 will give you sound advice that will save you time and aggravation in an emergency road situation. These are the kind of tips that could spell the difference between safety and danger for you and your family should a breakdown occur.

Your car will always be in top running form and more valuable at trade-in time when you lend an ear to these easy-to-follow hints.

Chapter 1

ENERGY EFFICIENCY

THERE ARE DOZENS OF WAYS TO GET BETTER MILEAGE FROM YOUR TRUSTY CHARIOT.

Slow Down

To save on gasoline, apply foot pressure on the accelerator gently and smoothly. If you visualize that a raw egg is between your foot and the accelerator pedal, you'll apply pressure so smoothly you couldn't possibly break the imaginary eggshell.

Whenever possible, it's best to speed up and slow down gradually because you waste gas when you suddenly floor the accelerator or slam on the brakes.

You'll conserve gas by anticipating red lights. Take your foot off the accelerator as soon as you know you'll have to stop, and accelerate gradually as the light turns green.

Gas consumption will be less if you shift into neutral when stopping for a traffic light. This takes the load of the transmission off the engine. Shifting into neutral is particularly important when you're using the air conditioner, because the engine idles easier in neutral and handles the drag of the air conditioner with less strain.

Since stopping and starting uses a lot of gas, try to maintain a steady speed that lets you make all the green traffic lights.

632

If you want optimum fuel economy, drive 30 to 35 miles per hour. At lower or higher speeds a car engine doesn't deliver its best mileage.

Learn to "trick" your automatic transmission in order to save gas. Here's how: As you accelerate to over 30 miles per hour, ease off the accelerator a bit, which will allow the automatic transmission to shift into high gear earlier than it would otherwise. Once it's shifted, continue accelerating, if need be, to reach your desired speed.

You can conserve gas when driving into the wind by slowing down. Fighting the wind wastes fuel.

When coasting down a hill or toward a stoplight, keep the engine running (it's needed for control of the car), but take advantage of gravity and, to save gas, ease up on the accelerator as you start down a hill.

If you want to reduce fuel consumption, don't rev the engine up to speed before turning it off for the night. You probably don't need to prime the carburetor this way, and the gas you pump into it will evaporate overnight, anyway.

You'll save on fuel consumption if you remove old spark plugs on schedule. If one plug out of eight is misfiring, you're losing 1/8 of the engine's output. Even if the engine misfires on one cylinder for only a short period—for example, at start-up when cold—you're running raw gasoline out of the exhaust pipe each time the crankshaft turns.

When you're driving at highway speeds, you can take advantage of the road draft created by large trucks. The air flowing over such large vehicles cascades down in a turbulent rolling motion that creates a draft toward the truck. This drafting is present behind a truck in an area beginning at a distance equal to the truck's length and extending back for two-thirds of its length. The effect is most pronounced and helpful four or five car-lengths behind the truck. If you can safely follow it at such a distance, you'll reap the benefit of a surprising 15 percent increase in mileage.

No Idling

You'll waste time and gasoline by letting your car idle excessively. After 30 seconds of idling, even in the coldest weather, your car should be ready to roll.

You'll save on gas if you get yourself ready to drive before starting the engine. Adjust the mirrors, the seat, and the radio, and put on your glasses and seat belt—*then* switch on the ignition.

Lighten Up

Because a heavy car uses more gasoline than does a light car, you'll save if you clear your trunk of unneeded tire chains, snow tires, sand-bags, golf clubs, and bowling balls.

A roof rack loaded with a few suitcases or boxes can decrease highway mileage significantly, but you can minimize the loss if you take advantage of aerodynamics and arrange items to minimize the load's frontal area.

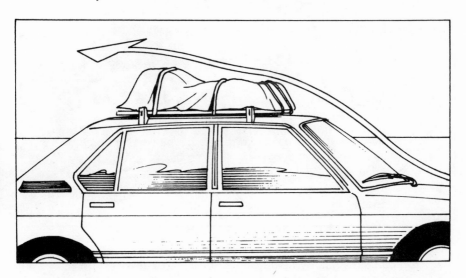

If you're looking for load room in a new car, you'll be ahead if you select a hatchback body. You'll get more load room per weight than you will with a conventional body design.

Tire Tips

For better mileage, use radial tires. They provide up to 6 percent better fuel economy than bias tires, and they roll more smoothly and last longer, too. On balance, the longer life makes up for the higher initial cost. A good set of radials will nearly duplicate the traction capability of most snow tires, yet they'll be more economical to run.

To extend the life of your tires, make sure you rotate them periodically.

At least once a week check your tires to see if they are under or overinflated. Also check tire tread for excessive wear.

You can save gas by riding on harder tires. Usually two pressures are given for tire inflation: one for an unloaded car; the other, as much as six pounds higher, for a loaded car or one that's to be driven long distances at high speed. Use the higher pressure for all your driving. You might not ride as smoothly, but the harder tires will roll easier, and you'll save gas.

Even the depth of your tire tread has an effect on fuel economy. Bald tires cause a loss of traction—and therefore a decrease in fuel economy—in rainy weather or on slippery surfaces, while a good tread grips the roadway well when the going is slick. Use the old Lincoln penny trick to measure the tread depth: Stick the penny into the groove of the tread, head first. If the top of Lincoln's head is visible, you have too little tread.

Keeping snow tires on during warm-weather months reduces fuel efficiency, too, because the heavy construction, tread pattern, and weight of snow tires make the engine work harder. So, when spring arrives, switch to standard tires as quickly as possible. (Snow tires also wear faster than standard tires in warm weather, since the rubber compound used for them isn't particularly suited to high temperatures.)

Way to Go

You'll usually waste gas by traveling a bus route, since buses make frequent stops that force you to stop, too. Each time you do, you waste gas. If you find that your regular route often puts you behind such a slow-moving vehicle, consider changing your route or your departure time.

Radio stations in most big cities broadcast rush-hour traffic reports. You'll save time and energy if you check these reports when you leave your house or work and then alter your route if there's a tie-up on your usual path.

If you drive to a particular destination each day, experiment with alternatives, because the shortest—and therefore the most economical—distance between two points isn't always the straightest line. Time yourself, consider how many stoplights or traffic jams you must wait for along each route, and measure the distance with your odometer. One route may take you a few blocks out of your way but allow you to bypass a bottleneck.

Fueling Up

Buying gas in the morning or on a cool day gives you more for your money because, like other liquids, gas expands when heated and contracts when cooled. At low temperatures, more gas will go into your tank.

Filling your tank only when it's three-quarters empty will save you weight—six pounds for each gallon you leave out—and allow you more miles per gallon. If you always top off your tank, you'll be driving with more weight than necessary.

It's best to keep the fuel level above the "empty" zone because, once it falls below that level, you risk dredging up the sediment that collects at the gas tank's bottom. This can lead to inefficient engine operation because of a clogged fuel filter and gas line.

Your car needs premium gasoline if its engine knocks, but otherwise, a lower-grade, no-lead gasoline might do just as well.

You'll save money with a rental car if you fill it with gas before returning it. Many car rental companies have their own gas pumps, but gas from these tends to be relatively high priced.

Weather Report

Parking in a garage saves on both heating and cooling costs. In summer, the shade cools the car's interior, so you don't have to turn on the air conditioner immediately. In winter, the engine stays warmer in a garage than it does outside, which means it starts more quickly and requires less time to warm up.

Accumulated ice and snow on your car put an extra load on the engine and reduce fuel economy. Because ice and snow on a car can reach a weight of 100 pounds, you should remove any accumulation before driving.

During winter in northern areas, try to drive during the warmer daylight hours rather than after the sun goes down and the temperature drops. The difference in mileage between driving in 75° weather and 25° weather is 1.5 mpg.

If your car starts slowly in wet weather, there may be a crack in the distributor cap allowing moisture to leak in and out of the ignition system. Take off the cap and examine it against a bright light. If it's damaged, replace it because it will decrease your mileage more than will a fouled spark plug.

If you're trying to choose between a heated-wire or electric-fan type rear-window defogger, the heated-wire type is the better choice for saving on fuel. The electric-fan type draws more electrical current than does the wire type.

When the engine is hot and the temperature outside is searing, you can avoid vapor lock effects by flooring the accelerator pedal as soon as you start the engine. Don't pump the accelerator. Just press it to the floor as the starter is engaged.

Because an engine that runs too hot wastes fuel, it's a good idea to keep the radiator completely full.

Before automatically turning on your car's air conditioner, try using the air vents because you'll save money if you do. Many newer cars have a ventilation system that can keep air inside the car fresh and cool even in hot weather.

Chapter **2**

BUYING NEW AND USED CARS

HERE'S HOW TO TELL A LEMON FROM A GOOD DEAL.

New Cars

Deciding what you want from a car will help you determine what size and model to purchase. If you're looking for economy, buy the smallest car that meets the majority of your driving needs. If you plan to drive the car for the remainder of its useful life, buy the mechanically simplest car available. If you plan to resell the car in a year or so, choose a model with popular options.

The fenders, doors, and other body parts of new and used cars are often aligned through the use of shims. At the factory, these shims are painted the same color as the car. However, body repair men often use shiny, new, cadmium-plated shims, which is a dead giveaway that a used car has been in an accident.

When choosing carpeting for a car or van, you might be happier opting for 100 percent nylon. Polyester carpeting looks beautiful when new, but deteriorates faster than nylon.

When inspecting a van you're thinking of buying, examine the paneling. Some builders use inexpensive pressboard panel with a thin, imprinted woodgrain veneer. Better shops, however, use real wood panels or wood panels covered by heavy vinyl with a woodgrain pattern. Vinyl paneling stands up well to wear and resists scratches even better than real wood panels.

It's better to select tires for a van on the basis of your driving needs, rather than style. Pay attention to the load range of the tire and tread pattern, because there are tires for highway driving, tires for off-road work, and all-terrain models. Keep in mind that larger tires with bold tread designs tend to be rough riding and noisy for general use.

Used Cars

It's best to check out the used car dealer before you check out the used car.

Since car troubles seem to multiply after three years, look for a used car less than three years old.

If a used car dealer has nothing to hide, he won't mind if you drive the car to your mechanic and let him look it over.

The odometer of a used car has probably been turned back if two or more digits don't align with the other numbers.

When buying a used car, make sure you check the exhaust. Put the car in neutral, press firmly on the gas. Look for white or bluish smoke. If you see that, the engine is worn and you shouldn't buy the car.

If there are new rugs or floor mats on the floor of the used car you're looking at, check underneath to see if they're covering rusted-out parts of the car's floor.

Never buy a used car at night. Used car dealerships usually have strings of incandescent light bulbs strung up all over their lots because those lights give "sparkle" to the cars. As you walk around the cars, the reflections detract your attention from any defects they may have.

Chapter **3**

BODY WORK

DON'T LET YOUR CAR DOWN. LEARN TO KEEP IT SHINY AND NEW FOR YEARS TO COME.

Rust

In checking your car for signs of rust, closely inspect any bubbles or blisters in the paint. If they are soft to the touch, the metal beneath probably is being eaten away by rust. Any rust should be treated quickly.

Nicks and Scratches

An ordinary wax crayon can cover scratches on your car's finish. Match the color of the crayon to your car and rub it over the scratches to cover them. Buff the area with a cloth.

Headlights

Headlights always seem to get covered with road dirt and bugs when you're traveling by car. To keep them clean, cover the headlights with plastic wrap in the daytime and in the evening take off the plastic.

Tires

If you want your tires to have a new shine again, clean them off and add a coat of clear self-polishing floor wax.

Don't spend a fortune on new snow tires. Buy recapped ones. The tread on snow tires is extra thick, so there's little danger of driving on thin rubber.

Interior

Keep your car mats looking new and make them easier to clean by coating them with a liquid wax shoe polish.

You'll protect your car seats from wet bathing suits by placing plastic cleaner bags on the seats.

Washing and Polishing

When washing your car, try to park it in the shade (or wait for a cloudy day) and avoid using hot water and soaps or harsh detergents, which can bleach the paint and cause streaks that are impossible to remove. A mild liquid dishwashing detergent is best.

You can keep the metal hose nozzle from hitting your car when you're washing it by slipping a rubber chair leg tip over the end. Just cut out the closed end of the tip and slip it on the hose.

To remove bird, insect, and tar marks from your car's finish, hold a cloth saturated with cooking oil over the area until the spot lifts off.

When you polish your car, you should park it in the shade. Otherwise, heat from the car's surface will interfere with the polish's cleaning action. Remember that you don't have to polish the entire car in one day, as long as you don't stop work in the middle of a panel, where a line would then be visible.

To make your own windshield washer, mix four cups of water, four cups of isopropyl alcohol, and one teaspoon of liquid dishwashing detergent. Store in a clean, tightly covered bottle.

A musty odor in a trunk will disappear if you leave a coffee can containing kitty litter in the trunk overnight.

Buy an extra kitchen mop to keep in the garage to use when washing the car. The mop will clean a wider area on the top, hood, and trunk of your car, and you won't have to reach or scrub as much.

Old bumper stickers can be removed from your car by rubbing them with lighter fluid or nail polish remover, then scraping gently with a razor or knife.

Windshield Deicer

Whenever you park your car outdoors in freezing temperatures, place your rubber floor mats over the windshield, and hold them in place with the windshield wipers. Later, you won't have to struggle with scraping ice off the windows.

Chapter **4**

ENGINE WORK

HIGH-LEVEL MAINTENANCE IS THE KEY TO A WELL-RUNNING CAR.

Cleaning and Maintenance

If you want to extend the useful life of your car significantly, change its oil and oil filter even more frequently than is actually recommended by the manufacturer.

You can sidestep sudden engine breakdown by replacing each fan belt or alternator belt you buy before three years are up. Like most parts made of rubber, these usually last about three years.

Check your air filter regularly and replace this relatively inexpensive part if it's clogged. If air is unable to reach the carburetor because of a clogged air filter, not only will the engine consume more gasoline, it will also be more difficult to start. And, if a filter isn't the proper size, dirt may pass through and harm the engine's internal parts.

When cleaning engine parts, use only cleaners designed for the job—never gasoline or lacquer thinner. Their fumes are toxic, and more importantly, highly flammable. Both gasoline and lacquer thinner have such low flash points that no spark is needed to cause them to burst into flame.

If you get in the habit of releasing your parking brake before you turn on the ignition, you won't damage your car by accidentally driving with the parking brake on. It's best not to rely on a dashboard "parking brake on" light, because its bulb may be burned out.

Battery

You should put away all smoking materials before cleaning your car battery's exterior. Batteries can be highly explosive due to hydrogen gas.

Check to see if the battery fluid is frozen before you try to boost a run-down battery. If it is frozen, jumper cables can damage the battery and possibly cause an explosion.

A light coat of petroleum jelly on battery posts and cable attachments retards corrosion.

Spark Plugs

Save money by avoiding so-called "super" spark plugs. They cost too much to be economical, even in the long run. It's best to stick to plugs recommended by the car maker and change them every two years or so, as the owner's manual directs. Economize by buying them at department stores rather than car dealerships, and learn to install them yourself.

When checking a spark plug's gap, use a round-wire gap gauge. A flat gauge can give you an inaccurate reading.

Pep-Ups

Even in early spring and late fall, old cars can stall repeatedly if damp, cold weather causes ice to form on their carburetors. Solution? Add a can of "dry gas" to your fuel tank. It's available under a variety of names at auto supply stores.

If your car is sluggish on winter mornings, use a hair dryer to blow hot air on the carburetor so the car will start better.

If you are tuning your car and a fastener refuses to budge or is difficult to remove, apply a little penetrating oil and allow it time to work. When you remove parts, arrange them in the order of removal and place them in a tray or other container so they won't get lost. This also eases reassembly.

Jump-Starts

When jump-starting your car's dead battery, line up the two cars so they're facing each other—but be careful not to let them touch. Touching can lead to electrical shorts and dangerous sparks.

If you back your car into the garage in cold weather, it will be in a good position for the use of jumper cables, if needed.

When purchasing a set of jumper cables, be sure they're equipped with a good electrical conductor, such as copper. Copper carries electrical current much better than aluminum and most other metals.

Chapter 5

SAFETY

KNOWING WHAT TO DO IN AN EMERGENCY IS HALF THE BATTLE.

Ready for Emergencies

Always keep an emergency box in your car. You should have a blanket, flares, an army shovel, kitty litter or sand, a sterno stove, dry soup mix, water in a plastic bottle, and a flashlight.

If your car door locks are frozen, hold a flame under the key for a few seconds and insert the key into the lock. The heat from the key will loosen the locks.

Keep an old belt punched with extra holes in your car trunk and the next time you haul something, you'll have a tie-down at hand.

If you don't have an ice scraper at hand, just take out an expired credit card.

If you keep plastic gloves and rubber bands in the glove compartment, you'll never have to get dirty if you have to tinker under the hood. Just slip the plastic over your hands and sleeves and hold in place with the rubber bands.

Keep an old window shade in your trunk. If you have some car trouble, like changing a tire, unroll the shade on the ground and you will stay cleaner.

An old nylon stocking kept in the trunk of the car comes in handy when you have a flat tire. If you rub the stocking around the tire, the hose will snag on the nail or tack that caused the flat, keeping you from hurting your fingers.

If you find yourself on the side of the road with a rusted jack and no oil can, take the dipstick from your engine and let the oil from it drip onto the jack.

If you've ever found yourself on a lonely road because you forgot to fill your gas tank, devise a memory jogger. Take a clip-on clothespin, paint it red, and print the word GAS on it. When your tank is low, put the clothespin on the gearshift and keep it there until you fill up.

Taking No Chances

If you have to pull over to the side of the road or highway, reflector tape strips placed on the inside face of your car doors will alert motorists approaching from behind you in the dark. Also, tape placed on the inside of the hood will make you noticeable to oncoming cars.

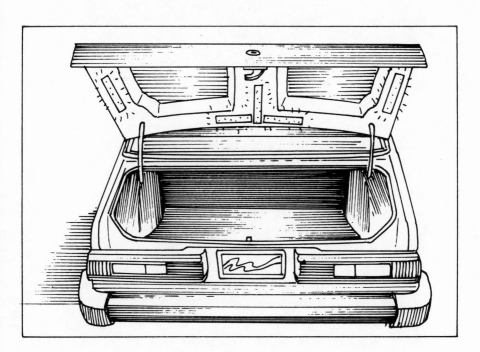

Putting an inch of baking soda in your car's ashtray will keep snubbed-out cigarettes from continuing to burn.

Keep a blackboard eraser in the glove compartment for cleaning off steamy windows.

Security Hints

Consider replacing the mushroom locks on your car door with tapered ones. They're more difficult for a thief to open.

In order to deter thieves from breaking into your car, always try to park in a busy, well-lit area.

To prove ownership of your car in the event of theft, drop your business card or an index card listing your name and address into the window slot.

Index